Affectionately, Rachel

William F. and Rachel Lillie Kerr Johnson's
wedding portrait,
Hookstown, Pennsylvania, June 5, 1860.

Affectionately, Rachel

LETTERS FROM INDIA

1860–1884

edited by

BARBARA MITCHELL TULL

The Kent State University Press

KENT, OHIO, AND LONDON, ENGLAND

© 1992 by The Kent State University Press,
Kent, Ohio 44242
ALL RIGHTS RESERVED
Library of Congress Catalog Card Number 92-4014
ISBN 0-87338-463-6
Manufactured in the United States of America

Library of Congress Cataloging-in-Publication Data
Johnson, Rachel Kerr, 1837–1888.
Affectionately, Rachel: letters from India, 1860–1884 /
edited by Barbara Mitchell Tull.
p. cm.
Includes bibliographical references and index.
ISBN 0-87338-463-6 (alk.) ∞
1. Johnson, Rachel Kerr, 1837–1888—Correspondence.
2. Missionaries—India—Correspondence.
3. Missionaries—United States—Correspondence.
I. Tull, Barbara Mitchell, 1932–
II. Title.
BV3269.J64A4 1992
266'.51'092—dc20
[B]   92-4014

British Library Cataloging-in-Publication data are available.

Contents

Foreword

WE KNOW VERY LITTLE about nineteenth-century missionary women. Those who have caught the eye of contemporary publicists and subsequent historians are those, generally single women, who were pioneers in evangelistic, educational, or medical work among women. On the other hand, those who went overseas with their missionary husbands, whose energies were directed primarily towards home and family rather than towards "the work," have been largely forgotten. Their obituaries in missionary magazines were brief, often vague and abstract listings of the Christian virtues they embodied rather than descriptions of real flesh-and-blood human beings. A secretary of the Presbyterian Board of Foreign Missions, Arthur Judson Brown, captured this form of remembrance in a single sentence: "The world does not contain nobler, sweeter women than the wives of missionaries."[1]

Thus we owe a real debt of gratitude to Barbara Tull for making available the letters of her great-grandmother, Rachel Kerr Johnson, who was a Presbyterian missionary in India from 1860 to 1883. Most of these letters are written to family members in western Pennsylvania rather than to the Board of Foreign Missions in New York City. As such they give us valuable insights into "the world" of Rachel Johnson, who was probably quite representative of many married missionary women of her generation. Barbara Tull's introductions, which draw upon other sources, place Rachel's letters in context and yet allow those letters to speak for themselves. I found that the resulting combination reads almost like a novel.

The first mission station in India of the Presbyterian Church in the U.S.A. was established in Ludhiana, Punjab, in 1834. By 1860 the Presbyterian Church had seventeen stations clustered not only in the central Punjab but also between the Jumna and Ganges rivers in what was then the Northwestern Provinces, later the United Provinces. Eleven of these

---

1. Arthur Judson Brown, *The Foreign Missionary: An Incarnation of a World Movement*, 369.

stations were the responsibility of the Lodiana (later Punjab) Mission and the other six of the Farrukhabad (later North India) Mission.[2] These missions were responsible not only for establishing stations and assigning personnel to them but also for setting mission strategy and providing oversight for the work carried out at them. Annual mission meetings combined business, worship, and socializing. All members were missionaries; Indians were eligible only for membership in the presbytery, the business of which was perfunctory during this period.

When Rachel Johnson arrived in India, women were not mission members, and work among women had not yet become a regular part, let alone a priority, of the Farrukhabad Mission. In fact, married women were not even listed as missionaries in the annual reports of the mission.[3] They were considered assistant missionaries at best and would not become voting members of the mission until the twentieth century. Women's missionary work had had modest and sporadic beginnings; it expanded only after 1870 when the newly formed Women's Board of Foreign Missions started sending single women missionaries to India in large numbers.[4] Prior to that what little women's work there was, in orphanages and schools, had been carried out by married women—usually in the face of local Indian opposition—during the time they could spare from their domestic responsibilities. Only two single women had been associated with the Farrukhabad Mission prior to Rachel's arrival. Jane Vandeveer came out at her own expense in 1840 and taught until an illness forced her to return to the United States in 1845. Mary Browning taught in Agra from 1854 until 1857, when she married the Reverend David Herron of the Lodiana Mission. In 1859 she helped found that mission's prestigious Christian Girls Boarding School in Dehra Dun.[5]

This definition of the missionary wife's "proper place," and Rachel's acceptance of it, helps us appreciate much of what is included as well as much of what is missing in Rachel's letters. Home and family were central in her life and provided the dominant theme in her correspondence. Even her vivid descriptions of India, whether written when in a mission station or while camping in villages, portrayed her home environment.

2. John C. B. Webster, *The Christian Community and Change in Nineteenth Century North India*, 14–15.

3. See the entry for the Fatehpur Mission Station in *Report of the Furrukhabad Mission of the Presbyterian Church in the U.S.A. for 1862–1863* (33). This begins by listing William Johnson as the missionary and then mentions the native assistant; wives are similarly omitted from other station reports.

4. Jane Tracy, "The Development of Women's Work," 67–70; Webster, *The Christian Community*, 142–45.

5. Webster, *The Christian Community*, 142–45; Helen Harriet Holcomb, "Sketch of the Furrukhabad Mission," 111, 116, 124.

One could argue that Rachel was only passing along to her family in western Pennsylvania the news she thought would be of most interest to them. Yet had Rachel developed other strong interests, for example in educating Indian girls or evangelizing Indian women, she would surely have shared these with her family. Rachel's primary missionary vocation was that of wife, mother, and homemaker; what her letters reveal is the way she sought to live out that vocation in circumstances very different from those in which she had been raised.

These letters also provide valuable insights into Rachel's social world. Because I found that missionary correspondence to the Board of Foreign Missions concentrated almost obsessively upon "the work," I looked to Rachel's letters for information about people, especially the Indian Christian people among whom she lived and with whom her husband worked. I did not find it. Social relationships between missionaries and Indian Christians seem to have been minimal, or at least not important enough to write about. Indian Christians did complain about missionary aloofness at that time, obviously not without justification.[6]

Much more is to be found in Rachel's letters about the social relationships between American missionaries and British officials in India. She strengthens my suspicions that social contacts were closer in places like Fatehpur, where the western population was very small and thus thrown together almost by necessity, than in places like Fatehgarh and Allahabad, where the western population was large enough for there to be separate social circles. Also in Rachel's letters are signs of a certain distance between the Johnsons and British society. One sign is Rachel's marked annoyance at British sympathy for and confidence in a Confederate victory in the American Civil War. After all, Rachel had two brothers in the Union Army. The other, less obvious but, to my mind, far more significant, sign is the remarkable absence of hostility towards Indians in her letters. The Johnsons arrived in India just after the 1857 revolt or "Mutiny," as it was known in British circles. The events of 1857–58 brought out in the British a marked suspicion and animosity towards Indians which continued for some years,[7] yet we find no trace of that, even in Rachel's early letters, despite the fact that her own brother-in-law and his wife had been put to death during the revolt. Her's was a less racist outlook. Rachel's negative comments on Indians are confined to discussions of their religious life. This was common among missionaries, and Rachel was less judgmental than most.

Rachel's primary social circle outside her own household was clearly that of the mission. Visits with fellow missionaries and mission meetings were very important events in her life. She valued the friendship of

6. Webster, *The Christian Community*, 87.
7. Thomas R. Metcalf, *The Aftermath of Revolt: India, 1857–1870*, 289–323.

other missionaries, and they looked after each other in times of crisis. The mission, spread out as it was, functioned as her extended family in India. However, she gives us only hints of the personality conflicts and disagreements over "the work" that went on in that wider Mission family, and those come out more clearly in letters to the Board of Foreign Missions.

Finally, these letters help us to locate Rachel in her own generation of missionaries. One does not find in her letters that inner conflict between vocation as a missionary and vocation as a homemaker which Jane Hunter finds characteristic of a later generation of missionary wives in China.[8] Rachel had already spent ten years in India and had given birth to four children (two of which had died) before she could begin to make comparisons between herself and the increasing number of single women missionaries who were working full time among Indian women. Nor are there signs that Rachel had been seriously challenged by the feminism of the women's missionary movement during the final third of the century. Rachel had obviously been nurtured in "the gospel of domesticity" and accepted its implications for her missionary life without apparent anguish or rebellion. Of the models of the minister's wife available to her in America, she took to India that of the companion rather than the sacrificer, assistant, or partner.[9]

Rachel Kerr Johnson remains a remarkable woman. By the standards of her day she was well, but not highly, educated. She sailed half-way around the world to create a good home for herself and her family in a culture and society totally different from her own. That was no easy task in the mid–nineteenth century. India then was very different from India today; the gulf between life in western Pennsylvania and life in the Northwestern Provinces, notwithstanding the presence of the British there, was far wider than it is now. One may conclude that Rachel never succeeded in bridging that gulf, but few, if any, of her contemporaries did either. There is pain, loss, and loneliness in these letters, but there is also wonder, delight, and deep contentment. It is good to have her story.

John C. B. Webster

8. Jane Hunter, *The Gospel of Gentility: American Women Missionaries in Turn-of-the-Century China*, 90–127. R. Pierce Beaver also makes a distinction between generations in *American Protestant Women in World Mission: A History of the First Feminist Movement in North America*, 48–115.

9. Beaver, *American Protestant Women*, 87–143; Barbara Welter, "She Hath Done What She Could: Protestant Women's Missionary Careers in Nineteenth Century America," 111–25; Barbara Leslie Epstein, *The Politics of Domesticity: Women, Evangelism and Temperance in Nineteenth-Century America*, 67–87. See Leonard I. Sweet, *The Minister's Wife: Her Role in Nineteenth Century American Evangelism.*

Preface

IT IS A RARE JOY to know great-grandparents as well as I have come to
know mine, Rachel and Will Johnson. Rachel's letters from India in the
nineteenth century painted vivid pictures of the India she and Will observed and loved, the stress of the Civil War on her family, the day-by-
day experiences of raising six children and losing two infants, and the
devoted support she gave Will while he was a missionary and, later, the
last white president of a North Carolina university for black men.

I first discovered a sample of Rachel's rich, descriptive letters after my
father's death in 1974; I found a box containing typed copies of a few of
her early letters from India. After reading those pages, I was hungry
to learn more about her life, times, adventures, friends, and especially
about why she and Will chose to sail half-way around the world to become missionaries. I had heard many fascinating stories about the three
generations of our family who had lived as missionaries in India, but I
found Rachel's letters especially compelling, immediate, and personal.

When my aunt, one of Rachel's granddaughters, and her namesake,
moved from the family home into a nursing home several years ago, the
task of sorting through generations of accumulated memorabilia fell on
my brother, mother, and me. From the basement up to the third floor,
we opened drawers, boxes, and trunks and found packet after packet
of letters and envelopes of photographs. It was overwhelming. Fortunately, early in this home-closing process—before we sold the house—I
opened a packet in the large roll-top desk in the living room and discovered the handwritten, fragile letters from Rachel. The handwriting
soon became familiar and I was able to sort her correspondence out
from the miscellaneous greeting cards and routine letters of several
generations. When the house was cleared, I had a sizable collection of
Rachel's letters and photographs from India, which, fortunately, my
aunt identified for me.

The actual letters and the typed copies of the originals are preserved
in the archives of the United Presbyterian Church U.S.A. in Philadelphia, Pennsylvania, for use in scholarly research. The intent here was to

focus on Rachel's stories and the personalities, actions, interactions, and feelings she vividly described over 100 years ago.

Most of Rachel's letters are contained in this volume. Several routine letters of little interest were deleted in their entirety. Ellipses indicate omissions of repeated requests for family and friends to write more often, repetitive descriptions, greetings, postscripts, sermonizing, casual singular references to people, or routine conversations.

Rachel's writing style reflected her times, her frugal use of paper, and her personal style. She seldom used paragraph indentations; her most common punctuation was a dash or a space, and she rarely used any other punctuation in her early letters. Rachel frequently used a single letter as a quick abbreviation for a place or a person's name that was familiar to her reader. Remaining as close as possible to Rachel's intent and meaning, as I was able to understand them after many readings, I edited the letters for clarity. Paragraphs have been marked, punctuation inserted, abbreviations expanded, an unfamiliar abbreviations (such as "c" for "etc.") changed to more familiar forms. In her early letters, Rachel used a great many underlinings; these have been deleted where this stylistic convention did not add to the clarity of her story. Spellings and capitalizations have been made consistent, except for those spellings that give special flavor and color. Long sentences have frequently been broken into two, three, or four shorter ones. Repetitive adjectives that dulled her descriptions have been deleted also. Very rarely have I added a pronoun, conjunction, article, or form of the verb "to be" to make a sentence more clear or smoother. Her prose has been essentially left unchanged.

Several of Rachel's consistent grammatical conventions have been retained. For example, no apostrophes were used in contractions or possessives. She never used the form "doesnt"; she always used "dont." To our twentieth-century ears, some of the words and phrases used in these historical letters may sound condescending, bigoted, or biased. I have not softened or changed those words (i.e., "urchins," "heathens"), for they were commonly used among her contemporaries and seemed to have very different connotations at that time than they do today.

One problem encountered in editing these letters was the spelling inconsistencies of the Hindi and Urdu words and name places, as scholars had just begun converting Hindustani languages into romanized spelling. All Hindi words have been defined where they occur in the text. My most common reference source to check the spelling and meaning of words Rachel used was a dictionary her daughter used, *A Romanized Hindustani and English Dictionary, Designed for the Use of Schools and for Vernacular Students of the Language.* The primary source for establishing a consistent spelling of place names in the letters was the "Map of India Showing the Missionary Stations of the Presbyterian Church" from the book *A Memorial of the Futtehgurh Mission and Her Martyred Missionaries: With Some Remarks on the Mutiny in India.* The book was written in 1859 by the Reverend J. Johnston Walsh, the Johnsons' first host and language teacher in India in 1860. A contemporary area map of the United Provinces of North India is enclosed as well. I chose to preserve Rachel's original spellings in the letters and to use current spellings in my comments. The two maps are included for the reader's reference and clarification.

Invaluable assistance in correcting my spelling transcription errors of the unfamiliar foreign words, providing spelling consistency and definition suggestions for them, and identifying photographic scenes from India was provided by several recently retired missionaries from Northern India and the Punjab: Joan Browne, Clara Wallace, and Ernie and Alfie Campbell. Anu Aneja and Blake Michel of Ohio Wesleyan University provided additional assistance in editing the Indian words and name places. The knowledge, skill, and personal interest of these readers contributed to the final product immensely.

Special acknowledgment must be given to John C. B. Webster, who wrote the introduction and provided sensitive recommendations following a care-filled reading of the manuscript. His observations and suggestions were particularly valuable since he is considered the world's leading authority on Presbyterian missions in India and is the author of the definitive history of Presbyterianism in India in the nineteenth century, *The Christian Community and Change in Nineteenth Century North India.* Much of John's expertise was gained as a student, pastor, teacher, researcher, and missionary in India from 1960–81.

Rachel's storytelling through her letters is, of course, the heart of this book. Rachel's gentle view of the world around her pulls the reader into her confidence and provides a unique perspective on a vibrant era. The tone of Rachel's letters varied with the readers: formal to her parents and community friends; fun-loving and teasing to her brothers; tender, businesslike, and confidential to her husband; and familiar, whimsical, and full of motherly advice to her children.

Although the letters generally speak for themselves, I have tried to set the stage by describing Rachel's early family life and have attempted to provide the bond between some of her letters and events of the day. Several letters from correspondents other than Rachel are included to give a fuller dimension to certain persons and events. Will was the published author and acknowledged scholar in the family, but, having served their scholarly purposes, most of Will's writings and translations must now be lost or forgotten on dusty shelves. I have, however, included selections from his extensive collection of photographs, several of his letters about pivotal events, and a few descriptive travel logs with the intent of fleshing out his character and enabling the reader to enjoy his considerable storytelling skills as well as Rachel's. Several chapter introductions contain information from Will's official mission reports and correspondence to the Board of Foreign Missions office in New York City. These work reports on what he was doing and his perspectives on the impact of their work in India are meant to complement Rachel's narratives about the Johnsons' home and family life.

On a dog-eared, refrigerator poster in our home is the anonymous statement "There are two lasting gifts we give our children—one is roots, the other is wings." This book is dedicated to our children—Rachel and Will's great-great-grandchildren. Here are a few more roots to inspire them to new heights in this generation.

With gratitude for the thoughtful ancestors who preserved these letters, I acknowledge with love and thankfulness the spirit of the current generations. My mother, Margaret Robbins Mitchell, who unfortunately died before this book was published; my husband, Dave; and each of our children, Craig, Stephen, Christy, Jim, and Anne, have provided immeasurable support and celebration in the evolution of *Affectionately, Rachel*.

Family Tree

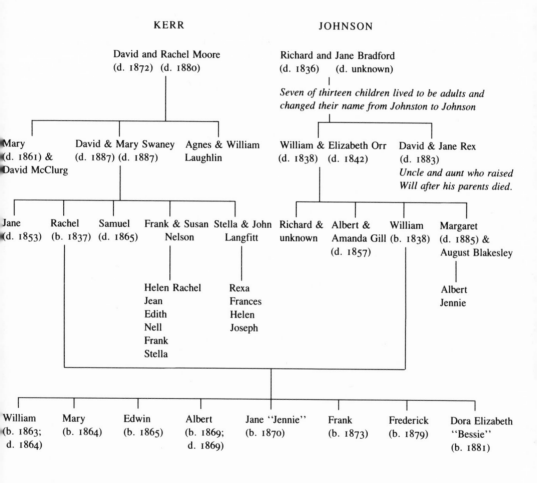

KERR

David and Rachel Moore
(d. 1872) (d. 1880)

Mary
(d. 1861) &
David McClurg

David & Mary Swaney   Agnes & William
(d. 1887) (d. 1887)   Laughlin

Jane   Rachel   Samuel   Frank & Susan   Stella & John
(d. 1853)   (b. 1837)   (d. 1865)   Nelson   Langfitt

Helen Rachel   Rexa
Jean   Frances
Edith   Helen
Nell   Joseph
Frank
Stella

JOHNSON

Richard and Jane Bradford
(d. 1836)   (d. unknown)

*Seven of thirteen children lived to be adults and
changed their name from Johnston to Johnson*

William & Elizabeth Orr   David & Jane Rex
(d. 1838)   (d. 1842)   (d. 1883)
                             *Uncle and aunt who raised
                             Will after his parents died.*

Richard &   Albert &   William   Margaret
unknown   Amanda Gill   (b. 1838)   (d. 1885) &
              (d. 1857)   August Blakesley

                                           Albert
                                           Jennie

William   Mary   Edwin   Albert   Jane "Jennie"   Frank   Frederick   Dora Elizabeth
(b. 1863;   (b. 1864)   (b. 1865)   (b. 1869;   (b. 1870)   (b. 1873)   (b. 1879)   "Bessie"
d. 1864)   d. 1869)   (b. 1881)

1837–1859

HOOKSTOWN, PENNSYLVANIA

𝒪𝒻 FAMINES WERE COMMON in the North Provinces of India, but the famine of 1837–38 was merciless. Gopi Nath Nundy ached with compassion for the starving, emaciated people lining the roadways. He was especially moved by the plight of the children. Nundy, a high caste Bengali from Calcutta, attended a Hindu college, converted to Christianity, and was baptized in 1833. He established a home in Fatehpur and visited the nearby villages and collected the children who had been abandoned by their parents or those whose parents had died. Mothers with tears in their eyes offered to exchange their children for a handful of flour so that they could die knowing their children would be cared for. Nundy took the starving children to Fatehpur, where Dr. Charles Madden, an Englishman in the medical service of the East India Company, used his own money to provide emergency care for the children. But when Dr. Madden's wife became ill and died, he could no longer continue his orphan project.

In a nearby village at Fatehgarh, Captain S. G. Wheeler, a British army officer, also saw the needs of the orphans and gathered a group together to care for them. The responsibilities soon became overwhelming for Captain Wheeler and he too looked for someone to take over the education and management of the children.

At just this time, the Reverend Henry R. Wilson, Jr., a new missionary from America, stopped in Fatehgarh on his way from Calcutta to a mission station further north in Lodiana. The three men, Wheeler, Nundy, and Madden, persuaded Reverend Wilson to combine the two groups of children in Fatehgarh and operate an orphan asylum until a replacement manager could arrive. Wheeler and Madden offered to pay Wilson's salary, while Nundy promised to assist him in providing training for the children. Reverend Wilson never did get to the Lodiana Mission; he remained with the orphan project until he returned to America seven years later.[1] Thus, the orphan asylum at Fatehgarh was

1. J. Johnston Walsh, *A Memorial of the Futtehgurh Mission and Her Martyred Missionaries,* 37–44; Webster, *The Christian Community,* 51–52.

the beginning of the Christian mission station that was to become so intertwined with the life of Rachel Kerr, born half-way around the world during that year of the great Indian famine.

Rachel Lillie Kerr was born early on a February morning in 1837 in the big brick house on the corner of Mill and Washington streets in Hookstown, Pennsylvania. She was the second daughter of David and Mary Kerr. Her sister, Jane, was two years old. Rachel's grandparents, uncles, aunts, and cousins lived around the corner or over the next hill on nearby farms.

Harris's 1837 Directory describes "Hook's Settlement" as "an industrious, flourishing village" with a gristmill, a sawmill, two tanneries, two blacksmith shops, a wagon maker, two tailors, two hatters, and a post office. With its mills and stores, Hook's Settlement served the farmers in surrounding Greene Township and was a comfortable rural community that was self-sufficient both socially and economically. Hookstown became its official name when it was incorporated in 1843.[2]

Mary and David, Rachel's parents, grew up in farm families outside of Hookstown.[3] Mary's father, Samuel Swaney, had a flourishing farm about a mile south of town on a branch of Mill Creek. About two miles further southeast, on Service Creek, was the Kerr farm, where David grew up. This fertile, rolling farmland of Green Township, in Beaver County, is hugged by the Ohio River on the north and by the northernmost tip of West Virginia on the west.

David worked with his father on the farm until he was sixteen years old. He learned the wheelwright's trade—building and repairing wheels—from his father, but he especially liked working with wood; so David Kerr left the family farm to serve three years as a carpenter's apprentice in Pittsburgh. After several years plying that trade in the city, David came back to Hookstown, bought two lots on Mill Street, and built a large brick house.

When the house was completed, David and Mary were married. While Mary busied herself making the house into a home, David built his shop across the street. From there he conducted his business of contracting and building, and in later years he devoted much time to oil exploration. He contracted and built most of the brick and stone homes in the county during the mid-nineteenth century. Many are still occupied and serve as monuments to his skills as the twentieth century draws to a close.

David's shop clung to the top of the hill before the land rolled on down to Moody's Run below, a gently meandering stream. Just out of

2. Denver L. Walton, ed., *The Beaver County Bicentennial Atlas*, 109.
3. The history notes of Rachel's family are primarily from Franklin D. Kerr, M.D., Records of the Kerr Family, chapters 1–7, Presbyterian Historical Society, Philadelphia. John W. Jordon, ed., *Genealogical and Personal History of Beaver County, Pennsylvania, at Its Centennial Celebration*, 157–58.

Fig. 1. Looking east into Hookstown from Moody Hill, the Kerr family home, the brick house with the wood fence around it, is in the center of this photograph taken in the 1870s.

sight around the bend on the west edge of town, the Run provided the power for the flour mill that gave the name to the street on which the Kerr home faced.

The Kerrs, Swaneys, Moores, Phillises, Pattens, and other relatives were, for the most part, second generation families in and around Hookstown. Most of the early families came to America from Ireland or Scotland to escape religious persecution, political relocations, increased taxes, and other discriminations by their English rulers. These staunch Presbyterians arrived in America with strong convictions about church, state, institutions, and society just in time to join in the American Revolution, in which they distinguished themselves. They lived an uneasy frontier existence with the Native Americans and watched their children die from hardships and disease. Seeking a pastoral home in America, they moved west until they found Greene County, Pennsylvania. They cleared the land for their farms; established the Mill Creek Presbyterian Church, the oldest church in Beaver County; started neighborhood schools in their homes; and helped build the community of Hookstown.

Jane and Rachel grew up in this secure, family community and made an easy transition from child's play, to playing house, to helping their mother with the cooking, washing, cleaning, spinning, knitting, weaving, sewing, and other household tasks. They joined their mother, aunts, and cousins in plucking feathers for the pillows, tending the vegetable and flower gardens, and canning the seasonal vegetables. When Rachel was four and a half, her brother Sam was born. Brother Frank followed two and a half years later. The girls took delight in the added responsibilities of helping their mother care for the babies.

In 1844, when Rachel was seven, her grandmother's brother, the Reverend J. P. Moore, established the first Select School in Hookstown. Now the girls could walk to school, instead of taking the long buggy ride to the rural schoolhouse on Uncle John Swaney's farmland, just over the hill from the Mill Creek Church.

Teachers in small towns in the early nineteenth century were often part-time preachers, men known for their education. Thus, on weekdays Jane and Rachel would learn their three Rs from the McGuffy readers with generous doses of an accompanying "Protestant ethic," which included instruction in the virtues of industry, punctuality, sobriety, frugality, and reverence for parental principles. On Saturdays, Father loaded the children into the wagon and took them down past Grandfather Swaney's farm and up the steep hill to the Mill Creek Presbyterian Church, where they spent the day learning and reciting the Shorter Westminster Catechism. They spent Sunday, or course, in church with their family.

However, life was not all happiness and order. In 1845 the "Hookstown fever"—probably typhoid—struck the little community and lingered for many months. Eighty-six of the 350 residents became seriously ill. Eight people died, including two doctors.

These were fearful times for Mary and David and their four small children. Mary was expecting their third son, Thomas, during the time of the Hookstown fever. Whether he died from the fever or some other cause is not known, but Thomas died in infancy in 1846, as did a fourth son, Sylvester, in 1848. During the hard times, the Kerrs turned to their faith and church for consolation; during happy times, for rejoicing and giving thanks; and during everyday times, for support, fellowship, and a view of the larger world through the eyes and the words of the educated men who passed through their community and spoke in their church.

Rachel was swept up with her family in the evangelical revival and reform movements of the Second Great Awakening in the early 1830s. These movements combined a contagious energy with a certain smug, self-satisfaction and a feeling of the moral superiority of Protestantism. The evangelical war on sin united the middle class who practiced their duties of faith, devotion, public service, and self-control. There was an element of disgust for frivolity, waste, and irresponsibility and for those who did not recognize sin and repent of it. The movement persuaded believers that the world is corrupt, but that it can be changed; a person had the responsibility through study and devotion to know God and the Bible, to serve humankind, and to build a life of truth and goodness.

Days short of her fifteenth birthday, Rachel wrote and illustrated a valentine. The carefully penned handwriting—with a few scratched out words—and the elaborate design on the cover sheet showed that Rachel labored over this piece with painstaking care. Her valentine mused on time, nature, the soul, and eternity. These seemed heavy, prophetic topics for a not-quite fifteen-year-old young woman.]

Miss Rachel Kerr   Valentine 1852
How silent and noiseless is the tread of time as he pursues his ever onward march, bearing all things before him and sparing none. Wherever we look around us we behold the traces of time and decay written on every object. Yet we find man always anxious to erect some monument or lofty pillar by which to perpetuate his glorious deeds, fondly hoping that these shall stand for a memorial of him, as long as time itself shall endure. But alas, how delusive are all his lofty aspirations to immortalize his name. For where can he find the monument which shall successfully withstand the ravages of time? But all will eventually mouldew into ruins.

He clothes the earth in a rich carpet of verdure, and decks the forest in its most lovely attire. He scatters flowers of various hews o'er hill and vale, and thus showers down blessings on human beings, to teach us his power and might. But soon he strips the earth of its verdure, and the forest resigns its grandeur and loveliness to the stern voice of time.

He traces deep furrows of sorrow and grief on the face of the lovely and the brow of the fair. Neither old nor young can defy his commands. They live in his kingdom, and die beneath his scepter. But the truth of the heart, this treasure, time itself cannot tarnish. It shall be as lasting as eternity itself.

The soul still remains unchanged amid all the wrecks of time. Like some vast rock whose towering forms rise in sublime grandeur amid the foaming ocean, whose waves constantly beat against it; yet it remains firm, unmoved and unyielding.

Day after day and year apon year is added to the cycles of glory, time, power and fame. Yet what is it, but the shadow of a man; a moment as it were of eternity; a fleeting Span which hasteth to be done, which soon will be lost forever. Lost on eternity's shore.

                                                        Hookstown

[When compared with letters from her brothers and sister at the same age, Rachel's writing seems more complete and complex in form and substance. She may well have been the apple of her Grandpaps Kerr's eye and the emerging scholar of the family. Although Grandpaps—as Rachel calls him in her letters—was a farmer, he and his wife were known to all in the area as "Uncle Davy" and "Aunt Rachel." According to family history notes, their home was where neighbors gathered to discuss "every subject which affected the welfare of mankind. . . . Religion and politics and the general interests of the country, as well as local matters, received their attention."

In Grandpaps's youth he received private or group instruction from a host of ministers or schoolmasters. The last school he attended was a night school in Frankfort Springs, Pennsylvania, at the age of sixteen. At seventeen his father died, and the care of the farm fell to young David. But he never set his books aside; they occupied his energies and attentions when daily farm chores were done. So when Grandmother Rachel's namesake came to visit and feast on her biscuits and sugar molasses, Grandpaps undoubtedly encouraged the child in her studies and nurtured her love of ideas.

After four brothers—although two lived only briefly—baby sister Stella, born in 1853, was a joy for young Rachel to cherish and spoil. Grief, however, tempered Rachel's joy that year. Four months after Stella's birth, her older sister and constant companion, Jane, died. Rachel was deeply affected by her sister's death; the happy, outgoing, resilient young girl was now serious and withdrawn, and her sadness was a concern to the whole family. Grandpaps proposed a solution: Since all recognized that Rachel was gifted intellectually and became stimulated and absorbed in reading and writing, he suggested that she be sent away to school to become a teacher.

This was a drastic decision for her parents. Female seminaries were generally reserved for the daughters of economically favored families and provided a finishing school for emerging young society women. Although David had constant work as a carpenter and builder of homes, he was not a wealthy man. Also, with two young boys and an infant daughter at home, Mary was very dependent upon Rachel's help and was reluctant to let her go. But Grandpaps found the perfect school: the Female Seminary in Steubenville, Ohio, run by the renowned Presbyterian preacher Charles C. Beatty and his wife. It provided coeducation at the secondary level and advanced training for young women to become teachers, missionaries, and homemakers. The curriculum promised to challenge the scholarship and imagination of Rachel with courses in "Intellectual and Moral Philosophy," "Evidences of Christianity," "Analogy of Natural and Revealed Religion," and instruction in becoming a teacher.[4]

4. E. B. Welsh, chmn., *Buckeye Presbyterianism*, 253.

In preparing their first child to go off to school, David and Mary's thoughts turned away from the lost children to the exciting prospects and futures of the four remaining children. Rachel was the first young woman in her family community to go away to school. While the women sewed, mended, and prepared Rachel's wardrobe, David was setting aside the $98.87 that was required for the first semester of schooling. This consisted of $60 for two quarters of boarding, $14 for tuition, $20 for music and use of the piano, $2.50 for books and $2.37 for miscellaneous school expenses.

When all was ready, Rachel, age eighteen, left her snug home and community, crossed the Ohio River, and began a boarding-student life with the school term of 1855–56. Her first letter from Seminary Hall in Steubenville, Ohio, was addressed to her mother. It was a formal letter ladened with elaborate expressions of gratitude and was signed with her proper first name, Rachel. As a child and young girl, Rachel was known affectionately to all her family and friends by her middle name, Lillie, but with her new mantle of womanhood, going off to Seminary, she adopted Rachel as her preferred adult name. The intimate signature of "Lillie" reappears years later in correspondence with her husband. The tone of her letter home to brother Sam nine months later is chatty, full of rambling narratives and requests for gossip.]

Seminary Hall
Feb. 22nd, 1856

My Dear Mother.

A leisure moment shall be pleasantly spent in writing a line to the dearest and best of Mothers. For who so kind, so patient and indulgent to our faults, our failings, and youthful follies, as she who has watched over us in our infancy and more mature years. No other earthly friend can supply the place of a kind and loving father and mother. May I be enabled to appreciate this blessing I enjoy, and may I never cause those hearts a painful thought who have given me the opportunity of improving my mind in the enjoyment of so many advantages.

How happy should I be even here, although I often long for the society of the loved ones at home, when I have the pleasing prospect, which many here have not, of returning to a happy and comfortable home. . . .

Your loving and affectionate Daughter
Rachel

Steubenville Female Seminary
Nov. 7th, 1856

Dear Brother,

Think me not forgetful of writing to you. I thought I would not write until I had got my room and roommate permanently fixed. Now here I am comfortably settled for another winter's study. I have a very nice room, nicely carpeted, with a stove and every convenience. Last, but not least of all, my roommate is a very pleasant one as far as present experience goes. . . .

There are a great many scholars here now, and more are coming in every day. I had a very pleasant trip coming down. I met with one of my teachers in the cars. We got to Steubenville about 8 o'clock same evening. We were met and taken to the seminary. Dr. Beatty and Mother Beatty gave me a very kind reception. . . .

Saturday morning I left for Springfield; got there about noon. I met Mr. Johnson on the way. I think he knew me—at least I did him very well. . . .

We have not got fairly started in study yet, but will soon. Jennie McCullough is not coming back, but there are a good many of my old acquaintances here. Lib Miller and Nora Bell from Pugh Town are here. I feel more at home than if all were strangers. Tho, of course, it is <u>not</u> <u>home to me</u>. . . .

Well doubtless you already know what is the result of the great election. If you do, you are better informed than I. We have only heard a rumor that "Buck" is elected—after all our trouble, convention, etc. What do you all do now for singings? I suppose there is something else on hand. Is Stella still a Fremont girl, ringing a few days?[5] I hated to go and leave her, but I will be back by and by.

And Samuel, how is the school flourishing? I hope you are studying hard, and Frank too. . . . My love to GrandPaps and all the rest of my friends . . . and everybody. Give me all the news.

> With much love, your Sister
> Rachel

Kiss Stella for me.

[William F. Johnson, first mentioned in this letter, was the new school teacher for her brothers and sister in Hookstown. "Mr. Johnson," Will, was to become Rachel's husband.

Will Johnson's ancestors came to America around 1770. They left Scotland because of religious persecution under James II, moved on to Ireland, then to America. The Presbyterian roots of Will's proud Scotch-Irish forefathers ran deep. Will's paternal grandfather, Richard, was

5. "Buck" was a nickname for James Buchanan of Pennsylvania, the successful Democratic candidate for president in 1856. The Kerrs were active in the new Republican party politics in Greene Township and supported local causes that had a distinct flavor of evangelical Protestantism. Stella, with her family, had participated in rallies and rang bells for Buchanan's Republican opponent, John Charles Frémont.

nine years old when the six Johnston children set out from northern Ireland for America with their parents.[6] Sadly, both parents died on shipboard and were buried at sea, leaving their children to face the New World as orphans. When the children arrived in America, they set up housekeeping together in the state of Delaware. Three of the older children married before the end of the Revolutionary War.

In the spring of 1791, the three married Johnston families and the three youngest Johnston children crossed over the mountains and settled in Washington County, Pennsylvania, near Canonsburg. This settlement was about thirty miles southeast of Hookstown, where Rachel's ancestors had established their homes. In due time, the three youngest Johnston children wed and started their own families. The Johnston families all remained neighbors as they homesteaded the land, joined the Chartiers Presbyterian Church, and became a vital part of the pioneering fabric of the North Straban Township community.

Richard Johnston and his wife, Jane, created a farm home for their family of thirteen children, nine of whom lived to adulthood. Among those nine was William, Will's father, who left farming to the others and became a medical doctor. Following his training, the young doctor and his bride, Elizabeth, crossed a few more hills and the Ohio River to establish their home and begin his medical practice in Cadiz, Ohio. According to *The Organ* of Cadiz, Dr. Johnston carved a "respected and cherished niche" for himself and his family; but in December 1838, when young Will was only nine months old, Richard died of "pulmonary consumption" at the age of thirty five, leaving Elizabeth with five children, ages nine months to eleven years.[7]

The young widow returned to the family circle in Washington, Pennsylvania, where she set up a milliner's shop and tried to keep her family together. But times were hard, and four years after her husband's death Elizabeth died also, family records suggesting that her heart was broken.

After the death of their parents, each of William and Elizabeth's children was chosen to be raised by a different aunt or uncle. Will, the youngest, at four years of age, went to live with his Uncle David, Aunt Jane, and eventually three younger Johnson cousins on a farm outside of Steubenville, Ohio. He lived on the farm until he returned to Pennsylvania to attend Jefferson College in Canonsburg. After graduation in 1856, at age eighteen, Will took a teaching position in Rachel's hometown of Hookstown.

In Hookstown, the attractive teaching newcomer and the vibrant young woman who went away to school to become a teacher undoubtedly

6. The family name was Johnston; the "t" was dropped during Will's youth by his uncles and aunts in western Pennsylvania and eastern Ohio.

7. *The Cadiz Organ*, Jan. 3, 1839.

heard a great deal about each other from mutual friends. After a proper introduction, they participated in a series of formal and informal social events and became better acquainted. Their attraction for one another grew.

Rachel's light-hearted letters to her brother Sam spoke of going sleighing with Mr. Johnson the evening she arrived home for Christmas vacation. Several months later Rachel boldly requested that Sam ask Mr. Johnson to delay the examinations so that she might be present. Their discreet courtship continued through personal letters; Rachel revealed this when she spoke of correspondence with an unnamed source—a thinly veiled reference to Mr. Johnson—who informed her that Sam had been chosen to perform in a school exhibition. Rachel never mentioned Mr. Johnson in letters to her parents. As their love bloomed, Rachel's and Will's stories joined into one.]

> January 6, 1857
> Steubenville Female Seminary

My Dear Brother [Sam],

I wish you all a happy new year. Such I suppose you have found it during holidays, when books were laid aside and seeking your own amusement would be your hardest task. But now we must all settle our brains down for the rest of the winter, with a better motive than merely to pass the time. We should still be trying to fill the vacancies that remain in the upper story of our craniums—not with mischief—but with something useful. Now brother, do not think I have turned lecturer, for this is all I will say on this subject at present. . . .

How are you improving the sleighing in Hookstown? Very industriously I hope. Perhaps you may have only one sleighing time as last winter. O yes, but that was a long time, if I do not forget. I guess I enjoyed the first sleighing this year, jolting over the clods in Mr. Johnson's sled the eve I went home.

Samuel, cant you slip down someday and give me a sleigh ride to comfort me. For we are all looking very wishfully at the sleighs as they go by with the merry bells keeping music to the times. They heed us not. But maybe if you had a sleigh pony and cart at your disposal, you would like quite as well to call on some of the little lasses at home. For I know they would be quite ready to draw down their bonnets over their faces and say, "Here am I. Take me."

I do not know of anything in the doings of our little Circle that is very interesting to write. I might say that yesterday evening I attended a meeting for the purpose of organizing a society of inquiry on the subject of Missions. It meets 2 a month. I was elected treasurer, an honor I would willingly have declined. We have not very much time for extra meetings. . . .

Your loving Sister
Rachel

P.S. Brother Frank. Your bookcase is hanging on the wall above the stand on which I am writing. The shelves are filled with books and it answers our purpose admirably. The girls are wanting me to <u>will</u> it to them when I leave. Which I will give it to is the question. . . . I have not yet decided. Goodbye.

Your sister, R.

Thursday eve, February 5, 1857

Dear Brother Sam,

. . . I was very glad to hear from you. I had some very pleasing intelligence in a letter the other day, which was that you are one of the chosen 12 to perform at the coming exhibition.[8] I hope you may do honor to yourself, also the society of the Literates to Young America, and lastly to your humble servant at the Steubenville Female Seminary—who had better be scaring up a few spare ideas for her oration or she might not come out 6 weeks hence.

Mine will not however need a very long time devoted to making gestures (practising the art I mean). The usual mode, you may not be aware, is to get up; look pale through your paint; have a slight nervous affectation—enough to give the impression that you are a sensitive plant (oh, sensible I mean); then let your voice resound so loud that it can be heard in the far side of your head and no farther. Then those ideas you have tortured your poor brain for weeks to find, will be appreciated by those fault finders, ready for the task of pointing out the beauties of your composition.

Enough. I need not anticipate. I soon must pass through these trying scenes myself. . . . It is 6 weeks from yesterday until our examination. . . . But "the wars will soon be o'er" and Ill <u>go home.</u>

Well, no doubt, I will miss the Exhibition, but <u>I wish</u> you all success. . . . Send me a Programmie. Dont forget.

Well Samuel, time and this paper admonish an adieu. . . .

Your Loving Sister,
Rach

8. In the nineteenth century, schools had celebrations or exhibitions on George Washington's birthday, Feb. 22. Entertainment for the assembled students, parents, and community members consisted of musical and oratorical selections presented by chosen students.

Saturday eve, February 28th, 1857
Female Seminary

Dear Brother [Sam],

I have just finished my work for this afternoon. Though I feel very much fatigued, after exercising my self for an hour or so, I think perhaps I will survive until after I get this finished. Methinks I hear you say that washing two or 3 collars is not quite as hard as chopping wood, which I suppose you have to engage in sometime on a Saturday afternoon. Oh no, I hear Frank say. It is I who helps Mother and Coz Paul in what makes the fire burn.

. . . We are busy thinking about examinations—studying a little too, to help along. We have quite a time. They do not allow us to study or stay up after ten. But Porr [Sepora Porter, roommate] and I break over this rule sometimes. After the bell rings, Mrs. Beatty comes skipping along to see if we are all snug in bed. Above each of our doors there is a ventilator—that is three panes of glass fixed on a pivot so as to turn—to let the air in; but, I think to let the light out seems the more important use. Coming as she is, we are some times ahead of her.

I will give you a little peek in side of 41 after ten. The fire is expired. On a chair in one side of the room is a box. In the box is a candle, and over the box is hoisted a large underline. Beneath, a seated book in hand, you will see two very sedate looking creatures: one of which is Porr, the other is myself. Our umbrella is a good one, whether raining or shining—we find more need of it in the latter case.

You have studied Philosophy and know the laws of reflection and refraction. They are the same yet, for if we had no umbrella, the rays might be reflected thru the crack of the door, and then refracted through the good old Lady's glasses. This might cause a commotion in the camp.

Porr always has a joke ready when occasion requires. Do not think we are getting frivolous, but we cannot afford to sleep so long as we wish when time is so precious. Some of our scholars however have carried matters a little too far. On Saturday last, 5 girls were suspended for attending the theatre. . . . They found their curiosity a little stronger than duty. This week one of our class was expelled—Miss Semple. . . . She would have graduated in 4 more weeks. I pity her, tho the fault was her own. There are only 12 of us left. We will have to be posted up pretty well, for the class is so small.

I have been having a good time with a tooth ache for a week or two, and feeling like having a little revenge on the troublesome member. I posted off to the dentist a few days ago and had my tooth extracted. Of two evils, this I thought the less.

Hug for Stella in her blue dress. Now tell her Achy [Stella's name for Rachel] has got a blue too. We will be matches as far as color goes. Our graduating dresses have just arrived. They are blue wool DeLaine, very pretty I think for school girls. Our class will all be dressed alike, as you know is customary. You can imagine what the call after getting a new blue is. Mrs. Beatty reminded us, for fear we would forget, that we must fork over the dimes. She always wants the girls to pay for whatever they get and not leave a bill at close of session. I will not get more than what I need. Ask Father if he will send me some money. He had better send $10. If there is any more than will suffice, I will keep it safe. Send in your next.

How are you getting along preparing for the Examinations? Do your best, for this child expects to be there to see the performance. Our Examinations will close on the 25th. We will then be Home on the next day at least. Now Samuel, ask Mr. Johnson if he will not be so accommodating as to appoint the Examination after the 25th. I, of course, do not wish him to go to any inconvenience to gratify my anxiety to be there, tho I want much to see you and all the rest perform. I tell you there will be a storm in the camp if I am too late for the fair. Dont forget this item.

I must close. Love to all . . . ,

Your Sister Rachel

[The Beattys, who ran the Steubenville Seminary, took a personal interest in their students. They assumed an *in loco parentis* role, as evidenced in the following letter that Mrs. Beatty wrote to Rachel's mother.]

Steubenville
July 19th, 1857

Mrs. Kerr
Dear Madam,

I write to inform you that your daughter has the measles and so she has not been able to write you. This week you will be looking for a letter.

They first made their appearance a week ago. On Sabbath morning she went to church as usual. In the afternoon she came to me saying she has some pimples on her face, but does not feel well. I told her she had measles, and must not go out. She thought not but I told her to stay in her room. In a short time they began to extend over her arms and body. Then she went to the nursery. I saw she was very sick, but not unfavorable symptoms. She had in addition her tooth ache and pain in her face.

She is much better, getting along as well as might be expected. We have a good nurse and our family physician has seen her several times. He says she is getting along very well. The nursery is warm and comfortable. The matron is a good nurse and I see her several times every day.

I hope with care, she will soon be well and back in school again. Several have had this disease and have recovered very well, and are in school again. I hope she will be able to write herself before very long.

She sends her love to all at home.

Yours truly,
Hattie E. Beatty

[There are no letters from Rachel to her family or friends from February to October 1857. After graduation Rachel returned to Hookstown for the summer before beginning her teaching duties in Steubenville in the fall. It is probable that Will found reasons to remain in Hookstown that summer, too.

The summer of 1857 was bittersweet for Will. The euphoria he felt following successful completion of his first year of teaching and in discovering his love for Rachel was overshadowed by the dark cloud of events around the world in India. His missionary brother Albert and Albert's wife, Amanda, were killed in the Sepoy revolt in Kanpur on June 13, 1857.

Although Will had been separated from his three brothers and sister when his mother died, the family maintained close ties. After serving in the Mexican War, James, the oldest brother, was a tailor in Kentucky, where he died in 1853 at twenty-five years of age, leaving a widow and young daughter. Sister Margaret, or Maggie, married a banker, and in 1857 she was living with her husband and infant son in Waterbury, Connecticut. Richard, a middle brother, ran away "out west" some years earlier and had not been heard from since. Albert, older than Will by four years, had grown up on a farm near Canonsburg, Pennsylvania, and had become a missionary in India. Albert and Will maintained as close a bond as distances allowed during their youth and young adulthood. They expressed deep affection for each other and great pain at being separated during their growing-up years. To strengthen their relationship as young adults, they made common educational plans. Will went to Jefferson College, which Albert attended before entering Western Theological Seminary in Allegheny, Pennsylvania.

In 1857, already two years in India, Albert and his wife Amanda were happily immersed in the daily activities of their adopted homeland. Like the other missionaries in India, Albert and Amanda were unaware of the potential impact on their community of Barhpur of the unrest bubbling just beneath the surface across India. India was not yet an independent nation; its history was replete with stories of conquering empires, power struggles between local rulers, and a more pervasive tension between separate, competitive communities with conflicting cultural ideals.

Fig. 2. Albert O. and Amanda Gill Johnson went to India as missionaries in 1855 and were killed in Kanpur during the Sepoy revolt of 1857.

The British entered India as traders in the seventeenth century. The East India Company was established to provide England with spices from the Far East. However, by the early nineteenth century, its managers had become like feudal barons ruling over large sections of India. The British government found this an increasingly unacceptable arrangement and in 1813 eliminated the Company's monopoly of the Indian trade, converting it into an agency through which Parliament ruled the Indian territories. Between 1813 and 1856 the British annexed a number of additional Indian territories and began administering them according to British procedures and in line with British interests. This often undermined local customs and local office holders, and the result was considerable discontent.

Following 1813, evangelical Christian missionaries began arriving from England, and after 1833 from America as well. At first the missionaries were not welcomed by Company officials, who did not wish to arouse the "religious passions" of the Indian people. But the missionaries soon became an accepted part of the Western presence in India. Their work in both education and evangelism posed a further challenge to traditional religious and cultural loyalties. While operating independently of the British government, and sometimes at odds with its official policy of religious neutrality, missionaries collaborated enough with local British officials for Indians to perceive them as part of a Western threat to the traditional Indian ways of life, whether Hindu or Muslim.

In 1856, an incident in southwestern India became a focal point for growing Indian resentments. A British soldier ordered a sepoy, an Indian soldier under British command, to grease his gun with animal fat.

Touching or using animal fat in this way was clearly against the Hindu religious traditions of the sepoy, and he refused. This single act of principle emboldened others and became the spark that ignited "The Mutiny," as Will, Rachel, and their contemporaries called it, or the "Great Revolt," as Indians refer to the event one hundred and thirty years later. On May 10, 1857, in Meerut, eighty-five sepoys refused cartridges greased with a combination of beef and pork fat. They were placed in irons and sentenced to ten years imprisonment. The next day, their comrades rose up in protest and released the prisoners, set fire to their station, and set off for Delhi, forty miles away.[9]

Albert and Amanda's letters first reflected alarm about the mutiny when they learned that Delhi had been burned and "insurgents" were marching 5,000 strong with an army of "thieves and plunderers" on Agra, eighty miles from their home. Lines of communication with the outside world were quickly closed. Another missionary couple sharing their station, the Campbells, with their two small children, returned with Albert and Amanda to join two other missionary couples in Fatehgarh. As the story was pieced together later, 116 British soldiers, civil servants and merchant families, as well as the four American missionary couples and the two Campbell children, boarded boats and set sail down the Ganges River toward Kanpur on June 4.[10]

They headed toward what they thought would be a sanctuary in Kanpur, the home of the Rajah of the area, Nana Sahib, a graduate of the Government College who professed to admire everything English. Many of the British leaders from Fatehgarh had been frequent guests in his home, gone hunting with him, and otherwise enjoyed his hospitality. But when the fleeing foreigners finally reached what they thought was friendly territory, they were greeted with a roar of artillery, which killed a British woman, a child, and an *ayah*, nurse maid. In confusion, the passengers left the boats to hide in the tall grass. Soon an army of sepoys gathered up the prisoners, tied them together two by two, and marched them off to Nana Sahib, who had assumed leadership of the mutinous sepoys in Kanpur.

Nana Sahib was in a dilemma. He was head of a Maratha Confederation which had ruled much of India before the turn of the century. Now he was being challenged to demonstrate where his primary loyalties lay: with the foreigners or with his own people. In his zeal to leave no doubt about his decision, Nana Sahib entered the British history of the revolt as the "incarnation of brutality and treachery." Among those

9. Metcalf, *Aftermath of Revolt*, 49.

10. Walsh, *Martyred Missionaries*, 41–43, 298–303; R. R. Cosens and C. L. Wallace, *Fatehgarh and the Mutiny*, 36–50. These two books—one using information from Presbyterian missionary sources and the other using British information sources—concur on essential facts but differ on some minor details.

giving counsel to Nana Sahib were advisors who suggested letting the merchants, planters, teachers, and missionaries go. But the voices that prevailed said, "No. Let the unclean foreigners be rooted out." When the British offered the sepoys 300,000 rupees ($150,000) for release of the captives, the response was, "It is blood we want, not money."

Thus, Albert and Amanda and the other bound prisoners were prodded, ridiculed, and marched for a day and a half toward the military station in Kanpur. At 7 A.M., June 13, 1857, the prisoners were taken out of the house and marched to the parade ground. There they were shot.

Will grieved for Albert and Amanda and their lost dreams, and he began reevaluating his own life choices. He did not fully understand the reasons for the sepoy revolt; he only knew that Albert and Amanda were caring, loving people who, by his standards and beliefs, were engaged in the most sacred responsibility—serving God and spreading His word around the world. More than a half century later, Will was asked what brought him to India. His answer quite simply was, "A grave." During those months of mourning in 1857, Will began to prepare himself to take his brother's place in the mission field in India. He resigned his teaching position in Hookstown, and entered the Western Theological Seminary in Allegheny.

After Will left for the seminary, Rachel returned to Steubenville for her first teaching assignment in a public school. Love relationships apparently were delicate topics and not suitable for family letters that would be read to all the aunts, uncles, and cousins, so there is little or no mention of "Mr. Johnson" in the following letters. Instead, she describes the antics of her students, her classroom, fellow teachers, and daily and special activities.]

School Room No 3
[September 1857]

My Dear Dear Mother,

School has just been dismissed. All are gone. I have swept and dusted my school room, and now I sit me down by my table to write to one of the dearest and best of Mothers. I am getting along very well. The first day was so dreary looking I almost got a "fit of the blues." Children can be noisy. But I am in very good spirits now. I heard the first evening, that some of the teachers were so much discouraged, they thought of giving up their schools. But I have not once thought of doing that. I will persevere. . . .

October 7, 1857

. . . I must go back a little to keep you posted in all my movements. In the first place, I got my certificate almost 2 weeks ago, after one week of suspense. It is a very good one, as high as any of the teachers got. And higher than some. It will last longer than my engagement here, which is all I wished.

I am now boarding at Mr. Junkin's, on the corner of 4th and Logan Streets. I have begun to feel quite at home among all. . . .

My school is flourishing. Scholars are getting orderly and I think in a little while my 60 urchins will keep as good order and pay as good attention as I could wish.

I had no school yesterday. The stove was being fixed and I could have no fire. I will not lose the time, for school was not dismissed on my responsibility. We only lose when we dismiss for our own pleasure, which will not be often with me, I am thinking.

On Saturday the teachers all meet together in the morning and consult on the best methods of teaching, and are drilled on the different branches. We hear lectures from some of the learned ones. These I think will be very profitable and interesting. The afternoon we have for ourselves.

We have had quite an exciting time among the schools since the certificates came out. The ladies, Miss Cuningham and Miss Griffin, had begun teaching over a week, feeling confident that they would get theirs. But they came blanks. And after teaching a week, they gave up their schools and went home. I pitied them, for their expenses had been large, coming a good distance.

There was quite an excitement a little while ago on our street. A house took fire and scared the people a little. But the fire was put out before it did any serious damage. The streets were thronged with people. . . .

> Ever your affectionate daughter,
> Rachel

Steubenville,
October 28, 1857

Dear Brother Frank,

. . . You know how it is in school. George has lost his book—Ben his pencil—Tom has left his at home—and Harry needs his back dressed for throwing stones at Sam. All these little things keep me flying round as spry as possible.

Our Fair came off last week. It was not very good. I was there two days for a little while. On Thursday 5 ladies rode. That was the best to be seen. One was an old lady who had no teeth—ugly as a mud fence. About as many ribbons on her as Nancy Smith would have, and a short riding skirt. She served for a laughing stock for the spectators. Some of the rest were very graceful and skillful riders. Our schools were closed 2 days for the fair. I suppose you had quite as good a one at Beaver. . . .

I attend the 2nd Presbyterian church and Sabbath school at 9 oclock in the morning. I have a class of about 20 juveniles, tho it will be divided after a little while. I hope the good folks [in Hookstown] have chairs provided for the basement again this time. I have one to sit on in class. And I can sympathize with those who have to sit on a six inch plank—for fear of soiling the nice cushioned seats up stairs.

Are you and Samuel both going to be at home, or out of school, I mean? I wish there was a good school at home for you.[11]

Frank, I do not think of anything very new or funny to tell you, unless I should mention one of our chief singers of sacred music, Euno, our little dog. Every time we have worship, when the singing begins, he throws back his head, looks up and then, with his nose pointing to the ceiling, strikes in. When we stop, he does. Then he begins again with us. He does not sing the same way, but varies with the tune. I never heard anything so amusing. If he is shut out of the room he will sit at the door. And the fun of it is, you might sing songs all day long and not a sound would be uttered, but if you strike on a sacred tune, then he tunes up. His is a serious organ, only sings psalm tunes. Enough of Euno.

I would like to know how Stella is getting along. If she was here, Achy would take her to school. But then how would Mother do without her too.

Mrs. Braddock told me she had seen Father in Waynesburg, and that you are all well. Where is Father working, or is he at home? Write me all the news from home. . . .

> Your loving Sister,
> Rachel L. Kerr

Steubenville
Wednesday evening, December 2nd, 1857
My Dear Brother,

. . . Well brother Samuel, perhaps you would like to hear how goes my experience by this time. But indeed I do not know that there has been much change the last few weeks, save in the weather. . . . Last Thursday was "Thanksgiving day" and all our schools were dismissed. We attended church part of the day, and Po Porter came up from the Seminary and spent the evening. . . . We spend our evenings pretty much at home, for there are so many of us here that we do not want for company.

11. Apparently when Will resigned his teaching position to attend the Western Theological Seminary in Allegheny in the fall of 1857, Hookstown was left without a teacher until a replacement was found the following spring.

Mrs. Beatty met with quite a serious accident a short time ago. She was thrown from their carriage. In her fall, she struck a post, which bruised her face and injured her so much that she has been confined to her room.

There was an entertainment given in the city Hall last week for the benefit of the schools. It was called a Cyclorama—something like those magic lantern shows you have seen, only on a much larger scale. The teachers were all privileged characters, admitted free. Of course we all went. There were some fine views of eastern scenery that is in the Old world.

Well Samuel, I spect you will think we are very grave and sober dignitaries down here if I do not spice my letter a little more. But we are the merriest of the merry. Jokes fly as thick as the coal soot in our little circle: "Can you tell me anything about Thanksgiving?" I asked. One of my little urchins said he guessed, "Noah appointed it." How I laughed at the little ignoramus! I wonder if turkeys hadn't something to do with it.

O, has Mother a turkey in the pen feasting on the countless ears of corn Frank and Stella are busy shelling and stuffing it with? I will likely be round about Christmas time to help catch him, and eat him. Tell Stella to keep the fowls busy pecking up.

. . . I say Good bye dear brother!

Your Loving Sister,
Rachel

[During Christmas vacation Rachel became increasingly concerned about the gap in educational instruction of her brothers and sister, since they had not attended school all fall. Rachel's particular concern seemed to be for Sam, who was sixteen, and she proposed that Sam come live with her in Steubenville to continue his schooling, which he did.]

Steubenville,
January 4th, 1858

Dear Father,

I have been making some inquiries today in reference to the high school. I will now give you the result, that you may consider the propriety of sending brother Sam here to continue his studies. I hope you may decide favorably, for I think it will be the best plan, and the cheapest of any other at his present advancement. I will enclose a circular which has the list of studies pursued. You will see that he is not too far advanced for the course of studies here. And he can improve quite as well here as at College, and it will not be so expensive. Besides, I think 'tis better to be pretty well advanced before entering College. Mr Sage has the reputation of being an excellent teacher. He teaches the languages and the more advanced classes. Miss Curtis, the assistant, was my room-mate part of this term. She is a very good scholar. The discipline in the school is good. Scholars are required to have their lessons as near perfect as possible. But I have said enough. Consider. I hope you may decide for the best!

Mrs. Junkin says she will board him on the same terms with us, $2.12 ½ a week. Tuition $8.00 per session of 21 weeks. And of course, he can study any of the branches mentioned in the circular. I think it will be a great advantage to board with us. You know how much has been said by great men about the good influence of a woman. If there is any good in that, he will have the good influence of 8 of the best—just think—5 of the learned profession. Now Father, I hope you will let him come. Think over the matter. I have given you a faithful view.

... Now with much love to you all, I leave you, hoping to hear soon.

Your affectionate Daughter,
Rachel

January 20th, 1858
Steubenville, Wednesday eve

My Dear Mother,

... Samuel and I are getting along nicely. He has begun his studies, and is very well content I believe—or at least I hear nothing to the contrary. He is now in his room studying and if he continues as diligent as he has begun, I think he will get along finely. He is in school all day until 4 oclock in the evening. He thinks they are a little more strict than at home.

... My school is progressing very well, and that is about all that occupies my attention. I spend my evenings mostly at home. Dr. Black of Pittsburgh lectures tomorrow night. His subject is the Berlin Conference of the evangelical churches of the World, which he attended at Berlin in Prussia. . . .

Affectionately,
Your Daughter

Wednesday, February 17th, 1858
Steubenville

My dear Father and Mother,

We received your letter on Saturday eve and were very glad to hear that all was well at home. Since last I wrote, all has not been so well with me. One week ago last Monday morning I took a severe spell of bilious colic. A physician was sent for and every thing done for me that could be. Yet still I suffered on. Nothing gave me any relief. . . .

My food last week consisted entirely of medicine, my drink of teas. . . . Dr. McCook attended all last week. He was here about 4 times a day. He is an excellent physician and a good Christian man. He reminds me of Doc Laurence in his talk. I thought he had better not write to you until I should get a little better, as it would only make you feel anxious while you could not be here with me.

. . . I have been treated very kindly by all since I took sick. I had every attention I could need. Yet, when sick, we long for the dear faces of home. One night I got a little impatient. Thought I ought to get better faster. And a little pettishly I told them that, "If Mother and Grand-Mother were here, they could do more for me than all the Doctors put together." Well I am getting along very well now. And I may feel thankful that 'tis no worse, and that again returning health smiles upon me.

Mr. Whitehills account to you of the small pox, was a little too large. I think he was scared worse than hurt. There have not been more than 10 cases in town altogether. Some of these were varioloid, and it has been confined to 4 or 5 families. There have been 2 deaths. These both were of the lower class of society, and through neglect they doubtless suffered. It was brought here by some rags sent from St Louis to the paper mill across the river. The man who died hauled them from the river and caught it that way. . . .

The Doctor told me yesterday that he did not know of one case in town now. Of the 14 public schools, 4 that are in 1 building, were closed for 2 weeks, because the small pox was in a house near by. Mine was not closed, as there was none in the vicinity of our rooms. The High School has not been closed. I think the danger is over. If we had thought there was any danger before, we would have written about it, and not have staid to risk such a loathsome disease.

The general health of the city is very good. We all got vaccinated over again, so we would be sure that we were proof against the Pox. The Doctor says the next time we want a sore arm, we may just as well take a splinter of wood and scratch our arms. For he has risked his vaccination 40 years, and intends to the rest of his life. He thinks once enough.

Samuel is at school. He is getting along very well, as far as I know; but I will save room for him to speak for him self when he comes back.

Several of my friends have called this afternoon. I find it rather inconvenient to talk. What a sad affliction it is for me to keep my tongue still. But I hope it wont be long. . . .

Your affectionate daughter,
Rachel

Steubenville
Wednesday eve, March 10th, 1858

My dear Mother,

I have not written this time as soon as I had intended, or as I ought to have done. For I could not find time to write. I have so much to do, going to church almost every night. There is preaching at night in every church in town but 2. The communion is in the 2nd Presbyterian church next sabboth. I expect a great many will join. Kate Doolittle and I go there and sometimes we go to the 1st church. The 2nd is rather the most fashionable, and the seminary girls go there. But I like the pastor of the 1st the best.

I heard good old Dr. Stockton preach last night. It seemed quite familiar to hear his voice again, though I believe I have not heard him since the revival in 1855 at home. I am so glad to hear that so many of my friends in Hookstown have come over on the Lords side. Would that all of our dear ones were brought to seek our Saviours pardon and blessing, that their precious souls may be saved! God grant that we may soon see that blessed day! . . .

My school will close the 26th of this month, or 2 weeks from Friday next. We all have a vacation of about 2 weeks. I thought this one would have been longer, but they give a long vacation at the close of next term. Most of the teachers prefer longer rest in the warm weather of July or August.

I have been very well since I went back to school. I earned enough since to pay my doctor bill, any way. My bill was $6.00. Very reasonable too, in comparison with the usual practice here—50cts a visit is the usual charge. If Dr. McCook had charged me at that rate, it would have been about 20 dollars. He is such a good man, a jolly one too. Looks a good deal like Uncle David Swaney and Doc Laurence together. So you may imagine how he does look.

He wants Miss Curtis, Kate, and I to sing in the choir of the 1st church, but we have never gone yet. We had a singing here at Mr Junkins Monday night. They wont sing any but Davids inspired Psalms in church, but I guess they think hymns set to metre good enough to learn on. We had a very pleasant meeting. . . .

I had the pleasure of a message from Jennie and Emma McLaughlin this eve. She tells me that Stella had been at a party and would not let the boys kiss her. Tell her she did just right. . . .

I think Jennie forgot the curl of Stellas she thought she had sent. And so the curls are all clipped off again. Save one for me.

I have not gone out much in the evenings, only to church. We have so much else to do. One evening I went to hear Madam Eloise Bridges give a Dramatic reading in the Masonic Hall. We had such a good time. Kate and I only were invited to go and we teased the rest of the family. When our company came, we started without telling where we were going; but they found us out afterward. . . .

Mother, I do wish I had the flowers that were in my summer bonnet. I wish you would get a small paper box and send them in it by mail. If you get a light one the postage will not be more than letter postage. I dont care about getting new flowers for spring, if you can send those.

Now Good bye to all the loved ones at home.

With love from Samuel and your affectionate daughter,

Rachel

Steubenville, May 24th, 1858

My dear ones at home,

. . . I was glad to hear that learning had revived in Hookstown, and would like to hear something more particular about the school. . . .

I have been enjoying myself, roaming a little during the last week. Our School Superintendent advises us to take our urchins out to the hills once in a while in the afternoon when they get tired. Of course this is very pleasant to both teacher and scholar. Miss B. (who teaches next room) and I marched ours up on the hill above town one eve last week. O how they scattered when we reached the grove, just like a set of wild deer. When ready to come home, we tinkled our bell, and the sheep came following after. We have just 6 more weeks of school, then vacation! This for schools—now for something else!

Presbytery of Steubenville met last week to ordain Rev. S. Sharp, as a Minister of the gospel to foreign lands. He leaves today for South America. The services were very solemn and interesting. Dr. Plumer from Allegheny officiated. He reminded me very much of some of the old patriarchs—Abraham, for instance—with his long white beard, which makes him look so venerable. Now I don't mean that I remember what Abraham did look like—I only imagined.

On Saturday I went with some 25 others over the river to what is called the town rock, a place where we have a delightful view of the city and surrounding country. We then went back some distance to a grove where the gentlemen or ladies spread out their provisions on a grassy spot that served for a table. And, having prepared some of that delightful beverage (coffee) at a neighboring house, we all partook with much mirth of the bounteous repast. The evening was pleasant. After enjoying to our hearts content the pleasures of such a trip, our jolly crew wandered back to Ohio. It was something like our 4th July picnic, only a little more so.

Samuel was along with his "Gray" [a horse]. I shan't tell any more of him. Frank may just ask him if he won't bet on the "Gray"?

There was nothing to mar our enjoyment, even the weather was propitious. Today, it rains, again. Here am I in my school room without an umbrella, and I can't think of getting my head wet. You know a person should be careful. Tho I expect my bonnet would suffer more than my head.

Stella, I will send a paper which you may give to Frank, and hear what is enclosed. Now Good bye. Love to all our friends, and to you all.

Affectionately,
R.L.K.

[Rachel hoped for a teaching position in Hookstown in the fall. The following excerpt is from the draft of a letter she wrote to the superintendent of the Beaver County Schools inquiring about the status of her Pennsylvania certification and the possibility of teaching in Beaver County in the fall.]

... In your note accompanying my Certificate, you stated that my marks entitled me to a professional [certificate], and that if you found my mode of teaching satisfactory, you would interview me.

I know your opportunity of judging was not very good. The time and circumstances considered, I hoped you would visit my school again before its close. But I suppose your other engagements have prevented you. The term for which I engaged expired on Monday 2nd. My services have been satisfactory to the directors, as far as I can learn. I think the progress of the scholars has been good.

If you esteem me deserving of a professional certificate, or if you have noted any faults in my behaviors governing teaching, I will esteem it a favor to receive your reply.

[The response was positive. Rachel spent the next two years teaching Stella and her neighbors' children in the Hookstown Select School on Washington Road.

Rachel's social life flourished in Hookstown. Church socials, school programs, and neighborly visits were occasionally complemented by special, formal evenings in town. These two invitations and the letter from her friend Jenni indicate that in addition to having many young women friends, Rachel was also popular with the young men.]

Friend Rachel,

Being too busy to call on you personally, I take the liberty of sending you these few lines to inform you, I am well, and hope you are enjoying the same blessing.

Well Rachel, I wish to say, that is I want you to under stand, that the young Ladies and Gents of this place and vicinity intend going up to Aunt Jane Jefferys this evening to have a jollification. And your company, as a matter of course, is expected, as well as earnestly requested.

The Ladies going are, Misses Stewart, Miss Gibson, Miss Maggie Hall, Sallie Laughlin, Sarah Wright, Nancy Durpon, and Cynthia Crothers.

Gents are Mr. William Miller, Samuel Miller, Marsh Donehoo, John Crafe, Sam Blackmore, Will and John Johnson, and your humble servant. You must attend by all means.

> Yours very truly
> Jim M.R.P

Miss Rachel Kerr,

You are respectfully invited to attend a singing this evening at the resadance of Mr James McLure.

> Wednesday
> March 23, 1859

> Thursday evening, July 29, 1859

Lillie dear,

It is now almost one long month since I saw you, and as yet I have not heard one word. As I was all alone this evening, I thought I could not spend the time more pleasantly than by writing to my little friend Lillie.

Oh Lillie, your old friend Doc McConnell was here last week. He talked so much about you. Said you were one of the best girls he ever new. He also said to tell you not to forget to answer the letter he wrote you three months ago. I promised him, when you come to see me, I would let him know. He is to meet us at the Harlem Springs.

Frank says to tell you to be in a hurry about coming, or he is afraid you will be married. There was a young lady told me a few evenings ago that you were to be married in a short time. I did not say one word, but thought you would not get married without letting me know it. And I think if you dont tell me, you will be real mean, for I feel as near to you as a sister. When you write, tell me all the news, and whether the report I heard correct or not. Frank says to tell you he is waiting right side up with care.

Well Dear Lillie, as I have nothing that will interest you, I will close. Give my love to your Mother, Father, Brothers, and kiss your dear little

Sister for me. And my love to all I know, and keep a portion for your own little self.

Now Lillie, when you write, tell me when you will come. Oh do come. I will do every thing in my power to make you happy. The family send their love—Frank in particular. Well, I will try and say good by. From your loving Sister,

Jenni

Write soon.

[Rachel had already made her choice of a life partner, Will Johnson. She filled her days with teaching, planning her wedding, and reassuring her family and friends that the decision she and Will had made to follow Albert and Amanda's footsteps to India was God's choice, and the right one for them.]

TWO

June–December 1860

AMERICA TO INDIA

⤷ RACHEL AND WILL'S WEDDING on June 5 was a major event in Hookstown that summer of 1860. It joined two young people who were well known in the community and who were setting out on a world adventure with an uncertain course. Closely following the wedding, Will was ordained as a pastor and commissioned as a missionary in his home church in Steubenville. Several weeks later, family and friends gathered to bid their anxious farewells.

The Presbyterian Banner gave the following account of a farewell celebration for Rachel and Will:

> . . . recollect the departure for India, in July last, of Rev. Wm. F. Johnson and lady. A short time previous to bidding adieu to all the home scenes of their native land, a Farewell Missionary Meeting was held in the Hookstown Presbyterian church, which was well attended, and marked by an unusual degree of interest. While none would have detained the missionary couple from going out upon their work of labor and love, the choking emotions of the soul, oft betrayed by the falling tear, testified to the fact, that there was a sundering of no ordinary ties.
>
> Mr. Johnson . . . had taught, for two or three sessions, the Hookstown Academy. During the period he was with us, he had endeared himself to many by his social qualities, and his hearty zeal for the missionary work. Mrs. Johnson is a daughter of Mr. David Kerr, of this place, and was a member of the Hookstown Presbyterian church, under the Ministry of Rev. R. S. Morton. In the family, in the social circle, in the school, and in the church, "none knew her but to love her." Many are the prayers sent up from our midst for the welfare of Mr. and Mrs. Johnson, and for their continued health and usefulness.[1]

The first letter home was from Cataract House in Niagara Falls. It was a brief, reassuring letter from both Will and Rachel, announcing that they had arrived safe and sound. Several days later, after they settled in

---

1. "Extracts from a Letter from India," *The Presbyterian Banner*, Feb. 23, 1861.

at the United States Hotel in New York City, they wrote a longer letter describing the first leg of their journey from Hookstown to New York City.

Between orientation sessions for their missionary work, Rachel and Will took several side trips out from New York City. One trip they particularly enjoyed was to Waterbury, Connecticut, to visit Will's sister, Margaret, and her husband, August Blakesley. Margaret and August accompanied Rachel and Will to Boston and waved farewell to the young missionaries as they sailed for India on July 28, 1860.

Rachel's correspondence during the voyage was returned to America in the form of a log she kept of their observations and experiences at sea. A large portion of this log was published as a news feature on page one of *The Presbyterian Banner* in February 1861. She described the beauty and wonder of the ocean, the southern stars, flying fish, sharks, dolphins, and albatross, and the changes of seasons, which sometimes occurred overnight. She wrote about the sailors and their lives on board ship; about her routines, sea sickness, and lazy days of reading and writing; and about special events, such as crossing the equator, spotting an island, and surviving a typhoon. After a sailing voyage of nineteen weeks—four and a half months—they welcomed the thrill of setting their feet on land again on December 8, 1860, and were delighted to discover that mail from home had arrived in India before their typhoon-delayed ship.]

United States Hotel, New York
July 21, 1860

Dear ones all in the old house at home:

This Saturday evening finds your absent ones comfortably situated in one of the great hotels in the great city of New York. We arrived here safely on Thursday evening and received a cordial welcome from Dr. Lowrie,[2] who made every arrangement for our convenience while we stay in the city.

After the last sad farewell, we turned our backs upon our dear old home and were soon in Wellsville. We took dinner and the afternoon train to Cleveland. About dusk we reached the city, and at once passed through the depot to the end of the dock. Here lay the *City of Buffalo*, the largest and most splendid steamer on the lake. The effect was as grand as white painting and gilding and good furniture could make it. Fine lace and curtains on the berths, etc.

2. Dr. John C. Lowrie, a former missionary to India, was secretary of foreign missions for the Presbyterian Church.

We were delighted with the trip on the lake. We went as much to ex-periment on the sea sickness question as anything else, but there was no swell. Though there was a good deal of wind and the waves rolled pretty high, we had to submit to the infliction of as good a nights sleep as we had for a week.

After breakfast we sat on the guard and enjoyed the beautiful lake scenery until we came to Buffalo. It possessed a great attraction for us as our first experience of being out of sight of land.

Wednesday we spent seeing the sights at Niagara. We were delighted with the grandeur and beauty of the scenery. As we gazed in silence and wonder at the rolling waters dash and leap over the great precipice, we could feel that it was really a world wonder. We captured a leaf and a twig here and there from the brink of Niagara, some of which we will enclose for you in our next.

We went over on the Canada side and down under the cataract. The water falls out several feet from the rocks and there is an L path under the torrent. We dressed in water proof clothes made of all yellow oil cloth, which were most ridiculous looking. Then we followed our guide down a long winding stairs and around under the horseshoe falls. It was a beautiful sight to look out through the great wall of water and down at the dashing spray.

We saw Blondin walk the rope across the Niagara River a hundred feet above the roaring torrent. It was a frightful sight. He stood on his head in the middle of that slender wire, hung down from it by his feet and loosed his hands, turned summersets backward and forward, etc., and came back safe. Then he walked it again with his feet in baskets.

There were a great many visitors at the falls as pleasure seekers from all parts of the country. Wednesday we took a parting look, and were soon rattling on the ridges, shooting over the bridges on the New York Central road. We traveled and slept very fast. Reached Utica in the morning, where we snatched a hasty breakfast.

The scenery down the Mohawk is beautiful. Sam, I suppose this is the Mohawk you sing about.

At Albany we changed cars, crossed the Hudson, and took the New York and Hudson train. This route lies along the Hudson River, where the scenery was grand and beautiful. The towering hills, the Catskill Mountains beyond the wide river, and floating on its bosom were so many sailing craft—sloops, barges and large steamers—dotting the banks beyond. West Point was on a high eminence, commanding a view of many miles of the Hudson. Many other places of interest marked the route.

Last of all, we are in this great noisy city. At the depot, greeted by the noisy cab men, we went on our way rejoicing to the Mission House. We spent the evening shopping and resting. Friday we spent in business.

Friday evening we accepted Dr. Lowrie's pressing invitation to visit his home, Astoria. Took an East River steamboat and went over, and enjoyed our visit very much. His family consists of his wife and two daughters—very friendly.

Astoria is a beautiful place. All the buildings are fine and surrounded by large and well cultivated grounds, ornamented by trees and shrubbery of every description. The streets are wide with trees planted on either side. Most of them were the drooping willow.

Saturday morning we returned to the city with Dr. Lowrie and went and got some photographs for our friends. In the Mission House, we saw photographs of all the Mission brethren and their wives lately gone out. . . .

Sabbath, we went over to Brooklyn to hear Henry Ward Beecher, the noted preacher. We heard two sermons from Mark, 6th chapter—38th to 40th verses—and John, 6th chapter—35th verse. They were grand. There was not much sleeping in his church. His style of delivery and expression all kept the attention fixed without wearying. The church seats about three thousand people and the house was full. The choir sang some of our good old tunes—"Where and When Shall We Meet Again," etc.

We have been so busy that we have not taken time to visit any of the sights of the city, except those that come in our business line. Today we expect . . . to [visit] some of the places of interest, and then we will leave for Waterbury tonight or tomorrow.

We do not know what day we will sail, probably the 1st of August. Dr. Lowrie gives us much encouragement about the ship being a very good one, which will add much to our comfort on our long voyage.

From the window where I now sit, I have a view of the East River. Just below us is the Fulton Street Ferry. On the opposite side of the river is Brooklyn. Ships, schooners and vessels of every description are lying in the harbor, and many others are plying the water. The street below is full of omnibuses, hacks, people and noise.

Mr. Johnson has gone up to the Mission House to attend to some other business, and I thought I would scribble a note to you while waiting. I have no pen and ink here, but maybe you can make out a word here and there.

Father, I found my purse alright. I forgot to leave my trunk key, but will send it. I must say goodbye. There is Mr. Johnson and he will add a line.

With much love for the loved ones at home and all our kind friends,
                                    Your affectionate daughter, Rachel
P.S.
I wanted to have written a letter to some of you, but we have been enjoying ourselves so well, I could not find time. I could not have believed

that Rachel could have borne all the trying scenes and separations of the last week with so much serenity and happiness. But the same Father, who bids us take up the Cross, gives Grace to bare it cheerfully and joyfully. I know it will cheer your hearts that your loved one finds the path of duty ever to be the path of peace.

Yours,
Will F. Johnson

Waterbury, Connecticut
July 25, 1860

My dear brother,

Since I closed the note sent you from New York, we received a dispatch from Boston stating that the ship, *Art Union,* on which we expect to go, will sail on Saturday next. We finished up our business in New York on Monday, and left for Waterbury on Tuesday morning at 8 o'clock. Arrived here at 12 noon. Our friends [Margaret and August Blakesley] gave us a cordial welcome, and have been devoting their time to our entertainment, so that our visit is very pleasant.

Waterbury is quite a large town, some five or six thousand inhabitants, I think. It is the most beautiful place I ever saw. The houses are all so neat looking, and so much taste is displayed in the cultivation of the grounds around them.

I had no idea that the New England villages are so different from what we are accustomed to seeing in Pennsylvania. The houses are not built so closely together, and they have room to display taste in the cultivation of flowers, evergreens, etc. The elm appears to be the favorite shade tree.

Mr. Blakesley got a carriage and took us out to visit the cemetery, which is about a mile from here. It is beautifully laid out with nice drives through every part. There are some very fine granite monuments (pure white granite). At the entrance is a beautiful fountain, the jets falling at different heights that look very pretty.

Waterbury is quite a manufacturing place. This morning Mr. and Mrs. Blakesley accompanied us to visit some of the factories. We visited the brass factory where they make pins, hooks and eyes, thimbles, rings, candle sticks, all kinds of brass wire—indeed, everything that can be made of brass.

We first went into the part where they were putting up and making pins by the bushel. It did look so funny to see great stacks of pins. The machinery for sticking them in the papers was very curious. Then there was a row of girls folding the papers in bunches as we buy them.

We then went in where they were making thimbles and saw them in every stage, from the little flat round piece of brass to the finished article all ready for the finger. The machinery for making hooks and eyes was our wonder. To see three or four motions of the little iron fingers roll them out, all finished, was indeed very fast work. But I cannot describe all that we saw. The nice bright buttons were some of the brightest I ever saw, etc.

This was all very interesting to see, but maybe not so much so to write about. We did not have time to visit the glass works. We were so tired when we got around those I mentioned, we felt like resting for hours.

We stopped in the Cathedral. It is a very fine building. Though not so large as the Cathedral at Pittsburgh, it is prettier. There are a great many fine churches in Waterbury.

Mr. and Mrs. Blakesley are going to Boston with us, to see us off. I will not close this letter until we reach there, where I hope we will get a letter from home. We got some photographs in New York for our friends as we promised. A package will be sent home, and I want them distributed as noted.

                                        Friday, July 27th, 10 P.M.
Mr. and Mrs. Blakesley went down with us on board the ship today and inspected our future home. The ship is a very good one. Our state rooms will be very comfortable. The cabin is nicely fixed up, but I will tell you all about how everything looks when I have time. By the way, we saw our Captain. He is a very pleasant man and a Christian by profession, and we hope in truth.

Now Father, Mother, Sam, Frank and Stella, all—I write you a last goodbye from the shores of our native land. I do not feel any fear or dread of launching out on the mighty ocean, ever since I have had a glimpse of its greatness.

We are rejoiced at receiving your letter, etc. today. Write often and faithfully to us. I think it would be a good idea if Sam and Frank would keep a journal of all the little items. If you would only write once a week in it, in a few weeks you would have a good long letter without the trouble of sitting down to write all at once.

I am so sorry that I could not get Grandfathers pictures copied. They were all sent with our trunks, and are stowed away in the ship. Here is a scrap of a Merino dress I bought in Boston, and my trunk key. Our Niagara relics are unfortunately stowed away in the ship too. But we will send you some from India when we get there.

Remember me in love to all our friends, and our dear Pastor's family. 'Tis very late. We sail at 9 or 10 A.M. tomorrow. May you all be kept safely by the same loving hand that supports us all.

                                        Goodbye. Affectionately,
                                        Rachel

Notes on the Sea—Atlantic Ocean
−13 days from Boston
August 9, 1860

A Greeting, loved ones, from your wanderers far out on the wide, wide sea!

Almost two weeks have passed away since we bid adieu to the scenes of our own dear native land, and set sail in the good ship, *Art Union,* for our distant home. The blue hills of America have long since faded away. And the ships that hovered in sight, the distant sails that were just visible on the horizon—all, all have vanished. And we see nothing but a wide waste of waters below and beyond, and the blue sky above. Alone on the ocean!

We came on board the ship Saturday morning, July 28th, at 9 o'clock. Mr. and Mrs. Blakesley, Mr. Rankin (Treasurer of the Board of Missions) and his wife, accompanied us to the ship. We finished fitting up our rooms, arranging our clothing where we could get it conveniently. Then our friends bade us goodbye and went ashore.

Mr. Johnson's sister felt very badly to see him go. The few days we spent with them were very pleasant ones though. Of course, our having to leave so soon, and for a foreign land, could but mingle sadness with our enjoyment. I liked Mr. and Mrs. Blakesley very much. But in my letter mailed the morning we sailed, I told you about our visit there.

At 10 o'clock the ship was loosed from its moorings, and piloted by a steam tug, we moved from Boston Bay. Our friends stood in a little group on the beach, waving hats and handkerchiefs as long as we could see them from the deck.

Although we gazed with tearful eyes on the shores of the country as they fast receded from our view, we felt that we would ever love our native land, wherever we would wander. Yet the ties that bound us to it were easily broken, in comparison with the strong bonds that clasped our hearts, home and friends. Those are the ones that seemed dear as life. Yet even those, however dear, must be given up at our Saviors call, if we would hope to be counted worthy of His love. It was a sweet consolation in the thought that we are sacrificing all for our Redeemers cause.

We had been jaunting about here and there so much after we left home, that we were tired and weary, and felt it a relief to be free to rest again. We did not expect to escape an introduction to the pleasures of seasickness very long after we got out to sea. But the first day we felt very well. The weather was pleasant and the sea very calm.

About ten miles from port the steamer left us. Now our ship glided along steadily with very little motion. And we all sat on deck watching the many ships around us. Some coming into port and others bound out.

A person gets such a good idea what a ship looks like from pictures of them, that I could hardly realize that I had never seen one before coming to New York.

The first night we slept soundly, rocked in the cradle of the deep. Sabbath dawned bright and clear, and we spent the day reading. In the evening a breeze sprang up that soon reminded us that we were not on stable land.

We number in all just 24 on board. Captain Norton, Mr. Kemp, first mate, Mr. Phillips (super cargo),[3] Mr. and Mrs. Wyckoff [fellow missionaries also bound for India], Mr. Johnson and I compose our table circle. The sailors eat their grub in the fore castle.

The accommodations on board are much better than I expected. The main cabin is about 16 feet by 10 feet, nicely finished off with the gilded cornice around the ceiling. In the center of it is a table, fastened to the floor with seats on each side, which are also screwed to the floor. Above it is suspended a barometer, lamp, and clock.

On each side of this cabin are three state rooms. One occupied by the Wyckoffs, another with our trunks in, and one by Mr. Johnson and me. The rest are used by the stewards. These are a little larger than the state rooms on steamboats. Each contains two berths, a little wash stand with pitcher and bowl, and a shelf for our books. A strip of carpet covers the floor. This large cabin opens into a smaller one where we sit, lounge, etc. This is a few feet lower down and in the stern of the ship. A bureau in one corner, writing desk in another, and a few chairs, table, mirror, and two wide lounges, comprise the comforts of our parlor.

Captain Norton is a great favorite with us all. He is so kind and sociable. Mr. Phillips is a very intelligent young man and has charge of the ships cargo. He is always ready for a chat. His father is a minister in the Congregational Church, and has trained his son up in the good way.

August 13, 1860

Now I must tell you of our experiences of sea sickness. That indescribable infliction is common to almost everyone that ventures on the sea. The second day after we sailed, one by one, we began to disappear from the table. Feeling a little twitching about the stomach, as though it was about to be turned wrong side up. Looking a little pale about the mouth, you tried to smile a ghastly smile. As our companions asked, "Are you getting seasick?" All feeling very unwilling to give in. But it was no use. We soon were lying stretched on our backs, too sick to care for anything

3. "Super Cargo" was an abbreviation for the title "Cargo Superintendent," the onboard representative of the merchant sailing ship's owner who looked after all the commercial business and cargo during a voyage.

in the world. We gave our whole attention to searching all the little corners of our stomachs for something that we felt ought not to be there.

As the dinner bell rings, it is the signal for renewed labor. The last crumb of your breakfast has long since been deposited in the little tin cup hanging by the bedside. And when the steward puts his wooly head in at the door to ask what you would like, you feel you would like to throw your shoe at him, if you were able, for merely mentioning anything in the eatable line. But common sense prevails. And you agree to try to swallow a little tea, and toast or gruel, which is hardly down, until it is (with an UGH) deposited in the cup again.

But in a few days we were on our feet and able to totter up on deck, feeling so weak and lazy, that it was a burden to move, speak or laugh. Everybody laughs at you, and you laugh at everybody else. For the sickness is never dangerous, though so very disagreeable. We are now all able to take our place at the table and do justice to that provided.

Our cook gets up things very nicely. Makes good bread, pies (pumpkin and mince), puddings, soup, cornbread, etc. We have not opened our jams yet. We are saving them until we get tired of everything else. The jelly Mrs. McGahan gave me is disappearing fast, and tastes very good indeed. We have on board several live sheep and pigs, and plenty of chickens and ducks. Vegetables: We have cabbages, potatoes, turnips, onions, beets, etc. Thus, you see we have a good variety of everything except fruits. Dried apples is all we have seen yet.

In the morning we go up on deck and exercise awhile. Breakfast at eight o'clock, after which we read and sometimes I sew. I cannot write but a little at a time. The rocking of the vessel makes it very unpleasant, but as I grow stronger, it will not be so.

Yesterday I saw some flying fish. They are five or six inches long, and have little transparent wings about three inches long on each side of their back. With these, I often see flocks of them fly up several feet out of the water. But as soon as their wings become dry, they fall back again in their briny home.

We see the little Nautilus sailing along with its beautiful pink sail, looking like a shell sailing on the water. Captain Norton says it's body is a jelly like substance and it is poisonous.

The weather has generally been pleasant since we sailed. Only a few rainy days and squalls of wind. We make about 7 or 8 knots an hour. A knot is equal to a mile on land [about 1.15 mph].

We do not know at what time we may meet a vessel going home. If we should, I will send you a message. For I know it will seem a long while to wait six months for news from us. But we must all learn the lesson of patience. And you, dear Mother, will have many lonely watchings. But I trust you are able to say cheerfully, "All is for the best." These separations are very sad to think of; but we know that all is well with us, if we have the good Shepherd to watch over us and protect us. I feel most grateful when I think that a mothers love and prayers are ours wherever we go. Separated we may be by land and sea, yet there is one place where we meet, to ask for blessings from the kind and faithful Friend who is ever present with us all.

Monday, August 20, 1860

Well, dear brothers—Sam and Frank:

This is a beautiful morning. And to enjoy its beauty and delightful breeze, that is tossing up great billows on the bosom of the old ocean, I have brought my portfolio and talking materials up on deck. In a little shady nook, I will spend an hour more or less in a social chat about life on the ocean waves.

If I could now sit down with you in our favorite seat under the shadow of the maples, and tell you of my travels and of the sights I have seen, I think your first questions would be: "What does the ocean look like?" "What kind of a life is a sailor's life?" So, this will be my theme this time.

The ocean—What shall I liken it to? As I look out over it, I see a wilderness of water, ever restless, wave chasing wave. Or if the breeze dies away, the water sometimes assumes a glassy look. Yet, they rest not, but rise and fall in a long heavy swell, which gives the ship a very unpleasant motion, until one gets accustomed to it.

The water is a deep, dark green. As I look far out over the sea, the water and sky seem to meet. As I follow that line around with my eyes, it is one unbroken ring. The bright blue sky our ceiling. The dark water our heaving floor. And our ship, with its white wings, gliding steadily on. But we still see nought but the same watery path day to day.

Yesterday the ocean was very calm and still. It sparkled in the sunlight like a sea of diamonds. Along side of the ship, it looked like a shower of fireworks.

The ocean presents some beautiful scenery. But I cannot but wonder that anyone should want to be a sailor. It sounds very nice to sing of the merry sailor lad, with heart both light and free; but I think poor Jack soon learns that there is more prose than poetry in the life on the ocean. His business is to be always ready to jump at the call of the officer with a ready, "Aye! Aye! Sir!" Then he goes about any work given him.

Every morning the decks must be scrubbed off, which he goes about in his barefeet, with his blue pants rolled up. Then all the brass fixtures must be scoured, sails mended, ropes tarred—which they do by dipping their hands in a mixture of tar and grease. They rub it on the ropes. He must run up the rope ladders to take in sail. No matter, rain or shine, Jack must be about doing up the chores.

The sailors are divided in two divisions called "Watches." One under the first mate, and one under the second mate. These are on duty alternately four hours each night and day. In turn, each man stands at the helm and turns the great wheel which guides the ship.

In the fore castle is a long room, with beds ranged along the wall where Jack sleeps. His meals he takes here, or on deck, as he pleases. For each sailor has a little wooden flat bucket, called a kit, out of which he eats his pork and beans. Besides, he has a tin pan for his soup. Everyone has a tin mug that holds about a quart. Out of this he drinks his tea sweetened with molasses.

I often watch them coming to the cook, who gives each one his portion, and he goes off, and sits down to his lunch. Twice a week they get some pudding too. How would you like to be a sailor, Frank?

Thursday, August 25th, 1860

A little shower interrupted my last mornings talk with you. But I will try to gather up the thread of my discourse and go on. I hope you will not find fault with it if there are a great many knots, for it must needs be broken off. Every little squall of rain that rises doesnt give you time for any "Yankee Speculation," as the Captain says. You see a mist out on the ocean, feel a sprinkle, gather up your traps, and run down into the cabin. By the time you get settled there, the breeze is all over. Sometimes I sit still, and take what comes, and have at least to go down with a wet head.

But I must tell you something more of the sailor boy. He wears a loose sort of jacket, a little cap, and blue cotton pants, to suit his taste and means. I used to think that sailors all dressed in uniform. But I find they dress quite shabby. And how could they do better, on $8 or $10 a month. They have a suit of yellow oil cloth which they wear in wet weather.

Our sailors are a mixed crew—some Irish, Dutch, Swedes and American. One grim looking fellow, Old Ben—we call "Santa Anna"—, says he is an American. But I should feel ashamed of him as a countryman. When they are pulling on the ropes, he pretends to be working very hard, but I dont think he would ever break many. He looks like some coal diggers we see at home. The mate likes to tease him, and Old Ben says he was too gay a boy to ever get married (He looks about 50). One boy, Charlie, is a smart, active fellow and has, I think, been raised among respectable people.

At first when I saw them climb the tall masts, I expected every moment to see them laid out on deck, a pile of broken bones. But they run up the ropes, active as a kitten, holding on by hands and toes.

In the evening, very often the sailors sing to amuse themselves. One, a Swede, is a splendid singer. We often listen to him singing his quaint old songs about his lassie over the sea. He is very fond of sentimental songs.

On Tuesday, our eyes were greeted with the sight of a sail. As it drew near, we found it to be an English Brig bound for the West Indies. The Captain ordered the sailors to hoist our flag, "The red, white and blue." It did make us feel good to see the stars and stripes floating over our heads. Yesterday we saw another sail in the distance. I hope we will soon meet one homeward bound.

This morning we are going at about $6\frac{1}{2}$ knots an hour. Sometimes we go as much as 11, when we have a favorable wind.

I have just been covering some books with paper muslin. We read a great deal. I have been reading Bayard Taylors, *Travels in India, China and Japan,* Primes, *Travels in the Holy Land,* Prescott's, *Conquest of Mexico,* and I must not forget, *Robinson Crusoe.* Mr. Wyckoff had a copy of it, unabridged. I enjoyed reading poor Crusoes haps and mishaps of land and sea very much—his sojourn on the lonely island where he had to be his own mechanic, farmer and Jack-of-all-trades, and his encounter with the pirates. Though an old story, yet it is one you find interesting. I have also read Mrs. Segourneys beautiful poems.

Now I wonder what you are all doing at home. Mother, I know is busy. As it is near dinner time she is doubtless getting up something to eat. Father has, ere this commenced, built the Temple of Learning, where the youth of Hookstown, for another score of years will learn wisdom. And Frank too is likely helping on the good work.

And Samuel, have you got Mr. Lincoln disposed of? I have a medal with Lincoln's embrotype on one side, and Hamlin on the other,[4] which Mr. Blakesley gave me. It was made in Waterbury.

And where is dear little Stella? At school, maybe, where I hope she will study hard and learn to write and read, so that she can write letters to me from away over the sea. Stella, I know, will try.

August 27, 1860

We are now only a few degrees from the Equator and what is called the Equatorial Calms. These are those calm belts extending around the Earth, each varying from 8 to 10 degrees in width. One is at the Equator, and one at each of the Tropics of Cancer and Capricorn. Between these belts of Calm are the Trade Winds, where we always have good winds.

The sea is now very still. Its surface is only broken by little rippling waves. Yet there is a heavy swell which gives an unpleasant motion to the ship, a heaving up and down. The calms are said to be the most unpleasant part of the voyage.

4. An embrotype was a chemically etched figure on metal. Hannibal Hamlin was Abraham Lincoln's vice-president from 1861 to 1865; the two men's faces were etched on Rachel's political commemorative medal.

Here in the tropic latitudes, it rains almost incessantly. It seems to pour down instead of falling in drops. The Captain and mates wear oil cloth capes. Umbrellas are of no use. For the first little breeze would carry it overboard—you too, if you refused to part company with your wet weather friend. When it rains, we are shut up in the cabin. We dare not venture further than to peep out of the door at the sailors paddling about in the water like so many ducks.

The last few nights we have been serenaded by the mosquito band. But our ears are strangely out of tune and we fail to appreciate their entertainment. They are greedy fellows too. In spite of many hints and warnings from slashing pillows, etc., they persist in presenting their bills. Nothing short of a feast of blood satisfies the villains.

We always have prayers in the cabin at eight o'clock in the evening; after which we usually go up on deck and walk, or have our chairs taken up, and sit and talk for an hour or two. If the weather permits, and though the thermometer may be 80, yet the evenings are pleasant as we could wish.

Our voyage will be tedious for a few days until we get across the Equator. With so little wind, we make little progress.

We are trying to beat eastward. Ships cannot safely cross the line west of 36 degrees, on account of a strong easterly current which endangers them being driven over on the coast of South America. There is a ship in sight steering the same course with us. The Captain thinks she is bound for California. She is so far off, he cant make out what she is.

September 3, 1860

We crossed the Equator yesterday, Sabbath. So we are up one side of the hill. Now we hope to slide down the other in a few weeks. We did not meet with any accident crossing over the line. The gentlemen did not get their hats knocked off, nor the old ship trip on it. So, I think we have pretty good evidence that our first impressions, when we began the study of Peter Parlay's geography years ago, that the Equator was a real line of some kind, stretching around this great ball called the Earth, were all wrong.

Yesterday there were a great many flying fish skimming around the bow of the ship. We were all watching for some, but they cannot be caught. The mate says they sometimes fly up and get caught in the chains on the side of the ship. Mr. Phillips has been trying to catch some of the larger fish with his hook and line, and a piece of sail cloth for bait. But they wont bite. Sensible fish they are.

We have plenty of salt fish to eat. Herring, mackerel, and our sardines are very good. I dont like the cod and never eat it. This morning we had mackerel for breakfast and it makes me so very thirsty.

The water is getting quite warm. It tastes like water that has stood in the house on a summer day. But it tastes pure and sweet. The Board put up a box of lemon and raspberry syrup, which makes a very nice drink. They also gave us a box of sugar crackers and several drums of figs. But we ate so many crackers when we were sea sick, now I cant bear the sight of them—nor of tea or coffee. At meals, I always drink water in preference.

It is just eight weeks since we left home. How much I would love to hear from you; but no, many weeks and months must pass ere I enjoy that pleasure. I hope you are getting a good long letter ready for us.

September 6th, 1860

40 degrees South longitude—32 West One third of our voyage is over. At least Captain Norton thinks we will not be more than 120 days. After wandering on the ocean for so long, sky above and waters beneath, you may imagine with what pleasure we greet the sight of land once more.

This morning, before sunrise, the Captain waked us with the pleasant news, "Land ahead." He called us to "hurry up and see the old Meeting House." We jumped out of bed, hurriedly dressed, and ran up on deck.

True enough. Far out in the mist, a dark mass loomed up, that looked very much in shape like some old meeting house with a tall steeple. We sat on deck in the misty morning light watching it, until, as the sun rose and poured a flood of light, our "Old Meeting House" resolved itself into a great towering hill, surrounded by a huge pyramid. Other smaller hills appeared. As we drew nearer, with our spy glasses, we could see trees growing among the rocks. Here and there patches of cultivated ground, and, on the upper part of the island, a town.

This rocky isle of the ocean is called Fernando de Noronha—a small island, only 7 miles in length by 8 miles in width, about 133 miles off the coast of South America. It is a place of banishment for Brazilian convicts. There are three forts on it, and vessels sometimes stop here for water. But the supply is uncertain, for very often they have no rain for two years at a time.

When we approached nearest to the island, which was five miles, you might have seen four or five artists, very busy with pencil and paper, sketching its rocky shores. When the task was finished, our sketches were all passed round and criticized. The unanimous decision was that we each had succeeded in getting a very striking likeness of Fernando Nerona. Thought it was our duty to preserve it for our friends edification or amusement, as the case might be. Mr. Johnson says, "Be sure to add that, though all looked much like the island, no two had the slightest resemblance to each other," which he adds very appropriately. But I will enclose mine. Judge for yourselves whether it is as the old lady said of her daughters painting, "either a cow or a rosebud."

September 10th, 1860

This morning we are again be calmed. For the last few days we have made 180 or 200 miles. But the wind has left us.

September 27th, 1860
Southern Ocean

For the last two weeks we have been deprived of our pleasant readings on deck. Shivering amid cold chilling winds when I ventured out, I was glad to muffle up with shawl, hood and mittens. My warmly wadded mandarin is so comfortable, I hardly know how I could do without it. I think we will not feel the cold so much in a few days, for we will get accustomed to it.

We have been rushing down toward the southern icebergs at the rate of 200 miles a day. The change from a warm tropical sun, to these cold west winds, that come fresh from the regions of perpetual winter, has been so sudden, that we feel it very much. We would love to see a bright, warm fire, but we have no stove in the cabin. The only fire on board is in the cooks "galley"—a little kind of kitchen, where the cook prepares our meals.

Mrs. Wyckoff and I go out there sometimes, but we do not stay long, for cook has no room to work when we two are there. He is a good-natured, black, grinning negro, and very fond of talking to us. He always asks us to come whenever we are cold.

The steward, who has the superintendence of the cooking department and is general housekeeper, is a little snappish sometimes. But we dont mind him, he soon gets in a good humor. He is an excellent cook and prepares all the nice dishes, so that excuses his bad temper. And he is often very kind.

These brave west winds make the ship roll and pitch, so that it is almost impossible to walk about in the cabin. You will probably get your pate battered against the wall by a sudden lurch of the ship, or your limbs blackened by a collision with a chair, stool, or box enroute for the other side of the room. I have often been landed in the one on the opposite side of the room.

October 10th, 1860

It is not only impossible to exercise in the cabin, but worse on deck. The upper deck, which is the room of the cabin, though level as a floor when the sea is calm, is now leaning first at this angle $/$ and then $\setminus$. It is rather inconvenient for locomotion. I have been trying to tie our water pitcher up so that it wont get rolled off under the bed again. Books on the shelf come tumbling down and everything is dancing about at a fearful rate. The spittoon has traveled all around the cabin and finally is tied up.

At dinner the scene is laughable. "There goes the soup over in somebody's lap." "Look out or a potato will give you a red nose." "Here are crackers all piled around your plate." The carving knife slides under the table cloth and hides itself.

Attempt to dip a spoonful of nice chicken soup, and just as you are about to smack your lips over the well seasoned dish, it goes in your lap, spoiling your new calico. And alas! the wash woman you will not find on board for lack of water. Then for the next course, you must hold on to your plate of roast pork with one hand and your glass of water with the other, and eat if you can.

But now the ocean, with its waves piled up mountain high, is grand beyond conception. Mr. Johnson and I go up on deck, muffled up in shawls and sit in the cold, breezy, air whipping against the ship. Now and then a great wave dashes the foam and spray up over the deck and into our faces. After we look out over the countless billows piled up on either side, we seem to be down in the trough of the sea, while the waters are a wall on either side. The waves come dashing over each other, forming beautiful miniature Niagaras.

Flocks of Cape pigeons, about the size of doves, with pretty snowy breasts and black and white wings, keep sailing around—never tiring—but now and then, dropping down on the waves to pick up a stray bite. There on the bosom of the waves resting gracefully for awhile, then up and away. The cook caught one with a hook and line. Then the mate wrote our ships name and the date on a little piece of wood, and tied it around its neck and sent it away. Huge albatrosses, measuring ten or eleven feet from tip to tip of their wings, are sailing around us.

We now see for the first time the Constellations of the Southern hemisphere. The Southern Cross, that everybody writes about who has been around the Cape, is the brightest of the constellations. But it has only two stars of any brightness. The "Magellan clouds" look like a fleece of wool floating in the blue ether.

We are still rushing along at the rate of 10 and 11 knots an hour. We spend most of the day shut up in our little room reading; sometimes, with a hot brick for a foot stool. We are getting fat and hearty and have astonishing appetites.

Indian Ocean
November 1st, 1860

I found it almost impossible to write when the waves were rolling so high. I have not tried for several days. We passed the Cape of Good Hope—several degrees south of it—and sailed easterly some 6000 miles in a direct line. Then changed our course northward and are now in the Trade Winds, that carry us along briskly.

We are enjoying delightful spring weather. We went to bed one Saturday night, our teeth chattering with the cold, and next morning waked to find a bright spring morning—all but the singing birds and green fields.

The Cape pigeons began to leave us. Only a few stragglers here and there are left. We amused ourselves trying to catch them with a hook baited with a little piece of meat. But the ship was going so fast that when they would dive down to catch the meat, it would run away from them. Although they paddled after, they had to give up the chase. Mr. Johnson called me up one evening to see one that was flying around with a little bottle suspended round its neck with a note in it. We were all very curious to see what it was, but could not catch it.

November 5th, 1860

We are now again in the region of the flying fish. Yesterday as we sat on deck the water seemed alive with them. Flocks of them would fly up out of the water, pursued doubtless by some greedy albacore in search of a dainty bite. These albacore are large and very beautiful. Mr. Johnson was out on the bow and saw some of beautiful bright colors.

I saw a dolphin leap up out of the water, a little away from the ship. This fish is said to show all the different colors of the rainbow when dying.

The great whales go spouting through the water. A few evenings ago, Captain Norton pointed out several to us, far out on the water, spouting the water high up into the air.

We saw quite a curiosity in the shape of a water spout at sea. These are something like the whirl winds we see often in the streets at home, carrying the leaves and dust up into the air. But in the water spouts, the whirling motion of the air carries the water up out of the sea to meet that pouring down from the clouds. They are funnel shaped at both ends and small in the middle.

A great ugly shark, with its triple row of teeth, great fins, and scaly body, followed us for a time. It came waddling, hoping some poor fellow would get overboard and give him a dainty bite. But he was disappointed. For we only offered our companion, with a fine open countenance, a piece of meat with a hook in it for its dinner. But he disappeared without gratifying us with further acquaintance.

Two little fish go before this monster, which are called pilots. When they see anything on the water, these sharp sighted little fellows go back and pilot the shark to it. In reward for their kind offers, he protects them from the larger fish. If they get in danger, they are said to get in under his fins or under his back.

November 8, 1860

I must tell you something about tropical moonlight and sunsets in the Indian Ocean. They surpass in beauty anything I have seen on the land. The atmosphere is clear and brilliant. The sunlight, a ball of fire, drops down beyond the water, leaving a flood of golden light. It colors every cloud in the most beautiful and gorgeous drapery. These clouds are of every hue and tint, floating to the zenith in clusters, while all around the ring of the sea. Some are of a delicate rose tint, others of a bright crimson, and many intermediate shades. I never imagined a sunset so brilliant. But there was not only this gorgeous coloring of the clouds, but beyond these, instead of the blue, I have seen the sky of bright green—a color I never saw in the sky at home.

We were all sitting on deck one evening, just after tea, when our attention was attracted by a new and very beautiful appearance of the sky. The sun had just disappeared below the horizon, when we observed beautiful pink bands diverging from the sun, and extending across the heavens, converging in the east. It was the prettiest sunset I ever saw. Those belts of light continued bright for sometime, then faded away in the twilight. Almost every evening reveals some new freak of the clouds, that calls for wonder at the Glory of God. His Glory is displayed in the heavens, where his pencil alone could trace those delicate tints and suffuse the touch of beauty we see in the fleecy clouds.

When the twilight fades into night, the moon rises in queenly beauty. We see far over the sea a silvery path reflecting back her brightness. The stars begin to pale before the flood of light that pours down upon us. We gaze at the little rings of light on the still water. Or, as the ship stirs the water into little ripples, they dance about—shooting and twisting into shapes like fiery serpents, chasing each other through the waters. This surpasses by far any display of fireworks I ever saw.

November 10, 1860

We are once more in the Northern hemisphere, but far away from the "Old House at Home," hid in the leafy maples. Now, while we are favored by the warm breezes of tropical clime, the cold November winds at home are howling, and the dear ones there are gathered round a bright fire.

But doubtless the excitement of politics is enough to keep the politicians warm. It seems but a little while since we were all singing Fremont songs together. Our gentlemen are all Republicans on board, so they can't get up any very warm debates on that question.

Laying politics on the table, I will tell you about the ocean on fire—at least it seemed so. A few nights ago, Mr. Johnson and I were promenading back and forth on deck about 9 o'clock. We were just about going below to retire, when the second mate, who was on watch, told us to come and look at the water over the stern of the ship.

We went and looked down into the deep dark waters. They seemed to be filled with balls of fire. As we looked ahead, at intervals, there seemed belts of light across the water. It was bright phosphorescent light. When the ship passed through one of these, the water seemed alive with fiery serpents, balls of fire and every conceivable shape of dazzling light.[5]

This phenomenon is often seen at sea and sometimes extends over several miles. "Maury," in his Geography of the Sea, calls it "White Water." He says they are caused by organisms of the sea. Whether wholly animal or wholly vegetable has not been satisfactorily determined. That geography of the sea is a very interesting and instructive book.

There is little of that monotony about the ocean that one would naturally expect. Its restless motion, change of form, change of coloring, all have contrary effect. But I must say, it makes one feel very lazy. Everyone of our company testifies to the same. When you sit down to write, you feel as though it were impossible to summon energy enough to record a single idea. Anything that requires thought, you feel unequal to the task.

But books are indispensable. You can doze over a nice story book or book of travels while a delicious feeling of laziness steals over mind and body. It leaves only the bare consciousness that you exist. This I think is owing to the change from an active bustling life in the noisy world to the quiet life on shipboard. Out of the world, you might say, for all the direct connection you have with it. Imprisoned, where you can only walk a few feet for exercise. It is not strange that this listless feeling takes possession of ones mind and body.

>Indian Ocean—Latitude 6 degrees North
>Ship *Art Union*
>November 13th, 1860

We are now rejoicing in prospect of soon reaching our destined port. Here in the region of calms, where we expected to make but 50 or 60 miles a day, we are sailing along with fine winds. We are making over 200 miles a day. We crossed the Equator on last Sabbath and are now sailing in the waters of the Bay of Bengal. This is less than a thousand miles from the "City of palaces" [Calcutta].

The rain is pouring down in torrents this morning. We are all busy writing, for it is not every day that we can rouse up energy enough. We are so lazy. Indeed, I dont think I ever realized the true meaning of that word, in all its force, until I became a sailor. But it is not strange. We are cooped up all day with only a few feet to exercise in. All we can do is eat, read, and sleep.

5. Rachel described bioluminescence, the emission of light from living organisms.

We are only about 200 miles from the island of Sumatra and 130 from the Nicobar Islands.

Yesterday a little bird came aboard. Mr. Johnson called me to come up on deck to see it. The Captain thought it was a land bird, but when he caught it, we found it was web-footed, as all sea birds are. He called it a "booby." Not a very musical name truly, but about as musical as its voice.

November 14th, 1860

It does seem as though our journey by sea is almost over, when we get to packing up. The weather being pleasant today, Mr. Johnson and I went down between decks and overhauled two chests. We packed up such things as we will not likely need until we get to our India home. I found my Merino dress and Mr. Johnson's pants, a little mouldy in spots. So, we gave them an airing on the upper deck.

I have been quite busy sewing for the last two or three weeks. I made Mr. Johnson a nice double study gown, which will keep him comfortable in the cool mornings and evenings. I also made him two Marseilles vests, which look very well, considering that I have not served an apprenticeship as a tailor. I miss our Finkle machine that used to work such wonders in that business.

We are only 36 days in making the passage from the Cape to the Equator, which is a very quick passage at this time of year. Sailors have a superstitious notion that if there are missionaries aboard, they will have a long passage. But there seems to be no Jonah aboard now that hinders their good fortune.

Thursday, November 15th, 1860

Our dinner of clam soup and roast chicken has been carefully stowed away. Now for an after dinner chat. This morning I gave my trunk a general clearing up. Among other things I found, was Fathers pale shadowy picture. How I wish we had good life-like likenesses of you all. I wish you would improve the first opportunity of getting good ones.

You could easily send them to Dr. Lowrie by mail—the postage would be but a trifle that far—then he could send them out with some box being sent to India. The missionaries are constantly sending for articles which they can get cheaper at home than in India. There are some 20 or 30 boxes on board this ship for missionaries in different parts of our mission there.

By the observation today we find that we are only about 500 miles from land. Only a few days until we enter the Hoogly River. Calcutta is about 100 miles from the mouth of the river.

What an important triumph of art is that which enables the mariner, in a few minutes, to figure out the very spot on the chart where the ships course lies. He charts his course far out on the pathless ocean, where he

meets no friendly mile posts to point him on the way—no footprints—
no wheel tracks—by means of a little instrument he can hold in his
hand, and by his observation of the altitude of the sun at different hours.
We can see on the chart just where our path crossed last years voyage.

Yesterday we made 230 miles and we are still scudding along at about
10 knots an hour with the wind aft. This makes the ship reel from side
to side like a drunken man.

The table is set for tea and the dishes are all dancing a jig: the crackers acrossing over into the meat plate; the tea cakes playing with the butter dish; and the spoon hopping round in the sugar bowl. The arm chair
in which I am sitting keeps sliding thump against the door, then against
my bunk (bed). It is blowing quite a gale. The great waves are rolling up
like mountains and thumping the ships sides.

> Bay of Bengal,
> Thursday, November 22, 1860
> 100 miles from Pilot

My dear Friends,

A few days ago we were congratulating ourselves in the prospect of
soon reaching port, without experiencing any of those terrible storms
that have invested the mighty deep with such terrors. But our hearts
have been taught anew the lesson, "Boast not thyself of tomorrow, for
thou knowest not what a day may bring forth."

Favorable winds were speeding us on our way so rapidly, that we confidently expected we could reach "Sand Heads," where we would take
the pilot, on Sabbath last, (18th). We were all rejoicing in our unusually
short passage from the Cape, through the calm belts of Capricorn, the
Equator and Cancer, and in fair winds in the Bay, where we expected
"head winds." The joy which filled the hearts of all was reflected from
every face. Light-hearted repartees enlivened each social meal as we
looked forward only a few days.

But we were yet to see God's wonders on the mighty deep exhibiting
his power on a sublimer scale than our eyes had ever witnessed. On Friday we had very strong winds which increased to quite a gale on Saturday. As we were approaching the "Sand Heads" very rapidly, we began to
fear that we would have to "lay to," if we should reach them while the
waves were so boisterous. There was also danger of being run into during the night by some of the ships that were cruising about in the Bay,
bound in like ourselves, but tossed about by adverse winds. Although we
had a light rigged on the bowsprit, yet in the thick darkness, mid the
rain and mist, this would only be visible a short distance. Saturday eve
the winds and rain were still unabated.

When we retired to rest, the dark, threatening clouds warned us that
it would doubtless be a night of peril, from wind and wave. The sails

were all furled, but the "spanker," "mizzon-topsail," and "main-topsail." These were "double reefed." With these precautions, the Captain came below. The 2nd mate and his watch were on duty. We all lay down to rest, perchance to sleep, feeling that our lives were in the keeping and watched over by the Eye which never slumbers nor sleeps.

We had all fallen asleep, when about 11 o'clock, we were waked by the mate calling the Captain. In a moment he was up and on deck. He is always called when a sudden squall comes up in the night, but this, we knew, was no trifling squall.

The wind was howling fearfully. The masts groaning and creaking. The vessel swaying from side to side. The waves dashing and thumping against the sides of the vessel, thundering in our ears. The sails we could hear flapping round the yards, all tattered and torn. All these, with shouting of the Captain to the officers, and they to the crew—striving in vain to make their voices heard above the blasts that almost took their breath from them—told us of the great danger that surrounded us in that hour of peril.

All hands were aboard, but the poor sailors were perfectly bewildered. In vain they were ordered to go up and furl the remaining sail. Dumb with despair they stood, unwilling to incur a more fearful risk than that which surrounded us all. But who could blame them, for it seemed certain death to venture aloft where they were liable to be swept overboard by every blast that lashed the tattered sails about the swaying yards. The 2nd mate, while trying to furl the top sail, had everything blown off him—pants, hat, everything, but a remnant of his shirt.

The sails now being all gone, there was nothing to keep the ship steady, and it was almost impossible for the helmsmen to steer and keep her to the wind. For if we once got turned round broadside to the wind, we would go down in five minutes.

Two men were at the wheel, and a sail was quickly lashed to the rigging on the windward side, to keep the ship steady to the wind. This and the strength of the wheel-ropes, were all we had to depend on now. When the wheel-ropes parted, the Captain was providentially just at hand. Four set wheel tackle, ropes passing over pulleys, were instantly hitched on to the tiller, which connects with the rudder, and all hands bore down on these ropes throughout the long night.

The dead lights were put over the windows to keep the seas that came dashing over the decks, from breaking into the cabin. The lights on deck were extinguished by the blasts of wind, and nothing more could be done but wait for the morning. The Captain's voice was heard inquiring for the time. And his oft-repeated reply, "Is that all?", told how little he expected we should ever see its light.

In the midst of these dangers, with peril on every side, we felt, as we never did before, the preciousness of that promise of our Savior, "Lo, I am with you always." As our earnest prayers ascended to our Father, we felt that He was able to keep us safely under the Shadow of His wings, safe from the storm and the tempest. We knew that if He had a work for us to do in India, He would bring us safe there. Or, if we were about to find a grave in the waters, He was able to bring us safe home:

> "Beyond the smiling and the weeping.
> Beyond the sowing and the reaping."

And there we hoped to find forever, "Love, Rest and Home."

It was indeed a night never to be forgotten. Those hours that we lay waiting for the dawn of an earthly Sabbath, which we knew not whether our eyes should greet, or whether we should enter on that long Sabbath that shall never end. Thus the hours passed slowly away. We kept our watch unwearied and sleepless.

At length morning came. Still the tempest raged with increased fury. We ate a little breakfast without the Captain, who remained faithfully at his post on deck, with only a cup of tea to refresh him after his weary watching.

The barometer kept falling lower and lower all forenoon, which warned us that the worst had not yet come. We sat round the cabin watching it with the most intense interest. Our ship looked sad enough by the morning light—the sails hanging in shreds, the braces swaying from the yard arms a tangled mass, while the winds swept dismally through the wreck.

The ship reeled from side to side until the yard-arms dipped in the water, and the sides dipped down until they scooped up the water on the lee side. The sea rolled up like great mountains, threatening to swallow us in the depths. At noon, the steward could not set the table, the vessel rolled so. We took a lunch, though you may well suppose, very little sufficed us.

But the end was not yet. A sudden crash announced that the main top-gallant mast was gone. Another, and the mizzen top-gallant mast was gone also. The ship has three masts, named mizzen, main and fore. Each mast has four parts, each carrying a yard and sail. Those four are the lower, top-mast, top-gallant, and royal. These last two parts of the main and mizzen masts were those that gave way. The fore-mast braved it out.

It was now a time of the greatest anxiety, for we knew not at what moment a sea might sweep over our house, and smash it in pieces. For the waves washed over into the fore castle deck, until the water stood knee-deep on the "lee-side."

Yet amid all this tumult, we were enabled calmly to look up to Him who rules the winds and waves and cast our cares upon Him. Our little company met together, and joined unitedly in prayer and praise. Mr.

Johnson read the 107th Psalm, then we all bowed together in earnest prayer around the Throne of Grace.

Then, while our voices joined in singing that sweet hymn, "Father Whate'er of Earthly Bliss," the glad news that the barometer was rising was repeated from one to another. The little prophet pointed out with unerring certainty every change in all the storm. The clouds began to break away, the wind to fall. When the sun went down, the heavens were suffused with a beautiful rosy tint.

The yards that were swaying from the sides were cut away by some of the brave sailors, and the sails that were close furled round them, were saved, after much hard exertion. The men worked bravely. Climbing over the sides of the vessel, hanging on by the ropes and rigging, they tugged and pulled at the sails to get them in out of the water, while the waves dashed over them.

Once they had almost got the main top-gallant sail tugged in, when it gave a lurch and got away. It went through under the vessel, and came up on the other side. All hands ran to catch it, but it got away from them.

The steward, a curly headed darkey, was down over the side. His locks usually so precisely laid, were standing out in all directions. He looked as though he was a fury coming up out of the waters. So frightful he looked. Every face was now lighted up with joyous hope, such as those only can feel who were delivered out of such perils as we had encountered for 16 long hours.

When the lamps were lighted, the tea-table was spread, and we all gathered around it with hearts glowing with gratitude to Him who again furnished us our table in the midst of the waters. The evening was passed in social converse, and then we kneeled at the mercy-seat and offered up our earnest, hearty thanksgivings to our Preserver. He had said to the waves, "Thus far shalt thou come," and had rebuked the winds that they were stilled. Tired and weary with our watchings, we lay down to rest, and slept peacefully until the morning.

Monday morn dawned bright and fair. The sea, so lately raging in such fury, was almost calm. The long heavy swell alone told of the storm that had so lately tossed it so fearfully. The ship was soon rigged out with all the sails left, and the men were at work repairing the losses.

The decks were strewn with pieces of ropes and sails. These were lashed in all kinds of knots. Great cable ropes tied into knots, impossible to untie, and new sails made of strong canvass were whipped into ribbons. Just think of strong canvass woven out of strong threads like twine. You would think it impossible to tear it.

I never imagined the winds could have such power as we saw them exert in this storm. But such storms do not often visit the seas. The Captain and 1st mate have been seamen for twenty years, and the 2nd mate for 30, yet they all say they never saw such a "blow" before. They have seen some pretty hard ones.

This kind is known by the name of "Cycloons" [cyclones] in the Bay of Bengal. In the China seas, they are called Typhoons.

Our vessel is so strong and tight that 'mid all the pitching and straining of her timbers, she did not leak a particle. It was well for us we had a good strong vessel, or she could not have lasted through the storm.

We have nearly all the sail set again, and are steering for the pilotage, as well as the winds will permit. But we have to tack East, then West, trying to beat again the winds, and make Northing.

Several vessels are in sight today. We have signalized two. This we do by means of flags. We first hoisted our ensign—the stars and stripes—to tell them we were from America. One vessel then showed English colors. A brig in sight showed American colors, and told us by her signal flags, that she was from the isle of Mauritius, bound to Calcutta, 34 days out. You have no idea how even such a little event as this, is hailed by those who have spent weeks and months without seeing any sign of living beings on the wide waters, but those of our own crew.

Yesterday we saw what seemed to be the wreck of a vessel, and the Captain gave orders to "bear down toward her." But we found that it was a native vessel, crowded full of people. They were not in need of help. At a distance their vessel looked as if it was dismasted. But it was a low-rigged vessel, which made it seem so. And we went on our way rejoicing in kind intentions, as they did not require our services.

"Sand Heads," Mouth of the Hoogly River
November 28th, 1860

Reached the pilot brig this morning. We have been beating about the Bay for the last 10 days, with such strong head-winds, when there is not a dead calm. We have only made about 150 miles northing in all that time.

The late storm had driven the waters up into the Bay, and the reflex current, flowing out, was so strong that it drifted us back faster than the wind carried us along. Vessels have been in sight for several days. Every new sail we hoped was the pilot brig. Once, indeed, we were in sight of it, but adverse winds carried us right away from it. Thus we have been beating about, each day thinking, surely today we will get a pilot.

The Light boat is anchored off Sand-Heads, and either furnishes ships with pilots or directs where they may be found. At night she shows a light every half hour. Last night while we were sitting on deck enjoying the moonlight, a bright light loomed up far o'er the waters, which we welcomed as the Light ship. A breeze sprung up and carried us along nicely all night. The Captain was so anxious about reaching it, that he did not sleep any. But we slept quite comfortably until six o'clock this morning, when we were greeted with the news that a pilot brig was bearing down towards us.

We hurried up on deck, and in a little while we saw them lower a boat, hoist signals, and put out for our ship. We "hove to," and the boat came up alongside, with the "pilot" and "leadsman" aboard, with their Hindoo servant. The boat was rowed by eight of these dusky sons of India. You may imagine with what interest we gazed for the first time upon these natives of that country where we expect to find a home.

These Bengalees are about as black as the majority of darkies we see at home. They are quite slender, and some of them were rather comely, while others were fierce looking fellows. The pilot's servant is now pattering round in the Cabin, helping the steward spread the table. He has about a yard of blue calico twisted round his head, wide pants of cotton cloth striped with red and green, a blue shirt over, and two or three yards of white muslin wrapped round his body, one end hanging down before.

He and the steward keep chattering together in the Bengalee language. The Captain introduced the pilot to us a few minutes ago. He is a regular "John Bull," a little pompous fellow with a fierce mustache, who puts on airs enough for half a dozen "Brother Jonathans."[6] He is Master of the ship now, until we get into port.

We are now lying at anchor, waiting for the flood tide. The current is so strong we can only make headway with it in our favor.

I went up on deck a little while ago to see a large Mail Steamer which passed quite near us. We flatter ourselves that it bears a message for us too. Oh how we long for letters from home! A vessel passed yesterday with troops on board bound for China, we supposed.

The water has changed so much in appearance the last few days— from deep blue of the Indian Ocean to a dark green, and then to a lighter green, and now it is quite muddy looking. The weather is delightful. Not very hot at noon and just cool enough to make a blanket comfortable at night. Pieces of logs, bamboo, cane and branches floating by, remind us that dry land is somewhere in this region. Several little birds have visited us. One has long slender claws about 4 inches long, and legs proportionably.

6. The nickname for the typical Englishman, "John Bull," a hearty, bluff, good-natured, and slightly pig-headed character, first appeared in a 1712 satire by John Arbuthnot. "Brother Jonathan" originally was a derisive British nickname for American Revolutionary War patriots. By the mid–nineteenth century it was commonly used by the British to refer to the United States or to any American man.

Off Sangor Island

Thursday, November 29th, 1860

Now here we are at the end of our voyage, after being tossed on the Atlantic, Southern and Indian Oceans, for 123 days. All are in excellent
health and good spirits, ready to welcome the shores of India. Here we
are, "strangers in a strange land."

We are now about 17 miles below Redgeree, and will not reach there
today. This morning our eyes were greeted with the sight of land once
more. We could see it looming up darkly against the horizon; the trees
standing out in bold relief. This Island is covered with jungle. It is a re-
sort for tigers and other wild beasts.

This morning we were sitting on deck, watching a large French Ship
being towed down by a steamer, when a boat filled with natives came up
alongside. They came aboard to help work our ship up the river.

Their boat is a long flat boat and their carpenter has joined it tightly
together, without a single nail. The pieces are fitted together, and then
holes bored. Strings are put through and tied securely. I can now see
their boat through the window, where it is moored astern of the ship. I
hear them chattering.

These are very uncivilized looking specimens. When we look at those
degraded creatures, we begin to realize that we are nearing a heathen
land. They have no clothing on their bodies except a piece of long cotton
cloth, about 4 or 5 yards long, which is wrapped several times round the
waist and brought up round the loins. The end is twisted in at the waist.
Thus, nearly all their body and the lower part of their limbs is exposed.
Some of them have their hair shorn, while others wear it long.

The sailor boys have been trading off their old clothes to them for
cocoa-nuts. One little fellow, they had rigged out in a full suit of "Jacks,"
but he soon laid it off and donned his own as far more comfortable. Another black fellow was strutting about with just an old satin vest on. They
looked quite ridiculous, you may well suppose. You have little idea how
strange they look.

I know my dear Father and Mother will rejoice to know that we are
not cast down and sad, but are ready cheerfully to enter upon our labors,
although every day we think and talk of the dear ones we have left.
Though we long to see you all, yet, we regret not that we have followed
what seemed clearly to be the path of duty. And I trust dear mother,
your heart will be cheered and comforted. I will write often and tell all
that concerns our life in this strange land.

And now a word to Samuel and Frank. I have already written some to
you on the ocean. But my brothers dear, do write us great long letters
about home. Everything will be interesting. The little things that are
constantly occurring at home is what we will most want to hear. For the
great events of our country we will learn from the newspapers.

And my sweet little sister Stella, I want a little letter from you. I will write you one soon. Now I can only tell you to be good. Dont play all the time with "Jimmy and Kate" and your other little ones; but help Mother, and learn to write and read.

This night, from the far off climes of India, we would bid our letter "good speed" across the wide ocean to our waiting friends, to bear them our messages of loving remembrance, and the good news that still "all is well." Mr. Johnson joins in love to home, and all our friends in Hookstown.

We will write from Calcutta, before we leave for Futtehgurh. The pilot says that all is quiet in India. The sailors are singing about going ashore as they pump. I guess the poor fellows will be glad when we get to port.

> Goodbye dear ones,
> Affectionately, Rachel

> Ship *Art Union*, Garden Reach
> 2 miles from Calcutta
> Friday eve, December 7, 1860

Dear Brother Sam,

A thousand thanks to my dear Mother and brothers for the good long letters that this day have gladdened our hearts. Captain Norton took a native boat and went up to Calcutta. He called on the agent who does business for the Mission House. As soon as possible he dispatched our bundle of letters down by his servant.

When Captain Norton came back and said there were letters coming, I was almost crazy with joy. Mrs. Wyckoff and I danced round the cabin clapping our hands and could hardly wait. We were so impatient to hear from our dear ones at home. In a little while the precious package came. With trembling hands, we broke the seals and devoured the precious morsels. Good news from home. None but those who have wandered for long months without a single message to tell that there was indeed a circle of dear friends far over the sea thinking of you, can tell you how— like cold water to a thirsty soul—is a letter from those you love in the dear old home.

Mr. Johnson and I were up on deck when the letters were handed to us. You would have laughed to see us scamper off to our own rooms to enjoy them alone. I almost broke my neck—I mean, I might have done it—for I tumbled down three or four stairs in my hurry. Oh! how happy we all feel tonight, for we all have good news.

Mr. and Mrs. Wyckoff are sitting across the table finishing up their letters, and Mr. Johnson is at my elbow writing. Captain Norton is reading. The steward just passed through. His hair is curled and his black face shining like his boots, his collar just so. He is going across the country to Calcutta to see his Dinah, who he has not seen for ten months.

A great roach, about two inches long, just stepped across my portfolio, without as much as stopping to look where he was encroaching. We have plenty of them on the ship, and a few mosquitos to sing for us. These, with the jackals in the neighboring jungle, keep us in music.

I closed my letter home on the 29th. That was a week ago yesterday. The next day, Mr. Johnson received a letter from Rev. Walsh, missionary at Allahabad, stating that the annual meeting of the missionaries in North India had just closed. We were appointed to the Allahabad station, not to Futtegurh as we had expected. The object in sending us all to Allahabad, was that we might have the best advantages towards learning the language. There we will have every possible help.

This is the arrangement for the first year. We cannot tell now what will be the arrangement afterward. We felt much surprised, for we so confidently expected to go to Futtegurh. But we do not feel disappointed at all. We feel that our ministers here know far better than we can what is best, and where we can labor to best advantage.

Mr. Walsh wrote a very kindly welcome to us. He says he was very much attached to Mr. Johnson's brother, Albert. He feels a deeper interest in Mr. Johnson, from being so intimate with his brother. Mrs. Walsh wrote a very friendly letter to me, giving us a hearty welcome to this strange land and to their home. She says she will almost feel that their lost friends have come back to them. We are to stay with them until we get our own homes ready.

Our voyage up the river has been delightful. We have been now more than a week drifting up the river. The river is four miles wide down near the mouth, and the tide is very strong. So we could only make progress when the tide is flowing up the river. It flows in five hours, then out 7 hours—ebbing and flowing alternately. During the seven hours we have to lie at anchor.

We expected to be towed up by a steam tug, but they seem to be all engaged. Every one almost had a ship in tow. But we are just as well satisfied that we did not; for we have had a better chance to see the country. Everything is new and charming to us salt water birds. If we had only had our letters, I dont think we would have grumbled a bit. As it was, we felt a little impatient. But we have such comfortable quarters on the ship that we ought to be contented.

There are plenty of fruits and vegetables. The natives bring oranges, bananas, pineapples, cocoa-nuts and vegetables on board every day. Bananas are of a golden yellow and taste more like pears than any other fruit I ever ate. The meat is soft like a muskmellon. Pine apples are delicious. And the inside of the cocoa-nut is filled with a sweet syrup called milk.

The natives make queer looking pipes out of the shell of the cocoa-nut, which is about as large as a small pumpkin. A pipe goes up from the top, with the bowl for the tobacco in the end. The shell is then filled with water, and there is a hole in the side to which they place their mouth, and draw the smoke down through the water. This queer pipe they call a hubblebubble! They keep it passing round as steady as an old maid in a chimney corner would keep the smoke puffing. This seems to be their comforter at all times.

The natives bathe always before they eat. I have seen them sitting on the boat, just astern of the ship. One would dip up a basket full out of the river and hold it over his head. After he had got completely ducked, then another. After oiling their bodies, the rice pot is brought out. Every fellow gets his tin pan or earthen dish, fills it up and takes a little handful of curry, which they make of fish or fowl and spices. Each one pitches in with his hands—no spoon or knife—but just scoops it in as fast as he can conveniently.

We have become quite used to seeing them about in their strange fashion, although we were shocked at first to see their scanty dress. Some of them are far from being repulsive. One brown fellow waits on the table and he is rather handsome and smart as a bee. I saw one the other day with a ring on his big toe, which he seemed to be as proud of as many a civilized dandy who sports one on his finger. They all have some ornaments—a string of beads round the neck, a ring round the arm above the elbow, or on their fingers.

Mr. Johnson has described our going ashore on a board seat, which was very amusing. When we were coming back, I was perched up on my seat, with only six of them toiling and groaning to get me on board the ship, thinking I would be tender hearted enough to notice their "bakshish mom sahib"—which means "Alms Mistress." I thought that 14 pounds divided among six need not extort so many grunts, so I only laughed at them. They are the greatest beggars ever was. Captain Norton asked one if he meant "bamboo bakshish," which is in plain English the same as a certain kind of hickory oil. But he grinned good naturedly and said "Nay Nay Sahib" (Master).

We had a delightful ramble of about three miles through groves of Cocoa-nut palms, bananas and the tall bamboo. The low mud huts of the natives, thatched over the roof with dried grass, were clustered here and there in groups. We went right through a herd of buffalos, where they were feeding peaceably on the grass. We went through a village, with one of the natives for a guide. You ought to have seen the women kite into their houses. Here we saw some telegraph wires stretched along, which spoke of some civilization. We walked up the river to Redgeree and there our boat was waiting for us.

We have done very little reading this last week. It seemed so strange to have something to look at beside the water, that we spent the time on deck spying out the country, and laughing at the ancient looking crafts that are constantly passing.

The Governors barge passed down a few days ago with streamers flying fore and aft. The barge looked like a house floating down. It has sloping roof on both sides and a nice looking cabin with all kinds of ornamenting on deck. It was towed by a nice large steamer.

I have seen the river all dotted thick with native boats as far as the eye could see, up or down. Their boats are round bottomed and very long and sharp. They look something like a new moon. Some have little cabins in. We have one called a Dinghy boat, in which we go ashore occasionally. They scoured it with sand until the boards are white and clean.

Mr. Wyckoff and Mrs. Wyckoff, Mr. Johnson and I went ashore in one on Wednesday. We rambled about awhile. Went up round the English Magazine where they have their powder stored. Received a polite salute from a native sentinel, who was on guard pacing back and forth, but could not speak a word of English.

You would laugh to hear us talking bad English when we are trying to trade in the fruit bazaar (Markets). When the Captain is along, he is our interpreter. He knows about three words of Bengalee and he explains the rest by signs and motions that would try anybody's face.

I now hear the town clock strike the first time for a long time. It sounds strangely on the still air.

Well, brother Sam, I am glad to hear you are still in the "pedagoging" business. I wish you good success and pleasanter walks than last winter. I cant drive over in the sleigh for you any more. Are you still choir leader? I am interested to hear from your little gatherings still. Though I am absent in body, I am often present in spirit. It seems to me that I feel a deeper interest and more anxiety that you and Frank should be good and useful men now, though the wide sea separates us, than ever I realized before. I feel that life is so uncertain. There are so many pitfalls for the young especially.

Now I know you do not think about the snares that are laid by the wicked one for tempting you astray; but I pray God that you may be His, that when my brothers are gone, they may still be remembered by what they have done—that they may be stars in Jesus Crown. Improve every advantage you enjoy, for we are blessed as not many are with opportunities of improving the talents given us, be they one or more.

And Samuel, dont give up going through college. You can help yourself some, and father will help you too. Keep the mark before you. And wherever you are, dont forget a sisters claims. Dont neglect to write often. I could write Oh! so much, but it is getting late. Your letter was very good. I was glad to hear that Hunter is able to go into business again. Give him my best regards, and all of your chums.

(Now I will add a line for Stella.)

Dear little pet,

I would love to see you, and kiss you once more. But the big water is between us. Lizzy Stewart says your class put a great many cents in the box to send Bibles to the little heathen. I want you to not forget them. Sister Rachel sees them every day. They have no clothes, no kind teachers, no books. That is the reason sister left those she loved to go to them, to tell them to be good, that there is a Savior—for they think pieces of wood are gods. Dont you pity them?

Now dear Sam and Stella, I must say bye bye and go and see you in my dreams, as I often do.

In our ramble the other day we drank some juice from the date tree. It is very good. Tell Aunt Agnes I dont like it quite as well as the nice Maple Syrup she stirred off the day Stella and I walked out to see her. We have some buffalo milk for our tea and coffee, but I dont think any we have seen yet will compare with the good rich cream Grandmother always made us help ourselves to so liberally. Tell her to save me a good big apple and I will bring her and GrandPaps two nice pineapples that will make their mouths water for a week. How I wish I could send a basket of oranges and lemons to dear Aunt Mary Ann. I know she would like these.

Rachel

[As Rachel promised, the following two letters are Will's. The first is an excerpt from his letter to her mother, with his version of their first trip ashore at Garden Reach. The second, to Frank, is full of Will's vivid description of the sights on one of his walks on shore with the Captain.]

Garden Reach,
Ship Art Union
December 7, 1860

Dear Mother,

. . . Lillie is just now writing a letter to Sam, and as we are writing at the same time and under the same impulse, you may find our letters much alike, but this you must excuse, . . . We are getting here just at the opening of the cold season. I trust we will get pretty well acclimated before the end of it. But such as it is! I never saw the like of it.

You may talk of pleasant weather in America, but one forenoon stroll, such as I have had today, would just put new ideas into any one's head about what constitutes pleasant weather. I can't describe it. Now when you are beginning to shiver round fires, I can put on linen clothes and tary by the hour on the ground under an orange tree with the greatest comfort. Or in the cooler mornings, I can put on a heavier coat and stone monkeys across the paddy (rice) fields—as I have done—with equal comfort. This is the Calcutta winter. But its just like June, early June, with you. There are cool nights and warm noons, but the skies are cloudless. The air is balmy and the gardens are brilliant with flowers. The ripe fruit weighs down the trees and all is gorgeous summer life.

On last Friday (Nov. 30) we went ashore: Captain, Supercargo, ladies, Wyckoff and I. It was just like letting squirrels out of a cage to get our feet on solid ground once more.

Each ship is attended and aided at the river by a native boat. Ours was manned by 11 Bengalees. This was brought alongside. The ladies were seated in a chair, wrapped up in our national flag, and then, by means of pulley, they were hoisted over the ships side and let down in the boat.

But if you could have a picture of our getting from the boat to the shore, I think it would set all Hookstown in a roar of laughter. Our ship was anchored just off Redgeree and the tide was down. There was a stretch of soft mud and water, of a hundred yards or more, over which we all had to be carried by the natives. Just imagine me squatted on the shoulders of a couple of slender black Hindoos, innocent of all clothing, save a breechcloth. With an arm round the neck of each, I seemed to be hugging them most affectionately.

The ladies were each placed on a board, with about a dozen men to carry and steady them. We all landed without any mishaps—though with much merriment at our awkward appearance. And away we started for a ramble on land.

I think this was the first time in my life that I ever esteemed mud a luxury. Such a tramp, through meadow and thicket and paddy field and bazaar. Everything was new and strange.

The land on both sides of the river is very low and is often overflowed. The people regulate this by large dikes parallel to the river. On these lay our path most of the way to Redgeree, where we were to meet our boat.

On the way we turned aside and strolled all through a Hindoo village. You cannot imagine what a fairy scene that was to us, who for months had not seen so much as a leaf or blade of grass. Here, at once, to be transplanted into a tropical village where we wandered through a perfect wilderness of those far-famed fruits, which makes these lands seem a very Eden to the imagination. Here stood the glossy leaved orange tree. Here a clump of cocoanut trees shaped most like a green umbrella with a very long handle. Here a date palm, lower but of like shape with its little pitcher strapped on its trunk to catch the milk—sweet delicious juice which exudes when it is tapped. Here is a banana tree or plantain with their huge leaves, like an over grown tobacco plant: the most delicious fruit I have yet seen—something between a pear and muskmellon. Here is wilderness of what seems overgrown cactus, with all sorts of outlandish roots away up in the air. Here is a thicket of the tall and graceful bamboo, which seems to have grown just specially on purpose for fishing poles and such things. Here is a mango tree with its bright little leaves— with hundreds more that I shall learn the names of soon. But I know your mouth is watering already. I dont want to make you break the 10th Commandment, so I'll say no more about fruit trees now.

Whenever we came near a native hut, we could hear a chattering among the brush, and the native women went gliding into the houses. You dont often get to see them. But the men mostly stay to greet you with a low bow, hand to forehead and humble salutation—Salaam, i.e., "on you be peace." You can see the little urchins running about at play, gracefully attired in a string of beads or a silver necklace. "Only this and nothing more."

The huts are built of Bamboo poles or mud, or both. They are quite low and dark looking, heavily thatched with rice straw. The floors are of mud, made nice and hard and kept neatly swept. Near almost every house, and generally buried in a wilderness of fruit trees, is a square pond of water—often with pond lillies growing in them, and other bright flowers.

As we came through, we stopped at the Bazaar, where there were half a dozen shops, like grocery stores somewhat. Here we butchered the Kings English by trying to twist it into bad Bengalee, until finally we managed to buy some nice fruits—getting cheated of course. After a walk of three or four miles, we all came off to the ship highly delighted with our first visit to the sunny plains of India, . . .

Yours ever,
Will F. Johnson

Garden Reach, December 7th, 1860

Dear Brother Frank,

Your sister Rachel undertook to answer the letters which she received today from you and Sam, while I wrote to your mother. But she is not through her letter to Sam yet, and it is getting late. The mail steamer starts for London tomorrow, so I will commence a letter to you and she may finish it.

Just think how this letter comes to you. While I tell you, trace it out on the map. First, by a large mail steamer it will leave here tomorrow—run down the crooked river Hoogley—out into the Bay of Bengal, down the coast to Madras, then up to Bombay, then by the Arabian sea to Aden, then by steamer up the Red sea—past where Pharooh was drowned; then from the head of this sea across the desert by carriages to Alexandria; then by steamer through the Mediterranean sea, past Malta, Cyprus, Crete, and Elba; then through the Straights of Gibraltar and up the Atlantic to Southampton, England; then by steamer to New York, thence by railroad to Georgetown—winding up with a trip up the celebrated valley of Mill Creek. So even this little letter, insignificant as it may seem, is yet quite a respectable traveler when it reaches you.

. . . The Captain and I went off in the boat one morning. In our ramble we found a Hindoo Temple with a school in it. We peeped in through a crack in the window at the idols, most of which were images of men without heads—one being devoured by a tiger. Finally the old school teacher invited us inside. We went in.

There was a neat Bamboo shed in the Court yard of the Temple, and just in front of the idols, was the school. For our edification the teacher set the scholars to writing. They were little chaps of Stella's size. What kind of copy book do you think they had? Each one had a little square on the mud floor, a yard square. This was nicely sanded and they wrote on the sand with a stick. They wrote well, considering that they had to keep one eye upon their visitors all the while. When we left, school teacher and all followed us out a good ways.

Going on a little ways, we chased three monkeys across a paddy (rice) field and finally treed one on a low tree, where we came very close. He grinned hideously. These were as tall as a large dog with tails 4 feet long, and they go with the funniest gallop you ever saw.

This morning we were lying just opposite the palaces of the Ex. King of Onde, which are just on the bank of the river. I got in the dinghy (or 3 oared boat which we keep for going ashore in) and went off. We tried to land in the yard of one of these houses. He has 5 splendid, big, brick houses, with fine grounds, to keep his 60 wives in. After being chased away from two or three of these, I at last succeeded in landing in one of the nicest yards, and walking until I had quite a crowd of natives jabbering about me.

When I had satisfied my curiosity as to the house and grounds, and condescended to understand the very plain intimations of these fellows, that this was "Beebe Zenana," or a harem, therefore forbidden; I got in the boat and went up to a lane which goes to the Calcutta road to Garden Reach. When I came on this road, here came a parcel of natives, leading two big black bears, two pretty monkeys, and one man had a huge live snake wrapped around his neck and breast by way of cravat. Scarce a hundred yards from here there was a huge Bengal Tiger pacing about in a big stone cage in the yard of one of those palaces. I was watching him this afternoon through the bars.

Your sister is ready to add her note now, so I will close.

Yours, Will F. Johnson

Good Morning Dear Frank,

I have so much to tell you this morning. What shall I say first. Well, I will follow your fashion—just give it as it comes—which is best of all ways.

This morning a great mosquito bit me so hard, and sung so loud, that I waked before the stars had gone to bed. Mr. Johnson and I got up and waked the Captain to get ready for a visit to the Botanical Gardens, which were just opposite where our ship lay.

We bustled round and read our letters over again by candle light, while the rest were getting ready. Then just as the sun began to peep over the hills, we started off in our dingy boat, rowed by three natives. The morning air was a little cool, so I put on my blue wool delaine dress and heavy shawl and shaker bonnet. With Captain Norton, Mr. and Mrs. Wyckoff, and Mr. Johnson, away we sped over the river.

We landed at the foot of the garden grounds. We walked up a long stairs from the water edge—entered a wide gate way and walked along the nice wide graveled walks which underneath are paved with brick. The scenery that greeted our eyes surpassed description. I wish my poor pen could paint the scenes of beauty that lay spread out before us. The tall graceful firs—the evergreen cedars—the palm and cocoa-nuts—the dark green orange trees—the bananas with the tattered plumage, and countless others of which we did not know the names.

But the greatest curiosity was the celebrated banyan tree with its 125 trunks. We had not time to count them, but some in the country are almost twice as large, so Bayard Taylor says. You know the branches send out little sprouts that grow down until they reach the ground where they take root, and grow to be great large trunks. We walked round between these, and Mr. Johnson plucked off a leaf for me, which I will put in this letter—not because it looks very different from many you see at home, but because it is off this famous tree which grows on the Hoogly.

We saw thousands of earthen pots with rare plants in them and many strange looking trees and flowers. One little plot of ground was set round with a hedge of the most lovely morning glories I ever saw. Their cup was as large as the face of your hand and their color was a bright blue. Then there were great crimson flowers as large as the crown of your hat, beautiful roses of a bright pink and crimson red, and little delicate flowers hid in among green glossy leaves, and flowers of every hue and kind blooming mid tropical fruits, which hung in clusters on the trees.

All this was on a December morning, when I suppose Frank is snugly tucked in under a blanket and comforter, dreaming of red noses and frozen toes, or merry sleigh rides over the fleecy snow with James prancing and jingling the bells about his ears, and Jennie or Emma or Lina tucked up in the warm Buffalo robe by his side. Well I doubt not we will often think of your jolly winters, and long for a cool shake with Jack Frost, but the weather we now enjoy is delightful.

We have reached the moorings of Calcutta Wharf. Far as the eye can see is a forest of shipping—ships from every clime. And the strand is lined with beautiful English residences, palaces you might better call them. But more of them and Calcutta again, when I have seen more than a birds eye view.

Goodbye Frank, write soon and often and think of your brother and sister in India.

Dear Mother,

I am so glad that you wrote so soon. Nothing could have been half so welcome as a message from my mother. Every word from you is so precious.

I should like to have helped you eat your nice "peach butter," but I suppose there was no trouble in getting it used up. Here is 2 nice large bunches of bananas on my shelf. I would like to give you and father some, they are so good. Mr. Johnson bought them for me from a native. We dont indulge very much in fruit, for we have been without it so long, we fear it would not be safe to pitch in just yet.

You say Mother, that August was a long month. I knew it would be. O—how much I thought of you. I know you have suffered much, and I would that I might never cause your heart to ache one moment, or your eyes to shed one tear. But Jesus has laid this cross upon us and we will bear it cheerfully, that we may glorify Him more. Mother, you know I love you all very dearly, but I can be happy in India or anywhere, if I know you are cheerful and contented. I am not friendless here. A kind and loving husband is mine, and you know how very dear he is to me. And I have another Friend who has never deserted me. One who never will leave us; who whispers peace to your hearts and to ours, tho we are so far from each other.

I am sorry to hear that there has been so much sickness. Remember us to . . . Aunt Abby—tell her we often remember her in her loneliness. . . . With love to all our friends, and dear parents, I close.

Affectionately,
Rachel L. Johnson

THREE

December 1860–August 1861

ALLAHABAD AND FATEHPUR

⁂ IN HER FIRST LETTERS from India, Rachel introduced her family and friends in Hookstown to the India she and Will saw, heard, and felt in those early days. She described their tours around Calcutta, the "city of palaces," which they visited for four days on their way to their mission orientation station in Allahabad.

Rachel and Will traveled west, inland, by train. The first quarter of their trip, to the end of the railroad line in Ranigunge, took them through the rice fields of Bengal. From the end of the rail lines, their baggage was sent on to Allahabad in the slow but reliable wheeled carts drawn by oxen. Rachel and Will traveled on in a gari—a pony cart, like a stagecoach—with their shipboard friends, the Wyckoffs. They traveled along the Grand Trunk Road, or Great Thoroughfare of India, as it was commonly called. The ponies for their gari were changed every four miles, providing a relay of fresh horses. At night they stayed in government bungalows, where they were provided beds and facilities to prepare their meals from foods they brought with them from Calcutta.

On December 18, 1860, after a journey of over 14,500 miles and five months, from Hookstown, Pennsylvania, to Allahabad, India, Rachel and Will finally reached their first home in India. They were guests in the house of the Reverend and Mrs. J. Johnston Walsh, who had been good friends of Albert and Amanda Johnson's. The Walshes' home was nestled in a grove of trees on the banks of the Yamuna River just above its junction with the sacred Ganges. Rachel described Allahabad as the new seat of government for the United Provinces of India, and thus they found they had many English neighbors. Much of their time in Allahabad was spent studying the Hindustani language and learning the customs of their new homeland.

Several months after they arrived in Allahabad the Reverend Gopi Nath Nundy, one of the founders of the Fatehpur Mission in 1838, died. Will's first official mission assignment in India was to replace Reverend Nundy in his station in Fatehpur, 80 miles from Allahabad. Thus,

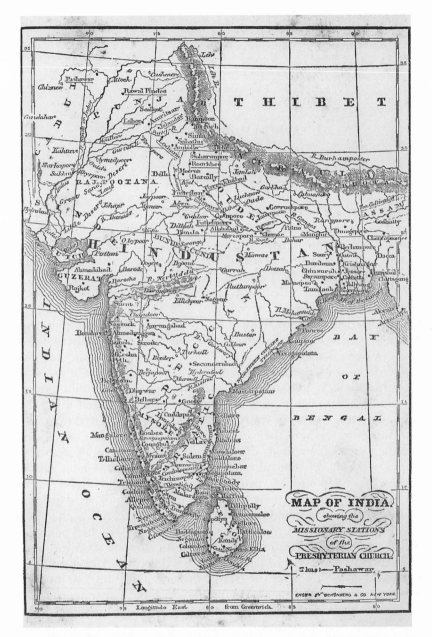

Fig. 3. "Hindustan," place of the Hindus, became anglicized to "India" in the nineteenth century. This 1859 map was familiar to Will and Rachel and reflects most of the spellings they used for the places they lived or visited. Their mission activities were centered in the north-central region labeled "Oude," a misspelling of Oudh, which became the United Provinces of Agra and Oudh, currently called Uttar Pradesh, meaning "north country." Courtesy of the Department of History, Presbyterian Church U.S.A.

Fig. 4. This enlarged map of the United Provinces of Agra and Oudh and several of the independent states still under ruling princes shows more contemporary spellings and locations of the mission stations and cities that Rachel and Will visited or to which they referred. Courtesy of John C. B. Webster.

four and a half months after arriving in India, Will and Rachel moved into their own home on the outskirts of the village of Fatehpur. Their home, a half mile from Fatehpur, was in a compound with four English homes and was surrounded by a cluster of homes belonging to Indian Christians.

In her letters, Rachel took her mother on a room-by-room tour of their new home and described the cooking and housekeeping utensils and practices in India. She took her father on a descriptive tour of the architecture and building features of the area and spoke of the school she had begun for the children of their village. In contrast to Rachel's letters, in happy, reassuring tones with her family and friends, Will's correspondence with the Board of Foreign Missions expressed doubts and concerns.[1] He "stoutly protested" the wisdom of sending him to Fatehpur. He felt it was the "hardest post to fill in the mission," and he was ill equipped for the responsibilities. Particularly, he felt he needed more time to learn the language, however, the older missionaries, who knew the language, wished stations with better homes, etc. Will and Rachel felt alone, lonely, and were unable to talk with the people with whom he came to work. Other "petty vexations" were that Gopi's widow was angry with the church, and "gave a great deal of trouble"; one of the readers, a primary support aide to the mission, "ran away"; preaching to the small group of English every Saturday required extra duty for Will, apart from his mission responsibilities; and the cost of living in India had gone up considerably since the Sepoy revolt. On this latter point, Will spoke in support of a colleague, who appeared to be smarting from the Board's response to the colleague's admittance that he had gone into debt to cover basic essentials. The Board of Foreign Missions in America advised, "do without things rather than go in debt for them"; Will responded with, "If forced to go into debt don't add to woes by reproaches."

As news reports of growing political turmoil in America reached India, Rachel and Will noted the irony of her family's concern for their safety, when it now appeared that her family was in far greater danger in Hookstown. In May 1861 Rachel wrote her parents that the British press in India reported that war in the United States was inevitable and that Lincoln had disappointed the people. However, she added that the Americans in India didn't put much trust in the British press, because it was obvious that the British were sympathetic with the cotton-growing gentlemen in the South, and these "gentlemen" were their prime news sources. As Rachel and Will reeled off bits of news they had about the war—"Sumter has fallen. . . . Eleven killed in Baltimore. . . . Washington is threatened. . . . The border states are aloof"—Rachel asked, "What next?" Still later she reported being stunned by the news closer to home that Harpers Ferry was occupied, that her father was serving in a home guard in Beaver County, and that the local volunteers had been ordered off to war.]

1. "India Letters, Furrukhabad or Lower Mission," *Foreign Missionary Correspondence of the Board of Foreign Missions . . . Presbyterian Church (U.S.A.)* (hereafter cited as "India Letters"), vol. 10, no. 57, May 31, 1861. This is the second letter in this volume from Will to the Board. The first (Jan. 1, 1861) described the "perils of the trip," already recounted by Rachel in the previous chapter. This letter from Will is summarized as dealing with "mission strategy."

Allahabad, India
December 24th, 1860

My dear Father, Mother and Brothers,

Here we are, comfortably settled down in our home, after many wanderings by sea and by land. And a very pleasant home it is, in the beautiful city of Allahabad. For a few months, the Wyckoffs and we find a
home with Rev. J. J. Walsh's family, at least until we learn something of
the natives language and habits.

We arrived here on Tuesday eve, December 18th. Were most kindly
received by Mr. and Mrs. Walsh and their good, hearty welcome made us
at once feel at home among such warm hearted friends. Mr. Walsh reminds me very much of Dr. Smith. He is quite as hearty looking, and a
real jolly man, loved by everybody for his kindness and hospitality. He is
the author of *Lives of Martyred Missionaries,* and was a very good friend of
A. O. Johnsons. Mrs. Walsh is not quite so lively as he, but very pleasant.
The more I see of her, the better I like her. They have 8 children, all but
two of which are in America. One, a little babe 5 months old, and little
Anna, about 4 years old. She is a little blue eyed girl that looks something like Stella did when she was her age. I do not often see her sunny
looks and blue eyes without thinking of a dear little one far away, that
used to nestle by my side.

But now I have introduced you to our friends. Before I speak further
of our home, I must tell you of our trip up the country from Calcutta.
My last letter was closed just before we left the *Art Union,* which we felt
half sorry to leave, after finding there a home for so long. Most of all did
we regret to leave our kind Captain, who had ever been so good a friend
to us through all our long voyage.

On Saturday morning, December 8th, Mr. Johnson went ashore with
the Super Cargo. He went to the Custom House, got a "permit" for our
baggage, and submitted it to the inspection of the Custom house officer,
who was very kind and only peeped into our trunks and chests, without
searching through their contents. Mr. Johnson was much afraid he
would lose some of his books, which were reprints of English works not
copyrighted in America. Some of the missionaries have lost the best
books in their libraries. Such books being seized at the custom house.
But they let us through without any trouble.

About 9 oclock on Saturday we bid goodbye to the *Art Union.* In a native boat we were rowed ashore. Mr. Shearin, the agent of our Mission
Board, had sent one of his native business agents (called sircar) to conduct us to lodging rooms at the Auckland Hotel. With him for our
guide, we threaded our way through the throngs of dark faces that covered the beach. All were jabbering in their unknown tongue. Each
wanted to offer their services and strange looking conveyancers for our

accommodation. To these we turned a deaf ear, and hurried up to the "garree" waiting for us. A garree is a four wheeled carriage, with a large square bed, covered and closed in front, with doors at each side. Inside are two seats, one facing each way. The drivers seat is outside, in front, like a stage coach. Mr. and Mrs. Wyckoff, Mr. Johnson, and I crowded into one of these, and with a turbaned Hindoo outside, away we went so fast as our bony old nag could carry us. We were now indeed in India. And in its city of palaces—the far, famed Calcutta. On every side strange sights and sounds.

Some of the English residences along the river were large fine looking houses. They were built of brick and covered with stucco work which, being painted white, looked very pretty peeping out from among bright green trees, and surrounded by gardens of brilliant colored flowers. From the broad carriage way that runs along the river, we soon turned into the narrow dusty streets of the city. They have no sidewalks, as everybody rides here, except the natives.

After a few minutes of careful driving through the crowds of people and queer looking carts, native buggies, etc., our carry-all stopped in front of a fine, large hotel. We were soon most comfortably fixed in the great, lofty, cool rooms, nicely furnished. Floors covered with straw matting, which looks as nice and is cooler than carpet, bed covered with mosquito bars, and every comfort provided for us. Our meals were served in our own rooms, English fashion, by a Hindoo servant with his white turban on his head, and his dress of wide cotton pants. Instead of a coat, he wore something that looked like a long shirt reaching to the knees, all of white.

The natives in the city wear more clothing than those we first saw, which I described in a previous letter. Some look quite nice looking. The higher castes wear fine muslin and look more cleanly dressed. All have either a long piece of cloth wound round their head or a little white muslin cap.

From the sun doors of our room, we had a fine view of the Governors palace, which is a large building built in the form of a cross. It is surrounded by large and beautiful lawns, with a large carriage way leading in to the palace. On each side of the entrance of these, there is an arched gateway, surmounted by the figures of wild animals. Over one was a large bronze lion crouching, as if about to spring on is prey. In front of these, an armed sepoy (native) kept marching back and forth as guard, to prevent the entrance of unbidden guests.

The houses are all flat roofed, except the natives, which are built of mud. The roofs made of bamboo poles, then covered with brick tiles. These are about a foot long, and are just like a pipe split in two parts. One layer first put on with the cup shaped side turned up, and the ends over lapping like shingles. Then another layer is over this with the round side up. This carries off the water pretty well, but such roofs need repairing very often after the long rains.

The first evening in Calcutta, which was Saturday, we spent sitting by the window of our room, looking down on the busy scenes in the street below. Hindoos and Mohammedans, with their strange costumes, white and red turbans, native women—with their long pieces of white cloth thrown over their heads and drawn round their faces for a veil—passing by with burdens on their heads, some with earthen water pots. These are all low castes, for none of the native women are seen in the streets but those of the lowest castes. Their liege lords do not allow them to expose themselves to the public gaze unveiled, they are so jealous of them.

There were long trains of bullock [ox] carts, made after the most primitive fashion, with clumsy wheels. The patient looking bullock walked slowly along, bearing the yoke on their necks. This was merely a piece of wood across the end of the tongue, with all the weight resting on the back of the neck. Between, on the tongue, was seated the driver with a sharp goad of bamboo in one hand, which he plied unceasingly. While with the other, he seized hold of the other poor bullocks fly brush and pulled it constantly. He shouted to them most unmercifully, while they plodded along unconcernedly. It was indeed a very laughable sight.

Countless garrees drawn by old rickety ponies, that bore little resemblance to the horse species, went rumbling by. Then there were the palanquins, or palkis for short, as they are often called. These are a native invention. They are nothing but a box, some six feet long and three broad, high enough to sit upright in. The bottom is cushioned and a pole extends out at each end, by which the natives carry the box with the pole resting on their shoulders. Generally 6 or 8 to each palki, they go along at kind of quick pace like a trot. I saw many of these passing by, with some English gentlemen and ladies quietly reading a book as they were thus being carried along.

Late in the eve, we received a note from Rev. Pourie, of the Free Church of Scotland, inviting us to attend his church on the Sabbath. This was very pleasant to us, to receive a welcome so soon from a Christian brother that knew us not. At an early hour we started in a garree, which we had hired for the day, and reached the Free Church in time for service at 10.

The church was large and very elegantly finished, seated with chairs, and very beautifully lighted with large chandeliers. This church has been built by Englishmen residing in Calcutta for their own accommodation. Rev. Pourie preached a most excellent sermon, which we were enabled to fully appreciate the privilege of hearing, after being so long deprived of the privilege of enjoying public worship in the sanctuary. When a colored man rose and led in singing one of the good old songs of Zion, we often had sung in our dear native land, I almost felt like looking round for the dear voices that had so often joined with me in this same sweet hymn of praise. I could not realize I was in a heathen land. At the close of the sermon, a gentleman and lady walked up the aisle, followed by a Hindoo servant carrying a little babe, which the parents had baptized. After service was over, Mr. and Mrs. Pourie and their daughter came and introduced themselves to us. They are very kind persons and have much of the true missionary spirit. We went again to church at night.

On Monday we went to the bazaar and made some purchases of such housekeeping affairs as Mrs. Walsh advised us to get here in Calcutta. I got a straw bonnet and trimming, for my poor old straw was all going to pieces. I never put it on, but at the risk of crown and front parting company. We got table cloths, mosquito bars, etc. I am very glad we got our hardware in New York, for every thing is so dear here, and the natives such sharpers.

Tuesday eve we took a drive on the strand. This is a fine broad carriage way along the river bank, with rows of trees on each side. From here there is a fine view of the best part of the city, and of Fort William, which mounts 1000 guns, commands the entire city, and protects it. Here on the strand, a plot of ground is enclosed with railing, where ladies and gentlemen exhibit their horsemanship. In the centre is a platform, where a fine band discourses sweet music every evening. Every person that possibly can get out of the city gathers here in the evenings. There are Englishmen and native merchant princes in fine carriages, with their turbaned servants mounted up on their carriages before and behind, garrees, palkis of every kind, down to the native buggies pulled by old, worn-out horses in rope harness, and people of every clime and color.

On Wednesday morning we took a drive out to what is called the Seven Tank Square. This is a beautiful place, just out of the city, owned by a rich old baboo (i.e. native prince).[2] The grounds are nicely laid out with nice flower beds. A little native boy brought me some beautiful roses. Here the baboo has a large palace built, with everything around him that his fancy craves. He has a private museum of curiosities for his own amusement. In front of the house is a large tank, or reservoir for water, with wide ghauta [ghat] (i.e. flights of steps leading down several feet to the water). In this there were fish, 2 or 3 feet long, so tame they came up and ate from our guides hand. For enclosures round, there were reindeer and other animals. One was a great ugly rhinoceros with

2. Originally Baboo was a Hindu title of respect, meaning mister, squire, master, or a person of distinction—as Rachel is using it. However, by the mid–nineteenth century it was more commonly used to refer to someone who was superficially cultivated or effeminate.

a great horn growing up straight out of its huge snout. Its skin lay in large folds over its body, and its feet were at least a foot in diameter. It ate some leaves from our hands and grinned very good naturedly in return.

Rev. Pourie sent us an invitation to meet a party of their friends and take tea with them. But after the days labor, we did not feel like going out again in the evening, and did not accept it.

Thursday morning we left Calcutta for North India, expecting to reach Benares on Saturday evening, and there spend the Sabbath. Our chests and boxes we sent by bullock train. We took the cars for Ranegunge, 125 miles from Calcutta, on our way to Benares, which is 428 miles from Calcutta. The cars were nicely cushioned. But, unlike our American cars, there is no communication from one to the other. There are only two seats in each division, one facing each way, and extending the width of the car. In this cozy little room we were locked up by the conductor, and went whizzing along over the level plains of sunny India, feeling very safe. There were no steep banks and dangerous precipices for the iron horse to leap over.

As we left the city, our track lay through rice fields which the natives were beginning to harvest. The country was all perfectly level, but diversified, with groups of palm and date trees and many others new to us. We had a birds eye view of native villages, houses of mud or bamboo, as we flitted by them.

About 5 o'clock we reached Ranegunge where the railway stops. Here we were to be provided with dawk garrees to take us the rest of the way. These dawk [dak] garrees are a regular institution of the country, just as coaches used to be in America. The garree is the same as I described before, except there are no seats in it, which is a convenience at night when you want to lie down. In the bottom we placed our mattress and pillows, and in one end our blankets, carpet bag, shawls, etc. Our trunks were mounted on top. These garrees have very good springs and the roads are perfectly smooth and level, so we were very comfortable. We traveled through the whole distance without changing garrees.

In a few minutes after we reached the station at Ranegunge, the Wyckoffs were installed in one garree and we in another, with an old rickety horse attached to each one, and two Hindoo coachmen mounted in front. You may think, with two coachmen, we were over stocked. But wait and see. The Wyckoffs started first. Soon a cloud of dust seen in the distance was all that was visible of their equipage. But our pony took a fancy to travelling backwards, and it took some 5 or 6 coolies to push him. One to pull at his nose and at each wheel, while the driver alternately beat and coaxed him. Once it threw itself flat down, out of the shafts. Mr. Johnson and I were just taking our lunch of crackers, cheese and cake, quietly laughing to ourselves at the ridiculous figures they made, when I saw "Barney" [the Kerr's horse in Hookstown] lying sprawling on the ground. I jumped out with my lap full of eatables, while Mr. Johnson stepped out to hurry them up.

By this time Mr. Wyckoff had got his coachman stopped and he came running back to see what was the matter. A few minutes more and we all started off on a "bee line" for the next stopping place. We had a fresh relay of horses every 4 miles. The next change, we happened to get the best horse. And while Wyckoffs were travelling crab fashion, away we went flying past them, our pony bound to beat on that race.

In India there are no hotels through the country. In place of these, there are houses called bungalows every 10 or 12 miles, provided by government for the accommodation of travellers. These are one storied houses, built double, with one good sized room containing a bed, chairs, and table. There are two other smaller rooms, one a bed room, the other a bath room. Here all travellers can claim shelter for 24 hours by paying one rupee, that is half a dollar. Travellers carry their own provisions and here find servants who will make them a cup of tea and coffee for a trifle.

In Calcutta we provided ourselves with bread, spiced beef, tea, sugar, cheese, jam, and cake for our journey. We traveled day and night, only stopping about two hours from 11 to 1 to rest a little, wash off the dust, and have breakfast prepared out of our provisions. With a little rice and milk we got at the bungalow, we all agreed it made an excellent breakfast fit for a king. At night we stretched ourselves out on our bed and slept soundly, only waked occasionally by the coolies calling, "Sahib, bakshish [slang for something between a tip and a bribe]!" They wanted this for "pushing the garree over the hill." The hill was perhaps an elevation of 6 inches or a foot. Horses all agree in this country that hills are insurmountable without 5 or 6 coolies to push them and the vehicle both over.

Now imagine us, all alone in the night, except these dark sons of India round us, horses cutting up such monkey shines, jackals screaming in the jungles, and yet we were sleeping as soundly as if we were in our soft couch at home. None of them knew a word of English and we as little of Hindustani. Mr. Johnson did get a little book in Calcutta out of which we picked a few words which we occasionally made use of. One was "jaldi jao," which means, "go quickly." These he shouted from the side door when they took a little too much time getting their "hubble-bubbles" ready.

One night we were waked by a voice calling, "Sahib! Sahib!" Then when he did not answer, they called, "Mem Sahib!" That was for me. We were both awake, but kept mum. They kept calling for a good while, but finally gave up trying to wake us. And the driver mounted and drove off, while we lay there shaking our sides laughing.

The grand trunk road, along which we traveled, is said to be "the longest and best in the world" (and I would say the dustiest too). It is the great thoroughfare of India, extending from Calcutta to the North about 1100 miles. We met long trains of bullock carts laden with boxes, bales, etc., and large caravans of camels with great packs tied on their backs. They were led by tall, lordly-looking Arabs, who were taking their articles of trade to Calcutta. Some of these trains I counted as they passed us, one by one, and there were 80 or 100 in one long train, with only 3 or 4 men to guide them. One went before, leading a camel, and the next was following after, led only by a cord tied through his nose. The cord passed back through the nose of the next, and soon through the whole train.

We also met natives riding on huge elephants, or passed a camp where they had stopped for the night, and were preparing their humble meals of rice and curry under the shade of a wide spreading banyan tree. We now began to realize that we were in the midst of Oriental life in the East, and were seeing sights that once only seemed like fancy sketches, when we read of them beyond the sea.

On our way, we crossed several rivers. Some were spanned by long bridges, others were only dry beds without a rill of water now, but are very wide and rapid in the rainy season. We couldnt see the propriety of paying toll for only crossing where there was a place for a river. But it was all the same, the cash had to be handed over.

Our coachman carried a horn which pealed forth its clear notes at every approach to a station where we changed horses. It seemed to cheer our poor nags wonderfully. After being pushed, and patted, and shouted at, they would go as if they were possessed, while the horn blew louder and louder.

After our long life on shipboard these adventures were very pleasant. Since we felt well, amid all our exposure, it enabled us to enjoy anything that turned up. Our horses proving such slow travellers, we did not reach Benares [Varanasi] until Sabbath day about noon. We had no choice but to hurry on to Benares, although we did not like to travel on the Sabbath. When we came to the Ganges, our horse was taken out, and we were pulled across the bridge of boats by coolies.

We stopped at the travellers bungalow and were invited to go to the Kennedys, missionaries of the Church of England. Rev. Ullman and wife, missionaries of our board just returned from England, met us here and we all spent a day pleasantly together at Rev. Kennedy's.

Monday morning we visited a native school which has long been under the care of Mr. Kennedy. There were 200 native boys being instructed by native Christian teachers. The school building was very large. In the center was a large square hall, very high and open at the top and covered with canvass. On the four sides of this hall were rows of little rooms, in each of which was a separate class or division, each with their teacher. Some were writing, some reading, some learning English, some Hindu, all studying aloud. It was a very interesting sight. Some of these little fellows were bright, intelligent looking fellows. The features of the Hindoos are European, although their skin is dark.

Benares is a large city about 500,000 inhabitants and considered a very holy city. I think you find a description of it in "Allens India."

From the school, Mr. Ullman conducted us through the city to the celebrated Mohammedan Mosque, built by Arungzebe, on a spot considered most holy of all by the Hindoos. We ascended one of the minarets which is 240 feet high. The ascent is made by winding stairs that are inside from the balcony. On the top we had a fine view of the "Holy City" with its mass of flat roofed houses that seemed all in one solid mass together. On a neighboring housetop, a tailor sat busily plying his needle. Flocks of little swallows and pigeons were twittering around, some peeping out of a minaret where they were building their nests.

From this we went to the most holy temple of the Hindoos, where there were crowds bringing their offerings of flowers and leaves. They were casting them on an image of stone, before which a light was kept burning. There were several of these images, all with their offerings sprinkled over them. They offered us wreaths of yellow flowers saying, "Wont you offer something too." Large bells were suspended from the ceiling. Each one rung one of these when they offered their gift, to attract the attention of their god. In this temple were the sacred Brahman bulls stalking round. These no one dares to disturb for fear of the wrath of the gods. Oh! how my heart sickened within me at the sight of their idolatries.

The domes of this temple are gilded. One is of pure gold, the other looked more like silver. Thus, the poor ignorant Hindoos will spend their all on their temples, thinking to merit a happy future. If Christians made half the sacrifice for their religion that the heathen do for theirs, how soon would every temple become a Sanctuary for our God, and these dumb idols be cast into the ditch to be trampled under foot, instead of adored as gods. O what a great work there is yet to be done in India alone. May Our Father grant us grace and strength to do something.

On Monday evening we were called on by some of the German and East India missionaries, who welcomed us to share their labors in India. We also met Rev. Parsons and lady, Mrs. Pierce and Miss Packer. They came to Mr. Kennedy's for tea.

Tuesday morning we set out for Allahabad, 75 miles distant from Benares. The country now looked more cultivated and became much prettier as we approached Allahabad. We travelled all day and reached the river Jumna [Yamuna] about 8, where we received a note from Mr. Walsh telling us where to find their bungalow. About 9 o'clock, on the eve of the 18th, we drove up to a white, neat-looking, one-storied house, surrounded by a grove of trees, on the banks of the Jumna. This proved to be the home of our kind friends, the Walshs, who were ready to welcome us to a comfortable resting place, after our long journey of many miles of land and over 14,000 by water. Need I say, we enjoy our rest after all these wanderings.

The Mission grounds are delightfully situated on the Jumna river, just above its junction with the Ganges. They are surrounded by a mud wall. This is called the Mission Compound. Within this enclosure is the bungalow. All English houses are called bungalows that are one storied and with tiled roofs. They are built of brick, then plastered with a kind of cement, outside and inside, and whitewashed. The rooms are large and airy and a veranda extends round on all sides. These make very comfortable dwellings.

A short walk from our bungalow, down among the palm trees, is a lovely church, where, every Sabbath, Mr. Walsh preaches in Hindustani twice—once in the morning at 10 and once in the evening at 3. The first Sabbath we were here there was one English service. We made a pretty large congregation of our own: Rev. Barnes and family from Lahore, on their way to America, Rev. Ullman and wife, with the rest of us, a few English families, and the native Christians.

It seems very strange to listen to a sermon in Hindustani, when you dont understand half a dozen words, and to join in singing a hymn that is unintelligible. The Sabbath School meets in the morning after service. The school numbered about 60 last Sabbath. Some of these are native Christians children and some are gathered up from the bazaars. I was surprised to see how orderly the little heathen children conduct themselves, and how promptly some little bright eyed fellow, almost naked, rose and answered the questions. I of course did not understand, but they seemed to answer properly. Within the compound there were also several native Christian houses.

On Sabbath eve at 6, there is service in the English Chapel in the city, where the Rev. Williamson, chaplain of the troops, holds service. It is a drive of about 3 miles from the Mission premises. We go as often as we can, and on Thursday evenings to prayer meeting. The church is generally full on Sabbath.

The seat of government has been removed from Agra to Allahabad and this makes the English population much greater here. There are several regiments of soldiers stationed here. The fort is a very large one. The railroad now extends from here to Cawnpore, and will soon be open farther.

The English see the importance of internal communication and are busy building railroads, which will make the country still more secure. Although everybody here thinks it is perfectly safe now.

The last telegrams from America bring sad news of our own dear country, that the election of Lincoln has roused up the south to rebellion. Senators are resigning, states pulling down the Union flag, volunteers being mustered, etc. We trust there will be more talk than fighting, and that we shall soon hear better news of our country.

We have not yet received our baggage, which was sent by bullock train. We expect it in a few days. Then we hope to get settled down and begin in earnest the study of the language.

Allahabad is a large city. We have taken a good many drives through it, but I have not seen it all yet. I will give you a general description of it when I write again.

We will write home once a month regularly, and I would like to hear from home at least that often. Samuel, I think you and Johnnie Johnson should keep up a correspondence.[3] Then when one of our families receive news from us, the other can too. Besides, I think you might both find it interesting, and I think you ought for our sakes.

Christmas Day, 1860

Oh! how I would love to give you all a Christmas greeting face to face on this bright morning, that seems to whisper, "Merry Christmas to all!" My thoughts wander back to the dear old homestead where Father, Mother, brothers and sister are gathered round the bright fireside.

I know you think this morning of the absent ones and it is sweet to feel that we are remembered; but I would not that your thoughts should be sad ones—though it would be a precious privilege, could we all be gathered there. Our Christmas is very different indeed from any that we have had. This morning two of the native Christians brought presents for Padres Walsh, Wyckoff and Johnson (Padre means priest, and they always address our missionaries thus). Each basket contained cake, oranges, plantains, sugar, almonds, pistachio nuts—these taste like ground nuts.

Christmas eve our families were all invited to take dinner with Mr. Middleton, a merchant and a warm hearted Irishman who has lived in India for many years. They have a large family and one daughter, a young lady. They live very nicely, have plenty of this world's goods, and give splendid dinners. We all went at 7 o'clock and spent the evening.

You will think 7 is late for dinner hour, but here the meals are very different hours from those at home. People rise early to enjoy the cool morning air, and take a cup of tea and slice of toast as soon as they rise, then breakfast at 9 or 10. If you want to go out on business or pleasure, you must go before breakfast. It seems so strange to us. After breakfast we must find employment in doors. We usually have dinner at 4 or 5 and

3. Johnnie, one of Will's cousins with whom he lived on the farm near Steubenville, was the same age as Sam.

tea at 8. The natives do all their cooking in the evening. The air is filled with smoke and fog, so it is not very pleasant to be out at night.

January 4th, 1861

I must close my letter today, for the mails leave tomorrow. Our boxes have all arrived.

Rev. Morrison is stopping with us on his way to Calcutta. He is going home by way of England. His health is poor, but he has labored here between 20 and 30 years and is a gray haired man. He lost his wife only a few days ago, and has the care of a little boy now all himself. He is the man of the Lodiana Mission who got up the Worlds prayer meeting. He will stay with us through the World Prayer services of next week, when we will join you and all our Christian friends in prayer.

This is our third letter to you, which I hope will all reach you safely. We have received but one letter from you, and of course, are anxiously looking for another soon. Letters and newspapers come in about 2 months.

Father, will you not send us the Banner regularly, after you have done reading it? The postage from New York is 6 cents a number, which we will cheerfully pay, if you send it. The letter postage is now, for any under $\frac{1}{2}$ ounce, 27 cents from New York here.

Stella dear, here's a kiss for you, for which you must pay me with another in a little letter. I must write to Grandfather and Aunt Agnes soon. Tell me about Aunt Mary Ann.

With much love to you all and all our friends. Goodbye.

Affectionately, Rachel

Allahabad
February 4th, 1861

My dear Friends,

... We are very busy studying the Hindustani language. A native teacher, called a "moonshee" [munshi], comes every day to give us a lesson. He spends an hour with the Wyckoffs, and an hour with us. We have learned the letters, and are now reading and studying the grammar. Our moonshee speaks very encouragingly of our progress. This is of course very gratifying, but we will need a great deal of patience and application.

The weather is still quite cool. Mr. Johnson finds his overcoat very comfortable when he goes out, and I can wear my warm shawl without any inconvenience in the mornings and evenings. But at noon, the sun is very powerful out of doors, where exposed to its rays, but cool enough in the house.

Next week we are going to move out into the tent and part of the College building, until we get our house repaired. The roof leaks, and Mr. Walsh is going to have the tiles all taken off and a new covering put on. It will be a new life for us, living in a tent, but it is very pleasant. Mrs. Walsh says every one prefers it in the cool season. The tent is now pitched under the shade of two large trees, a little distance from the house. It is made of thick canvass, which turns the water when it rains. Inside are two rooms, with a little veranda in front.

There is now a large mela being held at the point where the Ganges and Jumna unite, a little distance below our bungalow. This is held by the natives once a year. They flock here by thousands to bathe in the sacred waters of the junction of their most holy rivers. The roads leading down to it are lined with pilgrims, who have come many scores of weary miles to have their sins washed away in the holy water.

A few mornings ago, Mr. Johnson and I took a drive down to the Mela ground before breakfast. There, gathered on the banks of the river, were multitudes of these deluded people, and some of the most wretched looking beings I ever saw. Their faces were daubed with red and yellow paint and mud, until they looked more like fiends then men.

We strolled along the bank, stopping here and there to gaze at the strange sights around us. Here was the shopkeeper with his gaudy, colored chintzes, spread out in his little tent made of bamboo poles and straw matting. There was a seller of trinkets, with his variety store of rings for the toes, ears, nose and ankles, spread out before him on a piece of cotton cloth. Mr. Johnson bought some little trinkets. He is gathering up some curiosities which we will send home by and by.

Here we saw those wretched looking creatures, the fakirs, or holy men, so called. They are worshiped as such by the Hindoos. They are almost naked and their bodies covered with ashes and filth. Some have their faces all smeared over with yellow paint. They are as hideous looking as mortal could make himself. These pretend to be so holy, that all their passions are subdued, and outward circumstances have no effect on them. One poor wretch passed us who had one arm stretched up above his head. He had held it that way until it had grown stiff and lifeless as a log. His hand was all shrivelled and his fingers looked as though part had dropped off. Another was sitting in a little wagon, his feet bent up until his feet lay over his shoulders. Oh! how it made me shudder to look at these revolting sights!

The point of the river where it is thought most sacred, is covered with flags. Some are merely strips of red cloth, some striped, and some of every horrid device.

A little way above this is a row of sheds. Some are used for a bazar (market), where fruits and sweet-meats and different articles are sold. Others are appropriated to their pandits, who are learned Brahmans of high caste, who expound their Shaster—which you know is their most holy book. One of these we saw seated on a kind of rude throne. His head was crowned with a wreath of marigolds and a necklace of the same. These were brought as offerings by his worshipers. White flowers were scattered round him, and he, with his book, was jabbering away to a large crowd of men and women.

Nearby was a barber arranging the locks of a fakir, which were at least 10 feet long. I never saw such hair. It was all separated into little rolls, as thick as my little finger, and these then were wound round his head. There is one spot where a piece is fenced off and here the people come to be shaved, not beards only, but pates too. They think that they will please their gods by the offering, and they pay their priests for the privilege of being shaved. Their priests book them for so many years (some say a million) in Paradise, for every hair offered. Some have their heads shaved close, others have one little lock left on the crown, and some a lock over each ear.

Crowds were rushing into the sacred Ganges to bathe and wash away their sins in its holy water. Each one has a little brass pot which he takes away filled with water. This he carries often hundreds of miles to his home. Formerly a great many old people would come here and drown themselves, thinking they would be sure of going straight to heaven. But this the Government has prohibited, and a boat is kept to rescue any who attempt it.

Mr. Walsh goes down to preach at the Mela every day with Rev. Parsons from Benares, McKumby, an East Indian who speaks Hindustani better than any missionary in India, and Rev. Zeman, a German. They are all staying here and are busy preaching to the crowds of people. Mr. Johnson says he feels like pitching into the work too, but he fears not many of the people would find English very edifying.

Last year Mr. Walsh says there were 500,000 people gathered there. This year there is not so many, owing to the famine in the Northern provinces. There is very great suffering all over India. North of us, for want of food among the natives, hundreds are dying from starvation. Many of the poor creatures dig for roots to satisfy the gnawing of hunger. Multitudes are perishing. Great quantities are being sent by the "Relief Society." Mr. Johnson and I drove past the railroad depot, where we saw many hundreds of sacks of grain, which were all going up to Cawnpore to be distributed. But the means of communication with most parts of the country is by bullock train, and even these poor beasts are in a starved condition. The famine is caused by the drought, but in many places there has been some rain lately. The English are contributing liberally for their relief.

I was glad to hear, brother Sam, that you are engaged in the good work of teaching. I trust you will have much success. And brother Frank,

I sympathize with you in your "arduous labors," keeping the woodshed filled, the fire warm, the farm in a flourishing condition, "James" well fed, etc., and cultivating your mind too. But I hope your teacher will not permit you to "break your constitution," but lend you a helping hand to encourage you.

Father, if you were not so far away, we might give you a job. The house in which we live is a double house for 2 families, and has to be repaired. Such carpenters as these natives are, you never saw. More of them again.

Mother, we are almost ready for housekeeping. Mr. Johnson has been buying chairs, tables, and we will be very comfortably fixed. I never saw a more cheerful people than the missionaries are. They are so dear, Mother, that you need not feel anxious about us. We have everything but our friends from home. We hope to meet them someday, never to part again.

Remember us to all our dear friends with love. Goodbye. Very affectionately,

Your own Rachel

Allahabad
March 26th, 1861

My dear Father, Mother, brothers and sister,

. . . my good husband and self are both very well. We never enjoyed better health. The hot weather makes us feel a little lazy sometimes, but this, though a troublesome affliction you know, is not dangerous. Plenty of work pressing, generally effects a cure.

This is the beginning of the hot season. But as yet the mornings and evenings are cool and we find a blanket and sheet comfortable at night. I am just beginning to wear my thin dresses and Mr. Johnson has not yet put on light clothes. In the hot weather we must have a great many changes of clothes, for in a short time your clothes are wet with perspiration and soon become unpleasant.

I have become quite a tailor, Mother, and find it very useful to know how to make pants, vests, etc. Last week I made Mr. Johnson a nice black merino vest and several pairs of pants for the hot weather. We can get sewing done very nicely by the native tailors, or "durzis" as they are called. Most persons hire them by the month. Their wages are from 4 to 6 dollars a month. (How would our tailors at home like that!) These men will make any kind of mens wear and ladies dresses and, in fact, anything you give them. Their powers of imitation are surprising. Give them a coat, dress or anything you want copied, and they will make a garment exactly like it in size and work. They always take the measure from the garment itself. I was much amused to see them hold the cloth in their

Fig. 5. Household servants featured in this picture are, left to right: the *khan-sama*, the master's personal servant and "master of the household gear"; the assistant bearer or house servant; the *sircar*, clerk who keeps account of expenditures; the *dhobi*, washer man; the *durzi*, tailor (in back); the *mihtar*, sweeper; the *guawalla*, man who tends the cows or herds; the *peon*, errand boy; the *punka walla*, who pulls the cord of the *punka*, a large swinging cloth fan on a frame; the cook; the *mali*, gardener; and the *bhisthi*, water carrier.

toes—between the great toe and the next—a plan which you might suggest to our home tailors as quite an improvement.

Indeed, toes seem to be a very useful institution in this country—the carpenter holds the wood with his toes and picks up his tools—the washerman, or "dhobi," holds up the clothes straight with his toes when he irons them, which he does on the floor. Such a useful appendage is always graced with a nice big ring, or rings, as the fancy may be.

Although labor is so cheap, yet we missionaries have not rupees to spare. Living is so expensive to have work done, that we do what we can ourselves without injuring our health. In this country we cannot do the same kind or quantity of work we can in our climate at home. It has been tried over and over again by missionaries coming out, who at first feel like pitching into work of every kind, just as they would at home. The result has been, in a short time their strength is wasted, health broken down, and they have to go home. This, just as they are beginning to understand the natives and language, and to be of use in the Mission.

Thus, the great object for which they are sent is defeated. They are sent to devote their powers of body and mind to the instruction of this ignorant people, and to labor for the good of their souls. I say this because many people think, when they hear that our Missionaries have servants in this country, that they live extravagantly, and might live on less money. In fact, they barely get what supports them, and many find it difficult to make their allowance meet their expenses, economize as they will—while every person in our own country expects to lay by something.

Missionaries try to make their homes pleasant and comfortable, for that is their little world where they must find all their pleasure and enjoyment. Every family must have at least 5 or 6 servants and these all will about do the work of one good one at home. I now speak of our Mission families, for the English, who have good, fat salaries, have 3 or 4 times as many.

This abominable caste system is what gives the European so much trouble and expense. You might as well expect the cat to pull the carriage, or the horse to catch mice, as to expect the cook to sweep the floor, or the "dhobi" (washerman) to cook a dinner. For this reason, everything you want done, you must have a different servant.

I speak of men servants, because women are never hired as servants, except as nurses. They have all the drudgery of home work or work in the fields, but the women are never house servants, to do work in a family. You see them in the field carrying bundles of grain on their heads. She is indeed made a beast of burden, then abused, beat and knocked about as though she had no feelings, no soul. Poor women in India! Well might the heart melt with pity for her.

Another great pest with servants is their dishonesty. They will cheat you before your eyes—watch as you will. Everything must be kept under lock and key. If not, your wearing apparel will grow beautifully less. Your stores for the table will disappear as if by magic, and still the servants will all protest that they are innocent as lambs. Lying and cheating, the natives are taught from infancy to consider very clever, and necessary accomplishments. Indeed, I would much rather do all the work of any common family at home, than be bothered with such servants, if it were possible. But here we have to accommodate ourselves to the Indian climate, and adopt such customs as will be for the advancement of the work for which we left our native land. We are progressing very well with the language, and I hope we will in due time be able to take an active part in the missionary work.

When I last wrote, during the mela, I mentioned that we were about to move into a tent until our bungalow was repaired. We had 2 missionaries from Benares and a German missionary and his wife, who stayed with us for 2 or 3 weeks. Having so many, we gave the German family the tent, and we moved in the school building, which had several vacant rooms not used by the school. Here we are still. This home is what is called a "Kothi" [a single-family detached house of bricks]. The walls, floor and roof all "pakka" or solid. The walls are brick and the floor and roof are built of large smooth square stones. There is a stairway outside, leading up on the roof, which is a very nice place to walk in the mornings and evenings. Mr. Walsh says he has a notion to take his bed up there tonight. It is very healthy to sleep in the open air. The air is so dry, there is no danger of taking cold, as in our moist climate in America.

But I must now tell you of the great loss our Mission has sustained in the sudden death of Rev. Gopee Nath Nundy, native missionary at Futtehpore. He was a man of great worth, one esteemed by every one and of great influence among his country men. His labors among them have been much blessed. He was one of the first converts from heathendom and was ever a zealous Christian. During the mutiny, he and his family were obliged to flee from place to place. They were imprisoned in Allahabad, threatened with torture and death, if they would not deny the Savior and become Mohammedans. I have seen the place where they were imprisoned. It is in a "serai," or inn, a place for the accommodation of native travellers. It is nothing more than a large square plot of ground, enclosed with a high stone wall, and all round the wall are little rooms—just like a long porch divided into rooms. Europeans never stop in these places.

Gopee Nath had for a long time a disease in his head, which threatened his life, but finally he died very suddenly. Futtehpore is the nearest Mission station to us, only 80 miles, or 3 hours ride on the cars. His wife sent a telegram of his illness on Tuesday evening, the 12th. Mr. Johnson and Mr. Walsh started off next morning to see him, and they remained with him until he died, which was on Thursday, 14th. After funeral services they returned home Friday evening.

That station was now vacant. In order to consult about what should be done, Mr. Johnson, Walsh, and Wyckoff all took a trip last week up to Futtehgurh to see the brethren there. The result of their deliberations was that Mr. Johnson is appointed to take charge of the station at Futtehpore. We will likely have to leave Allahabad about the middle of April. You will begin to think we are great wanderers, but I think we will now be settled permanently—at least for a time. On last Tuesday Mr. Johnson and Mr. Walsh had to go again to Futtehpore on business. I accompanied them to see what is to be our home.

Futtehpore is quite a large city, but there are only a few English families there. They, and the Mission station, are very near together at a little distance from the city and near the depot. The few families who reside there are very good people. Although not many yet, they will form a pleasant society. Mr. Johnson was very well pleased with them during his stay there, and says we will find them very kind. The station is on the railway, which is quite an advantage.

We have had a very pleasant home with the Walshes, but I feel quite satisfied that we are now going to have a home of our own. We will then feel that we are really over our wanderings, and I think we will have a very comfortable and pleasant home at Futtehpore. We are busy making preparation for housekeeping—picking up a tea kettle here and a frying pan there, just as we can get them. When we get installed in our home, I will give you a description of an Indian kitchen, and cooking utensils, which are very different from our home articles.

Well, I think you would laugh to see some of the native inventions. We see the women grinding at the mill just as they used to do in Bible times. Steam mills are not plenty in India, but women are, and millstones too.

Saturday morning, [March] 30th
I have just returned from my mornings walk. Mr. Johnson, Walsh, and Wyckoff all started off about 6 o'clock to an auction and have not yet returned. Government officers are changing places so often, that furniture can often be picked up cheaper at these auctions than it can be bought elsewhere. There was a fine English shop here, where we could get almost everything, provided we were willing to pay 5 or 6 times its value. But it has just closed and the proprietor has gone to the hills in the northern part of India to remain during the hot weather. Mrs. Walsh and I went down before they closed to get some things we wanted. I wished to get a hooped skirt. Mine that I brought with me are much broken, and the extra sets I got in New York were not sent, through some oversight. And what do you think they asked? Only 12 rupees. That is 6 dollars! I did not purchase, since I sent to Calcutta for one with a lady going down. Such things are cheaper there, yet dear enough too.

Mr. Johnson brought with him from Futtehgurh, 2 books of his brothers, which were found there in a well after the mutiny. This, and a piece of china of their tea set, are all the relics that were found. We visited the well in Cawnpore where the women and children were thrown after they were murdered. We saw the house near which A. O. Johnson, his wife, and our other missionaries were shot. In Futtehgurh he saw the place where they had lived. It was, of course, but a melancholy pleasure for him to visit these scenes where they had lived and died, but he very naturally felt a strong desire to see them. A tablet is erected to the memory of the 4 missionaries and their wives in the Futtehgurh church. A picture of the church you may see in the "Memorial of the Martyred Missionaries." It has been repaired and is now as good as ever.

In Allahabad the "Church of England" has a very nice church, which was built by Government expense. It is built of brick, then plastered outside and painted a stone color. The spire is very tall and beautifully proportioned.

One evening we went down near the Ganges to see a very large heathen temple. It has cost a great deal of money. The temple is in the midst of a large garden which is surrounded by a high wall, built of stone. On the wall were large figures of statuary. The garden was laid off in nice walks and there were some very pretty flower beds. We entered through a high stone gateway, walked along a wide path to the middle of the garden, and there the temple reared its lofty dome. The painted minarets reflected the suns rays from its gilded points. The temple is built on a platform of nice smooth sandstone, about 4 feet high, which has broad steps leading up to the temple.

One of the zealous old Hindoos insisted that we should not go up these holy steps or walk on the platform, without taking off our shoes, which he said would defile the holy ground, because they were made of the skin of a slain animal. Mr. Walsh argued the case with him. Finally another man, who was a fakir, came and agreed that as we did not take our shoes off when we go into our own places of worship, therefore we might go on the platform, but not inside the temple where the idol was. This we agreed to, for we could see without going in.

The inside of the temple is divided in two small rooms, open on all sides like a porch. The floor has beautiful marble, and one of the idols was a marble figure of the Brahmin bull. On the walls were pictures of many different idols—frightful looking things. The ceiling was ornamented with paintings. Screens were hung round to prevent the sun from making their majesties uncomfortable. In another place was their god Ram and his wife. These just looked like 2 great dolls. Stella would hardly have had them for such, with their grinning faces. Oh! how absurd idolatry seems when you gaze upon its abominations.

You can scarcely imagine the low and degraded state to where man my fall. If Christians in our own land witnessed the sights that we do, they could not be so indifferent about sending the Gospel to the heathen. My dear Mother, rejoice that we have come to India; and dear parents, pray for us that we may not labor in vain—that God will bless us and make us very useful.

Well I must close my letter tonight, for tomorrow the overland mail goes. The last news from America by telegram announced the election of Davis, President of the South. We feel very anxious to hear of peace again being established.

Remember us to GrandPaps and Grandmother, Aunt Ag and Uncle and all our friends. With much love to you all. Goodbye.

Very affectionately,
Rachel

Futtehpore
May 15th, 1861

My dear Mother,

. . . We are now settled down in our own home, Mother, in Futteh-pore. Mrs. Nundy, Gopee Nauths widow, did not get out of the house as soon as we expected, and we remained in Allahabad until April 30th. A few days before, we sent off our goods and chattels by bullock carts. On the 30th we came up by rail. Left Mr. Walshs' at 6 A.M. and reach home at 9 A.M.

We found our house topsy turvy: some half dozen natives busy white-washing, etc.; our goods had not arrived; and here we were in a nice fix. But in a little while, one room was ready for us. In quite a jolly humor, we set about our first housekeeping in regular picnic style. Our breakfast was served up in a little time. Here was the quandary: our spoons, knives and forks, etc. were on the way, someplace between Futtehpore and Al-lahabad—where, we knew not—and the natives do not use such things. However, among them, they gathered up 2 cups, 1 saucer, 2 plates, 1 knife, 1 fork with one prong, and a teapot. With bread and butter, sar-dines, meat and a nice cup of tea, we made quite a hearty breakfast. We do not drink coffee in the hot weather. Tea is much healthier here, and we have learned to be very fond of it. But we never have such fragrant tea at home as we get here.

The afternoon we spent at Dr. Sherlocks. Our goods all arrived in the evening, and we soon got things arranged for spending the night very comfortably.

Futtehpore is a much smaller city than Allahabad. Still there is a na-tive population of 20 or 30,000. The English station, where our Mission property is, is $1\frac{1}{2}$ miles from the native city. There are but 5 English fam-ilies here. We are all very near each other. If you could stand in the door of our bungalow, looking from the front—about as far as from our house over to Aunt Abby Glasses—you might see the white columns of the courthouse. A short distance from that is Judge Edmunstons dwell-ing with a nice garden in front. About the same distance in an opposite direction is the large double bungalow occupied by Dr. Sherlock and his wife, and Mr. Anderson and family. The railroad depot is about equally distant. There is another house a little farther off, where 3 bachelors drink their tea in "single blessedness."

But enough about the neighbors house, come take a peep at our home. Oh! what a pleasure it would be, dear Mother, if I could, indeed, see you in our home. The Mission Compound is about 4 acres, enclosed by a wall, 3 feet high. I believe I have told you before that there are no fences in this country. If anyone wants a plot of ground fenced in, a wall of clay 2 or 3 feet high is sufficient. Our house is built almost square, with a porch or veranda extending round all 4 sides. The veranda is about 10 feet wide and supported by round columns built of brick, plastered, and placed 10 or 12 feet apart. In building, as little wood is used as possible, for it is so scarce and dear.

But Mother, come inside and see what a nice large room is in the centre. This is our dining room. There are rooms on all sides which makes it a little dark. But it is the coolest room in the house. The floor is covered with a carpet called a "darri" [duree]. It is woven of cotton chain and nicely striped. It makes a much nicer carpet than any rag carpet. On the walls hang several pictures. A door opens on one side into our sitting room which is a very cozy room, not so large as the last. On the floor is a woolen carpet, which we bought second hand, but it looks very well. In the centre of the room stands a round centre table and on each side a teapoy—these are English inventions I believe, as I never saw any in America. These are nothing more than a kind of 3 legged stand, used for holding books or any little nicknack. On the mantel ticks an American clock that just came out in a box from New York. Alongside are ranged the likenesses of some of our friends. So we have your faces ever looking upon us in our Indian home. Uncle Beatty and Mrs., and two large pictures hang on the walls. There is a large easy chair we brought from Boston and some cane bottomed chairs, which are the only kind I have seen in India, and which the natives make very nicely. They are made of a kind of reed entirely, which are very comfortable, but do not last long. Mr. Johnson got me a low one for a sewing chair, for which it suits admirably. A lounge covered with blue and white curtain chintz—and now you have a picture of our parlor.

Another door from the dining room opens into Mr. Johnson's study. The room is carpeted with printed cotton cloth made at Futtehgurh. It looks very well when new but dont last a great while. A door on the opposite side opens into a bedroom. One on the other side opens into another bedroom, which we will have for our own. The floor had to be made over and is not yet dry enough to occupy. We have carpet for it like the dining room. On each side of this room are 2 other rooms about 12 x 17 and another off the sitting room smaller.

The house is badly planned, with so many small rooms. In India we want large airy rooms. But as it is, we have a very cheerful looking house.

In every room hangs, suspended from hooks above, a *punka* or huge fan. It is made of a deep double frill of white muslin tacked on a nicely turned pole, or on a light frame covered with cloth. This fan is now in motion over my head, being pulled back and forth by a native out on the porch. The rope from the punka passes out through the wall. The doors have to be kept closed all day to keep out the hot winds. We hardly ever go out, even on the veranda, after 7 or 8 in the morning. Early, it is quite pleasant and late in the evening.

We have two tatties up now, which are large doors made of the roots of grass tied on a bamboo frame-work in layers. A boy stands outside and throws water on this all day, and the hot wind blowing through evaporates the water and makes the house quite cool. The hotter the wind outside, the cooler inside.

The church is but a few steps from the door, and the native Christian houses are all round the Compound. Only 2 families know any English.

Mrs. Walsh, little Anna, and baby came up last week and stayed several days. We enjoyed their visit very much. Mrs. Walsh is very kind to us and she is always ready to help us by advice and any way she can.

Dr. Sherlock and his wife called this morning. We see them every day. They are both young, and came out to India last December, though he had been here several years before they were married. They are from Dublin, Ireland. We like them very much.

I hope, Mother, you do not feel so lonely now as when we first left you. I know you will be glad to know that we are cheerful and although almost alone, yet we do not feel lonely. I feel very thankful that we feel so contented. We often—very often—talk about you all and think and wonder what you are all doing at home. We would love better than all things to see you. But we know we cannot now, for our work is here. Nearly all our Missionaries have found it necessary to go home and rest a little after a few years. Walshes were home 3 years ago, and we may someday see you all again, if our lives are spared.

I have not yet told you that we are both very well, as we have been ever since we came to India. This is now the season for fevers, and there was a good deal of it in Allahabad before we left. Mr. and Mrs. Walsh had both a slight attack. The head teacher of our Mission school has it now. He was in such a miserable place that we had him brought up in our house in a room we do not use, for Dr. said he would not likely get well where he was. He is a very good man, a native from Calcutta. The Dr. said his disease was not contagious and I trust he will soon be better.

Well Mother dear, I must say a few words to the rest, so goodbye for this time. Dont work too hard but get some help, you ought to rest now. I often see you in my dreams.

A word to Father: We were very glad to find a few lines from you in the last home letter. I suppose you are busy, altho you did not tell us what you were then doing. Have you got the schoolhouse finished? I think it would take the carpenters here an age to build a house of wood. We have one employed out in the Compound who has been 12 days working at a pair of doors and still they are not done.

The doors of the houses here are all double, the upper part is glass and answers in place of windows, which are not often made in a house in India. I have not seen a single door in India. The roof of our house slopes up to a point—like Uncle Billy Sterling's—and is first covered with a thatch of straw, then a layer of tiles. The heat here warps the wood very badly, then in the rainy season, every drawer and door will take a great swell.

The white ants are a great pest. They come up in a single night through the hard floor. You will see a line of fresh looking sand or clay under which they have a little gallery, where they carry out their depredations—always working under this cover which they throw up. Bookcases, bureaus, chests and trunks all have to be set up on bricks off the floor, or have a piece of tin under them. They eat all kinds of wood. Before we came here we had our chairs put in a lumber room. We found one chair had one leg quite eaten off, just a shell left. I could hardly believe at first that little ants could do such things. They work slyly but surely.

. . . The last news from America says war is inevitable and that Lincoln has disappointed the people, showing great inefficiency for the present crisis. But we dont credit all we see in the English papers about America. They talk a great deal about cultivating cotton more extensively in India now, but the cotton here is not so good as America. It too would be a long time before they have means of transportation as railroads, etc.

Thus my paper is filled. May God bless and keep you all.

Your affectionate daughter,
Rachel L. Johnson

[May 15, 1861, continued]

My dear brothers,

We have been so very busy since we came to Futtehpore that writing letters has been put off until now. There is little time and I will only add a postscript for you especially this time.

We are now in our own home. How much I wish you could come over and take dinner with us. I am sure I could give you something nice. The great Indian dish is rice and curry. The rice I know you would like, and the curry you would soon learn to eat. It is made of chicken and a great many hot spices, which almost burn ones throat, but we are very fond of it now. We had cucumbers for breakfast and muskmelons this morning, which were very nice. It is always best to eat fruit for breakfast in India. You know we dont breakfast until 9 or 10, and have dinner at 4 or sometimes later. Then a cup of tea and some toast when we get up, and a cup of tea when we go to bed—great tea tipplers we are.

. . . Mr. Johnson will write when he has more time. He is now writing a sermon. He is very busy and has to preach in English every Sabbath to the few who are at this station. Soon he will begin reading sermons in Hindustani.

Well Frank, what about West Point? And how is Emma, and Jennie, and Lina? I congratulate you on your escape from measles. I had a slight taste once, I remember. I hope our friends are all over them.

Now my dear sister Stella, you shall have a few words too. Did you get my letter I sent you about the bear dance? I wish you could come and stay with me and see the goats, guineas, geese and lizards too that run about on the walls and catch flies. You might be a little afraid of them, but they wont bite anybody. You would laugh at their funny long tails. I laughed very much one night at the way they fight. Two got in a little muss and the biggest one bit off the other ones tail. The poor thing had to run away a "bunty." . . .

Mr. Johnson joins in love to you, and to all our friends.

Lovingly,
Your sister in India, Rachel

Futtehpore
June 13th, 1861
My dear Brothers—Samuel and Frank [written by Will],

. . . You must not be surprised if in so long a journey a letter should once in awhile be lost. They ought to come through in 6 or 8 weeks. The mail brought me the World and Independent newspaper as late as April 13th. We can keep up pretty well with the political news from America,[4] but in these exciting times it is sad to be kept two months behind always. The Indian newspapers give us the most important news in about a month after it happens, but not the particulars. The news is telegraphed to Malta from London. The steamship and railroad bring it from Malta to Bombay. From Bombay it is telegraphed to Agra, Allahabad, and Calcutta, where our papers are printed.

When I stayed in Allahabad, I used to read the New York Times, Tribune, Observer, the Presbyterian, the Record, and Foreign Missionary. Now I only get the two latter and the World and Independent, which my sister sends me. The postage on every home paper that we take costs us 6 cents a number, or three dollars a year (except the Presbyterian, Record, and Missionary, for which the Board pay). So you can imagine how we devour every word of home news in them.

When the mail comes, in about the 7th and 21st of every month, we can scarcely take time to eat or sleep until we have devoured the home papers. We cannot afford to take any of the papers published here, but the Judge sends his round when he has read them. From the papers then we find out all the political news; but what we cannot find is what

4. The political news Will referred to was the erupting Civil War in America. The war came dangerously close to Washington when Virginia seceded from the Union on Apr. 17, 1861. As Will wrote his letter, the first great land battle of the war was brewing at Manasass Gap in the Blue Ridge Mountains of Virginia, twenty-five miles southwest of Washington. James M. McPherson, *Ordeal by Fire: The Civil War and Reconstruction*, 154, 208–13.

is going on in your neighborhood. We never hear a word of what happens in Hookstown, or in Beaver County, or Pittsburgh, unless from your letters.

I was very much interested in what Hunter McGahan told us of the oil excitement at Hookstown, and in the particulars you gave us of what was going on about town. About such things, and about everything which you think about, and talk about at home, we never get tired of reading.

Our life here still goes on in the same old way. The weather is still so hot that I dare not stand out on the porch, even in the shade, from 9 or 10 o'clock until 5 P.M. But inside we work away very busily and contentedly all day. Once in awhile the punkah fellow, who stands out on the verandah, gets almost asleep. The punkah begins to swing very lazily over our heads, and the air in the room is scarcely stirred by it. Almost before we know it, the perspiration will start from every pore in the body. Unless you will shout out to him, "Kainche" (pull), in a few minutes your clothes will be wringing wet.

But the only time when the heat is really very troublesome is just after tea for a few moments. We eat dinner at 4 P.M. and as soon as it gets cool enough in the evening, we take a walk or a drive. After we come back, after dark, we drink a cup of tea, but eat no supper. After drinking this tea we feel excessively warm. In five minutes our clothes will look as if we had been dipped in a pond. But as soon as this is over, we feel greatly refreshed inside. I do not know what we should do here without tea. People here eat very little bread. It is not the fashion to use it at dinner at all. Tea becomes the staff of life. It is the first thing when we get up in the morning. My bearer wakens me in the morning by crying out, "cha taiyar hai," or "tea ready is," and it is almost the last thing at night.

Rachel and I have splendid health and good appetites. You will think so too, when I tell you that she and I eat a quarter of mutton every two days, besides occasional chickens and fish. The principal things we have to live on are mutton, rice, and potatoes. It takes pretty strong rations of these to keep us going. In fact, we find that our chickens here are as unhandy as the Methodist preachers Shanghais—they are too much for one and not enough for two. I bought a goat the other day, which gives milk enough for our tea. I paid for it $62\frac{1}{2}$ cents.

And now Samuel, I am glad to hear that there is prospect of your going to college. I am glad of this because I cannot but hope that this will be the first step towards your coming out to help us in this blessed work. If you consecrate yourself and all your services to the service of your Savior, as I sincerely trust you will, I feel sure that you would think it a pleasure if God should allow you to come and live here. There is so much to be done for his service. But whether this shall be or not, I hope that you will at least make a proper use of all the advantages which you receive. Nothing perhaps would so much increase your power—either for good or evil—as two or three years of vigorous study at college.

About Frank, I was sorry to hear of your fancy for West Point. I think it very likely that the end of that career would be an early death, either in some unhealthy frontier post, or Indian squabble . . . or in some wearisome engineering expedition. I am sure it is not at all the kind of life that I would choose, even if it does offer a good education in Science and Mathematics. There are higher walks of life within your reach, if you were willing to try for them. But if you commit your way unto the Lord, all will be well.

About the political troubles, what can I say. I can see no future in store for our country but a season of fire and blood. Our National sins have been great. I fear that for them we are now condemned to drink to the dregs a bitter cup. You thought we were going away into danger—now you are probably in more danger than we are. How little we know of the future! But the path of duty is ever the path of safety.

Sumter is fallen. The mob has killed 11 men in Baltimore. Washington is threatened. The Border States stand aloof. What next? But there is one great security. God reigns. And amid the dangers of nations and the doubts as to our own duty, we have one unfailing resource—trust in Him. Do not my dear Brothers forget this.

Yours as ever,
W. F. Johnson

Futtehpore
July 26th, 1861

My dear Father and Mother,

This mail we send you the long lost letters, mailed to you in Calcutta almost 8 months ago. They have been lying in the dead letter office there ever since, along with all the letters written by the Wyckoffs during the voyage. When they learned that you had not received ours and as they have received no news from theirs, Mr. Wyckoff thought he would write to the postmaster and see if they had been sent. In reply he received a huge package of letters that he had been flattering himself was long ago gladdening the hearts of their friends. When I tore off the envelope and saw the thin paper—Oh! home letters, thought I to myself. But lo! When I opened them there was our own names signed. How disappointed I was.

But I was very pleasantly surprised one morning, for here came Frank and Stella peeping out from a nice long letter. Oh! how glad I was to see their dear faces—so good and lifelike. Frank looking so bright and pert. I almost expected to hear him speak right out and say: Well Rachel, I am pretty glad to see you after my long trip. And next came

Fig. 6. "Sweet little sister Stella," at age 8 in 1861.

Stella dear (fat, round face—looking as though she had been feasting on apple dumplings until she had grown almost one-half). Hers is very good indeed. Every feature so distinct. And they were both perfectly safe and sound after all their adventures. Where is Sam? Certainly he is coming out to see us. But perhaps you are all waiting to see whether Frank and Stella would get here safely. Be encouraged!

Mr. Walsh and Mrs. Wyckoff came up from Allahabad and I could not get a letter written to you. Mrs. Wyckoff has a little daughter, which is now about 3 months old. They have commenced housekeeping, living in part of Walshes house.

Mr. Walsh held communion service in Hindustani the Sabbath he was here, last Sabbath of June. This was the first time we sat around the communion table with our little flock of native Christians here. The service was all in Hindustani, but now we can understand a good part of what is said—enough to gather the general meaning. As we gathered round the tables in the aisle—like we use to do at Mill Creek—there were only 4 white faces there. But here was a little flock of the dark sons and daughters of heathen India, 17 in number, who gathered round the same table. They could say "Thy God is our God," if not, "Thy people is our people." But there were a few who remained seated when we rose to obey our Saviours Command, "Do this in remembrance of me." And who were they? Those bright, intelligent-looking, young men, that looked in wonder at us as we bowed our heads in prayer and sang the praises of our Lord, were worshipers of wood and stone. Their fountain of cleansing away their guilt is the muddy Ganges, that flows along a few miles distant. They often bow in prayer, but they call on a god who hears not. They sing praises, but it is to their god Ram, or some other incarnation. We felt that we were a little band. But we rejoiced that there was even a little band under the shadow of heathen temples to worship the true God.

One of those heathen boys I saw one morning in school with a wreath of flowers hanging round his wrist, which were for crowning some idol god. When he saw me notice it, he quickly tucked it up in his sleeve.

Mr. Johnson and I were taking a drive below the city one morning, when we saw across the open plain a huge pile of clay that looked something like the figure of a man. We thought perhaps it was an idol. A few days after, we went out the same way. Leaving our carriage, we walked across the plain to investigate the matter. As we drew near the monster, we found that it was a huge pile of clay fashioned into the shape of a man seated on a high platform of clay. On his head was a kind of crown. His eyes, nose and mouth were very large, and a moustache was nicely curled up to an exquisite point. His right arm was extended. But alas, for its beauty, the clay had begun to fall off and displayed some wisps of straw wrapped around a stick stuck into its huge side. The figure represented a giant of perhaps 25 feet high, if he was standing. Round the sides of the platform are figures of smaller size. At a little distance, in front of the platform, is another idol, also of clay, in the figure of a man in a lying posture. We walked along from his head to feet, and found it was about 40 feet long. A few weeks ago, the Hindoos had these all daubed with paint and decked in gorgeous array for one of their festivals, when they brought their offerings to this pile of clay.

We walked on from this place to a little Muhammadan Mosque, built over the grave of some of their saints. This was a small square room built of brick with a dome shaped roof. It was plastered outside and inside with the usual cement used here and white washed outside. The inside was painted in various figures. In the centre of the floor was a little marble block which marked the tomb. On this there was carved two little footprints, the design of which we did not know.

The Muhammadans make a great merit of visiting their tombs. They are even more bigoted than the Hindoos. They have just been celebrating one of their great festivals called the "Muharram," which is in commemoration of the death and burial of Muhammad [actually, the martyrdom of Muhammad's two grandsons]. They go through all the ceremonies of the funeral, having representations of his throne and his bier. They form processions with a great deal of tom toming on drums, etc. A great deal of tissue paper and tinsel are wasted on these occasions. Although they begin with a <u>fast,</u> it generally ends in a feast, and a row among themselves.

Saturday night, [July] 27th

We took a little jaunt down to Allahabad on the 9th. Came home on the 12th. A little change is necessary once in awhile and is better than medicine. Mr. Johnson did not feel very well for a week, but the change set him alright again. We came back quite well.

We have been much surprised at our getting along so well through this, our hot season, without feeling any ill effects from the change of climate. It is not everyone at home who gets along a whole year without having some ailment to complain of.

But I began to tell you about our visit. We started off one night between the showers for the Capital. The night before it had rained 8 inches! (all in one night). The country, nearly all the way to Allahabad, looked like a great lake. But our iron horse had a dry track and, snorting and puffing, away he sped. About 2 o'clock we found ourselves in Allahabad. Walshes carriage was waiting at the depot and a few minutes drive brought us back to our old headquarters. A little nap, and then we were bustling round seeing things old and new. We breakfasted with the Walshes, the Wyckoffs joining us, then all dined with Wyckoffs. Thus, we divided our time between them.

The 12th was the 17th anniversary of the Walshes wedding day, and they had a feast prepared of all the fat things of the land. They invited Rev. Williamson, Presbyterian Chaplain of the Army—a very good young Scotchman—to come out and dine with us. We all did ample justice to the roast fowls, guineas, chickens and oyster patties, vegetables, corn and beans, and the delicious fruits.

After dinner, Colonel MacPherson sent over an elephant and we all took a ride around through the city, mounted on the monsters back. You may imagine how dignified we felt, looking over the roofs of the houses or into the upper stories, as we passed through the crowds of staring natives below. Our elephant looked very gay too, with his great blanket of red and black patchwork, trimmed with silk fringe and tassels, which hung down over his great black sides.

On his broad back the "howdah" was firmly strapped by means of ropes and leather. This "howdah" is something like a small carriage bed with two seats in it. Each is capable of holding two persons. The elephant was brought up to the door by the "mahaut" (driver). He was a Mussulman with a great turban on his head, the usual native dress. His business is to sit on the animals neck, just in front of the howdah, and guide it. He does this by means of a piece of sharp pointed iron, about 20 inches long. He holds this in his hand and gouges it into the elephants head. He is also assisted by his toes, which he has firmly planted under each ear. If he wishes to turn to the right, his toes are pressed against the left ear; or if to the left, the right ear is gouged a little. To make the animal kneel, the iron is pressed on the top of the head; to stop, on the forehead. Another fellow, not quite so well dressed as the driver, runs alongside. This is the grasscut. He feeds, brushes and takes care of the elephant, doing all the hard work. If under a native master, he will have to paint the most ridiculous figures over the elephant in all sorts of gaudy colors. This pleases the eye of the natives very much. When the elephants are trained, they obey the word of command without anything more.

When our elephant had kneeled down, and a ladder placed along his side, Mr. Johnson, Mr. Williamson, Anna Walsh and I mounted into the howdah. Then the driver, astride of its neck, gave the command. With a little grunt, the elephant elevated himself, first on his fore feet—which made us feel as though we were going to slip off over his tail—then his hindquarters soon brought our seat level with the top of the house. Away he strode down through the branches of the trees. He took great long steps that shook our sides at first. In a little while we got used to the motion and felt very comfortable in our lofty state. After a little excursion we were lowered at the bungalow, and the rest of the party mounted. They went the same round. This was our first ride on the elephant. I told Mr. Johnson we would make quite a sensation in the streets of Hookstown, if we could appear before you as we then were situated.

We left Allahabad the same evening, about 9, and reached home safe and well. Since, we are busy as usual. Mr. Johnson reads a sermon in Hindustani on Sabbath mornings, and in the evening preaches in English. The native Christians have been sick a great deal with fever since the rains began, and he has to be doctor, teacher, preacher, in addition to all his patriarchal duties over our little community. . . . Then there is our daily lessons with the "munshi," and one of the Catechists comes to be instructed in English, etc. Plenty of work makes the time fly.

I have a little school of the children of native Christians, that I preside over every morning. Some are learning their A.B.C.'s, some are reading a little, and two of Mrs. Nundy's boys study geography, grammar and history. At first I had no books, but I succeeded in getting some primers in Allahabad. We will get along better now.

The weather is very pleasant now, altho we still have the punkas pulled. Almost every day we have some rain. This cools the air very much and makes the grass grow beautifully. This is considered the most unhealthy part of the year. The water stands on the plains, causing fever a great deal more than even the hot winds. In September the cold weather will again begin. Then we will have beautiful days and cool nights.

But I must not talk of every thing but the one great topic that fills your thoughts and causes us sad forebodings: the war that perhaps even now is raging around our once peaceful homes in America. I cannot realize that our peaceful hills may now be echoing the sound of the murderous cannon, and that those dear to us now need a "Home Guard" for protection. Very earnest is our prayers that the Arms of the Almighty may protect you and spare your lives—that peace may soon again be in all your borders. Oh! how eagerly we long to hear of the end of this sad struggle. The last telegram brings news that Harpers Ferry is occupied by the Federal troops, and that vigorous preparations are going on on both sides. How old this will seem to you by the time it crosses the waters.

There is a great excitement now about raising more cotton in India and making roads, etc. The Manchester cotton speculators will, no doubt, do something more than talk in the present emergency.

Well Father, I hope your company will not be called in to defend the homes in the quiet valley of Millcreek. And my dear Mother, may you have no need to be left alone to days and nights of sadness. I felt disappointed when I read the last home letter. The news was all about the war, hardly anything about home. But I suppose there is little else thought of, or talked of now, but war. The boys forget to say even that you are well. I expect we feel more anxiety now about you all, than you have need to feel on our account. May you all be kept in peace and safety.

With much love from us both to you all, and to our friends,

> Your affectionate daughter,
> Rachel L. Johnson

P.S.
Well brother Frank, you want to know how we liked your face. I am glad to say that we liked it very much, because it was just like you. I think you must have heard the drums beating when you were sitting for your picture. For your eyes look just as though you were wanting to pitch in to some of the traitors.

I love to think that my brothers love their country, but it brings the tears to my eyes to think of the possibility of you filling a soldiers grave. But if I felt sure that you were both soldiers of King Jesus, then the bitterness of even this thought would be taken away. May you be such! Write often to your affectionate sister—R.

Brother Samuel, I want you to send us your face. I am glad to hear you are going to college. Be diligent and keep from bad company, and make a good man out of yourself. You can if you will. Write often. Tell me all about your plans, doings, etc., as you used to do in our nightly chats. We have a nice comfortable home where we would love to welcome you, but this pleasure is not possible soon. Your affectionate sister, R.

Futtehpore
August 23rd, 1861

My dear Mother and Father,

. . . Well it seems from Frank's letter that you are all in good spirits, Samuel gone to college and all the rest busy as bees in the hive at home. And I am glad to say that all has been well with us too. I feel very thankful that we have never yet had anything but good news to write to you. And I hope you will not soon hear anything to make you sad. We have been blessed with health, and everything in our situation and prospects is hopeful. And my dear Mother, do not fear that we will only give you the bright side of the picture, but feel assured that we will truly tell you all things concerning us—our health and our circumstances.

. . . One of the native Christians has just called Mr. Johnson to give out some quinine for his wife, who has the fever. This one is our principal man. He is quite a genius, although he is about as ugly as he could well be. His name is Henry. He talks English and is 2nd teacher in the school. Lucy, his wife, can talk a little English too. But she gets a little crazy sometimes and then she scolds furiously. At other times she is very well behaved. A few weeks ago Henry was very ill with fever, and we had him brought over to our house; for Lucy had one of her wild spells, and would not do anything for him. After we brought him over, she came over to admonish him, but we sent her home. She thought she was much abused. But the poor woman did not know what she was doing. She always acts very respectfully toward us when well.

The natives have a strange fancy, that when they get fever, they must shave their heads first thing. Ananh Masih, a Reader, had his shaved a little time ago, as bare as your hand. He looked so strange with his bald pate, that we laughed at him and tried to convince him that, "the top of the head was the place where the wool ought to grow." But they say, "Its our custom." And that is the best possible reason for a Hindoo.

This fellow is a queer one. He is especially fond of medicine. He would rather take it than not, and looks very happy when we give him a dose of pills or castor oil! After taking a dose of the latter, he came and told us, "It was very good and he was particularly fond of it." You may well suppose we had a good laugh at his odd taste.

During the rainy season, the natives are constantly complaining of fever. We keep dosing some of them with quinine every day. Mr. Johnson says he has a good deal better practice than many a village physician, and he is quite right. Ever since the rains began, there are generally 4 or 5 in our Compound sick with fever. And it is not strange, for the whole country round Futtehpore is dotted here and there with ponds of standing water—green and slimy—that send up their poisonous malaria: fit food for "jungle fever." We have about another month of this weather, and then the cold will bring a healthier air.

Saturday Night

This evening we had a long drive. Our pony gets very frisky if we dont take him out every day. He wants to race with everything he sees—be it a little, long-eared donkey, an ugly, old buffalo just out of a muddy pond, or a foolish colt—no matter what. A trot of 3 or 4 miles however cools his ambitions, and he trots home very demurely. We called at Doctor Sherlocks and chatted a little while.

Now my good husband is writing a sermon and I am chatting to you, while the "punkah wala" on the veranda is pulling lustily. The great punka swinging over our heads helps drive away the mosquitoes and little sand flies, as well as to keep us cool—that is, as cool as possible, when the thermometer hanging on the wall is 89 or 90 degrees. The hardest rains are now over, but it still rains every few days. We have a shower or two, then the clouds scatter away, and the sun shines out very hot. The mornings and evenings are very pleasant. Only then the punka rests.

I have on a lawn dress and Mr. Johnson has thrown off his coat, yet the sweat is oozing out of every pore. Yet the heat is more bearable than you suppose. We need to change our clothes much oftener than in the cooler climate.

You will be surprised when I tell you that Mr. Johnson wears flannel underclothes, a fashion people here have adopted to keep themselves cool. Old Indian residents say it is far healthier, for it protects from sudden chills after perspiring freely, which you are almost sure to get if you go into a draft of air. I thought I would adopt the habit too and made myself a nice warm body long ago. It is folded up in a corner of the drawer, and I have been putting off the evil day as long as possible. Somebody was telling me the other day that an old man had been in India a long time. During the ten years in which he had always worn flannel, he had never been sick. "Very good" says I, "then surely it is a good thing." But half the story was yet not told. For my friend went on to say that the same hale, old gentleman laid his flannel by, and enjoyed as good health the next ten years without it. This was rather a poser, and left a little excuse for risking our lives to King Cotton.

But enough of this. I wonder what you are all doing this Saturday night. How I would love to take a peep at you. A good night to you all.

Monday Night, [August] 26th

Well my dear Mother, I promised you in a former letter to give you some idea of housekeeping in India. I gave you a description of our house. You will now go out a few steps from the back veranda, or porch, through a little grassy yard, and I will show you our kitchen—or "bawarchi-khana," as we call it in India. We enter a little porch, and then a room—not quite so large as our home kitchen. But why? you ask is our kitchen so far away. Well, although, we like a roast for dinner, we dont care about being ourselves the object. So we keep away as far as possible from the fire.

But where is our cooking stove? Look along the side of our kitchen at the mass of brick work. On the top of this platform are little places like this ∪∪∪∪ in which the fire is placed. We use charcoal instead of wood. Over these holes the brass pots are placed to stew, boil or bake. These pots are lined with tin and have to be retinned every month, which the tinner does very cheap—about 3 cents each. But it is a very thin coat, which is put on by heating the vessel and rubbing the melted alloy quickly over. We use no iron pots, but a teakettle, frying pan and a spit for roasting meat or grilling chicken. This is a long bar of iron, sharp at one end, on which the savory fowl is turned round over the coals until nice and brown. A little bake oven is built just outside, which is used for cake, pies, etc. We get our loaves from the baker.

I will not introduce you to the cook until we find him in the house, for he does not wear a super abundance of muslin in the kitchen. It is so hot, and he does not expect to be seen by visitors or any one, so simple breech cloth completes his attire. When we find him in the house he sports wide white pajamas (pants), a white chudder (a kind of tight sack reaching to the knee), an ample turban rolled round his head, and another roll around his waist of white, or some figured lawn, to match his turban. The cook is a Muhammadan.

Our "khansama" (house steward), who provides everything, we brought with us from Allahabad. We find him very useful. He understands our ways and our Hindustani, which is of course not very accurate yet. His name is Hafiz. He is pretty dark with keen black eyes. He is a little round shouldered and very active. He is quite a "swell" in the way of dress, but very anxious to please in his work.

It is very amusing to hear the eastern style of conversation. It is so full of extravagant, high-sounding words, and so very humble toward the "Sahib loge," as they call the white faces [literally, people of the world]. Hafiz came the other day and asked Mr. Johnson to give him leave of absence for a few days on account of his brothers death. His request was in this fashion: "If it please your Honor, I will go. You, oh Master, are my Mother and my Father and all my relatives, and when your Majesty pleases I will return. Your interests are mine, and I am devoted to you, etc. etc." This is a specimen of their way of talking.

The "mihtar," or sweeper caste, are Hindoos. They wear the cloth wrapped around the loins, a kind of round about of muslin. The brooms are made of coarse grass or reeds, tied like the sweepers you sometimes use for brushing the hearth. I do not suppose the sweeper in India ever saw a broom with a handle. He would not know what use to make of it.

I think I have told you about the "bhishti," who carried water in a bag of goat skin slung on his back. He draws from the deep well in a leather bucket, or hitches a couple of bullocks to the rope to pull for him.

The "dhobi," or washerman, carries the clothes off to a huge pond of water. He has a large flat stone for a washboard. He dips the clothes in the water, then beats them on the rock. Dips and beats, until they are cleansed. Then he spreads them out on the grass to dry. All the time he is washing them, he stands in water which comes up to his knees. You will think it is strange when I say a man does the washing in India, but remember that it is the business of a particular caste who only do this work. The dhobis wife helps too, and you may be sure she does the hardest part of it. For the Hindoos dont think their wives are fit for anything but work. When the clothes are dry they are made into a huge bundle. The patient, little, long-eared donkey that has been limping about the tank, hobbled all day—his fore-foot tied to its next neighbor, or maybe all three together—has his fetters loosed, and the bundle is thrown over his back. This covers up all but the long ears and sober, resigned-looking countenance, and four little shanks, that look as though they would break off under such a bundle. Now dhobi, donkey, dhobi's wife, and most likely two or three little naked urchins, wend their way home, followed by a lean, lank, sheepish-looking dog. In due time the clothes are nicely ironed, and sent to the Sahib. Wages are $2.50 a month. Not very much tis true, but one will wash for several families, and in this way will make plenty to buy his rice and curry.

We get very good rice for 2c a pound. Cheap enough is it not? But remember we are in the midst of rice fields. Sugar we get for 7c a pound, but it is not so good as the sugar you have. We have just received a box of Mocha coffee, for which we paid 18c a pound. Fruits are scarce now as well as vegetables. We have plenty of corn. We still have a weakness for corn soup and roasting ears, but we never indulge very freely in such things. Dysentery is the scourge of India and we always have to be very careful in our diet. Cholera has been very fatal this season in many places at Futtehgurh, Delhi and many others. We have escaped at Futtehpore with only a few cases among the natives, who often make their suppers on cucumbers and such things.

Now Mother, I am almost at the end of this sheet and yet, I have many things I would like to tell you about. How very unsatisfactory my pen is. It is so slow, I am so lazy, and the clock on the mantel ticks away the time so fast. It is now calling out 9, which you always used to tell was time for people who like to sleep in the morning to go to bed. I get up earlier now, but still I like a morning nap.

Last night we spent the evening with Mr. Tyrrels, who is assistant magistrate. It was late when we got home. Dr. and Mrs. Sherlock were there too, and Mr. Poiser, a bachelor, who is the highest magistrate.

Here we are invited to dinner at 8 o'clock at night. What a ridiculous custom. Then we go to bed with full stomachs and get up with headaches.

. . . Now dear Mother, Father, Samuel, Frank and Stella, I must bid you all good-night.

Let us hear from you often.
Rachel

August [31,] 1861

Well my dear Frank,

You gave quite a glowing description of the sweet spring time at the old homestead. Much would I love to hear the little birds that sing so sweetly in the maples; and see the nice box you have kindly made for the Martins; and see the nice, grassy yard you had trimmed so neatly. Yes, everything about the old house at home is very dear—and much more those in it.

You say that the Volunteer Company had been ordered off to the war. If I understand right, it is Captain Little's Company. When you write again, tell us who have gone that we know.

I think you were very sensible Frank, to accept father's offer about the work. I hope too that your wishes to get a good education may be gratified, and that when you get one, it will fit you for much usefulness.

You ask about the Wyckoffs. Can it be that I have been so extremely selfish as to fill all these sheets I have written to you just about self, and not a word about our good friends? I am sure I thought, Frank, I had told you all about the color of their eyes, the color of their hair and the color of the clothes they used to wear. A link must be missing somewhere. But to make amends, I will tell you that they are very good people, and very good friends of ours. Mr. Wyckoff is from Western Ohio. He graduated at the Seminary a year before Mr. Johnson. His talents are medium and he is earnest in his work. He is about the size of Mr. Johnson, has light hair and blue eyes. Mrs. Wyckoff is a little taller than I, and has black hair and black eyes, and is a very pleasant woman. She had lived in Memphis, Tenn., with a cousin of hers, for some time before she was married. Her father lives in Iowa, but her Mother is dead. She has a tolerably good education. I had a letter from her a short time ago, and she says they are getting along finely. They do not appear to feel the heat very much, and enjoy very good health.

Frank, I was very glad to hear that father has got gravestones for Jane's grave, and the little ones. You forgot to tell me what inscription is on them, and what shape are they.

Now my dear brother . . . I told you a long time ago we were going to send a box home with some Indian curiosities. As soon as we find it will not be in danger of falling in Jeff Davis' hands, we intend dispatching it.

I almost forgot to tell you that our boy Hafiz, of the huge turban, admired your likeness very much and made us laugh heartily when he asked if you were a "Padri" too (They call preacher, Sahibs-Padris). He wanted to know when you were coming to India. I was sorry that I could not tell him when to expect you.

With much love from us. Good-bye.
Affectionately, Sister Rachel

Saturday Morning, August 31st [1861]

Dear Samuel,

I am so glad to hear that you are at college, and I hope you will enjoy your life there very much. I have already written a long letter home, but I feel this morning I must add a line especially to you. You are now away from home, and I know you like to get letters as well as I do. I wish I could send you a little "chit" every week (that is what we call letters in India). Old Baldee, the man who brings the letters, comes up very often saying "koe chit na hai" (no letter). Tomorrow I hope he will produce a bundle from his wallet containing one from my good brother Sam.

. . . We are getting along finely, have good health, good spirits and plenty of work to do in the Mission. We feel a great interest in the success of our Country, and wait anxiously for every item of news about the war. We have news by telegram from America to July 4th. A long time ago, is it not?

This year we celebrated the 4th in a quiet way at home. I wonder how you spent it? Mr. Johnson has some pretty lively discussions on the American question with the "John Bulls" here. You know they dont appreciate our Republican institutions and government, as they do our cotton. They say the Union is gone—a little fact that we dont swallow yet.

Maggie Blakesley sent us a letter all spangled with stars and stripes by last mail. She says a great many have gone from Waterbury, and Mr. Johnsons Uncle Terry has enlisted for 3 years.

. . . With much affection from us both, and dont forget your sister.

Rachel

Sister dear,

One little corner left for you. Frank tells me you are a pretty good girl, and I am glad to hear it. I would like to send you a present of a nice Persian kitten, but I am afraid this letter would not hold it.

FOUR

October 1861–June 1862

FATEHPUR

℣ RACHEL AND WILL wrote chatty conversations to Rachel's family about everyday trifles in Fatehpur and in their lives. After the drought of 1860, Northern India was grateful for the rains of 1861, but the weather went to the opposite extreme. Long-time residents said 1861 was the wettest season in thirty years. The swollen, raging rivers wrecked another kind of havoc on the poor villages of Northern India that were built along river banks. Rachel said there was no escape to higher ground, as there was no higher ground in the flat lands of the river basins.

Both Rachel and Will spoke of the illnesses that plagued Fatehpur residents. Will said the health problems seemed to stem from the fact that Fatehpur was in a basin, lower than the level of the Ganges, and therefore without drainage. "The air is full of malaria . . . native Christians are constantly suffering from fever . . . and most Europeans have been sick."[1]

Will reported that he and Rachel were developing skills and comfort with the Hindustani language, but that study still occupied much of their time. Will said that he was now able to read a prepared sermon in Urdu at the Saturday morning services. He called on the Catechists to pray. The catechists and readers also went regularly to the bazaars and surrounding villages to preach.[2] Will continued preaching at an English service every Saturday evening, which almost all of the British residents in the station attended. Related to his work in the mission, Will's letter to the Board in August 1861 contained some continuing and mounting mission concerns. He concluded, it "looks as if the church were going to ruin in my hands"; the membership of the Christian community had decreased significantly since he arrived. Most of the Christians who were baptized just before Gopi's death "disappeared immediately." In addition, Gopi had paid money—on a monthly basis, like wages—and

---

1. "India Letters," vol. 10, no. 83, Aug. 29, 1861.
2. The catechist taught the basic principles of the religion; the reader read the Scripture.

provided housing to inquirers into the faith. Will had no money for this purpose. When the monies stopped, the inquirers "ran away." Another problem was the work behaviors of the local Christians. Many had been discharged from their jobs for "bad conduct." Will said "the reputation of native Christians here is so bad here that . . . I cannot get places for them."[3]

In contrast to Will's mission concerns, Rachel presented a proud account of the formal end-of-the-school-year ceremony for parents and the community, which showed off the accomplishments of the young male scholars in their mission school. On the anniversary of their first year of living and working in India, Rachel reported that they were glad they had come. Rachel talked of visits, walks, and activities with their good friends, Dr. and Mrs. Sherlock in Fatehpur. She talked also about their small circle of missionary friends, with whom they visited between train stops at the depot, or when Rachel and Will made an occasional trip to Allahabad for a change of scenery or to escape the hot weather. Each letter had added notes for Stella and her brothers. In notes to Stella, Rachel described whimsies she thought Stella might particularly enjoy, such as a visit from a giant, a tame bear who danced, and a fight between a snake and a weasel. In letters to Sam and Frank, Rachel asked for reports on their schoolwork, friends, and community activities.

War preparations in America made significant cuts in the funds provided to support mission projects and personnel in India. Each letter from the Board of Missions urged Will and his colleagues to be even more frugal in the management of their meager mission funds. To save money, the Presbyterian missionaries in India made a major sacrifice in 1861: they canceled their annual November meeting. This was an immense professional and social sacrifice for couples like Rachel and Will, who felt isolated in their small villages. They had few opportunities for conversation with people who understood their cultural backgrounds, hopes, dreams, and commitments.

The war being fought in the States also heightened tensions between the British and Americans in India. Will and Rachel smarted at references from the English to the "fighting clowns in the North" and the "brave, generous, clear-headed aristocrats" in the South, who were fighting for a free tariff and longing for governance by their British king. Painfully, these reports were also accompanied by taunts, jeers, and sarcastic remarks from their British neighbors.

Rachel and Will followed the progress of the war at home on maps August Blakesley sent them. Rachel wrote of their dismay over the Union defeat at Bull Run; their concern that General Fremont—the man they had strongly supported for president in 1856—was described

3. "India Letters," vol. 10, no. 83, Aug. 29, 1861.

as incompetent as a field commander; and their sadness at hearing that many of their friends at home had gone off to war. In April 1862, Rachel expressed elation over the apparent turn of events in the progress of the war. She cited news of Federal victories that indicated the North was ahead again. Thus, the press reports they received in India began to change the minds of their British neighbors toward the Union.]

Futtehpore, India
October 1st, 1861

My dear Mother,

. . . The telegrams, papers and letters bring sad news from our beloved country. Oh! how it makes our hearts sick within us when the telegram comes in with: "Great Southern Victory," "Northerners Totally Routed," "Grand Army of the Potomac Flying Panic Stricken," "Washington in Danger." These blaze forth in large letters in the papers, accompanied with taunts and jeers and sarcastic remarks from sympathizing (?) John Bulls. The defeat at Bulls Run does indeed appear to have been most disgraceful. The more to be lamented as it will encourage the traitors. But we hope our Country will come out right in the end, and then be not only a wiser but a better nation.

Wednesday Morning,
[October] 2nd, [1861,] 6 A.M.

Mr. Johnson has gone to attend the funeral of a poor man who died yesterday evening. He was a physician from Banda, about 90 miles from here. A friend of his was taking him to Calcutta, hoping that the journey on the river would revive him a little. But when they reached our station, they were obliged to stop. The poor man was too much exhausted to go on. They stopped with Dr. Sherlocks. After lingering a few days, he has gone on the long journey to his last home.

On Sabbath morning Mr. Johnson visited him and talked with him about the interests of his soul, but he was too weak to hear much. It seemed very sad for a young man, just beginning life, to be cut down far away from home and friends. . . .

We rose this morning while it was yet dark, and my husband drove up to the Doctors, that they might get through the services before the sun gets hot. I have just been standing on the veranda watching to see the little procession leave for the grave yard. They have now passed out of sight. In front was the corpse in a palki, (a long box) borne on the shoulders of four coolies. Following were 5 or 6 men walking, with their carriages following after. Walking is pleasant in the cool of the morning. The grave yard is almost 2 miles from this part of the station. They will perhaps be gone an hour. I could not help feeling sad as I watched the little procession moving along—all strangers—bearing the dead to rest among the bones of strangers. No mother, no father, no brother, no sister, no friend to shed a tear over his grave. Perhaps all of these dear ones are waiting in his father land, and longing for tidings from him, who never again will greet them by message. But I must not dwell on such sad thoughts.

My little table is brought out on the veranda, and I sit writing to you while the birds are all chirping their morning song over my head, peeping out from their nests in the eaves of the house. A saucy, old, black crow is stalking across the yard, cawing over a fine breakfast he has picked up. The chickens and geese are busy hunting among the grass for theirs. And the ducks are quack, quack, quacking about something. Three or four "bails" (oxen) are nipping the grass. All are busy as bees.

I see Jacob, our catechist, and Henry, one of our native Christians, chatting together. And there goes the old bhishti, or water carrier, with his goat skin bag on his back. A little black fellow is driving our flock of goats off to pasture in the jungle. There are about a dozen goats in all. Three are ours, and the rest belong to the native Christians. We use no milk but goats milk. It is much better than the cows milk we get here.

This morning is cloudy, and I think we will have rain today. It is a good thing that the rains are continuing so long, for we will have more cold weather this year. This has been a remarkably wet season. The oldest inhabitants say there was not such rains for 30 years. You may imagine how welcome they are after the drought of last year. But, welcome as they are, they have also done much damage in many places. The rivers have risen suddenly, and rapidly overflowed their banks. And the country, for hundreds of miles, has been covered several feet in many places with water. Great numbers of villages on the banks of the rivers have been swept away, leaving not a single, mud wall. Many lives have been lost. Thus, many of the poor natives have lost all, and are left to find shelter wherever they can. In many of the stations the people were obliged to go about the streets in boats. You must remember that the country is flat and level. There is no chance of running up on a big hill to dry spots. Many of the embankments, which are thrown up along the river banks, gave way, and the water rushed over the surrounding country causing fearful damage.

We are situated in the basin, between the Ganges and Jumna, and several feet below either. If the "bunds" or embankments had given way, we might have had occasion to go on a boating excursion. Fortunately they held out.

Mr. Walsh was up here on last Sabbath to administer communion to our native Christian church. He says that the Jumna washed part of their chabutra away. A chabutra is a nice, paved, porch, that extended out from their door to the river bank; a very pleasant place to walk and sit in the evenings.

We are still plodding away at the Hindustani. Moonshi comes every day, and we read with him. We also read in the Testament in Hindustani, along with the English version. Mr. Johnson is getting along finely with the language. Of course it will require a long time to become familiar with the different uses of the words. Every day we find ourselves picking up something.

The time passes very quickly. It seems but a little time since we came, and yet almost a year has slipped away. We feel well satisfied with our Station. I am sure we ought to be encouraged, for through all the sickly season, we have had the best of health.

The troubles at home must needs cripple more or less our missionary operations. The Board writes that they may have to cut the missionary part of their salaries. The missionary brethren think that they will have to give up the usual Annual Meeting, which is a great disappointment to us all. We have been looking forward to that meeting with much pleasure, hoping to meet all the missionaries and their wives. Then we would feel more interest in each other. I received a letter from Mrs. Brodhead, wife of the Missionary at Mynpoorie, and she says they will be much disappointed if we do not come. This year the meeting is to be at Mynpoorie. If there is one, the missionaries will not be able to take their wives with them, and probably they will not meet at all.

When the cold weather fully sets in, we will go out through the district, camping in tents, which will be a novel life for us. The Catechists and Scripture Readers will accompany us, preach and distribute tracts and testaments, etc., to the villagers. But more of this again when we begin our Camp life.

Afternoon . . . it has been rain, rain, raining, just like an "election day." Mr. Johnson has just finished settling his accounts for last month. He has the Mission expenses, the boys school, the girls school, Relief fund for the poor, the Widows and Orphans fund, and the Bible Society, etc. These give him at least a days work at the beginning of every month to keep them all straight. I keep an account of all our family expenses, and give in my account once a month, so that we will know just how our private accounts stand.

When this reaches you the cold December winds will be chilling you, and you will be gathering around the bright warm fires. How we would love to meet you all there. I dreamed of seeing you all the other night. I thought you had all come to India. I was badly disappointed when I awoke and found it was all a dream. . . .

Very affectionately,
Your daughter,
Rachel L. Johnson

Futtehpore,
October 31st, 1861

Dear Ones All,

I send you a Christmas greeting, hoping that you will receive it about the time that merry old gentleman known as Kriss Kringle comes. He comes "in his sleigh with eight tiny reindeer," and pops down the chimney; fills the little folks stockings with candy and kisses, and all thats nice; and fills the older ones tables with turkey, pudding and pies. Altho we are not with you, to help you enjoy the Christmas cheer, our hearts will wish you a happy, happy one. We will join you on this side of the world in feasting on the good things of the land. We hope that if old Kriss finds it poor sleighing, he can come on an elephant or hump backed camel, which will do quite as well. I will then tell you what he has brought us in his pack.

We are now having a foretaste of winter. The mornings and evenings are cool, like September with you. It is delightful to have ones teeth chatter once more, after being heated in an oven so long. We go out early and take a brisk walk in the fresh morning air, which makes one feel full of life all day. But if we stay until the sun gets high, we need an umbrella to keep off its rays, even if the air is cool. All the Europeans have their umbrellas covered with white muslin, as black absorbs the rays and white throws them off. The natives sport every color and kind.

Have I ever told you about their strange and ingenious ones made of leaves? A straight stick or bamboo, which is smooth and round for a handle; some rods running out from the top for ribs; then strings stretched round, and one layer of leaves tied on, and then another, and so on. You need not laugh about this rude contrivance, for it keeps out the hot rays better than a nice silk one would. Stella, how would you like a parasol made out of bright maple leaves. Give Frank a job. But I forget. They are all hid in their bed of snow. Other specimens I see made of splits like a basket. But the native dandies have fancy colored ones, often red, yellow and blue, all in one—something like a gay patchwork quilt.

Now that the weather is getting cold, I pity the little children of the poorer classes. It is their fashion to wear nothing at all, but one little knot or bunch of hair on the back of the head. A few evenings ago we were coming home from a drive round the city, when we saw one of these little chaps kicking up the dust and throwing it over himself. As we passed him, he stopped and made a most polite salam. Another little group were playing under a tree. I see one little fellow in our Compound in the same cool dress—the child of a poor, half-witted, old woman—and I am making a warm, little coat for him. I gave Sukhi, the mother, an old dress of mine, which pleased her very much.

Almost every day some poor distressed creature comes asking the "Protector of the Poor" to give them something to fill their "pate" (or stomach), and some "kapra" (or clothes) to make them "garm" (or warm).

We were amused yesterday morning at an old fakir, as they call their holy men. He came to the door lamenting, "Sahib, bahut bhuka hun, bahut gharib." That is, "Master, very hungry—very poor." Mr. Johnson said to him, "Very well, will I give you some bread to eat?" (You know the Hindoo would not eat anything we had even touched for that would break their caste.) The old man raised his hands beseechingly, while a grim smile spread over his face, and said, "nahin," "nahin" (No No), "Sahib. Paisa mangta." (I want money to buy in the bazaar.) Mr. Johnson then asked him what those streaks of mud on his forehead were for, and he said to please his god. Mr. Johnson said they looked very dirty, and made him look like a fool. The old fellow good-naturedly began to rub it off, saying apologetically that it was put on very early in the morning, as tho he was not quite awake when he did it. The Sahib then gave him some "pice" (money), and sent him on rejoicing.

It is very strange how bigoted they are about caste. I was reading a story yesterday in the paper about a Hindoo, who, a few weeks ago, started on a voyage to the Isle of Mauritius. The voyage being longer than he expected, his stock of rice was all consumed long before the ship reached port. The crew offered to share their provisions with him. But "no," he said. "He would die rather than break his caste by eating their food." And day after day the poor man lingered, starving, but still holding fast to his faith, until death at last put an end to his bodily sufferings. Thus, these poor deluded ones vainly cling to their bigoted love for their false religion and idol gods. And the Muhammadan part of this race of people are even more bigoted. They have a deeper hatred of the religion of Jesus, that dear name they never speak, but to blaspheme.

. . . Well dear ones, here I have been chatting away almost to the end of the sheet. Mother dear, what are your busy hands about? What are you making? What have you got new—a new bonnet or dress? Where have you been visiting? When were you at Grandpaps? What is Grandmother doing, and Aunt Agnes, and all our neighbors?

I have a thousand questions to ask, but no room.

With love to you all, and all our friends and neighbors. Goodnight.

Very affectionately,
Rachel L. Johnson

P.S.

My dear Stella,

I have no little letter from you for a long time. Where is the post office now? Do you like to go as well as when you tried to beat me, and get all the letters first? I send you a kiss to put in your stocking for Christmas.

Tell me about your little friends, and give a kiss to all my friends for a Christmas gift from India.

Your Sister Rachel

Futtehpore,
October 31st, 1861

To Father and Mother Kerr and the Boys [written by Will]:
My dear Friends,

It almost startles me to think how the time has slipt away since first we set foot in this benighted land. Alas! How little have we accomplished! How sad is the retrospect! But still I keep flattering myself that next year I shall be able to preach in Hindustani, and then I will be able to do more. I still plod on reading with the munshi. He is a real, pleasant-faced, young Hindoo, who came up this morning in a warm, long coat of light, blue merino, and jaunty little cap of the same, instead of his usual spotless muslin robes. He is the head Persian teacher. I am quite fond of him. I dont think his faith is very strong in idolatry, as he laughs sometimes when he tells me about the women worshipping snakes, etc.

I generally spend some time each day translating with one of the Catechists. By myself I could turn the words into Hindustani fast enough, but without long practice one cannot get the idioms of the language. They are absolute necessary to one in preaching. This is tedious work; but the prospect of being able to speak to the people in their own tongue of the wonderful works of Christ, makes it quite a labor of love. The language is very different from ours. To say "Khub Fajr," "good morning" in Hindustani, would make a Hindoo stare. He would wonder why you called that morning any better than another. But say "Salaam," "May peace be on thee," he understands at once.

It is droll to hear familiar words with such different meanings. For instance, the popular proverb that "every bail is worth $5" is here literally true. Here bail (oxen) draw the carts, plough the fields and make themselves generally useful. What they call a "house," would be rather an unpleasant place to live in. It is a pond of water. You will be surprised that our chief article of diet is the "bear" (sheep). Our cook would be greatly astonished if we told him to cook "maize" for dinner. He would probably reply, "Oh Protector of the Poor, whatever your honour's order is, that I will do. But pray tell me, how shall I cook the table?" It sounds strangely to tell the servants to put the "saws" on the horse, when you mean the harness; or to put some "tail" in the lamp. But the chap would not smile if you told him to "lay" an egg and cook it. (Take it and cook it.) The first salutation when a native calls to visit you is to tell him to "bite." Thereupon, instead of taking hold of you with his teeth, he obeys you by sitting down. Perhaps you put a piece of paper before him and say "lick," and he takes a pen and writes. Some one calls out, "Billy is in the pool"; and you turn around, and find the cat among your flowers. People here have "knocks" instead of noses, and every hair is a "ball." You say "Kerr" the coffee, when you mean to make the coffee. I might extend the list to any length.

This is a wonderful country for what Beecher calls "varmint" of every description. Some time ago, the Dr. sent us down a basket containing 4 beautiful Persian Kittens with their mother. The Persian cat is generally black and white, with very long silky hair and a very bushy tail. They are much prettier than our home cats. We enjoyed the play of the little fellows very much for awhile. Such agility in kittens so young. I certainly never saw such desperate plunges and falls as they went through by the hour! We began to think them perfect tigers. But finally the old cat found some fleas somewhere. It was in the rainy season—the swarming time—and almost at once the house was beset with fleas. We put the kittens out for a few days into the room where Hindustani books are kept. But soon we had to put them out of doors and keep them out. For several weeks the floor in that room was almost black with fleas. I didnt dare to enter. However the cold of these last few mornings is beginning to tell upon them. Today, the first time for a long while, I opened the door. But the room was so full of big, venomous-looking, yellow wasps, buzzing angrily about, that I had to beat a hasty retreat. If I think of it after dark tonight, I will have a fine hunt with my leathern flapper.

The other day I was studying with one of the catechists when I happened to look down, and there a big scorpion was running from his feet toward mine on the carpet. It is a wonder he didnt sting one of us. This same scorpion is a curious fellow. When he runs, he carries the sting at the end of his tail curled up over his back in a very defiant way . . . ever ready "to kick." I have seen a native very dexterously pick up one in his fingers, by quickly nabbing the end of the tail. But on the whole, I would much prefer that they should stay out of the bedroom. Flies and mosquitoes have not troubled us much, but in the rains the air is filled with all manner of bugs and flying insects. When the lamp is lit at night, they are a great nuisance.

But of all these things, bugs, fleas, scorpions, cobras, hornets and flies, we are nearly free now for six happy months. Now you can sleep at night without the lazy punkah waving over your head. Now you can take a walk in the cool mornings, if you take care to get home before the sun gets on hour high. Now the doors can be kept open without danger of headache. From this to the middle or last of March, the weather will be delightful.

Almost every evening when we go out to ride, we see a little fox running about within a rod of the road, apparently not much afraid of us.

They are very innocent, interesting-looking creatures. I think they are much smaller than the American fox. The jackals make their appearance about dusk, and are very plenty. They are more like a large fox than a dog. They are excessively impudent, yet great cowards. They come around the house in the evenings often, and howl by the hour. Sometimes they disturb the service in church by their noise outside. The other day one came in broad daylight. It chased a chicken all about the yard and would hardly desist, although two or three people were yelling at him.

One evening Mrs. and Dr. Sherlock went with Lillie and I to take a drive on our usual route, the Banda road. Nearly two miles from home, what should we see lying in the road, but a huge wolf. As the carriage came closer, he stepped to one side a little till we passed. When we returned, he leisurely walked across the road in front of the horse, and then stood and looked at us. The Judge was telling us that the other day he was walking not far from the court house, when two huge wolves, like calves, trotted across the road in front of him. Today, an elk is running about through the yard. Altogether, you see what fine times I might have if I had a gun. But I cant afford it.

I have taken up all my letter in describing these trifles. Perhaps, after all, these are what you like best to hear.

We enjoy living here very much now, and would be sorry to be sent anywhere else. The troubles of our Board at home made it necessary for us to give up our usual annual meeting this year. This was quite a disappointment to me, as I wished to take Lillie to see the city of Lucknow, the most wonderful city in India perhaps. If we are spared, we may be able to go next year.

You cannot imagine with what interest we read at this time everything relating to the troubles in our own, old, native land. I think we are at least as patriotic now, as when we used to sing Fremont songs in the Glee club at Hookstown. By the way, I see by the last telegram, that Fremont was a little too fast in his proclamation in Missouri. I hope they wont recall him for it. The telegram also speaks of General Lee's repulse at Cheat Mountains—a small affair I suppose.[4]

4. On Sept. 11, 1861, Lee mounted a surprise attack on the Union position on Cheat Mountain Summit near Elkwater [W.Va.]. However, heavy rain made the difficult terrain almost impossible to cross, and the Union forces held off a Confederate attack.

Frémont, driven by excessive unrest in Missouri during August 1861, proclaimed martial law over St. Louis on Aug. 14. On Aug. 30 he extended his proclamation to seize all property and slaves that belonged to any Missourian who supported the Confederacy. Lincoln believed that Frémont had gone too far, beyond what was permitted in the Congressional Confiscation Act of Aug. 6. When Frémont refused to modify his course, Lincoln removed him from command. McPherson, *Ordeal by Fire*, 161–64.

But the mail is to leave this eve. I must close. I hope in the exciting times at home, those may not be forgotten who wait with itching ears for every echo from across the Atlantic.

Yours ever, W. F. Johnson

Futtehpore
November 27th, 1861

My dear brother Sam,

. . . While my good husband is writing a sermon (seated across the table), I will chat with you. The clock on the mantel points with its long finger at 20 minutes past 7, and this is a Wednesday night of cold November. I dare say you are muffled up in a corner, close to a warm stove, poring over your books. You dare not peep out without a warm comforter to protect your nose.

Here in India, we have all the advantage of an entire change of seasons, all in one day. In the morning—this morning for example—we got up when the sun was beginning to peep, and bustled round with our teeth almost chattering. Mr. Johnson dons his heavy clothes and I my woolen dress (my blue delaine, you remember), and over that, a warm sack of gray flannel which I have just made for the cool mornings. Hafiz brings some toast and a cup of hot tea, which encourages us to try the frosty air outside. Mr. Johnson gets his "sola topi" (hat for the sun), which is a curiosity, or was to us when we first saw them. The foundation of the hat is pith—just like what you used to punch out of a weed to make a pop gun. I dont know what bush this is taken out of, but it is moulded into this shape and is covered with light gray alpaca, and lined with green inside the rim to shade the eyes comfortably. Well, he dons his tall hat, gets his cane, and I, with my warm coat and brown straw hat and warm gloves, are ready. Away we go up the long level road for a walk. We have to walk pretty briskly to keep warm.

The cold is much like the cold, biting wind of November in the old home, except that we have no cold rain or sleet. The sky is perfectly clear and the air dry.

This morning we walked nearly a mile and a half. Sometimes we go two and three, just according to how lazy we feel about it. This exercise makes us strong. We have to lay in vigor now for the next hot season. At 12 o'clock (if you were on this side), you might see Mr. Johnson strolling round with an umbrella over him. Even now it is not safe to go out at noon unprotected from the hot rays of the sun. Then, in the evening, it is quite cool again, and I find my light woolen shawl very comfortable.

But enough about the weather. You know now to bring your overcoat and comforter and fan along with you, if you come to spend a few days with us this month.

Since our last letter, written a month ago (in which Mr. Johnson and I both wrote), we have both been very well, excepting a little cold from the change of weather. We have not been to visit any of our Uncles or Aunts or Cousins, but in place of this we have taken a run down to Allahabad. As our Missionaries had not any Annual Meeting this year, on account of the troubles at home, making the Board short of funds, everything of Mission expense has to be economized. Mr. Johnson had to go down to see Mr. Walsh on Mission affairs, making up yearly accounts and estimates for next year, etc. And, of course, I went along.

We went down on the 15th. Left here at 10 P.M. and reached Allahabad about 3 in the morning. We wakened up Walshes watchman, who was busy sleeping. In a few minutes we heard our jolly old friend Mr. Walsh, bustling out to welcome us. The Walshes were staying at Mr. Williamson's bungalow—the same young Scotch Chaplain I have mentioned in former letters. Mr. Williamson was fitting up a new house to receive his bride, a Scotch lassie who had come from Scotland. He had gone to Calcutta to meet her and get the knot tied. The Walshes had kindly lent their assistance to arranging his house affairs, and were waiting to receive them.

We staid there with them a few days, and Mr. Johnson preached twice on the Sabbath in English. After he came from morning service, I went with Mr. Walsh to the Hindustani service down at the Jumna in the Mission premises. It was about 3 miles from where they were staying. Mr. Johnson had to preach in the evening, and did not go along. We stopped a little while with the Wyckoffs in our old home. Then we went to church, just across the yard. Mr. Walsh preached to the native Christians.

After church we went into the Wyckoffs, and waited for the carriage to go back. We heard a step on the veranda, and looked round. There was a stout, little man with a ruddy, smiling face, who we recognized as Mr. Ullman, one of our Futtehgurh Missionaries. The same who we met in Benares, when we were coming up the country from Calcutta. He was returning from England to India, after 2 years of absence. He stayed a few days in Allahabad with us. Mr. Ullman joined our Mission, altho he is a German and his wife is from England. He is a good Missionary, has an excellent knowledge of the language, and works hard. But his wife is a crotchety body. She is always complaining about the ills she thinks she suffers. But she looks well and hearty, and everybody that knows her thinks she is a victim of her own fancies, so the poor woman gets little sympathy. They are now traveling about, hoping a change will do her good. They stopped with the Wyckoffs and we went back to the Walshes.

In Allahabad, there are churches of 3 denominations. The Church of England (same as our Episcopal), the Roman Catholic and Presbyterian. The soldiers are marched to their different churches in companies, to the music of the band. They look very gay in their "red coats." I suppose they wear the same kind of uniform that they wore when "Brother Jonathan" gave the John Bulls, gallant scions, such a warm welcome; and left on record the first "Bulls Run," as Harper calls it in a late "Illustrated Weekly."

When I saw the soldiers parading, I could not help thinking that many perhaps of our old family friends were now, in our own once peaceful land, marching in the soldiers ranks; suffering a soldiers hardships; and many perchance now filling a soldiers grave. May God speed the right and hasten the day when peace shall again bless our dear country!

We read with eagerness all the news about the war and keep well-posted in regard to all the movements of the different parts of the Army, by diligent reading of the papers and examining the maps of the seat of the war. We have some very good maps that Albert Blakesley sent us from Waterbury. "The Banners" have not reached us yet. We will have to have a vacation to read them when they all get here.

I see a notice in one of the Calcutta papers of the arrival of our old Ship, the *Art Union,* from Boston again. But our good Cap't Norton is not along this time. She brought 2 or 3 boxes of goods and chattels for some of our Missionaries. We have not heard yet that there was any package for the Johnsons from the old country.

28th.—Well brother Sam, I come to say good evening to you again. I am well and I hope you are too. And if you are sitting in your room tonight talking to me as you ought to be, I will be very well pleased 2 months hence.

One year ago today, we were on board the *Art Union* looking out for a glimpse of the shores of this heathen land. Early in the morning we saw the welcome pilot ship and oh! what a bustle there was as we neared her and hailed for a pilot. How we gazed at the rude native boat that put off for our ship with the pilot in his fine broadcloth and kid gloves. But most of all were we interested in the dark-skinned, half-naked rowers, the first of Indian dark children our eyes looked upon.

Now that a year has passed you will say, "What think you of India?" First, I would say, "I am very glad we came to India." Here is plenty of work, and thus far it has pleased God to give us excellent health to go on with our preparation for labor here. We find Missionary life a very pleasant, happy one. The climate is hot and trying for several months of the year, but with all the appliances for keeping cool, the heat is bearable. . . .

We have many comforts that I did not expect we would find in a heathen land. Indeed, if you could peep into our home, you would say it is a very snug and cozy one.

The houses all look somewhat dingy after the rains. For the dust storms that come before, laid one good coating of dust and sand. The rain washed it off—much after that fashion I have seen little folks wash their faces, leaving some clean spots, and a good many dirty ones. So we have called the "raj" (mason) to put on a clean white face with his white wash brush. Remember our houses are plastered outside.

An old gaunt, long-legged fellow has been pottering at the church for a week past, altho he had an assistant and two boys to stir the lime, bring water, etc. He has just got over it, and now is at work on our bungalow. I think the principal part of the time was devoted to smoking the hooka; and a good deal of the rest to story-telling and gossiping, of which this people are very fond. The more marvellous the tale, the better. But just think of a head mason working for 12 cents a day. The poor fool ought to have time to indulge in a puff at his hooka. (I have just stopped a few moments to help Mr. Johnson with an orange.) The church now looks very white and neat, and our bungalow will be much nicer looking after a new coat.

Mr. Johnson has had the carpenter making a wheel barrow, which I suppose the natives here never saw before. They carry everything on their heads. Each one, man or woman, who does coolie work, which is carrying all sorts of burdens—be it bricks, clay, a box, a trunk, or a load of wood—has a little pad that he or she puts on the head, then hoists the load on top. It is surprising how much they can carry. But generally when doing work by the day—say carrying clay to make bricks—a very, little pile, in a little, flat basket, is their custom to carry. One load in a wheel-barrow would be perhaps as much as one man would carry in a day, pacing back and forth with his little basket on his crown.

Mr. Johnson was getting some work done in the compound (yard) when the wheel barrow was finished. 2 or 3 coolies were at work, so he told one of them to use the wheel barrow. He showed them how. But the old fellow made all sorts of excuses. First he was sick, he said, but that was no go. Then he said he was a Brahman, and it would break his caste. But Brahman or no, he had to try his hand at wheeling—much to his disgust with these new fangled customs.

A story is told of one of our missionaries up the country, who got a wheel barrow made and set some coolies to work with it, leaving them to themselves. When he found them, busy carrying the load in it, they were carrying wheel barrow and all on their heads. This is vouched for as a true story, and I dont doubt it.

Well dear, here is the last line, and the clock strikes nine. So good-bye tonight. "Salaam"

Sister Rachel

Futtehpore
December 2nd, 1861

My dear brother Frank,

. . . Mr. Wyckoff has had much the easiest time this year, for he had nothing to do but study the language, and he had Mr. Walsh to assist him; while we were thrown on our own resources in a station by ourselves. None of our missionaries are within 70 miles. Mr. Johnson has all the responsibility of being a patriarch of a flock from the beginning. But this initiation, tho trying at first, has really been an advantage to him. He has picked up the language better and quicker, for practical purposes than if he had been studying all the time.

. . . Well Frank, you say that Billy Miller wants to know what we have to eat. Tell him to come over and dine with us, and he shall have such a dinner as Mill Creek never saw. Roast deer (and the horns to take home with him), wild ducks, pigeons, chickens, turkey, goose, mutton, beef, as you please. Hams we procure at 50c a pound. They are brought from England. The hogs in this country are a dirty, mean, low-lived herd. The sight of which would put you out of the notion of ever trying to eat pork made of them. Those in America are beauties beside these.

Of fruits, we have now oranges, limes, custard apples and plantains (dont imagine they are like the plantain growing in the yard). They are called "banana," or the last is generally a little better variety of the same fruit. I have told you about them before. They are long, like sweet potatoes, and the meat is quite a little like a pear. The tree grows something like a corn stock, but very much larger. And the leaves grow like a corn blade, but are 5 or 6 feet in length, and two or more in breadth. The leaves are of a bright green and glossy appearance, and from some cause, the leaves after a while get all slit in ribbons—just as though you had gone over them and torn them in shreds, leaving them hanging on the stem. They look very graceful and pretty, even when drooping tattered and torn.

Mr. Johnson and I walked over to the public garden at the Court House a few mornings ago and we saw some tomatoes growing, but we have not got any to eat this winter yet. We have the Irish potato, and sweet potatoes can be gotten after a little. Eggplant, onions, radishes and cabbage, by and by, and so forth. With all, we have plenty to eat. I am sorry we cannot have your friends to share with us some of our Indian dainties.

I am sorry to hear that Johnny Ryan has gone to the war. He is so young, and I know they will feel very badly about it. Give our regards and sympathy to their family. Well Frank, I might send many messages to you all, and many of our old friends, but I have little room and less time now. Give our regards to all our friends.

Stella, I am always glad to get your little chits (Hindustani name for letter. There, you can tell Mother you know one word that the little Hindoo girls use).

You told me about your summer hat; what do you wear now in the winter? I have just been making over my green, winter bonnet on a new frame, for which I paid $1.25. That is almost as much as a new bonnet at home. But my bonnet looks very nice—almost as good as when Father brought it from Pittsburgh.

How are Grandpaps, Aunt Aggs and all our friends? I will write to Father and Mother next time.

Mr. Johnson joins in love to you all.

> Very affectionately,
> Your sister, Rachel L. Johnson

> Futtehpore
> Monday Morning, December 30th, 1861

My dear Mother,

You do not know how glad I was to find a letter from you in the last package of home letters received December 3rd. I had not been very well for a few days (feasting a little to freely on oranges and fruits) and was dozing on the lounge, when Mr. Johnson came home from the city. He asked me if I would like to have a home letter. As we had received a letter from you two weeks before, I thought he was joking, and said I would not have one. "Very well," then he said, taking out two large packages from his coat pocket. I soon changed my mind. There was no more dozing that morning, for there was a good long letter from home.

My dear Mother, it does not matter if you cannot now write as well as when you were young, and your hand was not so shaky. Every word from you is as precious to your absent children as tho every letter was rounded, just to the mark. We will be very glad to get anything that comes from our mother.

And so you, Stella and Frank, have been off on a jaunt to Beaver, and having a good time. I am glad to hear that. Father must have been very busy, being housekeeper along with all his other trades. I expect he would be glad to see you home again.

So Stella was pleased with the old iron horse, and thought it trotted along very briskly—quite as fast as old "Bet." There is one that comes puffing along past our door every day. How much I wish it would bring you along to see us. It comes now snorting along its long level track through the rice fields. But, it is an idle wish that can never, never be, however much it would gladden our hearts.

I told you in my last, that Mr. Johnson had sprained his hand, and was not able to write with it. I am glad to say that it is better now, altho he can use it very little yet. I have had to do all his writing for him for the last month. We are both very well and these cold mornings give us fine, red cheeks and blue noses.

We have delightful weather now, and every evening have a cheerful little wood fire to chat by. In the day time it is comfortable in our warm clothes without a fire. We buy our wood in the city, and pay for it by the pound. It is rather a funny way of measuring wood, is it not? We get 3 maunds, or 240 pounds, for a rupee or half dollar. And the natives sell milk the same way, by the pound, or "seer," which is equal to 2 pounds. Milk is 3 cents for a seer.

Here comes our munshi, or teacher, making his graceful salam. He comes every morning. Mr. Johnson reads with him his Hindustani lesson. I either read to him or with Mr. Johnson. We are getting on very well with the language.

You would think our munshi is a very gay fellow if you saw his fancy new coat of light blue delaine, bound with yellow chintz. His pants are of pink and white calico, and he has a gay little cap on the top of his crown. He has a very pleasing face, and speaks very politely. He teaches in the Persian department of the boys school.

Lucy, one of the native Christians, has just brought me a couple of nice fish, which I must put away. She talks a little English and is able to read and write. She is now employed as teacher in the girls school, which we have in the city. She has 16 girls under her care now, all heathen children, and teaches them spelling, reading, sewing, etc. The natives are very unwilling to send their girls to school, as they think they are not capable of learning, and at any rate are better without it. You may judge of the state of feeling, when I tell you that we have a flourishing boys school of over 100 scholars. The girls school only numbers 16.

The session of the boys school closed last week with a grand examination, which was very interesting, as well as creditable to the scholars and teachers. The boys seemed to take as much pride in trying to show off to advantage as our boys at home do. The school building, as I told you before, is built with little rooms on four sides, leaving a square plot of ground in the centre, thus 1 being the little yard or court, and all the rooms opening into it. For the occasion, this little yard was changed into a room, with an awning of cloth stretched above to keep out the sun, and a carpet laid over the grass. Thus we had a nice large room. The side rooms were newly whitewashed and looked neat. Against these were hung the school maps, some colored pictures, and illustrations of Bible stories. These were given to Mr. Johnson for the school. There were seats placed in front for the visitors. The boys were seated in rows in back, leaving some room for the classes to stand in front.

We drove down in the morning and found the boys all assembled in their gayest attire. Some of the wealthier ones with their fine embroidered tinsel caps, shining like gold, had large and beautiful shawls thrown gracefully round their shoulders. One little fellow I saw dressed in finely embroidered bobinet, which I thought was rather cool, even if over his muslin.

The classes in Hindoo and English were examined in their different studies, from the little fellow beginning to spell, up to the learned ones who were able to demonstrate a problem in geometry, or trace out the different countries of the world on the map. The classes were all examined on the Bible and Testament, and Catechism, for these are taught in every class as regularly as the other studies. The promptness with which many of these heathen boys answered questions on the Bible and Catechism would put to shame many a boy in our Christian land.

Dr. and Mrs. Sherlock were present at the examination, and a great many of the native Baboos, who are respectable native gentlemen. Some of them occupy good situations under the government. We were much pleased to see so many of the natives come out and show an interest in the school.

Several of the friends of the school had offered prizes of books, etc., to the most proficient in the different classes. At the close of the exercises, these were distributed to the fortunate ones. A native gentleman rose and made a nice little speech to the boys, expressing great pleasure with their progress. The boys looked very happy with their prizes and are very ambitious to gain them.

I was much amused at one little fellow with great black eyes, and rings of black paint round them, and very bright looking—not near as large as Stella—who, when the names for the prizes were read out, came rushing up along with the larger boys for a prize. But he found he had not been called. The teacher laughed and gave him a scrap of paper, and the little fellow good-naturedly went back to his seat along with the rest, taking his disappointment as a joke and laughing with the rest.

New Years Day, 1862!

A happy New Year to all in the dear old house at home! I trust it finds you all well and gathered together for a good New Years dinner. I know you are thinking of us today. I have just been making a nice cake to eat along with our oranges this eve. How I wish I could send you a nice basket full, dear Mother. Doesnt it make your mouth water to think about it?

On Christmas day we received a great many presents from our native friends. There were oranges, lemons, limes, pomegranates, Christmas cakes, etc., until we were quite over-stocked. In the evening we sent a present of cake and oranges to each family of the native Christians.

A gardener brought his present of fruit and flowers and decorated the veranda with a long string of flowers, which he tied to one column and stretched along to the next, and so on. No doubt he thought it very beautiful. But I must say, I thought the poor flowers hanging from the string, looked rather forlorn. But we indulged the poor fellow in his fancy, and, as he was poor, gave him a small present in money for his trouble.

Christmas eve, Mr. Posier, the Magistrate, gave a dinner to all the Station, which was a very grand affair. He gets 1000 dollars a month, and lives in very elegant style. Dr. and Mrs. Sherlock came down and spent part of Christmas day with us, and in the evening we all went in our carriage to the dinner at 7 o'clock. There were eleven gentlemen present and only 3 ladies. All the good things of the season were provided for the occasion. After feasting on the Christmas turkey, plum pudding, and a few of the many delicacies provided, we came home to dream of all sorts of hobgoblins, after such a late dinner.

Today, we will spend at home. We will enjoy our own quiet dinner quite as well.

Everything goes along quietly in our Mission Station. We have our regular Sabbath service, Thursday evening service, prayer meetings, and every day the two Catechists and two Scripture Readers go out to the city and villages to preach to the people. They generally listen well, and many acknowledge the truth of our religion, but have not the courage to give up all for Jesus. Many are joined to their idols, going down to death, unconvinced and unsaved.

Rachel L. Johnson

Futtehpore, India
January 16, 1862

My dear Friends,

I wrote to you two weeks ago a long letter which I hope will reach you in good time. Now when I know that there is a possibility that soon the mails may be interrupted between America and England, I must let no opportunity of writing to you pass by unimproved.

We have news from England down to Dec. 10th, and we fear that the rumor of war between England and America will be confirmed by the next telegram, unless indeed a more conciliatory spirit is shown by our Government, than by England. The English papers clamor for war to avenge the "insult" offered to the "British lion." If "Brother Jonathan" is as independent as in other days, when the old lion was faced, I fear his wrath will not be mollified.[5]

---

5. This close brush with war with England in the fall of 1861 was known as "The Trent Affair." Two Southerners, James Mason and John Slidell, were sailing for England on the British mail steamer *Trent* to represent Confederate interests in Europe. The American

The English and Indian papers are exhausting their indignation in long Articles on "America": They are calling the Yankees hard names, ridiculing our government as rowdies ruled by the mob. Our President is a weak imbecile raised up to his present station because he was one of the common herd. Seward is destitute of principle. McClellan is an upstart who only waits the chance to seize the reins of government, and proclaim himself "Dictator." The Army is totally demoralized. The Western States are just waiting to follow the example of the rebel South, etc. etc.

While, on the other hand, the South are Aristocratic (which covers a multitude of sins in English eyes), brave, generous, and fighting for a free tariff. They are clear headed, far seeing, and indeed so wise, that they already turn their longing eyes to the Oracle of Wisdom across the sea. They look for one of her "young Scions" to come and accept the title of King. The traitor Jeff Davis is a hero, and all his counselors are very Solomons. The Army of the south is well disciplined, brave, and determined. What is more, there are hosts of "the flower of their youth," who have gone forth wearing "the gold ring," the "goodly apparel," and who drink the "choicest champagne" from "silver goblets." Why should these not put to flight the "clowns" of the north?

But enough, you may judge of the spirit of the British press—excepting one or two papers, who favor the north. You can judge how encouraged we feel, after perusing these articles about the dear, old country. Imagine how trying it will be if war breaks out between the two countries, for then we will only get one side of the story.

If war is declared and you should not hear from us as regularly and often as heretofore, you must not feel troubled and anxious about us. We will be perfectly safe here. We may be able to send letters round some other way, thru some other country. It will be a great trial for us if we should be deprived of the privilege of hearing from you; but we trust that it will not come to such a sad pass. I only write this now by way of encouragement, feeling there is only a possibility of this state of things.

Mrs. Walsh writes that Mr. Walsh has gone to Calcutta, hoping that a trip of a few weeks on the river would improve his health, which has been very poor since months past. The Wyckoffs are well, and they are expecting Mr. and Mrs. Ullmann to stop in Allahabad during the mela or fair. Mr. Ullmann would preach in Mr. Walshs absence.

Mr. Scott, who is at Futtehgurh, writes that he, Mr. Broadhead (Missionary at Mynpoorie), and their families are out traveling, preaching to the villages. Villages only hear the gospel when the Missionary takes a

_____

ship *San Jacinto*, under Capt. Charles Wilkes, accosted the *Trent* off the coast of Cuba, and on Nov. 8 a boarding party from the *San Jacinto* seized Mason and Slidell and took them off in triumph to Boston. Wilkes was proclaimed a national hero in the North. The British threatened military action and demanded an apology. Lincoln wisely ordered the release of Mason and Slidell, and tempers cooled. McPherson, *Ordeal by Fire*, 221.

tour in the cold season. They travel from place to place taking tents with them and stopping a few days here and there. It is very pleasant they say, traveling thus; and the change is very beneficial.

I hope Mr. Johnson will be able to preach again next cold season, when I trust we will take a tour. We have sent Qasim Ali, one of our Catechists, and Anand Masih, a Scripture Reader, out on a tour today. They took books with them to distribute among the poor, ignorant heathen. They will preach and read the Scriptures to them. Old Qasim came in last night and intrusted his family to the care of the Padre during his absence, with a very ceremonious salam. We could not help laughing. This morning, perched on a native cart drawn by two bullocks, they started for a journey of a few weeks.

Well, here is a note from the Doctor wanting us to go up and help them dispose of some roast beef at 3 P.M. So, I must go and get ready and finish my letter when I come back.

8:30 P.M. Here I am again. The roast beef, cabbage, peas, potatoes, and pudding have been stowed away. After which, Dr. and Mrs. Sherlock, Mr. Johnson, and I took a little walk of $3\frac{1}{2}$ miles to help the digestion. Yesterday, we walked about 5, part in the morning when the air was biting cold, and part in the evening. We are laying up strength for the hot weather, when it is impossible to take much exercise. I have got such a bad cold tonight that my poor nose is like a young beet. The weather is so, even here, we are scarcely ever troubled with colds. Every evening we have a nice wood fire, and sometimes in the mornings, but our walk generally warms us without it.

I found a little cypress flower in the last letter. Was it from Stella? Did you ever get the letter with the banyan leaf in it? What are you all doing I wonder? Father making houses? Mother busy as a bee? Do rest this cold weather. How I wish old Betsy could bring you over to your childrens home.

Sam at College, tell me about your chums, your college debates, your studies, your teachers, your enjoyments, and your plans. Frank, how do you like the new school house, your teacher, your books, your Bible class, the girls etc.? Stella, I must tell you a little story by yourself now. Bye Bye to one and all, with my loving remembrances, from your

Affectionate—W and L Johnson

My dear Stella,

I was very glad to see a line from you in our last letter from home, for it told us you had not forgotten us. I think of you very often and wish I could see you. Have you grown any taller? Do you help Mother everyday? Do you go to school? Had nice times riding on your sled this last winter? Write and tell me.

I saw a tame bear a few days ago, that could dance and do many funny things. We all laughed heartily to see the bear dance. Another man brought a snake and weasel, which he made fight. The poor snake got whipped badly, which you will be glad to hear—for I remember you do not like snakes very much.

Well dear sister, Goodbye. We sent you much love and a kiss. Give my love to our little cousins.

Your loving sister,
Rachel

Futtehpore, North India
Feb. 14th, 1862

My dear Brothers,

When we wrote to you a month ago, we were expecting that "old John Bull" would succeed in picking a quarrel with you, and would refuse to carry our messages for awhile, until he had got a sound whipping. But I am happy to hear that all this bluster has been for nothing, and we still have a free pass. . . .

We are now beginning to feel a little lazy as the days grow hot. The mornings are cool, but the sun is very hot at noon.

The Rev. Ullmann and wife are spending a few days with us and are then going back to Futtehgurh. Mr. Ullmann is an excellent preacher in Hindustani. We like him very well. He is such a working missionary. But we dont like Mrs. Ullmann at all. She is a real selfish Englishwoman. She lived in London and thinks it the hub of the Universe. She is now sitting at the table near me, talking to me while I am writing to you. She is fat and little, fond of dress, and she quite tires one with the relation of all her ills and ailments. There is not as stout and hearty a looking woman in the Mission. But I must not be gossiping so. I was feeling tired and a little worried.

This morning we walked out to the grave yard, about two miles from here, and visited poor Gopee Nath's grave. From that, we walked over to the old Mission Compound, now in ruins. There are the ruined walls of the church, the Mission house, and the native Christian houses, just as they were left in the Mutiny. The yard is all over grown with weeds. We walked in among the ruins. The floors of some of the rooms have large holes dug, which we suppose had been dug to bury their valuables from the mutineers in 1857. After the mutiny, the Mission was removed to where we now live. This is a much better situation, the ground being higher and not so much standing water in the rains.

As we were returning home, we saw some most beautiful birds. One little one had gold covered wings and a head that shone beautifully in the sunlight as it flitted from bush to bush.

Feb. 20th, Thursday

. . . The Ullmanns left us on Tuesday morning and we are again settled down in our quiet little home. It is quite an event when anyone stops in our little station, for we do not often have the pleasure of entertaining friends. Indeed, I might say that the circle of friends in India is so very small that we cannot expect to see them often.

Mrs. Walsh passed by a few days ago, along with Rev. Williamson and his wife. They were going to Lucknow. As the station is quite near to us, and the train stops a few minutes, we met them at the depot. With a cup of tea for their encouragement by the way, we had a little chat with them. Mrs. Walsh had had a slight attack of fever and had accepted the Williamson's invitation to accompany them on a tour to Lucknow. We are all so well that no change is needed.

Mr. Johnson has been having rather a troublesome pet for a few days. Mr. Ullmann and he took a fancy to be vaccinated one day when they were at the Doctors. For several days they have been nursing their arms very tenderly. Mr. Johnson's was so painful that he could not rest at night, but is now getting better. Now in a few days I suppose it will be my turn. Mrs. Sherlock and I were vaccinated today. We thought it was best to be vaccinated again, for in the hot season there is almost more or less small pox among the natives in the city. We never know where we may be exposed to the infection. I have not heard of any cases yet, but it is very common among the natives. They seem to mind it very little more than any other disease. The Doctor has great trouble in persuading them to bring their children for vaccination. We have all been vaccinated from Hindoo children. An Irish wit here insists that, of course, there will be a change in our complexion. He tells his wife that he notices a perceptible change in the way she speaks Hindustani every day.

One morning while Mr. Ullmann was here, he and Mr. Johnson went down to the bazar of the city and preached to the people who were gathered in the streets. A large crowd soon collected round them of Hindoos and Mohammedans. Some of the latter were disposed to dispute. But most of them listened attentively.

Several respectable looking natives came up one morning and asked for testaments. Mr. Johnson gave them each one and made them promise to study them, which they readily did. Some of these came back while Mr. Ullmann was here, and he had a long discussion with them. They are very zealous Mohammedans, and cavil a great deal at the doctrine of Salvation thro Jesus.

There is a poor man at the hospital whom the Catechists have been visiting, who seems to be concerned to learn something of the true religion. His case is a sad one. He was traveling to some distant place, and one night, during the cold weather, lay out under a tree unprotected from the cold. Shortly after, he was seized with paralysis. From his body downward he is dead, his flesh all decaying. He knows he must die soon, and is very willing to listen to the plan of Salvation thro Christ. At the 11th hour he may, like the dying thief, be brought to believe on Jesus.

A very intelligent Hindoo and his family came here a few days ago and professed to be anxiously seeking a knowledge of the Christian religion. Mr. Johnson told him that if he became a Christian, he must be willing to take up the cross and bear reproach and perhaps persecution for the sake of his Saviour. Mr. Johnson explained to him that Christians must bear trials and losses for Christs sake. But he still affirmed that he was determined to be a Christian, and that his wife and brother also would come with him. Mr. Johnson then told him to come and live in the Compound with the native Christians. If after he had learned more of religion, and we had evidence of a work of grace in his heart, he would receive baptism.

He has an excellent pronunciation of Hindustani, and for the present we have employed him as our Munshi. We are much pleased with him. He is so particular in giving us all the true sounds of the difficult letters. We cannot read the heart, but this mans words are very good. Whether he will prove sincere or not, we cannot tell.

Thursday eve. [February] 27th
Yesterday the long lost "Banners" and the "Stewarts Chronicle" came. . . . The news is a little old, but there certainly is a good deal of it. All the numbers of April, May and June and one of March are in the package. . . . Mr. Johnson is sitting reading one of the Banners now. We would enjoy reading them very much if they would come as our other papers do. . . . The Board sends us the Presbyterian, free of charge, but we dont care so much for it as for the Banner, for it is an old friend.

We are glad to hear that you receive our letters so regularly. In our last we enclosed a little specimen of Hindustani character that we read. I hope you were edified with the contents.

Brother Sam, how are you getting along at College? Do you like it? What are you doing? Where are you staying? Come dear Sam, I want a long letter about all the little odds and ends about yourself. The more you have to say about Sam, the better. I want to hear about him.

And brother Frank, how do you find hard study agreeing with you? I am glad to hear you have a good teacher. Hope your bump of knowledge is developing itself laudably. Hope you will both make a good mark in the world. What do you study? Dont forget to drop us a line often, we are always ready to nibble.

How much we would love to see you all. How I would love to take you round and show you every nook of our Indian home. Do you get any idea of what it is like from my past descriptions? Anything you would like to know about, scratch it down when you think of it, and I will answer your Catechism. There are so many things to tell you, that when I come to write, I forget what I have already written about. And now dear brothers, with much love from us both, I must bid you goodnight.

Affectionately,
Rachel

Futtehpore, India
Friday night, [February 28]

My dear Mother,

We have just come home from Dr. Sherlocks. Mrs. Sherlock sent for us to come up and dine with them today. The weather is getting hot, and then it is no pleasure to leave our cool house to go through the burning wind to visit our friends. So we do all our visiting in our <u>winter</u>. The doctor lives about as far from us as from Mrs. Crosses to you. Yet we would not think of walking up there at 12 o'clock even now, not from laziness, but from prudence. The suns rays have such a sickening effect. In the house we are cool and comfortable. We had a pleasant chat. Mrs. Sherlock and I sewed, and our husbands helped with the chat and the dinner.

Mrs. Sherlock and I were vaccinated last week, but it did not take. This is the third time I have been vaccinated, since the time I had to march out from behind the kitchen door to have my arm scratched, when I was a little one. Stella ought to be, if she has not. All the little ones in our Compound have been.

I received a letter from Mrs. Wyckoff this morning, telling us that they will be here tomorrow morning. Mr. Wyckoff has not been very well, and they are coming up for us to cure him. We will be very glad to see them.

Mr. Johnson is now reading with the Munshi. I have not read my lesson because I wanted to write a line for you. I would be so glad if you could come in for a talk. You would be glad to find us so well and comfortable in our home. We often long to see you all, but we could not be better contented with our work or situation in any other part of the world.

How are all our friends? I hope Grandpaps and Grandma are well. I have written twice to them and once to Aunt Agnes. Remember us to them all.

Saturday eve

The Wyckoffs have come, and I have only time to close my letters for the mail, dear Mother. Goodbye. Much love to Father, Stella, and yourself.

Very affectionately,
Rachel

P.S. Stella darling, here is a kiss for you from Sister Rachel.

[Another companion letter from Will serves as an introduction to a brief note from Rachel.]

April 15th, 1862

My dear Mother Kerr,

... I had a light attack of fever one day, and felt pretty seedy for a week or two afterwards, so we took a trip to Allahabad for a change of air. After we had been there several days, Walsh would have us stay to help him eat the turkey on his birthday, "April 4th." As turkeys are not to be seen every day in this country, we consented. So we were there about 10 days. We purchased a number of things which we can not get in Futtehpore. . . .

We are more and more convinced now, that it was very well that we came to Futtehpore. It is much more expensive living in Allahabad, and the air is so filled with smoke and dust from the city, that there is little pleasure in taking a drive or a walk. Here you would think us wonderfully industrious: getting up and dressing by candle light; having our tea and toast; and far out upon our long walk before the sun is up. But the fact is, if we are not out by dawn, we cannot walk at all. Now it is only 7 o'clock in the morning, and the thermometer is 83 in the room, and eversomuch more outside. In two or three hours, the hot winds will set in. Then if the boy outside keeps the tatti well watered, the house will be much cooler, though the heat outside is something fearful.

Did Mrs. Johnson—I ought to say "Rachel"—tell you about the visit which we had from the Banda giant? I was told that a native wished to see me on the verandah one day. When I went out, behold, some huge mountain was towering above. I was so surprised, I could hardly tell for a moment what it was. When I saw that it was a man, I could hardly help feeling frightened to stand before him. I suddenly seemed to myself such a puny, insignificant mortal. However, Goliath condescendingly backed himself up against the wall for my amusement, and mounting on a chair, I marked his height on the wall. On measuring, I found he stood 7 ft. 3 inches, without shoes and stockings, and with a bad stoop in his shoulders. That is, he was about equal to a straight man in boots of 7 ft. 5 inches! 6 ft. 5 is extraordinary, but put on the top of that a head like a half bushel, and let it glare down on you with only one eye, and you can imagine that you would not care to meet such a person in a grave yard on a moonlight night.

We good Americans here are all crowing over the late good news from home. Victories crowding on each other now in fine style: Somerset—Roanoake Island—Elizabeth City—Edentown—Forts Henry and Donelson—Bowling Green and Nashville—Manasses evacuated—

Columbus burnt, etc.[6] The only regret here is that something of this was not done months ago. It would have saved the sowing of a great deal of abuse upon every thing American, which will be likely to bear bitter fruit some day. But to all these pictures of glorious victories, there is a sad reverse. The telegram which bids a nation rejoice, does not tell us how many homes are desolated to win that victory. It does not tell how many bright hopes, how much happiness, is buried upon that battle field— and well indeed, that it does not. When duty calls, nothing has any right to stand in its way. Better a mourning household, than a debased, degraded, despised people.

I believe we told you that the long lost Advocate and Banners had arrived. The fault was mine. I forgot to tell Lowrie to put the necessary 6 cents stamp on each one. So he lets them accumulate until a box is sent out here, and sends them in that.

We are looking every day now for a package containing books, stereographs, etc., which my sister, Maggie, sent out to Calcutta, in the ship *Albert Gallatin*. The ship arrived there nearly a month ago. But now the water in the Ganges is so low, that if our things were sent up by the steamboat, they will not reach Allahabad for some time yet. If they were sent by ox carts, they ought to be here soon.

In missionary work we are not making much progress, except that we both can now read Hindustani quite fluently, both in the Arabic character and in the Roman. I am not able to write sermons up in it yet, as the idiom is so difficult. But I hope to commence before very long. I have had several inquirers here under instruction, but as yet, none have given much evidence of a change of heart. Many there are who know the truth. Oh! that the truth might make them free!

. . . I know my Rachel will want to say a few words, so I will leave a page vacant for her to fill up. . . .

                                        Yours ever, W. F. Johnson

My dear Mother,

I fear you will think we are getting lazy, as we have not written for 6 weeks. Last mail time we were in Allahabad, with neither of us feeling much like writing. Mr. Johnson had not got over the effects of fever, and I had a very sore finger. It was something like a felon, but not so bad. It was so painful I would have been making wry faces all the time, if I had

6. A host of significant Union victories, cited by Will, occurred in Kentucky and Tennessee and off the North Carolina coast in January and February 1862. The western victories began with the battle of Somerset or Mill Spring in eastern Kentucky on Jan. 20. Union forces captured Fort Henry on Feb. 6 and Fort Donelson ten days later. These actions opened the Tennessee and Cumberland rivers. In the east, successful army-navy operations by Union forces resulted in victories on Roanoake Island, N.C., on Feb 8 and in Elizabeth City, N.C., on Feb. 10. McPherson, *Ordeal by Fire*, 179–81, 223–26.

tried to have a little talk with you just then. My finger is now quite well, and I have nothing worse than an old pestering toothache to growl about today. Mr. Johnson has been coaxing me to have the Doctor apply a little cold steel to the troublesome grinder, but I have not quite got my courage up to the point of parting with my old friend.

I must tell you how Mr. Johnson came to get the little touch of fever. One morning he took a fancy to do a little job of tinkering—out of his line of business. We had a clothes press that was not varnished, and he had it moved out on the veranda. With his little pot of varnish and brush, he set to work varnishing it. After a little he felt too hot, and laid off his coat. Altho he kept his head out of the sun, he allowed it to shine on his back. The consequence next day was that he had his bones full of fever, and for a week he was laid up in the house.

You must remember that this was in the morning, just at the close of the cold season, and I do not think he was exposed to the sun more than an hour. This will give you some idea of the withering effects of a tropical sun on us foreign plants taken from the cold latitudes. But, if we take good care of ourselves, and keep in the shade, we enjoy just as good health as anywhere. The judge over the way is as regular as clock in his habits, and I do not think he has ever been seriously ill during the last 20 years of his life in India.

We had a very pleasant visit from the Wyckoffs. They spent nearly 2 weeks with us, and they all felt much better for the change. Mrs. Wyckoff's baby is a frail little thing, and I hardly think she will be able to keep it long in these scorching winds.

Mrs. Fullerton and her children are up in the hills at Landour, and she says she and the little ones are much improved since they went there. I had a letter from her a few days ago. She said she was writing by a nice large fire—while we have our tatties constantly wetted to cool the air inside. Mr. Fullerton is at Futtehgurh, going on with his work. She says it is very lonely being separated from each other.

Here is our Munshi, trying to master the wonderful mysteries of our new door latch—like the one on the old kitchen door. I suppose he never saw one like it before. Mr. Johnson is showing him how to open it. We have our old Munshi back again now. He was sick for awhile.

I cannot write much, but more soon.

> With much love to you all,
> Rachel

> Futtehpore
> May 15, 1862

My dear Father and Mother,

The hot days have come again and it requires a strong motive to induce any one to do much letter writing, when the thermometer is at 91 in the coolest corner of the house. But you will be looking for a letter, and that surely is motive enough to the laziest child. Since our last letter mailed a month ago, we have both been quite well and going on with our work as usual.

. . . The telegram brings us glorious news of Federal victories, following one upon another so closely, that we hardly quit waving our hats over one, until another comes. The English and Indian papers are full of the doings of the brave little *Monitor*.[7] Old John Bull is rubbing his eyes to see if he is truly awake, and very loath to realize the fact that the despised Yankees are ahead again; and that he must go to work on his wooden walls and build them all over again. But bitterly as the press has ridiculed and abused the North, the tone is fast changing, under the new order of things. A few more victories, and Johnny Bull will be bowing very blandly to Brother Jonathan, and reaching out a friendly hand of congratulations.

Our latest news from London, April 18, announces: the capitulation of Island No. 10—Victory at Corinth[8]—Federal loss 25,000 and Confederates 35,000—Beauregard wounded and Johnston and 3 generals killed—100 guns and 5,000 prisoners taken—and General McClellan's advance to York town. What a horrible butchery that battle at Corinth must have been. With all the rejoicing over victory, what sad wailings from the bereaved ones will be mingled. May God in mercy speed the end of this sad war.

We have just received a 2nd package of Banners (10) sent out in a box from the Mission House, so now I suppose all the strays have reached us. By last mail, Mr. Johnson sent you an India paper, enclosing a wrapper off one of the papers we receive regularly, so that you could see how they are put up. I do not suppose you would find much to interest you in the paper, but we thought it might interest you merely as a specimen of the papers the English publish in India. There are a few native papers

7. The Mar. 9, 1862, sea battle of *Monitor* versus *Merrimack* was the first naval battle between two fully armored warships. On Mar. 8 the Confederate ironclad ship *Virginia* (previously the Union ship *Merrimack*) sank two Union sailing frigates and was moving in on a third that was stuck on a mud bank when night fell. By morning, a new, much smaller Union ironclad ship, *Monitor*, had moved in to defend the stranded vessel. In an intense and dramatic battle, the *Monitor* and *Virginia* battered each other with cast-iron shot. After five hours each withdrew, and the Union maintained naval control of the Chesapeake Bay. McPherson, *Ordeal by Fire*, 181–82.

8. Rachel is referring to the Battle of Shiloh, fought on Apr. 6 and 7, 1862. This battle was fought near a country meetinghouse known as Shiloh Church, a little more than twenty miles from Corinth, Miss. At the time it was the bloodiest battle ever fought on American soil. Rachel's figures from immediate news reports are distorted; although the Federal troops won the battle, they also sustained the greatest losses. Historians place the number of persons killed, wounded, or missing at the Battle of Shiloh at 13,047 Federals and 10,694 Confederates. Mark Mayo Boatner III, *The Civil War Dictionary*, 757.

printed in native characters, but not many. The Hindoos are not yet a newspaper reading people, except the few more enlightened ones.

. . . Last week we had quite a jubilee over a little box that came from the other side of the waters, sent by Maggie Blakesley from Waterbury. The box was filled with little knicknacks that she could get in Waterbury. Among other things, some beautiful melineotype[9] likenesses of the generals in the army, and other "lions" of the day. They are not in cases but each one has a little ring to hang by. So we got a large white card and frame, and 24 of your great men now grace the wall of our sitting room. I said 24, but I must say, less two; for Jeff Davis and Beauregard are of the number, and we cannot call them great men—unless killing people makes them so. There were also some beautiful stereoscopic pictures, views of the grand scenery on the Hudson, and some winter scenes that almost makes one shiver to look at the huge icicles and trees all covered with ice. Books, pins, patriotic envelopes, etc.

. . . Last Sabbath, Mr. Walsh was here to assist in the Communion services. The little orphan girl, Simme, was baptized. This is the one whose father and mother died on a pilgrimage to Juggernaut. She and her little brother are now both baptized members of our little flock. When she came, she could scarcely talk. But now she is able to repeat the Lords Prayer and a little hymn very prettily, and has learned her ABC's, and can spell words of 2 or 3 letters. She comes to school every morning, and when I am teaching the larger girls to sew, I also give her a needle and thread and a little piece of cloth to keep her out of mischief. She sits on the floor very patiently, sewing a stitch, and then threading her needle—which takes up most of her time. She was much pleased with a new pink calico dress that I made her last week, and a new muslin "chudder," or veil, which the little Hindoo girls wear instead of a hat or bonnet.

Her brother was baptized last Communion, and he rejoices in the name of Saimuale (Hindoo for Samuel). The little fellow did not understand being baptized, and when the questions were asked of his guardian, he spoke out himself, saying, "Han Sahib" (Yes Sir). I could scarcely repress a smile.

We have had a good deal of trouble lately with Lucy, one of the native Christian women, who has become deranged. We are preparing to send her off to Benares to the Insane Asylum. I expect we will have some trouble getting her off without her children. But we do not think it safe to let her run about any longer.

18th. You will perhaps think it strange when I tell you we are very cool and comfortable today, because the hot west winds are blowing—

9. "Melainotype" was the term used for ferotypes or tintypes for a short time after they were first introduced in 1857. The name came from the Greek *melas* and described the black background required for early photographic images to appear positive.

but so it is. We have not had such steady hot winds this month, as is usual at this season. So our tatties have been of little use. The tattie doors are made of the kus kus grass, so when new, the house is filled with the fragrance of the grass.

Our friend, Mrs. Sherlock, has just got a new Harmonium, and we enjoy an evening with them very much. Altho it is a little hot going over, the music is too great an attraction to deny ourselves. We went up last Monday evening and again on Wednesday eve, and had a little singing party of 4.

The moonlight these nights is so bright that we rather enjoyed a little walk home from the Sherlocks at 9 o'clock. The first night, however, our enjoyment of the moonlight was broken in upon by a little adventure, that put an end to observations on the beauty of the night rather abruptly.

We had left the Doctors and were walking along the quiet road towards home, when we heard the spattering of hoofs behind us. Looking round, we saw Mr. Anderson's large Sambar [a large Asian deer], with its great horns bounding down the road after us. This animal has head and horns something like a deer, but its body is large and strong. Mr. Anderson caught it in the jungle, and keeps it to watch the growth of its horns.

It was tied up under a tree, near which we passed, and it managed to get loose, and followed us. It came charging up towards us, and Mr. Johnson could find nothing to frighten it with. Neither stick nor piece of rock were to be seen, and all he could do was to flourish his hat, which it seemed to think was a challenge. It reared up on its hind feet, and threatened to come at us with its great horns. We could not turn to move on, for then it would come close after us. Only by flourishing hats and shouting at it could we keep it at bay. Mr. Johnson told me to run back to the Doctors, while he would keep it back. But as soon as I started, it darted after me. I had to stop and run back to him again. He called to some natives, who brought a long bamboo, which soon convinced the sambar he must not come too close. But he would not be driven back. All the way, we had to fight him with the bamboo pole. He seemed determined to have a little brush with his horns at my skirt, and I suppose too, he saw I was afraid of him. I did the running, and Mr. Johnson the fighting. When we got to the gate of our yard, I ran for the house, while Mr. Johnson stood with his pole in the gateway. But as soon as he noticed me, the sambar circled round, leaped over the hedge—and you may judge there was a little running *a la* "Bulls Run"—, but I got into the house. Mr. Johnson followed, after giving the sambar a parting salute with the bamboo. It came up on the veranda, and when I went to sleep, it was exploring round outside, enjoying its moonlight ramble no doubt much better than we did.

Now I must devote a part of this sheet to Sam and Frank, or they will have a large bill against me for any delinquencies. I trust you are both well and that we will soon hear from you again, dear Father and Mother.

And now dear brothers—Sam, Frank, and Stella too.

. . . Brother Sam, we were very much interested in your journal, and heartily wish you would oftener send us a few notes of your experiences. When we were in Allahabad, we met a Missionary and his wife (Rev. Barr), just from America. They belong to the Associate Church and were on their way to some station in North India. Mr. Barr hailed from Canonsburg. She told me her name was Black, and she knew a good many of the Johnson connections at Canonsburg. We only had a few minutes to talk with them, as it was after church on Sabbath night. We had a drive of 3 miles awaiting us, and they were going off on the train next morning.

I hope you are getting along nicely with your studies.

By the way, if you would like to read an entertaining book on sea life, get Dana's, Two Years Before The Mast. The descriptions are most graphic and life like. All the details of ship life are noted down, so truly, that when I read it, I almost fancied it was sea life on the *Art Union,* he was telling about. But the abuse he speaks of that the poor sailors received was very different from the treatment on the *Art Union.* Altho the discipline was strict, yet our Captain was kind. You and Frank ought to read it. It will give you a good idea of a sailors life.

. . . You are now exulting, I suppose, over the Federal victories. I think Seccession will soon succumb. Jeff Davis must be shaking in his boots, when he hears of all the disasters of his armies. If his likeness tells the truth, he is a fine looking man. But it is not a mans looks, but his doings, that tell of the man.

. . . This morning I saw a funny little sight that would have amused you. A man was riding along on a gray pony, and what do you think was riding on behind? It was holding on, not to the man's coat tails—for he had none—but to the roll of muslin around him. It wasnt a little girl or boy, but a funny, grinning, little monkey. There it sat, just like a little girl would, holding on with its two forefeet, that it uses for hands. I suppose it thought it a very nice way of traveling, for it looked pleased.

Affectionately, Rachel

Futtehpore, India
June 13th, 1862

My dear brothers,

You must not expect many sheets of "foolscap" from me until these roasting days are over. The rains will soon be here, then we will have a little time to cool between the showers, when I hope to have some long chats with you. . . .

Last letter, I sent you a piece of my new coat. How would you like one of the same? It is very fashionable among Hindoo hopefuls, to have coats of such material. They deck themselves out in as many colors as the gayest ladies.

My better half and self are quite well and enjoying the hot weather as well as possible. Under the punka we write, read, eat, sleep, study or sew. The old fellow with the little top knot, who pretends to keep us cool, has to sleep carefully, so as not to stop pulling; or "top knot" might have troublesome dreams.

We are preparing for the rains, getting the roofs mended of our house, the church, and the line of native Christian houses. The hard storms blow off a few thousand tiles every season, and these have to be replaced with new ones. The church is finished.

I see an old ragged vulture has esconsed himself on the highest point, overlooking the job, or perhaps on the lookout for a stray fowl for his dinner. These ugly birds, thought despised, are our best friends. They gather up all the carrion, which in this hot climate would be a deadly pest if left to decay and pollute the air.

The jackals are very troublesome. They are so impudent, they will come in daylight, and steal off our chickens, while we are shouting at them to frighten them away. Chickens here are not very expensive. We often get them for 2 annas, or 6 cents, a piece.

This is the season for the mangoes. Here is a dish full of large golden ones that Mr. Johnson brought from the bazar. I would be glad to share them with you. There are two kinds in this district. One is called Bombay mangoes that are very large and they taste delicious. We cannot always get them, but the other day the old judge sent us over a good basket full that would have made your mouths water. The trees look very pretty with the golden mangos peeping out among the bright green leaves.

The station and city are remarkably free from the usual diseases that come with the fruit season. The hot season agrees with me remarkably well; but Mr. Johnson feels it more this year, making him nervous (his nerves never being very strong). The rains will set in soon, and the weather will be pleasanter.

Did I tell you about the leopards that we saw in Allahabad? One morning Mrs. Walsh, Mr. Johnson, and I walked over to a Rajas Garden to see his amiable pets that had been brought from the jungle. In a large iron cage were 2 beautiful spotted leopards, about the size of a huge dog. They are just like very large cats in body, head, eyes, tail, and all their motions were catlike. One of them exhibited his accomplishments for our amusements. He would walk off to one side of the cage, and then spring towards us with a fierceness that made me inquire of his stable keeper whether the bars of his cage were strong enough. We all admired him very much—in the cage.

Here is the Munshi making his salam. I will leave the reading to my good husband. He has been sermonizing all morning, and had just settled himself for a nap on the lounge to rest after his studies. But he says he will read while I finish my letter.

You must not think us lazy if I tell you we generally take a nap during the day. We must get up very early, and our bodies need the rest in the heat of the day. It seems to be a necessary food for the body in this climate. The natives would much rather lose their sleep at night, than their nap in the day. When we first came, we pooh poohed the habit, as only a lazy one. Now we have learned from experience that it is very beneficial. We will soon be regularly Indianized in our habits. We have not changed our color yet, however. We are not exposed to the Indian sun enough to test his coloring qualities. . . .

Monday morning, [June] 16th
This is a morning to please the most fastidious duck. The rain is pouring down beautifully. All the geese and ducks are out waddling about in the yard in high glee. A poor little calf is scudding along before the wind, and does not seem to understand what a rainy day means.

I was quite surprised, Frank, to see that your school is patronized so extensively from "Dixie" to "Bear Creek." (I hope that Bear Creek is not dangerously near to you.) Well my good brothers, I have not room for many more wise? remarks, and I have not time to write you a longer letter by this mail. Dont be critical of this scrawl, for I am writing for brothers eyes, and I dont expect them to view me with a critical eye. With a great heart full of love for you all.

Affectionately,
Sister Rachel L. Johnson

FIVE

July 1862–December 1863

FATEHPUR

℘ TWO YEARS AFTER leaving Boston for India, Rachel reported that much of the novelty of their new homeland had worn off. It was no longer a curiosity to see elephants, camels, and bears in their village, or to eat a regular diet of mutton, curry, rice, mangos, and other foods their family in Hookstown had never tasted.

In response to their families' continuing concerns, Rachel and Will reported that they saw no evidence of military unrest in India in 1862. The British presence in India had doubled in the last five years, the Sepoy army had been disbanded, and the Indians had been disarmed. Painful memories of the mutiny were ceremoniously laid to rest for Will when he took a trip, as a guest of the British government, to attend the laying of the cornerstone for the Memorial Church in Kanpur. The Memorial Church was built on the site where Albert and Amanda Johnson had been shot to death five years earlier.

Rachel and Will's concern about the war news from home heightened when they learned that both Sam and Frank had gone off to war on August 14, 1862. When the war began, Sam was at Jefferson College and Frank was at Washington College. Years later Frank's daughter recalled her father's account, that "they literally dropped their books and ran to Hookstown." In Hookstown, Sam Kerr was instrumental in organizing his relatives, neighbors, and friends into Company H, 140th Pennsylvania Volunteer Infantry, to serve the Union cause. For his organization, Sam was assigned the rank of orderly sergeant. Frank was too young to carry a gun, so he went as a fifer. Soon, because he was a good rider, Frank became a message carrier for a general. Rachel and Will read the English newspaper accounts of the battles at Fredericksburg, Chancellorsville, and Gettysburg, learning months later that Rachel's brothers had fought in each battle.]

Futtehpore, North India
July 18th, 1862

My dear Mother,

I have just finished a second reading of Sam's and Frank's letters of May 10, received about 10 this morning. Glad to hear good news from both. When your letters come, we hurry over them as fast as possible, to hear what is the news. Then we go over them again more leisurely, and have a talk about you all. . . . I found your little geranium leaf peeping out first thing when I opened this letter.

Yesterday was the anniversary of our parting with you all. Two years have glided away, and how very quickly too. It seems but a little time, and yet, we have lived a life full of strangeness and new experiences. We have not been without our trials in these years of new life, but we have been very happy mid our labor and look hopefully to the future.

Yesterday there was a grand ceremony in Cawnpore, the laying of the corner stone of the Memorial Church to be built by the Government in commemoration of those martyred at Cawnpore during the mutiny. There was a special train from Allahabad to Cawnpore, provided by the Lieutenant Governor, to convey the passengers. The regular trains run at night now. Mr. Walsh wrote that he and Mr. Wyckoff were going up, so Mr. Johnson thought he would go along with the rest. We had an early breakfast, and about 8:30 in the morning the cars came rushing along full of people from Allahabad. They stopped a few minutes at the depot, where Mr. Johnson and two or three others joined the company. Then they were off to Cawnpore.

This is the first time I have been left alone, since we had a home of our own. But I did not stay alone very long. The Doctors wife had invited me to spend the day with her. So about 10 o'clock, I went up to the Sherlocks and spend a pleasant day with them. . . . The train from Cawnpore was expected back about 10 at night, and the Sherlocks would not allow me to come away until almost train time, so I just got home in time to have tea ready before Mr. Johnson came back, bringing Mr. Walsh with him. Mr. Walsh was to remain over Sabbath, which is our Communion Sabbath.

Mr. Wyckoff went on to Allahabad, and could not stop with us. Mrs. Wyckoff has another little daughter, which she calls Mary. The other, which is still a very little babe, only a year old, she named Lizzie. They are all very well now.

Futtehpore, India
August 3rd, 1862

To Father Kerr [from Will],
My dear Sir:

I hope you will not forget to add a letter from your own hand occasionally when the boys are writing. We are wonderful lovers of news in this part of the world. Though generally we have not much news to give in return.

India is now very quiet through its length and breadth. Some months ago, when there was war between Afghanistan and Persia, there was some little stir among the Mohammedans here. They hoped that this country would become embroiled, but the sensible ones among them saw that, with the overwhelming power of the English, there was no chance of doing anything, so the matter was quietly dropped. If they could not succeed in 1857, how could they now that the Sepoy Army is diminished one-half, and kept away from all the forts and artillery, and the European Army doubled? Besides this, the natives have been disarmed.

The Magistrate of this place, named Power, with his brother, were in Mynpoorie in the mutiny. They ruled that district with a rod of iron, and kept it down, until every district around had risen in rebellion. Some time ago when this excitement among Mohammedans was at its height, Power heard that several native zamindars (i.e., wealthy landholders) had been conversing together about what happy times it would soon be, when they should again be rulers, as they once were. Power marched these gentlemen up to court, tried them, and sentenced them to two years in prison for seditious language. You may well imagine that there was no more of that kind of talk when they found it was so dear a luxury.

Two weeks ago I went to Cawnpore to see the laying of the Corner Stone of the Memorial Church, which the Government is building to commemorate those who were so foully murdered there in the mutiny by the rebel Nana Sahib. The Government provided a special train from Allahabad—with free tickets. At Cawnpore they had carriages waiting at the depot to convey us to a large house over in the city, where huge tables groaned under the weight of all manner of eatables. There was ice water, soda water, sherry wine, brandy, etc., and fruits in abundance, even cigars for all who wished. All free.

Walsh and Wyckoff came up from Allahabad, and we three went together. We three chose a nice two horse carriage with coachman and two outriders, and kept it all day. We went everywhere we liked, visited, shopped, and went to see the new Gardens about that well, in which the mangled bodies of women and children were thrown, when Havelock approached Cawnpore. Over this well a most beautiful monument is

Fig. 7. The Angel of Resurrection statue stands in the middle of the memorial well monument in Kanpur and commemorates those who were killed in the Sepoy revolt in July 1857.

being erected by the Government. We passed the earthworks thrown up by Havelock when he retook the city, and in which he was for a time besieged.

Then we returned to the eating house, had our dinner, and drove to the old intrenchment of General Wheeler where the church is being built. The ceremony was at 6 P.M., and we were early. So we wandered about, viewing that scene hallowed by the blood, the patient endurance, and the death of so many brave men, women, and children. Here in the middle of a vast plain, we could trace the line of that low mud wall, not breast high, which was all that for weeks defended the doomed Wheeler and his men from the ferocious crowds of the Sepoys. One of the old barracks still stands in the fort—all battered and shattered as it was then. Close beside it was a flat stone to mark the position of an old well. Here were placed the bodies of those who first fell during the siege. But soon they found it impossible to bury the bodies inside the intrenchments. We passed out and across the plain. At some distance we came to a large stone cross, with two smaller crosses at the sides. These mark the site where all the bodies were afterwards thrown. It was a service of much danger, to carry the dead and throw them in here. It was always done at night.

Between these two monuments, we examined the well where the besieged used to draw water, at the eminent risk of their lives. It was a prominent mark for the rebel cannons. The upper part of the brick work, about the mouth, was mostly shot away. We could still count the places near the bottom where 8 or 10 pound cannon balls had struck. Half were bedded themselves among the brickwork.

It was in the midst of such scenes as this, that a large crowd of ladies and gentlemen, civil and military, from Cawnpore, Allahabad, Agra, and Lucknow, came to witness the laying of the first stone of the new church. Regiments of soldiers were drawn up all around, and a crowd of natives stood off at a respectful distance.

After the usual services, the Brigadier laid the stone, with a silver trowel. The band chanted the 118 Psalm. The blessing was pronounced. Then we all returned to the eating room, for a little more pie, cake, and ice water; thence to the depot again, where we took leave of our "turn out," and soon were in the cars on our way home.

It is not an every day occurrence to be feted at Government expense, so I thought you would like to hear about it. But my paper is done.

Yours ever,
W. F. Johnson

[Rachel continues the correspondence.]

Friday, 25th
We have had a very pleasant, rainy day. It is not very hot. I have just eaten a hearty dinner, Mother, of roast mutton, curry and rice, potatoes, spinach, etc. I fear I will not be able to write very much, but every

little helps. We are both very well (as said joint of mutton might testify if you could see it), and have felt much better since the rains set in. I fancy you now are enjoying a little warm weather (not hot weather, for you dont know in Hookstown what real hot weather is). This is the time too with you for berries and apples. It makes my mouth water to think about them.

Just now we have very little fruit or vegetables. The mangoes are done and other fruits are not ripe yet. We got a few guaves today, but they are not very ripe. I like them very well, because they are tart, and almost all the fruit here is sweet. We have had a few cucumbers, but the Doctor here, as I believe everywhere else, says they are not much better than poison. A very pleasant one to take, I think.

Since the rains began, we have had to take in our one small chimney. One morning we were almost deluged with the rain, pouring in through every little nook about it. The wall, which is made of sun dried bricks, began to fall in, splashing the muddy water over carpet, pictures, and everything. I chanced to be near, when a large brick came down, breaking the mantel piece. It tumbled into a pan set to catch the water, splashing it all over me. As soon as the shower was over, we got some coolies to work taking down the chimney, and by the time the next shower came, we had all made tight and safe.

It is very hard to make these tiled roofs keep out the hard soaking rains altogether, or indeed any kind of a roof. For the water pours down until everything is saturated with it. We are having plenty of rain this season, and the plains are now covered with grass, which makes the poor bullocks and buffalos look very happy. They keep nipping the fresh grass all day. Some of them look as if they had been living on hope for a good while. Every evening there are great droves of them winding their way down towards the city, followed by their herdsman, and large flocks of goats.

We have some half dozen goats now. I have to watch the milk very sharp, to keep the servants from stealing it all. A few days ago, I found out one of them was taking more than half for himself; so I relieved him of the responsibility of taking care of any of it, much to his grief. I often wish it were possible to get along in India without the pest of servants, but we could not do it. So we have to put up with their trouble. We are going to send our cook away. He is such a stupid fellow. We think he eats opium. The natives are very fond of it, and after they have used it a good while, they cannot do without it, and are miserable unless intoxicated by it.

Monday 28th

Two years ago today we sailed from Boston. Then we scarcely knew there was such a place as Futtehpore. India seemed like a very visionary land. Now the novelty of these Indian scenes has almost quite worn off. We look upon a string of camels with about as much curiosity as you would a drove of oxen. We look out on an old elephant waddling along as an every day affair. An old native brings a huge, shaggy, black bear to the door, which he has taught to dance and play many tricks; but we hardly think more of it than we used to at home when an old organ grinder came along. . . .

Mr. Johnson has just been arranging his paper in his writing desk, and found a collection of old steel pens which he threw out of the door. A Hindoo boy, who is watching some bullocks feeding on the grass in our Compound, saw them and gathered them up. He and the old punka wala now have had a great consultation over them. We were peeping out at them, shaking our sides laughing; while they, in innocent wonder, were turning them over and examining them very carefully. They were whispering to each other, and rolling up their eyes, wondering what those strange things could be. Doubtless they never heard of such a thing as a steel pen. The natives use pens made out of reeds—just like a little rod with the end sharpened. Instead of laying their paper on a table, they make a writing table of their knees, and much prefer it to any of our new fangled inventions.

Mother, I wish you could get Frank to copy some of the best receipts for making cakes, etc., from that good old cook book of ours. You will know what I would likely care to have. Remember we have plenty of oranges here. I think there are some good receipts for marmalades, etc. Frank might slip a few in several letters, out of the different departments of cookery.

Servants here have learned to cook after English ideas for the English, but we like our American dishes best. I have taught our cook to make several, and often make them myself. You know we have not many of the old home fruits here. We miss the apples so much. We have no fruit that fills their place to us. . . .

My good husband ought to have written some this time, but he is busy now with Jacob, a Catechist who is learning English. With much love from us both, to our ever dear Mother and to all our friends.

Very affectionately,
Your daughter Rachel

P.S.

A word to Sam and Frank: Salam Bhaion! Come tell me, with all your Latin and Greek, translate my greeting. You see, if your sister is not so proficient in the dead languages, she has acquired a few words of another language. We could now quite puzzle you with our Hindustani chit chat. Salam is the universal Eastern word of greeting; and Bhaion means brothers.

Last mail we were very glad to receive letters from both of you. Sam, can't quite forgive you, if you let 4 months slip away often without a line from you. Snatch your pen once in awhile. Dash off a few lines. Enclose it to Frank, and let him send it with his—just to let us know you are Sam Kerr, our brother yet.

Frank, go on and prosper. Always glad to hear from you too. So you have been making improvements, papering my old room. What is the color of the paper? Tell me so I'll know how it looks. Remember us to all the girls.

Much love,
Rachel

My dear Stella,

. . . Here is a pot of peach butter just made this morning and some mangoes. How I would like to give you one of these nice yellow ones. The peaches we got from the gardener are such a strange shape, just like little flat tomatoes, and the seeds are flat too. I did not think they were peaches at all when the man brought them, but they taste very good.

We have had a good deal of thunder and lightning yesterday and to-day, and plenty of rain. The little birds that have built their nest under the roof of our veranda are chatting and singing very merrily about the nice rain. The rain makes the little worms, bugs, and ants come up out of the ground, so they get a good dinner off them. Mr. Johnson just called me to see two pretty canary birds that a man brought in a cage to sell. He wants 50 dollars (only) for them. I think we will content our-selves with the little chippies that live in the veranda, if their voices are not so sweet.

. . . But Stella dear, I must say goodbye. Tell Father and Mother, and Grandpaps and Grandmother, that we are well, and send much love.

Your own sister, Rachel

[In addition to bouts with malaria, another of Will's recurring health problems was his deteriorating eyesight. Beginning in the fall of 1862 and continuing for about a year and a half, there were frequent refer-ences in Rachel and Will's letters to the "weakness" of Will's eyes. In Feb-ruary 1863 Mr. Walsh wrote to the Board of Foreign Missions that "Mr. Johnson's eyes are very bad." In June Will wrote to the Board, "My eyes are improving slowly. . . . I cannot read at night. . . . The glare of sun light is very trying." Malaria itself is not known to cause eye problems; however, quinine derivatives—and Will spoke of commonly giving qui-nine to persons with fevers—do cause permanent, irreversible damage to the retina. He may also have contracted a viral infection or one of a wide variety of other ocular conditions that would cause a temporary vision problem, since a permanent vision problem was never mentioned in later correspondence.¹]

Futtehpore, North India
November 3rd, 1862

My dear Father and Mother,

. . . We are both very well, but Mr. Johnson's eyes are not very strong yet, which hinders him in his studies. We hope the cold weather will soon restore them to their usual strength. The cold weather had been late setting in, but now we hope it has made a real beginning. If my nose is a good thermometer, I should say it was pretty cold this morning before the sun got up. When we were out, I was glad to muffle it up. The sun is still very hot at the middle of the day, but the wind is cold. The natives look distressed these cold mornings, and muffle up their heads carefully, while the bare legs are left to enjoy the weather as it comes. They suffer a good deal from fever now, as the weather changes. Lucy, one of the native Christians, has just come in and Mr. Johnson has given her some quinine. She is the one that was crazy, but she is quite well now.

We are getting ready to go to the Annual Meeting of the Missionaries, to be held at Mynpoorie, where Mr. Brodhead is stationed. There will be 3 missionary families from Futtehgurh, one from Agra, and 2 from Allahabad, and my good husband and self. We expect a very pleasant meeting with our American brethren and sisters. It will seem jolly to have a little party of Americans together once more, and I dont know a jollier set than the missionaries of India, from what I know of them. But I will tell you all about them in my next.

Now for our plans. The meeting at Mynpoorie is the 12th of November. The Walshes and Wyckoffs will leave home on Monday 10th, and reach our house on the 10 o'clock train in time for breakfast. They will stop with us until next morning, and rest the little ones. Then we will all go to Shikohabad on the cars. This is a days journey. From there we will go by "dak gari"—one of those vehicles that brought us up from Calcutta. While the Missionaries will hold a Presbyterial Meeting, and do a great deal of work, their wives will do a great deal of talking, no doubt, and amuse themselves as profitably as they can.

So much for our projected trip. More again. This week my husband must settle up his Accounts, and make out a report of what he has been doing the past year. He must prepare estimates of what he will require for the next year to carry on the work.

1. Emil Mitchell Opremcak, M.D., director, Ocular Immunology Laboratory, The Ohio State University, interview with author, Columbus, Ohio, Nov. 26, 1990.

We were getting quite discouraged about the progress of the war at home, when the news came of Popes defeat, and Stonewall Jackson and Lee marching on to Washington so fast, and invading a corner of Pennsylvania. What next? Is Jeff Davis likely to be installed in the White House in Washington? But the last telegram says McClellan defeated Lee at Hagarstown, and that Confederates are retreating. President declares slaves of rebels all free in January next, etc.[2] These are dark days for the dear old Union, and sad ones too. But all will yet end well.

Our hearts sicken when we read the tales of slaughter and carnage, and think of the sufferings of our brave soldiers, and heart breakings of bereaved hearts left behind. But ours is a cause worth suffering for.

. . . With our united love to our dear ones.

Affectionately, Rachel

Futtehpore, India
December 3rd, 1862

My dear Mother,

We have had everything topsy turvy for a few days, moving out of our house into a tent pitched in a grove of trees, just across the road from home. Our house needed a new roof. As that had to be done this cold season, Mr. Johnson got the sanction of the Mission at the Annual Meeting to make some changes in the arrangement of the inside of the house. It will make our home much more comfortable and convenient. The house was built by the late native Missionary, Gopee Nauth. It is agreeable to native ideas, but is cut up into a good many small rooms, which are neither healthy nor comfortable for any but natives in this hot climate. But I will tell you all about the new house, when we get it finished. For 2 or 3 months, you must imagine us living out in the woods, among the bright, green-leafed mango trees.

We have a nice Swiss Cottage tent, which has one good sized room and two little rooms in it, where we can live very comfortably as long as the cold weather lasts. You know we have no snow, sleet, hail or rain to fear all our winter days. It is all bright sunshine.

But come Mother, and I will show you what a Swiss Cottage tent is like. We will leave the dusty bungalow, where 10 or 12 coolies are busy pulling off the roof; walk down across the yard; over to the other side of the road; and here, peeping out from among the trees you see the white canvass tent. It has a peaked roof, which slopes down in front making a

2. On Jan. 1, 1963, President Lincoln signed the Emancipation Proclamation, which was not a popular decision with many in the North. In 1861 Lincoln had made it clear that the preservation of the Union was his goal; now a second major goal was the abolition of slavery. McPherson, *Ordeal by Fire*, 296–97.

little shady porch. We left the screens serve as doors in the day time. You notice they are made of reeds, woven together with thread, and bound round the sides with red chintz. These keep out the glare of the sun in the day, and at night these heavy canvass doors, now rolled up, are let down and tied at the corners.

We now raise the screen and go inside. This large room, perhaps 12 by 16, is for the present, our parlor, bedroom, dining room and study. Look how nicely the tent is lined with a gay print of yellow and brown cotton cloth. The sides are about 6 feet high, to where the roof begins to slope up. Notice the roof and all are lined with cotton print too. We laid some coarse cloth on the ground, and then put our carpet over that. In this corner, by the door, is the writing desk. In the opposite one, the dining table. The bed is in a back corner, with a white spread—which reminds me of Mrs. Morton. Here is our new rocking chair, which we got from Futtehgurh. The easy chair, that will fold up, we brought from Boston. And the lounge is very cozy, if one feels tired or lazy. These, and a few extra chairs, are all that this room will conveniently hold, and at the same time not crowd our hoops. In this little back room, the shape of a half moon and not more than 4 feet wide by 12 in length, you see a dressing table, a bureau, and three boxes or trunks containing clothes, etc. In the other little side room, is stowed a box of provisions.

Well dear Mother, what do you think of our tent? Not a bad place is it? As we only moved in yesterday, I cannot tell you much about tent life yet, but I think we will like it.

We promised Dr. and Mrs. Sherlock that we would go up and dine with them this afternoon at 3, so I must run away and get ready, although I would like to have a longer talk. Last week I dreamed that we were going over to visit you, but I expect my husband will think the journey a little too long for us. . . .

Stella, I have a visitor, a little squirrel, peeping in at me. Wouldnt you like to have his pretty tail for a brush? It is such a long one, he might spare you a piece.

Thursday, December 5th

Dear Mother,

I am alone this morning. Mr. Johnson has gone down to the city, to the School, and I will write a little more to you. We received your September letter just a month ago, and with it the first news that the dear boys have gone to war. It was with a sad heart and tearful eyes I learned that they too must go. Altho it is a bitter trial to give them up to the trials, temptations, and dangers of a soldier's life, yet I cannot but feel that they but did their duty. They are giving themselves to the service of our dear country, in this, her hour of peril. May God in Mercy keep them from danger and temptation, and bring them back to us in safety, not having served in vain. How anxious we feel about them. You will know by your own feelings.

I know you will feel lonely, and have many anxious hours. Our hearts feel for you, dear Mother, in this trial. We trust that you will be enabled to cast this burden too on the Lord, and He will sustain you, and comfort you. It is indeed a comfort to know that their Captain is a good man, and that so many of the young men of their Company are good, young men. Hookstown must seem very lonely and deserted, when so many have gone. God grant that the day of peace is near at hand. We weary waiting for the end of these horrible battles, where so many of our good and true are sacrificed. Our latest news is of the advance of the Army of the Potomac into Virginia in pursuit of the Secesh [Secessionists].

. . . We have been away from home two weeks, attending the Annual Meeting, which was held at Mynpurie. I meant to tell you all about our trip in this letter, but it will make it too long. I will leave the particulars for our next. I will only say that we met all our Missionary brethren and sisters, and spent a week very pleasantly together. We then went over to Futtehgurh, and staid a week longer with the Fullertons and Scotts. Now we are back home again, feeling much better of the trip.

Mr. Johnsons eyes are much stronger, and he is busy as he can be. He has had to dismiss the head teacher in the school, on account of want of funds to support him. Now he will be obliged to teach some himself. This will be a good deal of additional work, with his studying, preaching, and overseeing the repairing of our house.

We are both quite well, and hope to get all the good that is to be gained from the cold weather out in our tent. Tent life is considered the healthiest in the cold weather. We would be glad to have Father give our carpenter a little instruction in hurrying up his part of the work in getting our house ready. Smoking the hooka is his greatest concern. . . .

Very affectionately,
Rachel L. Johnson

Futtehpore, India
New Years Day, 1863

My dear Brothers Sam and Frank,

A Happy New Year! And where are my brave soldier brothers today? At home, in camp, or on the battle field? May our Fathers love protect and bless you!

It is now two months since we received your letters, telling us that you had enlisted, and were then on your way to Camp Curtin. How anxiously we are waiting for tidings from you. . . . In a letter from Hunter,[3] he said that he had heard from you both, and that you were at Oakton, on the Baltimore railroad. I did not think you would be put into service so soon, but would remain in Camp for a few months drill first.

How do you like a soldiers life? Not a very easy one is it? You will doubtless have many hardships and privations to endure, but keep brave hearts, and serve our country faithfully in this, her hour of trial. We will hope and pray that you may be spared to enjoy the blessings of a free country, and a lasting peace.

When I knew that you, dear brothers, had gone, my heart was very sad. When I think of the dangers that will surround you, and all the temptations of life in camp . . . I am sad. Think of all the suffering that wicked men have brought upon our once happy country, and of the many precious lives that must be sacrificed to purchase again the blessings of peace.

You will know, if you received our last letter, that we too are enjoying tent life. Our tent is pitched in a nice grove of Mango trees, and we will remain here during the cold weather, when we hope to have our house ready to occupy. But our winter is like a long "Indian Summer" in America, so it is no hardship to spend a winter out under the green trees.

The long-tailed blackbirds, the pert, little wrens, the busy, little, brown minas, the noisy crows, and the cunning, little squirrels are our neighbors. The crows go out during the day to visit the farmers grain fields (the grain we feed our horses with). In the evening, a little after sun down, we see a black cloud approaching. Presently every tree is covered with crows. The cloud is literally black. Thousands of them settle themselves in this one little grove, for a nap; and then, what a cawing and gossiping among the Jim Crow family. At dawn of day, the first sound is their chattering debate, as to whether we will call on neighbor "Chuckerbutty," or "Ram pershad," to levy our "black mail." This being decided, there is a noise of many wings, a rushing sound, and away goes our black colony to the labors of the day.

But neighbor crow is not to be caught napping, as our Company of Jim Crows find. There, in the midst of his grain, perched on a bamboo shed towering above the coveted morsels, sits a figure in white—that you might mistake for a bale of muslin. But every few minutes, an unearthly howl from the bale of muslin admonishes "Jim" that danger is near. So he cocks one eye at the suspicious looking watchman, and sidles off.

3. Hunter seemed to be a family friend who corresponded with Rachel, Sam, and Frank.

Neighbor crow makes a hop, step and jump, to a distant corner, where once in awhile he snatches a mouthful. Then he darts away, over the plain, to swallow it. Then he comes back for another, until he manages to make a pretty good breakfast of stolen grain, which he doubtless thinks very sweet.

The honest little minas, in the meantime, busy themselves hunting ants and bugs by the roadside. Satisfied that honesty is the best policy.

January 2nd

... In my last letter, I promised Mother that I would tell you of our visit to Mynpurie and Futtehgurh. We, in company with the Wyck-offs, left home on 11th. . . . We went on the cars from Futtehpore to Etawah, where we expected to get bearers to take us the remaining 30 miles in palki to Mynpurie. . . . We got off the cars at Etawah, and made inquiry of an old fat baboo at the post office, as to how soon he could get a conveyance for us to Mynpurie. He very cooly told us, in 3 days. Not less. For he would have to send word on ahead to the villages on the way, to provide us with relays of coolies, to carry our palkis. . . . As we could not wait so long, we telegraphed on to friends to engage the carriage for us, and we would come on next day by train to Shikohabad.

So, we could do nothing, but wait a day in Etawah. We went down to the dawk ghurr, or Government Inn. . . . A native cook is always ready to provide something for you to eat, and by paying half dollar, you have the privilege of the house for a day and night. Anything that the cook provides, you pay him for. We stopped at this Inn until next day, when we went on to Shikohabad. We got there about sunset, and found a carriage (the same kind that we travelled in coming up from Calcutta) waiting at the depot.

We got our quilts and pillows arranged inside, and our baggage stowed on top of the gari, and so prepared for a nap. We ordered the man to drive on to Mynpurie. He started off at a furious pace. Went about 2 miles, then stopped at one of these Inns for a fresh horse. The man led off the horse. We waited a long time, but no horse came. Mr. Johnson went to try and find the stable, but no horse could be found. After about an hour, the driver came leading an old horse back. Now we thought, we would be off. Away we went, helter skelter, coachman shouting and his assistant blowing furiously on his horn with everything clearing the track. This went very well for a mile, then, all at once, a dead stop. We looked out, and there was a blacksmith taking off the wheels of our gari. What's wrong now? Old coachman declares it impossible to go on without the gari being greased. We submit—as no choice is left—and after a little while the bugle notes of the horn peal out merrily, and away

Fig. 8. At this riverbank, local people washed their clothes, bathed, and collected water for drinking and cooking.

we go again. We dash on 8 miles; the horn peals out its notes again. A new horse is waiting. It is hitched on, and on we go. We dash on until about 12 that night. We see in the moonlight that we have come to a city. It is Mynpurie.

We drive down a long narrow street, and turn off into a nice, large, grassy, plot of ground. Among the trees, we see a little church, and drive on a little further. The Mission home peeps out from behind the trees. Our gari stops, and Brother Brodhead comes out to welcome us. He gives us a snug little room to ourselves, and we settle our brains for a nap. So good-night till morning, and we will be introduced to our Yankee brethren and sisters in India.

Well, we have had a good nap. So we will greet our friends: Mr. and Mrs. Brodhead are both young Missionaries, come out 2 years before us. He does not look older than my husband, and Mrs. Brodhead is a nice looking little woman. . . . Here are Mr. and Mrs. Scott of Futtehgurh. He is the oldest man in our Mission—a hale, hearty looking man, who reminds us some of old General Scott as we see him in his pictures. Mrs. Scott is his second wife, and much younger. She is very pleasant looking, and a very intelligent woman. Mr. Fullerton is younger than

Mr. Scott. He has a frank, jolly-looking face, full of fun, and is quite a large, stout-looking man. His wife did not come to the Annual Meeting. Mr. and Mrs. Ullmann, I have told you about before, when they visited us last winter. He is a German and she English. And the Walshes, and Wyckoffs, you know already. Mr. Owen reminds me of Dan Donehoo, but is an older man. Mrs. Owen is a daughter of General Proctor, of Revolutionary fame. But if a daughter of a Tory General, she is a very, nice, old lady, and very fond of her Adopted Country, America, which she has visited.

Now I have told you something of all the brethren and sisters, but the Johnsons. I leave you to form your own picture of them—with the reminder that they have added $2\frac{1}{2}$ years of wisdom to their stature since you saw them. So of course, they must have become quite grave.

We thought Mynpurie a very, pretty place. A little river winds along below the city, which gives a little variety to the scenery. The city is about as large as Futtehpore.

The Synod met every day, and had a busy, pleasant meeting. A number of changes were made. Mr. Brodhead will be sent to Futtehgurh, and Mr. Wyckoff will go to Mynpurie. Mr. Owen, from Agra, will go back to Allahabad. Mr. Ullmann is sent to Etawah, to begin a new station. Mr. Scott stays at Futtehgurh. Mr. Walsh at Allahabad, and we at Futtehpore. Mr. Fullerton is obliged to go to the Hills for his health with his family.

On Sabbath, we all sat down together to the Lords Supper. It was a precious season of communion to our souls. At noon we had a prayer meeting, to pray for our dear, native land. Mr. Fullerton conducted the services, and made some very feeling remarks on the condition of our unhappy country. Then several prayers were offered for our country, our president and rulers, and the dear ones who have gone forth to fight our battles. Need I say that the fervent prayer of our hearts was for a speedy peace.

On Monday, the business all being done, the Futtehgurh brethren started home. We arranged that we should all return home by way of Futtehgurh, as there was but one dawk gari running to Futtehgurh each day. Mr. Walsh and Mr. Johnson went in the mail cart; Mrs. Walsh, Anna, Hammie, and I followed after our husbands in the dawk gari. Then, next day, the Wyckoffs and Owens came on in the same way.

We spend a week with the Fullertons and Scotts, and had a delightful visit. Mrs. Fullerton, you know, is a sister of Rev. White, and is a lovely woman—one of the kindest and best. They have 4 little girls, and a little boy. The oldest is about 10 years of age, and I never saw a nicer behaved little flock.

The Fullertons and Ullmanns houses are in the same compound or lot. Mr. Ullmanns house was Albert Johnsons. Mr. Fullertons is the

Campbells house.[4] Both houses have been rebuilt since the mutiny. As we walked around in their old paths, and looked on their old homes, we felt sad to think of their cruel deaths—cut down by those for whose sake they had left all that were dear. But they are only home a little sooner than we who come after. Perhaps their deaths shall glorify their Savior more than their lives could have done.

January 16th

Sad news of the Federal defeat at Fredericksburg. How I long to hear of the end of this horrible war. How my heart longs to know if all is well with you, dear brothers. May God protect you in the day of battle!

I wish I could hear from you often, and write to you often, for I know you will prize letters from those whose hearts love follows you anxiously out in camp, or battlefield. . . . We want to know what regiment, company and division you are in, and all about your movements and commanders. Remember us to all our old friends with you in the Army.

I dreamed last night of seeing you come home from the war. One of those big, black buffalos I see every day was standing in the yard. Frank pitched into it with might and main. It was trying to vanquish you with its long horns. Then I woke in the midst of the fracas, in a great fright. . . .

Write often as you can. With our united love

Affectionately,
Sister Rachel

Futtehpore, India
January 20, 1863

My dear Father and Mother,

. . . Very soon you may expect a little box of Indian curiosities. Just such trifles as we could gather up from time to time, that we thought would interest you as curiosities because they are from India. They are ones not too easily broken, or too bulky, to be battered round in a little box for many thousands of miles. . . . We hope they will reach you safely. They were shipped in November, but we did not tell you before, for we did not want you to have the suspense of looking for it long before it came. The ship ought to reach Boston in 4 months, unless some of Jeff Davis pirateers takes her. . . .

On the opposite side I give you a list of the little nicknacks sent you in the box. They are all put up in little packages, numbered with the names of the articles marked on each, so that we hope you will be able

---

4. David and Maria Campbell and their two children, Willie and Fannie, were also killed on the parade ground at Kanpur with Albert and Amanda Johnson.

to know what each is. In addition to these, you will find a few figures in clay, that give a very good idea of native dress—if they are not broken before you get them.[5]

Your affectionate daughter,
Rachel L. Johnson

[Rachel missed writing her monthly family letter in February 1863. Will's letter in early March explained the unusual circumstances and announced the birth of their first child, William Kerr Johnson, who was born on February 21. There had been no hint of the pending birth in any of Rachel's letters home; she later explained that she did not tell her mother because the family already had enough anxieties.]

Allahabad, India
March 4th, 1863

My dear Friends,
Although I am almost interdicted these days from reading and writing, on account of the weakness of my eyes, I must at least send you a line to announce the birth of our son, Willie Kerr Johnson. I feel sure that the dignity of being grandparents will certainly add an inch to your stature.

As it was growing too hot to stay longer in tents, we came here on the 2nd of February, to our old home on the Jumna. Rachel wanted to be with her old friend, Mrs. Walsh, who, besides the greatest kindness of heart, adds the additional qualification of being the mother of eleven children. (By the way, our next neighbor here is the mother of 15!)

Our boy was born February 21st. Today Mrs. Johnson is able to walk about the room a little, so you see she is getting on very well.

The baby is very good. He sleeps nearly all night. He is going to look like his mother, I think.

We expect to return to Futtehpore next week, by which time our house will be about finished. . . . I hope by next mail, Rachel can write you a long letter.

With kind regards to all who remember us.

Yours ever,
W. F. Johnson

5. The list of curiosities from Rachel included: "3 toe rings, 1 brass inkstand, 2 eardrops, 2 nose rings, shells used as money (called cowries), 3 custard apples (dried), a sail knot tied by the wind in the storm in the Bay of Bengal, and 2 idol gods for the Steubenville Seminary."

Futtehpore, India
March 21st, 1863

My dear Mother,

If you received our last message, you will now be rejoicing in the dignity of <u>Grandma</u>. As Mr. Johnson could only write you a little note to tell you of the birth of our little boy, I know you will feel anxious to know further particulars, and how we are getting on. So my dear Mother, I will write this letter for you, and our own family—and not for the public eye.[6] For I know you will feel better satisfied, if I write freely, as I would talk to you if sitting by the old home fireside.

I did not tell you that I was expecting my confinement, because I felt that you had anxieties enough already. I would only be adding to them needlessly. My health was very good, and there is no need of borrowing trouble before it comes.

We went down to Allahabad, Feb. 2nd, and stayed with our kind friends, the Walshes, until last Wednesday (18th). Baby is just a month old today. He is a very, bright, little fellow. Of course, there never was such a <u>wonderful baby</u> in our eyes. I know Grandpa and Grandma would agree with us, and Great Grandma and Great Grandpaps too. The boys may now appropriate the title of Uncle Sam and Uncle Frank, and Stella is dear Aunt Stella. We have named baby, Willie Kerr Johnson.

Now I must come back to myself. I was taken sick in the morning, and baby was born at half past 8 in the evening. I got on very well. On the 12th day I was able to go out of my room and enjoy my dinner with the rest. After being up a day or two, I was taken with chills and fever and was obliged to go back to bed again. The Dr. gave me plenty of quinine, which soon broke the fever. In a few days I was able to be out again. Since I had fever, I have very little nourishment for baby, and am obliged to feed him with goats milk. But he seems to be thriving very well.

We came back to Futtehpore on last Wednesday, and have been staying with Dr. Sherlocks since. We will go into our own house on next Monday. It looks very nice and comfortable now—much improved by the new arrangement. Our rooms will be large and cool for the hot weather, which is fast coming on.

Mr. Johnson thinks his eyes are a little stronger than they were. He has a bad cold now, but hopes to be quite over it, and ready to fix up our house next week.

We were so glad to hear from you by last mail and to hear from the dear boys. Oh! how I long to hear that this sad war is over and our dear

6. It was a common practice in Rachel's day to pass letters among family members and friends. While addressed to one person, each letter was frequently read by many. Rachel's letters were often read at church as well.

ones gathered home again. Dear Sam and Frank, I think of them enduring all the trials of a soldiers life, with an aching heart.

. . . We are beginning to feel a good deal discouraged at the prospects of the war. The Federal army seems to meet with so many reverses. The generals are so very unfortunate that their laurels wither quickly. One mail brings news of McClellans resignation, and Burnside is the idol of the day; the next brings tidings that Burnside has resigned, and Hooker is in command. What next? Poor Mr. Lincoln must be at his wits end.

I suppose the war is beginning to bring hard times to you all. We dont see how the Missions will all be supported long, if, as at present, more than 50c out of every dollar has to be paid on foreign exchange. But perhaps the more urgent the call on God's people, the more willing and liberal will be their contributions to help with the Lord's work. They may all feel safe in lending to the Lord, for He will repay in full measure, while Gov't Banks and State Banks may prove shaky concerns. . . .

I am writing now with baby on my lap and he begins to remonstrate rather loudly, so I must hurry on . . . With our love to all.

Your affectionate daughter,
Rachel L. Johnson

April 20th, 1863

My dear Mother,

Since I wrote to you a month ago, I have had my troubles. I have suffered a great deal from sore breasts. One has gathered, which you know is no trifling matter. The Dr. lanced it last week, and it has been better since.[7] As the soreness is not all gone, I feel anxious for fear it gathers again. I have had a troublesome cough too, but now it is a great deal better. I hope to soon be quite well. These troubles coming before I had regained my strength, and at the beginning of the hot weather, have kept me down. So I do not feel very strong yet.

I was obliged to give up trying to nourish baby myself. As long as I had anything for him he got on very well, with the help of the goats milk, but I did not like to risk feeding him altogether. It would not be safe when teething time comes. So I have been obliged to do as a great many here have to do, get a native woman to come and nurse him. She gives her own babe to some one else, and comes here, and stays as one of the family, until baby is old enough to wean. I give her food and clothes, and $4\frac{1}{2}$ dollars a month. Her work is to give baby plenty of nourishment.

---

7. "Gathered" was a layperson's description of a swollen and inflamed breast, the result of an infection caused by milk being unable to get through the nipple, forming a crust inside the breast. Doctors commonly relieved this "gathering" by making an incision to release fluid and relieve pressure in the infected area.

It was very hard to give the dear little fellow up to any one else to be his comforter, but it could not be helped. He is growing finely, and is a very good baby.

 . . . An affectionate good-bye.

Your loving,
Rachel L. Johnson

Futtehpore, India
April 20th, 1863

My dear Brothers,

 On Thursday last we were again gladdened by good news from you. . . . Yours was dated Feb. 2, near Fredericksburg, Frank. I hope you are quite strong again and will not be obliged to become an inmate of the hospital again.[8] And Samuel, I am glad to hear that you are getting on so well. The war does, indeed, drag slowly on, and the telegrams bring no news of peace. But I trust the end is not far off. We know the dark hour often is just before the dawn.

 The home papers seem to anticipate trouble with old Bonapart. I think our Gov't has their hands full of Secesh, and had better settle this family quarrel, before getting mixed up in another. The last telegram says Wilkes has been pitching into another of "Johnny Bulls" ships. Poor Lincoln, if he steers safely among all these breakers, he will deserve another 4 years in the White House and a pension to retire on.

 You say, you think McClellan is the man. So do we. We hope Hooker will be more fortunate than his predecessors. We were glad to get the names of all your Commanders of Divisions, so that, from the papers, we can tell something of the movements of your division and corps, etc. We look with anxious hearts for the coming of every mail, and for news from you.

 When we wrote home a month ago we were stopping a few days with Dr. Sherlocks, until our house was ready for us. We are now at home, and have a very good and comfortable house to live in. I do not feel very strong yet, but am getting better. Mr. Johnson's eyes too are a little stronger, but he has to be very careful not to read very much with them. The munshi comes and reads Hindustani to him every night, so he is still making progress in the language.

 And now you would like to hear something of the wee Willie Kerr, I know. He is growing finely, and promises to be as wonderful a boy as either of his two worthy Uncles, Sam and Frank, when he gets as old. He talks in the coo coo language, and has a great deal to say. He makes up

---

8. In other family correspondence it was revealed that Frank was hospitalized with dysentery following the battles at Fredericksburg and Chancellorsville.

a very, sweet, little story, out of the few, little ideas that have begun to shoot. Mr. Walsh came up 3 weeks ago Saturday, and on Sabbath, held communion service and baptized baby.

Mr. Walsh's health has failed him so much, that he has been obliged to take a change for a few months. He has gone to England, and will perhaps be gone a year. The doctor did not think it safe for him to stay here this hot season. We hope he will come back with his health restored. Mrs. Walsh is still in Allahabad, at home, and will remain here. It would have been too expensive for her to go along, and her health is very good here.

Mr. Fullerton and family have gone to the Hills for the hot season. The Wyckoffs baby had a slight attack of small pox, but is now well again.

We are going to lose our good friends. Dr. Sherlocks are ordered by Government to Etawah, about a hundred miles from here. This is the new station our Mission has taken up. We are so sorry. They have been such kind friends to us, and we have been with them 2 years. We will feel their loss very much in every way. Indeed, when they are gone, we will feel that we are left almost alone in the Station. The Judge and his wife have been here but a little while, and we feel that they are strangers yet. I do not suppose we will soon again meet as good friends as the Dr. and his wife have been to us. But we cannot hope to keep our earthly friends near us. Our paths in life meet, and perhaps for a little way, they wind along together; then they part, and we meet no more until they again meet on the "shining shore." The Dr. too has been very liberal in helping support our Mission School. Unless the rate of exchange soon changes, we do not see how the Board at home can sustain our Missions all. Just think of it, out of every dollar sent to India or China, at the last mail, 72c went for exchange. At these high rates of taxes on everything at home, it is not likely that the subscriptions will be much increased. But the Lord will provide for his own work, and will do all things well.

We cannot see how this sad war and bloodshed is to work out good for His cause and people. But He knows and sees the end that all is for the best.

I am glad to hear that you do not suffer for want of the necessaries of life in your part of the Army. Hope the Army Contractors are obliged to wear paper soles out in the snow, if they really are as mean as some of the papers say, and furnish boots with paper soles for the soldiers. But I suppose most such stories are merely to produce a sensation. If you get the <u>needful</u> things, you can get on without many, little comforts that you once had, and I hope will soon enjoy again.

. . . We are now enjoying the hot weather. We have strong west winds that whistle through the tatti, and make the house very cool. One of the catechists, Qasim Ali, has just come in to read to Mr. Johnson. He wears spectacles, and is very anxious that we should get him a new pair out from America. He is very fond of books, and every new one Mr. Johnson gets, he wants him to give it to him. He is a very good preacher, and a great help to Mr. Johnson. He has a flock of little boys. He calls them Abrahim (Abraham), Izhak (Isaac), Yaqub (Jacob), etc.

Well I must rest awhile, for my back is very tired sitting so long. I must bid you Goodbye. Hoping to hear from you both very often. With our united love to you dear brothers, and our regards to all old friends with you in the Army.

Your Affectionate Sister,
Rachel L. Johnson

Futtehpore, Northern India
May 16th, 1863

My dear Father and Mother,

You say that your eyes are getting dim. I will try to write very plain, so that you will not feel it a task to read my letters. It is now 2 months since we had a letter from home, but hope, when this mail comes in, that we will have one from you. We feel so anxious to hear from the boys.

There was a rumor here that England had declared war against America. But it seems from the last telegram, that it has not yet been done. There is a great deal of bad feelings, and many hard words on both sides. We hope that it will come to nothing more. Hard words break no bones. The prospect of peace at home looks very dark to us. May God speed that happy time!

We are now in the midst of the hot winds today. The wind howls like December winds at home. Although the weather is very hot, we have not felt it nearly so much as we did last year. Our house is much more comfortable, I suppose this is one reason why we do not. We feel the want of a horse very much now, and have been trying to find a good, quiet one to buy. We have given up all hopes of finding our nice pony that was stolen.

We have been pretty well since I wrote last month (to the boys). I now feel pretty strong again. My breasts gathered a second time, as I feared, but has got pretty well. Mr. Johnson is busy at his work, reading, translating, etc. He cannot use his eyes all day for such close work, so he puts in a little time painting the doors, etc. Then our little Willie takes up some time.

Willie is growing to be a fine, big, double-chinned boy. He has always been very well, and is generally very good. Sometimes he shows signs of a pretty strong will of his own. Whether he inherits any of that from his mama, you will be able to tell.

Mr. Scott from Futtehgurh, spent a night with us this week. Mr. Sayre, the new Missionary, lives with them. Mrs. Sayre has a little babe, and has been so very ill, that for several days her life was despaired of. She is now getting better. She had convulsions and was blistered, bled, salivated and had her head shaved. Poor woman, she suffered greatly. We met them in Allahabad. She is very young, and seemed like a little girl.

Mrs. Walsh writes that she has just received the likenesses of her 7 children in America. They think of bringing their oldest daughter out to be assistant missionary. She is about 18, and has not yet left school. It would be very pleasant for them, for they have been separated from her so long.

We have had a catechist and reader out traveling through the country, visiting the villages, preaching, distributing tracts, etc., for several months. They have just come back. Jacob, the Catechist, is a very good man; and the Reader, Anand Masih, is very zealous in doing his work. One place they visited, they went to visit the native magistrate, and were received rather roughly. He asked what they came there for? And who told them to come. He ordered them to leave the place. The Catechist thought that they had better go to some other place, but "no," the Reader says. "We are in the work of the Lord, and we must preach here." The Catechist said, "When we are persecuted in one city, we must flee to another." But the reader said, "No. We must preach the Word of the Lord, whether men will hear or forbear." He is a very good worker, and we trust, a sincere Christian.

We have some hopes that the Head teacher in school will yet forsake Mohammadanism, and become a Christian. He professes to believe the Bible, and not the Koran. He comes every night to read with my husband, and seems to be very sincerely inquiring the right way.

We were walking in the yard a few evenings ago, when two old Brahmans came over in great distress. They had just arrived on the train, and had gone over to a well to get a drink, being very thirsty. When, by some slip of the rope, their brass lota, or drinking vessel, fell in. They were left without any way of quenching their thirst. My husband said he could give them some water, but no, they would not dare accept that. It would break their cast. At last, I believe, they found a brother Brahman of the right degree of holiness, and borrowed a lota of him.

Your affectionate daughter,
Rachel L. Johnson

Futtehpore, India
June 15th, 1863

Dear Brother Sam,

Many thanks for your shadow, received a month ago. Very good. Looks like Sam, with a little spice of dignity, which becomes the blue coat and brass buttons very well. We were very glad to see you, and not less so to hear from you yesterday (Sabbath). We had just come home from church in the morning, when Mr. Johnson spied a home letter lying on the table. He quietly slipped it in his pocket; then began to discuss with me the prospect of getting home letters this mail. We were not expecting the mail for a day or two longer, so I did not think of looking for one yet. You may imagine my pleasant surprise when the large, yellow envelope emerged from his pocket.

Since last I wrote, nothing new or strange has happened in our little world. We have all been well and busy as usual. There has been some sickness among the native Christians. One of the lambs of the flock, a little girl, died of small pox. The rest have, all through Gods Mercy, been preserved from it. Mr. Wyckoffs children both had it, but very lightly. They are now well again.

One of our Readers, Anand Masih, has just gone to Futtehgurh to seek a helpmate for himself. He has been importuning us for a long time to get him a wife, so my husband applied to Brother Scott of Futteh-gurh. He said there were several young damsels there in the market, and if Mr. Johnson would send Anand up, he might be able to find a help-mate to please him. We have not heard yet from him of his success.

Baldu, our Mission chaprasi [a servant], has been out in the jungle. He brought home 2 banyan sprouts to plant out in our Compound; so, if they grow, and we live to grow old in India, we may see it spread itself until it becomes a respectable grove. We have not been very successful in getting our trees to grow. Mr. Johnson has had some planted out every year during the rains, but most of them have died. The goats nip off all the leaves they can get at. It is amusing to see how nimble they are at climbing. They seem to delight in getting up on some fragment of a bro-ken wall, where they can show their skill in peeping over precipices with-out tumbling down. Our old white one regales itself off an old tree in the corner of the yard. Standing up on its two hind feet, it nips off all the leaves it can reach. I almost expect to see it step up into the tree, it seems so much at home on two legs.—But enough of this.

I suppose that long ere this, you have exchanged the monotony of camp life for active service. The last telegram brings news of battles in Virginia—Hooker defeated twice—but we have no particulars until the English papers come in. Then we will have a garbled account, making matters as bad as possible for the Federals. We anxiously wait to hear from you dear brothers. What of the battle?[9]

I am glad to hear that you enjoy camp life so well as you do. We trust that soon we shall hear of brighter prospects of peace. But pray, do

9. The Confederate victory at Chancellorsville (May 2–6, 1863) was one of the most remarkable victories in American military history. The Confederate army, outnumbered 2 to 1 and led by Lee and Jackson, thoroughly demoralized Union forces under "Fighting Joe" Hooker. It was a costly battle for both armies. The Union counted 17,278 men killed, wounded, or missing, the Confederates 12,821. Boatner, *Civil War Dictionary*, 140; McPherson, *Ordeal by Fire*, 318–21.

not think we belong to the party you have dignified with the title of "Copperheads."[10] We long to hear of an honorable peace.

Now dear Sam, I must say my little say to Frank too, so a wag of your hand, and goodbye. God bless you dear brother, and keep you ever.

Affectionately,
Sister Lillie

Futtehpore, India
June 15th, 1863

Well my dear brother Frank,

. . . We are always glad to hear about your camp life. I suppose you have pretty hard times sometimes, and not many delicacies to tempt you. If you could drop in among us today, we would be very happy to share with you some of the sweets that filled three large trays, brought by a native gentleman the other eve. You would have thought him quite a "Beau Brummel" if you had seen his shining hair, oiled to perfection, his faultless mustache, ending in very fierce looking points, the spotless fine muslin of his robe, and heard his fine speeches and smooth words, as he urged the reception of his offering of sweetmeats. There are raisins, almonds, nuts, candy, crystalized sugar in little trees, fruits, etc. It would indeed have been a favor if he had not brought quite such a bountiful supply, for there is more than I know what to do with.

Young Master Willie has not got his sweet tooth yet. He is getting to be a very roguish little fellow, fat and saucy. He lies here kicking up his feet, and trying to swallow his two fists. He is scolding a little because I am not devoting myself to him, instead of writing to Uncle Frank. Well Frank, I am tired sitting, so I will go and make a pudding for dinner, and finish my chat again, when perhaps my steel tongue will run a little faster.

Tuesday Morning

Good morning brother Frank, I am ready for another chat. So put away your fife, and sit down and listen. I had my hat and umbrella ready to go up to see Mrs. Goddard, who is sick. But a little shower caused me to repent of my good intentions, so I will have a little talk with you before breakfast.

Yesterday, there was a swarm of the winged ants. They come with the first rain in swarms out of the ground, until the air is full of them. It reminds one of a snow storm, when the air is full of large flakes of snow. This morning I do not see any trace of them.

10. "Copperheads" was a term used for Northern Democrats who opposed administration policies and favored a negotiated peace; it was often used as a derogatory term for all Democrats.

This year India has been visited with the plague of locusts in many parts. They came in such numbers that trees were stripped of their leaves, grain destroyed, and the larvae they deposited were gathered in bushels by the natives, and destroyed before they were able to fly. There were none in our district, but I saw a great cloud of them passing by towards Allahabad, where there were a good many. The natives use them for food, and consider them a great delicacy. How would you like some roasted locusts for diner for a change? Our old Catechist, Qasim Ali, says he has eaten them and likes them very much. But he is much horrified at our fancy for the unclean beast, and gives some very expressive grunts, as we discourse on the delicious flavor of roast pig. I suppose a native would enjoy a slice of pork about as well as we would a piece of roast dog. What is taste, but education, after all. A Russian or Chinese thinks a young puppy a delicacy; a Hindoo, his locusts and wild honey; and not long since, there was a society in France whose professed object was the introduction of horse flesh, as an article of food; while we fancy the flavor of roast pig, roast beef, etc. All, a matter of taste.

We were sorry to hear of the death of Davie Nelson. It makes one sad to think of the many noble lives that must be sacrificed for this wicked rebellion. May it please God to soon bring it to an end and prosper our country again. But if you dear brothers must lay down your lives for our country too, God grant that you may be taken to a better country, and be heirs to that crown that is far above all crowns of glory, the crown of life. And may we all have grace to bear our burdens and come off conquerors in the end.

We are glad to hear that our box got home safely, and that the clay figures were not all broken. Our papers have just come. Harpers Weekly has several pictures of Hookers headquarters. One Company is drawn up on parade, perhaps, it is the 140th Penna.

With affection always,
Sister Lillie

Futtehpore, India
July 1863

My dear Mother and Father,

We received this morning your letter of June 8, and the boys of May 11. I can now write with a lighter heart. For I felt very anxious to hear if the dear boys came out of Chancellorsville safely. "Our Regiment" was certainly favored in getting off so well.

A little more than a month ago we received Mothers letter with Franks photograph. We were very glad to get the boys photographs, and will be equally pleased when we get Father and Mothers and Stellas. When are they coming? Father, you have been working hard all summer, so pray take a little rest, and with Mother and Stella, take a jaunt up to

Fig. 9. Frank Kerr, photographed in his fifer uniform, joined the army in 1862 at age 17.

Pittsburgh. While there, call in at the best Artists saloon, and get us your pictures. The change will do you all good, and I know these days of suspense must be trying to you both. The trip will be a pleasure to you all, and Stella, I know, wants to see the smoky city. My first visit to it was, I remember, a great event in my young life. The iron horse will take you along without going to sleep, as we all did when we went with our old "gray."

It is now a little more than a month since we wrote to you. . . . Baby Willie is growing finely and is busy among his toys just now. He is beginning his troubles of teething, which makes him want a good deal of attention for a few days past. But as it will not be long until the cool weather comes, I hope he will get on well. We have had some very hard rains, that make the rice fields across the road look very pretty and green. We have had very few mangoes this year. Indeed, I have not seen one in the many groves around us; but the Judges wife has sent us some very delicious ones, that they had sent them from Lucknow. The trees do not bear every year abundantly.

Our old friend, Dr. Sherlock, now living in Etawah, has sent us a present of a nice buggy horse—an iron gray—that he used to drive himself when they lived here. A very nice present, was it not? A horse is a necessity in this country, if you want to save a Doctor Bill. We go out every evening now on our smooth level roads. We think nothing of going several miles in an evening. . . .

Rachel

My dear Brother Sam,

I was very glad to see your familiar fist, or at least, the work of it, this morning. I was glad too to hear that you and Frank were safe through the battle of Chancellorsville. But when I know that long ere this, you have probably been in many other engagements, it takes something away from my hearts ease. But I hope for the best. We will feel interested in your notes of the battle, and will hope to get them by and by. We see by telegram that Lee has marched across the river for an invasion of Penna. and Maryland. We hope that the Army of the Potomac will be able to give a good account of him. Jackson was a great loss to the Rebels. We see by our papers that the 2nd Corp (Couchs) did good service, and is checking the panic of Howard's Germans.[11] You did honor to your country. We rejoice in your bravery—Vicksburg holds out a long time. We thought several weeks ago, surely the next telegram will bring news of its fall; but (to quote Mr. Lincoln), "They are still pegging away." Your Company got off well, with only the loss of a finger and toe. We will feel anxious to hear of your own adventures.

We are quietly plodding on here in India, enjoying our day of peace. Seed sowing now, and praying for a speed harvest time. Our boys school is not so large now. My husband had to cut down expenses and we have fewer teachers. We hope to be able to keep the school from going down entirely, for the sake of our native Christian children and teachers. The later would then be out of employment, and it is hard to get any work for them here.

We are always so busy that the days glide away very fast, and time never seems to drag. Our boy is flourishing, rejoicing in short frocks, and soon I suppose the pant(ees) will follow. So time goes.

You will, I know, be glad to get home from the war. May God speed the day, and bring you home safely and spare you for better things. I

11. Stonewall Jackson was fatally wounded by his own men at Chancellorsville on May 2, 1863. Darius Nash Couch was the commander of the Second Federal Corps. O. O. Howard, commander of the Eleventh Corps, took the brunt of Jackson's attack on May 1 at Chancellorsville.

must leave room for a few words to Frank. As this is a family letter you must be content with your share of the crumbs. Goodbye, with love.

Affectionately, Sister Rachel

Well my dear brother Frank,

Thanks for your two pages received this morning, and yourself by last mail—or all that was left of you, after going through so many batterings on your journey over. You look a little thin, but very natural. We were much pleased to see you in your regimentals. We have several carte de visits now, and not the least prized are my soldier boys. You were very happy in being able to minister to the wants of others after the battle, and in not needing that care yourself. What harrowing sights must meet the eye after a battle. My heart always sickens at the details, but how much more horrible the sights of suffering and anguish must be.

Just now a syce [stableman or groom] led up to our door the little gray mare that Dr. Sherlock has sent us. The man says he has been 7 days on the way down from Etawah. Mr. Scott of Futtehgurh had lent us his, while he is at the hills. It seems a long way to borrow a horse of your friend, more than 100 miles distant, doesnt it? But we think nothing of distances now, when we have got so far round the world.

Our Reader has brought his wife home. She is a nice looking woman, very young. They came over to see us next day, and brought a large plate full of sweetmeats.

Munshi Qasim Ali is now reading or translating with my husband. Mr. Johnson has explained to him about mills in America that grind flour. You know the women have to grind it here in a little hand mill, daily, as they want it. Qasim amused us by proposing that we should get one sent out for the native Christians. He says it would be a very good thing. But the cost of one rather astounds him, in comparison with the cost of two round stones. . . .

But I am so very lazy, the days so very hot, and my space is so very small, I must say goodbye. The Lord keep you!

Ever affectionately,
Sister R. L. Johnson

Futtehpore, India
August 21st, 1863

My dear Mother,

We have just received our home papers, so I suppose there will be no home letters this mail, for they always come a little before the papers. You will know how anxious we feel to hear from the boys, seeing that the 2nd corps took such a prominent part in the battle of Gettysburg. They have done nobly and earned a glorious name for their bravery and valor.

But alas, what fearful sacrifice of gallant lives. How anxiously we wait to hear of our dear ones there. God grant that they are spared! I see that General Zook is among the gallant fallen, and Hancock wounded. From the position of the 2nd corp, they must have lost sadly. We think, and talk, and feel as much interest in the progress of our armies, as though we were not on the other side of the world. We are rejoiced by the news of the fall of Vicksburg, and Port Hudson, and Rosecranz victories in Tennessee, and Lees repulse.[12] We begin to hope that the end is soon coming. . . .

We are now enjoying the rainy season. We had one rainfall a few days ago that exceeded any thing I have seen in India; for three days and nights the rain poured down incessantly. I do not think it stopped a minute. The railway Station Masters wife had a little baby born on one of those rainy days, and as she was quite alone and friendless, I went over often to see her. Her little babe only lived 3 days in great suffering, and it seemed very hard for the poor woman to have no one to stay with her but a native woman who she could not talk to. She has a nice little boy about 8 years old, and he is all of her three that is left now.

September 15th

Mother, this letter is very slow getting off, but I could not get it ready for last mail, so it has had 2 weeks to wait. We are all well now. Last week my husband had an attack of fever, that did him up for a few days; but he is well again, and preached yesterday.

Last Sabbath was our Communion season. We had Mr. Owen from Allahabad with us. He preached morning and afternoon in Hindustani, and at night in English. Mr. Johnson felt so badly in the morning, that he was obliged to come home. The rest of the day he had to stay in bed. He had such hard chills and fever.

Mr. Owen did not bring Mrs. Owen with him, but she hopes to come up in the cold weather. Perhaps we will all go out in tents when Mr. Johnson and Mr. Owen talk of going out through a neighboring district to preach. Of course we will go with them.

Baby Willie is still growing finely and has very few troubles as yet. But I think he begins to feel his teeth coming, for he wants to bite everything he gets. He has such good health, which is a great comfort and blessing. The mornings and evenings are a little cool, so I must get something warm for him to wear.

12. Brig. Gen. Samuel K. Zook was mortally wounded at Gettysburg on July 2, 1863. Winfield Scott Hancock was also seriously wounded at Gettysburg, but he survived to become the unsuccessful Democratic presidential candidate in 1880, losing to Garfield. William S. Rosecrans led successful Union army campaigns from Murfreesboro to Tullahoma, Tenn., in June 1863.

Our Catechist lost a nice, little babe, a year old, last week. He was ill about 3 weeks, the illness from teething. Rachel, our Catechist Jacobs wife, has been suffering from rheumatism for a long time, and thought she would try some native medicine. She got some that an old paragon of wisdom prescribed for her, and now she is so badly salivated that her teeth are all loose, and she finds his cure worse than the complaint.

Lucy came over a few nights ago with a bad pain in her side, and Mr. Johnson prescribed a mustard plaster. But she was afraid it would burn. However, we persuaded her to have one on, and kept her a little while, to give it a chance to burn, for fear she would take it off. Sulbi, the Readers wife, had fever, so she must have some quinine, etc. You see my husband has to minister a little to their bodily wants as well as spiritual wants. He will soon be qualified for a doctors degree.

The hard rain made sad havoc on our little church; the ground got so soft that the pillars of the veranda sunk, and part of one fell down. Another almost toppled over and had to be propped.

On the 11th of September we had a grand wedding in our Station. Judge Bolderos sister in law, Miss Wilson, was married to a rich banker, Mr. Parry, from Delhi. We were present, with some 12 other guests. They were married with the Church of England Service, with the ring and all the other forms. The bride looked very nice in her lace skirt, white silk bodice, bridal veil, and orange wreath. They were married at 5 in the evening, and we had a grand dinner at 8.—The English always call their principal meal, "dinner." And their dinner parties are always at night, 7 or 8 o'clock.—The bride received a good many nice presents from her rich friends: diamond rings, bracelets, broaches, watch chain, and a great many handsome things. The jewelry, made at Delhi, is very beautifully set, and the work very delicate.

This is a rainy Monday morning and we could not get out for a walk. I see pilgrims from the mela, or fair, at the Ganges straggling by. They are happy no doubt in the hope of another good work laid up as a claim on Ram for future happiness. Poor deluded creatures. May God speed the day when they will look from the Ganges to the blood of Christ alone to cleanse their guilty souls from sin.

Our missionaries at the Hills are somewhat improved in health, but we fear some of them will have to go home. Mrs. Fullerton writes that Mr. Fullerton feels a good deal discouraged about the prospect of his health being restored. She has another little son, and has been very slow in getting strong, but is better.

Now I must run off and see about some breakfast, before I write any more. . . .

Your affectionate daughter,
Rachel L. Johnson

P.S. Kisses from Baby.

Futtehpore, India
Sept. 19th, 1863

Dear Sister Stella,

... Our baby Willie grows so fast, and gets up every morning at 5 o'clock to go out with his papa and mama to get the cool fresh air. Then when we come in, he gets a bath in a large tub full of water, which he thinks fine fun. He kicks, and crows, and laughs. Then after he is dressed, he gets his breakfast, and goes to sleep and sleeps a good while. Then when the little girls come to school, he goes too. He is much pleased to be with the little girls. He pulls their muslin veils off their heads, which makes them feel very much ashamed, for they think they ought to keep their head covered as much as their bodies. His papa got a little wagon made for him, and Maryann and Georgy often pull it for him. This generally makes him so sleepy, that he forgets all about school and goes to sleep. Do you ever get sleepy at school?

Your affectionate sister,
Rachel

Futtehpore, India
October 21st, 1863

Dear Brother Frank,

We were sorry to hear that you had been an inmate of the hospital, but hope you have, long ere this, got quite well again. You must be very careful about what you eat, if you have a tendency to dysentery. Be temperate in all things. If you have been on a long march, and are very thirsty, dont drink all you want. Wait until you cool off. If you have been very hungry, and come across a feast of fruits, melons or vegetables, dont eat all you want. Put the last half away for another time. These stomachs of ours are like our backs, they wont be imposed on by too heavy a load, and especially if it is a kind of load they have not been used to. But I am not a doctor, so I will not tender much advice—although, unlike theirs, mine is gratis. I will only say, boys, be careful of your health. Without it you cannot do much towards helping brother Jonathan out of his troubles, and I think one more long pull—a strong pull, and a pull all together—and the old Union will be righted, the Secesh overboard, then, "Hail Columbia, Happy Land."

But we want not only the Union saved, but we want the dear boys who have battled so bravely, and long too, to be saved to enjoy the good time coming. You have been waiting long, but we hope that with the dawn of the New Year, a brighter day will dawn for the good, old Union. So my dear brother, I would say, keep in good heart. The clouds begin to scatter. Are not the victories of Vicksburg, Port Hudson, Gettysburg,

Charleston (we take this for granted, as Fort Sumpter has fallen),[13] and East Tennessee, but glimpses of sunshine that herald the coming, clear, bright day, when the stars and stripes will again wave over the land from Maine to California, with no traitor to pull them down. We will hope on. The Hand that guides the helm knows the best time, and we must wait cheerfully.

Now Frank, I would you could come away over the ocean to a quiet corner of India, where there is no war; where the days are quiet, sunny days, and now for months, not even a storm will disturb their quiet repose. The bright, cool days are coming on. I cannot but wish you had our winter for camp life, for it is delightful—no mud, no sleet, no freezing rain, no soft snow flakes. It would be nice to have the snow, but for the rest, it is more comfortable without it in camp.

We expect to take our tents and go out in the district during the cold weather, visiting the villages where the glad news of a Savior has never come. Mr. and Mrs. Owen expect to go with us, and we hope to have a pleasant change. You will hear all about this when we go, so I will tell you about something that has happened.

The other day, when we were eating our dinner, the air was suddenly darkened with a great cloud of locusts. We left the table and went out on the veranda. There, over to the Northeast, was a great dark cloud moving on toward us. Soon the air was a full of great red locusts, as ever you saw it of flakes in a snow storm. Some stopping with us, and those higher up, moving on. The ground and trees looked quite red, and was literally covered with them. The native boys and girls were out running and shouting like school boys when the snow first comes. Some, with sticks and cloths and baskets, were beating them, and stowing them away in bags and baskets for roasting and eating, or for making a curry of. Henry, who has a large garden near by, was building little fires to smoke them off his vegetables. Some more natives were running here and there beating tin pans and shouting, to keep them from settling on the things. On they came in clouds. Mr. Johnson walked out across the yard, and at every step, a cloud of them rose up about his feet. Thus they came in millions, for about 2 hours, until everything was covered with them; yet the air was full of those passing on that did not stop. I caught some in my hand, and I think they were near 3 inches long, and quite red.

Dr. Sheetz and Mr. Anderson had some made into a curry, and said they tasted very nice, but we did not try their virtues. I would prefer something else. The natives roasted them in great numbers. They passed on a few miles, and stopped for the night among some cotton

13. This was a mistaken conclusion of Rachel's. Throughout the summer of 1863, Union forces attacked Fort Sumter, but the fort was not captured, nor was Charleston.

fields. They destroyed a good deal of that precious article, but the planters say that the plant was so young, that they hope it will sprout again, and that there will at least be half a crop.

Now dear Frank, I have devoted so much space to the locust family, that I have not much room left for the Johnson family. My husband goes out some times with a Catechist and Reader to the villages that are scattered about 3 miles of Futtehpore. They preach to them, read the Book of Books, and they gather around them to listen; but, as yet, they cling to their idols. Some are Muhammadans, and they think they worship the true God, and Muhammad is as good a prophet as the Savior. So they reject the only Savior who can save them from their sins. The Hindoos are generally more kindly disposed, and willing to listen; but alas, how often does the Missionary come home with the sad, "Who hath believed our report?" "They are joined to their idols." But we know that the heathen will be given to the Lord in his own good time. Pray for us dear brothers, that we may be faithful laborers, that we may do what we can to hasten that blessed day. Dear Frank, I trust that you are trying to live near the Saviour in camp, or wherever you are. . . .

Now I have only a corner to say goodbye. With our united love to you and kind regards to any of our friends in the Army.

Your affectionate sister,
Rachel L. Johnson

A Merry Christmas and Happy New Year.

Futtehpore, India
October 21st, 1863

My dear brother Sam,

We were glad to get some notes of your march in our last letter from home, received 2 weeks ago. We felt very anxious to hear from you after Gettysburg, and were so thankful to hear that you were both safe. It must have been very trying on you, making such long marches, especially with sore feet. We do begin to feel some hopes that the war is coming to an end; for surely the rebels cannot hold out much longer. God speed the day. . . . Keep a brave heart and bear a cheerful hand, for the good old ship is coming round, and you will share the honor of helping to right her. The eyes of the world are watching, to see whether indeed liberty has cradled sons who will prove staunch in storm, as well as sunshine.

. . . Where are you now, and do you think Lee will make another attempt to take Washington? Our Indian papers still cherish the forlorn hope that Lee will take Washington. The papers here are very Secesh in their tastes, and hold out, that in spite of all our northern victories, the South will not be much hurt, if the northern armies do take Charleston, Savannah, Mobile and a few other strongholds. Jeff Davis is even more sensible than these English blockheads. But I must not wax warm over their blundering stupidity, for we have given up punkas, and sent our punka pullers away, so it is proper to keep cool these days.

By the way, you have had some very hot weather, and I suppose felt it far more than we do the heat here, for we are prepared for it. Now let me give you a hint about marching in the sun—as learned from customs in India. Here no one goes out in the sun with a common felt or straw hat, without a long piece of thin white muslin wound several times round and over the crown. Thin, to be light, and white, as it does not absorb the suns rays. Now if you boys would to this on a march, there would be far less danger of sun stroke, and your head would be far cooler. Try it. In hot countries this is universally the custom. The native does the same, except that he has no hat, and winds the muslin round and over his head into a pretty picturesque turban.

But I forget that when this reaches you, it will be winter. Well this will keep until another summer, and you instead can remember to save all your newspapers to put over your blanket, which is said to be equal to another blanket.

If any of you boys have trouble with your big toe nails growing into the flesh after so many hard tramps, dont forget what "Dr. Hall" says in his journal of "Health." Dont clip off the corners, but cut a notch in the middle, and the ends will soon grow right. Now Sam, you will think maybe that these are very practical remarks about very little things, but our comfort is made up of just such little trifles.

Now dear brother, I will come back to India. We are just getting our first taste of the cold weather and right glad of it. We hope soon to go out itinerating, but perhaps not until after the Annual Meeting at Futtehgurh next month. We all feel quite brisk now in these cool mornings and evenings.

I was amused yesterday evening to see a great elephant shuffling along making a sad attempt at a run. Whether he felt cold, and was afraid of getting the rheumatism in one of those great legs, or a cold in his chest (trunk), which was more exposed, I cannot say. But he was getting over the ground sharp, from some cause. A little after too, I saw a camel mounted by a red turbaned policeman come rollicking along at a brisk trot. I thought from the jolting that man got, perched on the top of that hump, I would rather feel like giving "sir hump" a twitch of that rope that was fastened in his nose, until he was content to move his soft pads a little slower. Our little gray does not like meeting these ungainly creatures, and politely gives the road to them.

Young Master Willie still flourishes finely, and today rejoices in having completed 8 months. He is fat, hearty, and very fond of books and newspapers, and has no objection to pulling out a lock of hair, when he gets the chance. His own locks are very thin yet, only enough for one little curl on top of his head. He sends his salam to Uncle Sam, and hopes he will some day have the pleasure of knowing him. . . .

> Ever your affectionate sister,
> Rachel L. Johnson

[In November 1863, Will received the news that he had been reassigned to the mission station in Fatehgarh. Although Will and Rachel had hoped initially to go to Fatehgarh to take his brother Albert's place, they were now reluctant to leave their first mission home, community, and church in Fatehpur. But Will was prepared to go where his colleagues felt he would be most useful, so he took over the responsibilities of managing the boys' school and the Christian village at Rakha.]

> Futtehpore, India
> December 7, 1863

My dear Friends,

You will no doubt be surprised to hear by our letters of this mail, that we are to be transferred to Futtehgurh. You will not be more surprised than we were a week ago, when the matter was first broached to us. We went from here on the 21st of November to attend the Annual Meeting at Futtehgurh, of which perhaps Rachel has told you something. We had rather a hard trip in getting there, but the meeting itself was about the most pleasant one I have ever attended of any kind. We left Futtehgurh on Wednesday afternoon to return and reached this on Thursday morning, about 20 hours travel. Lillie and Willie had bad colds, otherwise we came back all well.

The reason of our promotion to this new place, is on this wise: J. L. Scott—one of our oldest and best missionaries—has for many years been stationed at Rakha, which is the large Christian village of Futtehgurh. It is considered on many accounts as one of the most important and responsible positions in our Mission field. His health failed last year, and very unexpectedly to me, he last week asked to have leave to resign his position there, which was too laborious for him. This was granted. After a long discussion, during which many plans were suggested and disapproved of, it was at last unanimously decided that we ought to go and take the vacant place.

Two years ago I should have been glad to go there. The surroundings of the families there are much more comfortable than elsewhere, and there are two of our other Mission families at Barhpur, only three miles away. One can have pleasant society occasionally. It was the scene too, of Alberts short labors, and he and Walsh built that fine church at Rakha—

Fig. 10. The church at Rakha, the Christian village outside of Fatehgarh, was built by J. Johnston Walsh and Albert Johnson, among others, and was served by Will Johnson from 1864 to 1870. The Rakha community gathered for this photo taken in the 1860s.

which is shown in Walsh's book—and I should have preferred to go there. I told my brethren that I had gone to Futtehpore rather unwilling, or at least very much against my views of what was proper and fitting. At that time it was acknowledged to be an exceedingly difficult post, and I then knew scarce a word of the language. But, I had gone there, and after some severe labor at first, and set things to rights, and was now very comfortable and very happy there. I was attached to the place, and did not wish to leave it. But I did not intend to set up my wishes against the decision of the Mission. While expressing my preference to be left alone, I was at the same time ready to go wherever they thought I would be most useful. So it was decided that I should go to the new station in January, and that Brother Sayre should take my old place.

I look forward with considerable hesitation and trembling to the increased care and responsibility of that important post. But He who has hedged my way round, so that I could not avoid going there, will give me strength to do what is required of me.

We have just heard of more movements of the Armies of Lee and Meade, accompanied by some fighting and much hard marching.[14] We are always anxious after these reports until we hear of the safety of the dear boys.

We are sorry to hear of Rosecranz removal. We think him, over here, one of your very best Generals; though he may not have done so well at Chickamauga as elsewhere.[15] We think the time of fearing any war with England has gone past. She hates the North still, but she is fast getting to hate the South still more.

Our new Governor General here, Lord Elgin, has just died. He was a fine man. I believe it is not yet known who will be his successor.

I presume Rachel has told you what little news there is to give. My kind regards to all who remember me.

Yours ever—W. F. Johnson

14. Gen. George G. Meade replaced Hooker as Union commander on June 28, 1863. The armies fought for three days, July 1–3, after which the Confederates, under Lee, withdrew. Meade cautiously followed, but the Confederates were able to cross the Potomac on July 13–14, much to Lincoln's anger.

15. Rosecrans was defeated at Chickamauga, Ga., on Sept. 20, 1863; he was replaced by Gen. George Thomas on Oct. 20.

February 1864–August 1865

FATEHGARH

c⅓ DEPARTING FROM FATEHPUR in November 1863, Rachel, Will, and Willie, together with several fellow missionaries and Indian readers, took their first extended preaching tour through surrounding villages. They took a southern loop and traveled eighty miles in three weeks. The missionaries usually walked, prepared to talk with any small gathering they found along the way, while the women and children rode in dak garis to the next campsite eight or ten miles down the road. The servants walked or traveled by ox cart with the tents and supplies. Like a traveling, small-town carnival in America, the entourage stayed in each campsite for two or three days before moving on to their next stop. These camp tours were refreshingly adventurous and social times for the missionary families. The children played with their playmates and the wives visited endlessly with good friends, who shared their language, values and heritage. It was a rewarding experience for the missionaries also; they were encouraged by the attentiveness the village residents showed, either out of curiosity or sincere interest, in the preaching of these itinerant messengers.

After their tent tour and the annual meeting in November 1863, Will, Rachel, and Willie moved into their new home in Fatehgarh in January 1864 full of hope and anticipation. When Will was originally assigned to Fatehgarh in November, there were to be two missionaries in that station, as there had been in the past, but circumstances had changed. Since monies were so tight, new missionaries had not been coming to India to replace those on leave or retirement. By February there were only six missionaries for seven stations, where nine had served before. Again Will prepared to serve alone in his new assignment in Fatehgarh. In a report to the Board of Foreign Missions on February 18, 1864, Will reported that "men are breaking under the work." With a note of satire, he added, "Perhaps indeed the Millenium is about commencing and the harvest of the world is henceforth to be gathered <u>without</u> laborers."

In a July 11, 1864, letter Will responded to an apparent question from the Board regarding the gloomy reports coming from their district. Will wrote that the missionaries understood the drain of the war, but, "the Church must not get the idea that all is progressing finely. She ought to know that as soon as the home struggle is over, there is a great work here to be done—which is all this while awaiting her convenience." This report was in contrast to most reports the Board had received. "Few missionaries of this period would admit to a sense of discouragement; to do so would have been to deny their confidence in God's power to change the hearts and minds of men."[1]

In every letter Rachel expressed grave concern for their families and the progress of the war in America. She expressed great frustration in the delayed delivery of news from home. In their latest news, Sam had been promoted to captain and was considering staying in the army as a career, much to Rachel's concern, as she had been urging him to consider joining them as a missionary. Frank was at Harpers Ferry and was planning to get out of the army after the war to continue his education. This was not Frank's first choice, however. He had been recommended to President Lincoln for appointment as a cadet to West Point, but Frank was still a minor, and his parents withheld their consent.]

Futtehgurh, India
February 5th, 1864

My dear Father and Mother,

Moving is not half as nice as I used to fancy it was when I was a little girl. It will be some time before we get our house in order yet, but will begin as soon as the Scotts get their packing done. We have a nice, comfortable house and a beautiful garden, and will, I hope, find Futtehgurh a very pleasant place. It is considered one of the healthiest stations in this part of India. The weather has been quite cold since we came up here, and we have had fire every day. We burn wood, as coal is very scarce in India. Wood is expensive too, for trees are precious, but we need fire a very small part of the year. For cooking we use charcoal.

We are expecting Dr. Morrison, one of our old Missionaries who has just returned from America (the same one who was Moderator of the General Assembly) with Mr. and Mrs. Henry, new Missionaries. They are on their way up to their station in the Punjab. We want very much to keep Mr. Henry here in Futtehgurh, but they want him badly in the upper Mission. So we do not expect that we will get him.

Mr. Fullerton has gone to Dehra—which is near the Hills—in Mr. Herrons place, who is obliged to go home with his motherless, little ones. Mrs. Herron died about two months ago. Mr. Fullerton hopes to be able to remain here longer, now that he has been placed at a hill station.

1. James P. Alter, "Presbyterians in Farrukhabad, 1838–1915," 1.

But his health is uncertain. We feel that Mr. Sayre will be obliged to go home, on account of his wife. This will be bad, for he has just begun to preach in Hindustani, and to be able to work. We hope she will get well enough to remain.

Mr. Johnson has not been well for a few days past. He had a slight attack of fever, which has made him feel quite used up, since Saturday; but he is better today, and thinks he has got rid of the fever. He has just gone to the funeral of a little child of one of the native Christians.

Willie is creeping around, climbing up by the chairs, tumbling down and bumping his head; stealing his papas hat and sitting down on it, pulling out the lining; and getting into all sorts of mischief. He is a great little busybody, and has to be watched every minute, or he is getting into trouble. He has four teeth and more coming, I think, very soon. They have not troubled him very much yet, but the dear boy will have a harder time I fear in the hot weather when his double teeth come. We tried to get his picture taken for you in Allahabad, but did not succeed in getting a good one. So we will have to wait until some artist comes to Futtehgurh.

We have not heard from you since November but this mail will surely bring a letter. We are rejoiced to hear from the telegram that there is a prospect of peace. We only fear that the news is too good to be true. The cotton speculators get up so many canards.[2]

Our roses are all in bloom Mother. And there are some little peach trees in the garden covered with blossoms.

We were glad to hear that Frank had got into such a good place in Frederick City, and that Samuel was climbing up through the ranks to a higher place. I hope the dear boys are both well, and all the rest of you. Stella, I suppose, is going to school, and Father and you keeping things straight at home. . . .

> Your affectionate daughter,
> Rachel L. Johnson

> Futtehgurh, India
> February 22nd, 1864

My dear Brothers,

I was intending to send you a little journal of our itinerating tour in tents from Futtehpore to the old fort of Kaliujur, in Bandelcund; but I

---

2. The false or unfounded reports by the cotton speculators were probably based on wishful thinking. With the South cut off by the Northern navy, the British mills turned to India as a chief source of cotton. Cotton growing thrived in India during the Civil War but rapidly declined after the war, since the cotton fibers of India were shorter, and less desirable, than those grown in America. Robert A. Divine et al., *America, Past and Present,* 431–33.

have been so busy, that I cannot get it ready for today's mail. So instead, I will write you a few lines to acknowledge the receipt of letters from you by the mail 2 weeks ago.

We were glad to hear that you are both so well and doing so well. Since that time the Army of the Potomac has doubtless seen more hard work, but I hope it may please God to spare your lives and bring you back home safe again.

You will see by my date that we have anchored in another port. We now hail from Futtehgurh, the "fort of Victory," instead of Futtehpore, "the city of Victory."

We came here on the 14th of January to take the Scotts place at Rakha. Our Mission here, like in Allahabad, is located in two places, about $2\frac{1}{2}$ miles apart. Rakha, the station near the town of Futtehgurh, is the largest Christian Village. There is a great deal to do here, looking after so many schools, etc., but it is one of our most interesting and pleasant stations. The other station, where the Brodheads are now placed, is near the city of Furrukhabad. There are not so many native Christians there, but the Missionary there has charge of the large city school, etc. There are two missionaries there generally, and their houses are in the same lot or compound.

Mr. and Mrs. Scott, with their little ones, will leave for Landour on Thursday next. Mr. Scott has been in India a little over 25 years, so he is beginning to break down; but hopes to be able to stay 2 or 3 years longer at the Hills, before he goes home.

Dr. Morrison was with us part of last week. It was pleasant to see somebody just from America. He has been absent in America and England, just as long as we have been in India. We met him on his way home, just after our arrival in Allahabad. He had a great deal to tell us about the state of things at home, as they seemed to him after his long while in India. All his children are now in America. His wife sleeps her last sleep in Cawnpore, where she died of smallpox, when they were on their way home. So he goes back to his work alone. It seemed sad to look upon his white hair, and think how thrice lonely he will feel when he goes back to his deserted and lonely home to labor on alone.

Now my dear brother, I fear you will think this sheet a very little one, but I do think the next will be larger—so hope on—and send us big ones to encourage us.

Master Willie has just celebrated his birthday. He attained to the dignity of his first year yesterday, the 21st. He stands alone, and makes a great effort to walk, but wants a little help yet. He is full of mischief, and often comes to grief through his exploring propensities; but gets on very well through all his little troubles. We are all well and enjoying the cold weather.

The last mail brings no special news about the war, but as the President says, "I suppose you are pegging away," and we will hear of the end soon. I hope Frank, you will be able to stay in Frederick City. You seem to have met a good place. And Samuel, we were glad to hear of your promotion—"Many returns of the same!"

. . . Now Goodbye. With our united love.

Your Affectionate sister,
Rachel L. Johnson

[Rachel's bright, happy accounts of Willie's development took an abrupt change when he developed bronchial pneumonia. After five weeks of suffering, Willie died on April 6, 1864. In all likelihood Willie died of malaria, for in the nineteenth century malaria was frequently misidentified and treated as influenza and was a great ravager of infants and children. Rachel and Will's worry and then grief was understandably profound, as evident in this letter from Will to his sister, Maggie Blakesley.]

Futtehgurh, India
March 19th, 1864

My dear Sister,

You must not expect much of a letter from me today as poor little Willie is lying very low with bronchial pneumonia. For more than a week, our hopes of his recovery have been but trembling hopes at the best. Sometimes he seems better, and again worse. Once the inflammation went to his head, he grew very rapidly worse. The Doctor, just then coming in, was able to check this. Poor boy. He is so patient. He has had a blister on his head, and two on his breast, and much of the time linseed poultices on his chest every hour of the day and night. The Brodheads are very kind, and help us to sit up every night, but loss of sleep is very trying in this climate. This is Willie's first spell of sickness, and it is a very hard one. It will be a very hard trial if we have to give him up.

Mr. Wyckoff has just come over from Mynpurie today to see and help us. Mrs. Johnson is feeling pretty well—though, of course, much worn out.

There is no news of importance. This country seems very quiet now that Europe and America seem all ablaze with war and rumor of war.

Please send this half sheet to David Kerr, Esq., Hookstown, Pa., as Mrs. Johnson will not be able to write them by this mail.

Sincerely, your Brother,
W. F. Johnson

Futtehgurh, India
April 5th, 1864

My dear Father and Mother,

We received our home mail yesterday—letters from Father, Sam, Frank. We were glad to hear that you are all now well, and hope that you dear Mother, will have no more trouble with your throat. Diphtheria must be a very painful disease. Stella is fortunate in getting over the measles now, while she is so young. I thought they were bad enough as I had them. The boys too are getting on so well, which is cheering news. I hope Samuel was able to run over home as he expected. Frank is sensible in denying himself furlough, however pleasant it would be for him, at the risk of losing such a good situation. We are sorry to hear of the death of so many of our old friends.

You will perhaps have heard by last mail of the illness of our dear babe. . . . Since that time, poor Willie has been a great sufferer. I hoped that we would have more cheering news to write before this mail, but there seems to be little change for the better as yet. 5 weeks ago he took a cold in some way, I cant tell how. At first it seemed to be nothing serious, but as he got to coughing hoarsely in a few days, we called the doctor in. Now for 4 weeks, he has faithfully attended twice a day. The cold settled in his lungs, and he has had a distressing cough that sometimes almost threw him into spasms. Indeed, one night he had several. The disease developed itself in what the doctor calls bronchial pneumonia. He has had three blisters on his breast at different times, and then when his head seemed in danger, the doctor put one on the back of his neck. After this had relieved his head, and got well, the doctor had to put on another. This is still sore. Then we poulticed his chest for more than a week at times. He has been salivated too, and is now, I think, on the point of it again, as his mouth seems to be getting sore again.

Now for 4 weeks, day and night, we have watched over our darling child, through all his sufferings, with what heartaches and agony of suspense you will know. Days full of hopes and fears, sometimes cheered for a little time with the hope that he was taking a turn for the better. Our hearts are full of bitterness at the thought of losing our dear little Willie, whose loving ways have so twined about our hearts, and made him the pet of all who knew him. He was always willing to make friends with everyone, and this made him a favorite with everyone.

Willie was just beginning to try to walk alone. He would get up alone in the middle of the floor, stand a little while, and sit down without help. Sometimes his little heart found courage to toddle on a step or two, but it will now be long before the thin little legs will be strong enough again—if God in his mercy does spare him to us.

His cough is now much better. The Doctor says the inflammation in his chest is decreasing; but he still has some fever every day, and we are anxious about his head—keeping cold applications to it all the time. For some days and nights he has had no sleep scarcely, but yesterday, and last night, he slept almost all the time. Today he sleeps a good deal, but wakes once in awhile and takes a little nourishment. We hope he is a little better, though very weak and low.

This has been a heavy trial to us, but our Heavenly Father has mingled mercy with our affliction. He has graciously given us health and strength for all our watchings over our dear child all these weeks, and given us sympathizing friends to help us. Mr. and Mrs. Brodhead have come every night, to share the care and watching. They could have done no more for their own, and they have been very kind and faithful. We have a kind, attentive physician, and skillfull too. But we know that only the Great Physician can bless the means used, and restore our child. On Him we strive to cast our burden. We know that "He doeth all things well." Oh for grace to say from a willing heart, "Thy will be done."

Now I cannot dear Father and Mother, write you more at this time. Our hearts are very heavy, and full of anxiety, but we must leave all our ways in God's hands. He will not afflict us above that we are able to bear, if we commit our way unto Him. . . . Hoping that the next mail will bring you better tidings of us all, and I hope then to write to the boys too, and Stella.

> With our united love to you all,
> Your affectionate daughter,
> Rachel L. Johnson

P.S. The war you see mentioned in your papers was some disturbance among the Himalaya tribes and is over long ago.

> Futtehgurh, India
> April 8th, 1864 (Friday)

My dear Mother,

With a heart full of grief, and eyes full of tears, I come to you my darling Mother, to tell you of our first great sorrow—the loss of our beloved little one—our darling Willie, that has been the light of our home for only little more than one short year. I wrote to you a few days ago all the particulars of his long illness. Though at that time my heart was full of forebodings, yet there was still so much of hope mingled, that I had not yet realized that God was, indeed, so soon to take him from us.

Indeed, on Tuesday night (I wrote the letter on Tuesday) while I was watching with our darling, I felt more hopeful than I had for several days. He was very weak and had taken little nourishment for several days, but while I was with him, he nursed very well several times. As his disease seemed subdued, I thought there was every hope that he would rally from his weakness. But about 5 in the morning, there seemed a change for the worse. His pulse became very weak, and he seemed sinking. He lingered only till 9 o'clock, when, with scarcely a struggle, the little spirit burst through its bonds of clay. While we wept over the dear, little, earthly form we knew, a little angel was born in Heaven. Willie was safe in our Saviours bosom. Our loss is his gain.

Lovely in his life, he was no less lovely in his death—a sweet smile, full of peace and rest, settled over the dear, little face, as though he would still speak comfort to our smitten hearts. At sunset, dear little Willie was laid in his grave, to sleep till Jesus calls him. Now with hearts full of grief, we are left to realize the desolation of our home without our darling.

You dear Mother, know the bitterness of such a loss, and can feel for us. How the heart keeps half expecting him, forgetting that he is not here. How everything speaks of him: his little toys, his little shoes, his little clothes, his little empty bed; the little birds that came on the veranda that he used to call—stretching out his little hand, beckoning them to him in the garden; the flowers that he loved. In one corner grew a bunch of little white lilies that he always seemed to care more for than all the rest of the flowers. The last time he was out in the garden, they were in full bloom. Now they too, like him, have passed away. We looked to see if one was left, but they are all withered and dead. Wherever we go, we miss him.

We have never felt grief like this grief. But in the midst of all our bitter sorrow comes the sweet thought that though he can not come to us, yet we shall go to him. This sad affliction comes from our Father's hand, and we know He doeth all things well. There is mercy no doubt in it all, and though now, in the first bitterness of our grief, blinded by our tears, we may not be able to see the light. Yet, He who has broken, can also heal. God grant that it may be sanctified to our souls. Now that the Good Shepherd has taken our lamb to his fold, may it be the means of leading us to follow more closely.

Dear Willie, his sweet and winning ways will always live in our hearts. How we wish you could have known and loved him too. What a comfort it would have been if we could have had you dear Mother and Father, with us in our affliction. But God did not leave us friendless. Mr. and Mrs. Brodhead were with us every night during all Willies illness, sharing our watchings, and doing all that could be done by sympathizing hearts. They too have felt the bitter trial of losing their first born—a little boy, 9 months old. He too died here in <u>this house</u>, while they were here on their way to Mynpurie, their first station. He died of smallpox, and they had to bear their burden <u>alone</u>, and see their little one suffer and die from a very loathsome disease. As Mr. Brodhead told us, we had much to be thankful for, that our little one was such a comfort through all his illness; that we could look back with only pleasant memories of his sweet face, sad as they are. Our two dear ones sleep near each other in the little Mission graveyard, just a little way from here, a short walk. It is a privilege to have them near us, and Futtehgurh will now always be linked to our hearts by a strong tie, for here sleeps our little Willie.

May 31st

My dear Father and Mother,

... When the next mail came, we were in Mynpurie with the Wyckoffs—whither we had gone to stay a few days, hoping a change would do us good, after our sad watchings and bereavement. We stayed a week, and came home again to our work. . . .

I told you that we had tried to get a likeness of dear little Willie for you when we were in Allahabad, but as we did not succeed in getting a good one, we did not keep it. After he was taken from us, we wrote to see if we could not get the one he had taken in Allahabad; for we felt that anything that resembled him in the least, would be very precious to us now. The artist had fortunately kept one of the impressions, and from it we had a few copies taken, one of which we send you enclosed in this letter. Although it gives you but little idea of what a sweet lovely child Willie was, yet it is something like him, and will help you realize that there was a little Willie. He was sitting on my knee, and as we were obliged to sit outside in the glare of the sun, I could not look at the camera all with my eyes open; and Willie, you see, has his head down. He is looking up under his eyebrows. His teeth too were troubling him, so he has his under lip all drawn in, as he kept biting his lip to ease them. But withal, he was laughing and crowing very happily, and I could scarcely hold him still on my knee to get a picture taken. But although this is not such a picture as we would have wished to have of our little darling, it is precious. For it is all that we have left of him save that other that will ever live down in our hearts, and come back in our memory. I know you will be glad to have something of him. Here is one little lock too of his hair. At first it was dark, but it had grown lighter as you see.

Now I must close this letter. I cannot write to you of other things now. . . .

Your affectionate daughter,
Rachel Johnson

[A month and a half later, Will wrote the following happy announcement to his mother-in-law and family in Hookstown.]

Futtehgurh, India
July 14th, 1864

My dear Mother Kerr,

I have some good news for you—at least it is a very pleasant affair to us. We doubt not you too will be glad to hear of it. On Sabbath night, the 10th, we had a little daughter born to us. We have employed a Mrs. Montgomery to attend on Lillie, until she gets able to be up. Rachel and the baby are both getting on very nicely.

We have had, for a month or so, almost unprecedented hot weather. The thermometer generally standing at 96–98 degrees, all day and all night. The rains, which should have set in a month ago, only began last week; since which time however, it has been comparatively cool.

We hope, if all is well, to spend much of the ensuing cold weather in a tour, among the villages of this district, to carry the Gospel to them in their homes. We, with our dear friends, the Brodheads, expect to take carts and tents, and march by short stages over to Etawah, to attend the Annual Meeting in November. We will go via Mynpurie, and the Wyckoffs will join us there. This will make a month of preaching. After we come back, we are talking of getting a large boat, and spending a month in sailing up and down the Ganges, preaching at the numerous villages on the banks. There are only plans however, and how often the best laid plans fail.

You have heard, no doubt, of the sad news from the Lodiana Mission. Two of our very best missionaries have fallen by the hands of natives. First Brother Janvier was beaten to death by a fanatical Sikh, for some fancied injury received from some European. The Sikh has been hanged, I believe. Then Brother Lowenthal was shot in the night, by his own night watchman—intentionally it is thought, but this could not be proved on the trial. In Peshawar, thieves are very bad, and the watchmen carry guns. If they see any one prowling about, they challenge him. If he cannot account for himself, they fire. Lowenthal was accustomed to take a walk about the house and verandah in the night, and the man seeing him, fired without a challenge. These things give us no uneasiness, for they would just be as likely to happen anywhere, as here. And even if there were danger, why should not the Missionary be as ready to face death for Christ, as our patriot soldiers are to face it for their country.

I am sending you, through my sister, a photograph of the place we are now living in Rakha. This is one of the pleasantest missions homes to be found anywhere. The house is large and very comfortable. As it now is, it was rebuilt with "Mutiny Compensation Funds" received from the Government. The grounds are beautiful, and the garden excellent. We have had an abundance of apples, peaches, grapes, mangoes, plantains, etc., from it. There is some fruit or other, all the year round.

We have just heard by telegraph of battle after battle before Richmond, and that Grant has pushed Lee back into the city, and crossed to the South of the James River.[3] We are much rejoiced at victory. But Oh! how anxious to hear of the continued safety of Samuel and Frank, both of whom we suppose to be with Grant. They are in God's hands however, and we trust he will bring them safely through all this terrible fighting.

Lillie sends love to all the dear ones at home.

Yours sincerely,
W. F. Johnson

Futtehgurh, India
August 13, 1864

My dear Sister Stella,

Your letter for our dear little Willie came, but dear Willie had gone to be an Angel in Heaven. Now you will never know him here, and I hope that we shall all one day meet, in that happy home, where our little Willie is now a happy, little angel. I was glad that we could get a picture of his sweet face to send, and hope you now have it safely in your album.

You have now another dear little one, who will someday, I hope, be able to say Aunt Stella—our dear little "Mary" which we think of naming her. As much of the name as Mother dont claim, will be for you. She is a good, little babe. She has pretty, blue eyes and a little cap of brown hair. She talks very loud when she is getting her bath and clean clothes on, but sleeps almost all day and night. When not hungry, she seems very content with herself and all the world.

It must be very nice to have Grandpa and Grandmother, so near, so that you can run over and see them often.[4] I would like to go over with you too, but the road is too long; so I can only send a message of love for them. Tell them we have not forgotten them, and would like to see them very much. . . .

How do you like going to school? I hope you are learning fast, and help Mother a great deal. How I would like to steal in quietly and surprise you all. It seems a long time since we left you. But though we

3. These references were to the Battles of the Wilderness, Spotsylvania, and Cold Harbor; the crossing of the James River; and the beginnings of the siege of Petersburg in May and June of 1864. On Mar. 12, 1864, Lincoln appointed Ulysses S. Grant General-in-Chief of the Union armies. Grant observed that for all the maneuvering and human losses sustained, the war was about where it had been three years earlier. Thus, with a much larger fighting force, he began a relentless campaign of attrition against Lee, which, at great cost, ended the war.

4. In the summer of 1864, when their farming days were done, Grandpaps and Grandmother Kerr moved into the old McFerran home, a sturdy brick house Rachel's father had built many years earlier in Hookstown.

would love best of all things to see you all, that would be the only thing that we would like to go home for someday. For we are very happy and content to live in India, and try to do something for the good of these poor heathen. . . .

Have you any singing schools or teachers to teach you to sing? What little playmates have you? What do you study at school? In our Girl's School, we have some little girls about 4 or 5 years old, and all sizes up to the first class, who are 16 or 17. There is one little blind girl, about your age. Her name is Niddia, and she has learned a great deal from listening to the other girls. She knows a great many hymns, and sings like a bird, though she cannot see any. She always seems happy and cheerful. How thankful we should be that our Father in Heaven has given us eyes that can see. Yet, how many forget to thank him for this good gift.

Dear Stella, now I must say Goodbye. A kiss from our little Mary and much love from us to you, dear Sister.

Your affectionate sister,
Rachel

Futtehgurh, India
August 12th, 1864

My dear brother Sam,

You will have heard by a former letter home, that you have a little niece now, a month old. So you will accept this piece of news as the apology for my not writing to you sooner. Last mail we were glad to find in our home letter, one from you too. I am glad you dont forget that you have a sister on the other side of the world who is always listening for news from the Army of the Potomac, with eager interest and affectionate longing, for tidings of "Lieutenants" Sam and Frank.

These have been days of suspense, since we read of the many battles in which the gallant 2nd corps has acted so noble a part. . . . Now I would like to have a long letter from you telling us what you saw, and what part you have borne in these bloody battles. Can you not tell us any personal incidents of those we know, for you will imagine with what deep interest we would read anything concerning the doings of the boys from dear, old Hookstown. . . .

We were very glad to get your likeness, and think it very good—much better, and more like you than the other. You say you would like to have ours, to see what changes 4 years have wrought. We will certainly try and send you one sometime. We have no artist here, but one may come along, or we may have an opportunity elsewhere. You would doubtless see some change. I think we are both much thinner than when we left home, but I do not think we are any darker—though we have spent 4 years amongst the dark, brown Hindoos.

We like Futtehgurh very much, though this has been a year of sad and bitter trial to us. It was but a little while after we came, that our darling boy was taken ill; then followed that month of agonizing suspense, while we watched by the little sufferer, and saw our hopes buried with our darling in the graveyard near by. Then followed these months of bitter bereavement, so that our short life here has been overshadowed by this much sorrow and sadness, that we have scarce realized that our home and surroundings are the most beautiful and cheerful for situations of all in our Mission. We are as comfortably situated as we could be anywhere.

A walk through our garden, under the shade of several large mangoes and along a path fringed with roses, out at a gate, and across a little grass plot, brings us to our neat, pretty-looking church. . . . The rebels destroyed all they could of it, but there was so little wood about, it could not be burnt down altogether. So they tore out the windows, and did all the damage possible. They tried to knock down the gilt ball from the top of the steeple, but it still stands triumphant, with only some round holes in its sides, that tell of the abortive attempts of the rebels. Here on Sabbath, and on Thursday evenings, is gathered a nice, respectable-looking congregation.

Starting out from home in an opposite direction, here, just across a large grassy yard, stands the Boy's School building, and the girls School (they are never taught together in schools here). Then back of these are some nice-looking, native houses, built something like our own, with verandas and flat roof, nicely whitewashed outside. These belong to some of our native Christians who have succeeded well in business, and are able to make themselves very comfortable. As we continue our walk, we find a large piece of ground enclosed and houses scattered about, some in rows and some alone. This is our Christian Village. Over these Mr. Johnson is placed as pastor, with full patriarchal powers. He cares for everything of a temporal nature which is referred to him to decide and control. There are perhaps 250 in the village now. Fancy the amount of patience required to guide and control all the little differences that would necessarily arise in any community of that size. Then remember that these have been surrounded all their lives by heathen influences, and some brought up in heathenism, and you will at once perceive how difficult the task must be to keep the scales of justice even. But we have among these some good, substantial men, who help to bear the burdens of the day and relieve Mr. Johnson of many of the little cares. Among the women too, there are many, very good, neat, and quiet ones, who exercise a very good influence over those who yet have a good deal of the old leaven in their hearts, that sometimes get them into quarrels and trouble.

One of the orphan girls was married two weeks ago to a young native Christian of the police in Mynpurie. My husband tied the knot. This is the first he has officiated, as here a minister must get license from Government to perform the ceremony, and go round an immense amount of red tape, before he has legal right. Until we came here, he never applied for license. They were married in the church, as has been customary here for convenience. Those who have the means, have a grand time feasting their friends for a day or two after, of which feasts native sweetmeats form an important part. We have never learned to like their sweetmeats much, for they have too much ghee—a kind of butter—in their composition. Some few kinds are pretty good. They often bring large platters for the missionary, and do not like to have their offerings refused.

Well brother Sam, I have only today to get letters ready for the mail and I feel little like doing much, for I have taken such a bad cold, that I feel quite too tired to make an effort to gather up any interesting ideas or items of news. I have a very, sore throat, and so you will not expect me to lengthen out my chat this time. I intended to write a sheet to Frank too today, but I do not feel well enough to write this time, so I will add a line to you in partnership. Either you may send this on to him, or Stella may send him a copy.

I would like, Frank, to know the history of your campaign in the Shenandoah; for I suppose your regiment has been in active service during these last weeks. I hope you like your present position better than that of private in the ranks. . . . In all your hard, weary, marches in the heat of battle, in the monotony of camp life, remember that loving hearts follow you with their earnest prayers, and a fervent, "God bless our boys."

Hoping to hear good tidings from you both. With our united love. Your affectionate and waiting sister,

Rachel L. Johnson

P.S. I will try to write to Frank next mail. We have been rejoicing over the fate of the Alabama,[5] and hope the Confederates will soon come to a like end.

Futtehgurh, India
August 12, 1864

My dear Father and Mother,

We were glad to hear by your last letter, received 3 weeks ago, of the continued prosperity of all our dear friends at home, and that as to that time, all was well with the dear boys. We wait with trembling hope for news from them, now after all those bloody battles where so many of our

5. The *CSS Alabama* was sunk by the *USS Kearsarge* off Cherbourg, France, on June 19, 1864.

brave ones have fallen. So many more hearts and homes left desolate. Every day, many times, the thought comes up: how is it in the dear old house at home? Is it too a house of mourning, or has God in mercy spared you this bitter cup? May you find his grace sufficient for what ever trials come.

. . . You will have heard by Mr. Johnsons letter of last month that we have a little daughter, born on July 10th. She is a fine, healthy babe, growing nicely. I cannot tell yet who she will look like. She is a good, lit tle darling, spending most of her time with her blue eyes closed in sleep, as all good babies should. I have not gotten very strong yet, but have escaped the former troubles this time, and hope soon to feel quite well again.

We were down at the Brodheads last evening for tea. Mr. and Mrs. Wyckoff have just been over from Mynpurie to visit us with their three little ones. They can come over in about 6 or 8 hours by dawk carriage. We expect Mr. Walsh and two new missionaries and their wives from America within 2 or 3 months. Mr. Walsh intends bringing his oldest daughter out with him. She is now about 17 or 18, and will be a help to them, and will soon learn the language or recall what she has forgotten. Children who have been kept here until they talk it, readily learn it quickly. If they return though, they at first may seem to have forgotten all. All children here learn Hindustani before their Mother tongue, hearing the natives talk, and being with them so much they soon pick up the words. Then, as they learn their own language, at first they make a strange mixture of the two. But this is, of course, only when they are very small. For soon they master both, and speak their own tongue as if taught at home.

The rains have at last begun in earnest, and the country now looks like a garden. The vegetation is so rich and luxuriant. Our garden looks beautiful with its wealth of flowers and orange trees and lime trees laden with fruit. The sweet limes are just beginning to ripen. They are sweeter, but no so luscious as the oranges—the last are green yet. The mangoes are about done, though we still see some of the poorer kind hanging in the top of the trees by the roadside. A few evenings ago, in passing one of the mango orchards, we saw the fruit piled up in heaps under the trees; looking, as Mr. Johnson said, just like an apple orchard in the fall. If they had been apples, I think we would have called on our neighbors for a few.

Our next Sabbath, we expect to have baby baptized. Mr. Brodhead will come up to assist my husband with the communion services, and baptize her.

The last time we saw Mr. Walsh was when he came up to Futtehpore to baptize our dear Willie, a short time before he left for Europe and America. Mrs. Walsh writes that her children have all had very sore eyes.

Mrs. Fullerton thinks of taking her children home to America next year. Mr. Fullerton will remain here longer, if his health will permit. Mr. Scotts health has been better since they went to the Hills.

Our schools are all prospering, and work generally. At the coming communion we hope to receive one of the Orphan boys into the church. Two of them are studying with my husband, preparing to become Readers, and seem like very good young men. These are orphans that were picked up in time of the famine 4 years ago. There are 21 boys in all. Some will, we hope, become very good useful men.

... With our united love to you all and nice kiss from your wee granddaughter.

Your affectionate daughter,
Rachel L. Johnson

Futtehgurh, India
October 5th, 1864

My dear Father and Mother,

You will be looking for a letter from us again, so I will improve the cool of the morning to write you a few words. First, let me say we are all well which is the most important news always. We had letters from you a month ago and OH! how glad we were to hear that all was well with you too, and that up to that time, dear Sam and Frank were safe and well. May it still be so with you all. . . .

The weather is now beginning to get cool, and we are all very glad of it. We were all looking forward to a pleasant meeting with our Missionary friends next month at our Annual Meeting, and to a long tour itinerating through the destitute parts of the country in our district. The Wyckoffs were to join us from Mynpurie, and with them, the Brodheads, and our staff of catechists and Readers. We hoped to do good, and receive good too, from a few weeks life out in the open air in our tents. But now we must not only give up our accustomed Meeting, but perhaps our usual itineration this season too, on account of the dark prospects at home. Exchange is at such a ruinous rate, costing nearly 3 rupees to send 1 to India, that our Board will have great difficulty, if indeed they are able to keep all our Missionary work supplied with the means to carry it on. They certainly cannot, unless there is a change soon for the better. Though we are so sadly in need of more laborers (here we have 2 missionaries to carry on the work of 4), yet the Board will not likely be able to send the 2 new Missionary brethren and their wives, who are waiting to come. . . . The Missionaries will have to give up this year a very important part of their work, their preaching to the destitute villages, that can only be visited during the cold weather. . . But perhaps our husbands will be able to go out alone, leaving their families at home.

This will lessen the expense a great deal, as they can rough it better without the little ones.

Mrs. Brodhead has a little babe now, about 5 weeks old. Her other little boy, Claude, has had a good deal of fever, which has made him look thin and pale. Mrs. Wyckoffs baby too has been very ill (teething), and Mrs. Walsh writes that her nice fat baby, that we saw when we were in Allahabad last, is now a poor skeleton—just lingering along between life and death. He is so reduced with his troubles teething. She is very anxious about him, and it will be very sad to lose her babe, just as she is expecting Mr. Walsh back. He has never seen this babe. It was born after he left for America. So you see we all have our troubles, though here, we have no war.

Our little Mary Ella keeps very well, has few baby troubles as yet, and is growing very fast. She is getting as fat and round cheeked as our dear Willie was at her age, and looks a little like him now. She is very good and sleeps all night, only waking once. . . .

And now dear Mother, what tidings of our own dear boys?. . . Our last accounts by telegram, give us a little more hopeful view of Grants prospects of taking Richmond, and Sherman of taking Atlanta. Lee has given our good old Quakers in South Eastern Pennsylvania a sad scare.[6] I should think they would begin to gird on their armor to save their homes. Some of the papers seem to charge them with being rather slow to do it, but I am sure Western Pennsylvania has come up nobly to the work, if the other counties have done as well as Beaver.

Father, are you all followers of good Abraham in Hookstown, or have you some Copperheads among you? We are all Lincolnites in our Mission Circle, though I suppose our good husbands votes wont count again. They travel so far. We all have to fight battles for our country here, among these perverse John Bull-ites. The papers here, of course, echo the sentiments of the English papers, and are bitter against the Federals. Our Americans sometimes try to set them right, but you know that, "He who is convinced against his will, is of the same opinion still." But we hope that victory will come to our armies, and then Sir "John" will become more respectful in his words.

Now I must give a little part of this sheet to Stella, so I will close with our love to you all and to all our friends.

Your affectionate daughter,
Rachel

6. During the summer of 1864, Grant became bogged down in his siege of Petersburg. Sherman's Atlanta campaign, begun May 6, was finally successful on Sept. 1, 1864. Rachel's reference to Lee and the Pennsylvania Quakers is not clear. Perhaps she was referring to a Confederate cavalry unit that raided Cumberland and Hancock, Md., in early August before retreating into West Virginia. Grant kept Lee busy in Virginia skirmishes around Petersburg and Richmond during the summer of 1864.

[Will's mission work with the Christian village and the boys' school in Rakha seemed to go as well as he could expect with his reduced funds and personnel. Will was a scholar, and he was anxious to maintain a quality school. Thus, reluctantly, Will applied for and received financial aid from the Indian government to hire more teachers. Will became increasingly uneasy about this move when he discovered that with these monies came government rules and inspections. Will reported that the inspectors were not Christians, knew very little English, and were not educators but that they always had many suggestions. He began to feel the autonomy of the school and its educational goals for the students slipping away from the mission. There was increasing pressure for private schools to become part of the government educational system, which was primarily interested in teaching basic skills and in disseminating the civilization of the West. Mission schools taught basic skills, secular subjects from a Christian standpoint, and the Bible. Other private schools, which were usually sponsored by Islam or the Sunni, also taught the philosophy and ethics of their religion or sect.[7]]

Futtehgurh, India
October 6th, 1864

Dear brother Frank,

Well dear Frank, I wonder where you are today—safe and well I hope. You have doubtless seen some hard fighting since you wrote last to us from Frederick City. We would like very much if we could know all about your doings, but I suppose you have little opportunity to journalize while you are making raids through the sacred soil of Old Virginia. How do you like your present service in the Cavalry Corps? You must not let the Rebels catch you in any of their escapades.

But you would perhaps like to hear something of our doings here in India. Everything goes on quietly, and prosperously. Our Boys school has lately much increased in numbers. Mr. Johnson has got a "Grant in Aid" for it from the government, of a certain sum of money to aid in making the schools more efficient. It does not relieve the Mission of any expense, but is only to help by giving the means to employ more teachers. If you spend 100 dollars more, government will give you another 100, but you must engage to still spend the $100 you have from the mission, so it only enlarges our operations. One condition not desirable, is that the government officials have the right, if you take the Grant, of visiting and enquiring into the regulations of the schools. These worthies, being generally natives, not Christians, with a little smattering of English and a great idea of their own wisdom, often give annoyance.

7. Webster, *The Christian Community,* 152–55.

Some are, however, really interested in the progress of the schools, and of course, they are always welcomed.

We have about 20 orphan boys. Some of them very promising. They were mostly picked up during the famine a few years ago. But boys are boys the world over. There is one, just returned from trying to feed on the husks for a few months past. He and another took a fancy that, altho' fed and clothed and taught well here, they would like to see a little of the outside heathen world. So one night, they decamped. We let them go. Now after wandering for a while about, here comes the prodigal, dirty, and hungry, begging to be taken back. Mr. Johnson tells him he will let him come this time, but if he gets tired of his home again, he will have the privilege of taking care of himself.

There are a number of little orphan girls too. Some of them are bright and learn well. But there are a few dummies too, that find it very difficult to master their a.b.c. Some of the older girls will soon expect to be married off. They think it a dreadful thing not to be married in this country. Robinet, one of the native Christians, has a nice looking daughter, that was to have been married more than a year ago. Then the young man was not doing well, and the engagement was broken off. His daughter since was very ill with a fever, and it left her with a weakness in one limb that makes her limp a little in walking. This being considered a fault by the marriageable young men (for you must know that Hindoo youths appreciate beauty and grace too), he has been in great trouble for fear she would be left without a husband, as the poor girl was getting to be an old maid of 17! But he has found a husband at last for her. They manage such matters very queer in this country. He, the father, goes to the father of the marriageable young man, and proposes his daughter as a suitable match. The father being agreed, they make all the arrangements, and so in January next, they hope to have the knot tied. The engagement is made known to every body as a matter of course. But enough on the subject of matrimony.

. . . So Frank, we hope you soldier boys will soon bring the Rebels to terms. We were glad to hear that you have got in so well, and hope you and brother Sam will continue to deserve well of your country, and receive your reward.

But dear Frank, I hope that in all this turmoil and strife, you do not forget that you have enlisted as a soldier for the Great Captain. Be faithful in his service, and seek not only your own spiritual welfare, but that of your companions in arms. If by your example you lead others to enlist in the service of Christ, blessed will be your reward. I could not wish for you, my dear brother, more than that you may be found among those who have fought well the good fight, for whom is laid up the crown of life.

Affectionately, your sister,
Rachel

Futtehgurh, India
November 16th, 1864

My dear Father and Mother,

We were glad to hear by last mail good news from you all. We feel very anxious always about the boys, and indeed I feared to read your letter after the accounts we had read of so many fearful battles. But our Father has graciously kept them safe and so may it please him to keep them until the end!

We have all been very well. Mr. Johnson has been suffering a good deal from toothache for a few days. Though this is not usually counted on the list of sicknesses, yet, I think it is harder to bear comfortably.

Our little Mary is growing nicely. She sits up very strong, and can make herself heard all over the house, though she is generally a very, good baby. She begins to count her toes, or at least tries to put them in her mouth; and she devotes a good deal of time to one little thumb, that she seems to think particularly sweet. She now sits on my knee, and is very busy trying to make pieces of an old letter. She interferes a little occasionally with my attempt at writing to you. . . .

We will perhaps go out on our tour about the last of this month. We will be out more than a month perhaps, or as long as the funds appropriated to this part of our work will allow.

I told you in my last letter of the illness of Mrs. Walsh's babe. She had made arrangements to try a change of air to see if it would rally, but the very day she had intended to start, her dear babe died. This will be sad news for Mr. Walsh, who she now expects in a few days.

Mrs. Owen of Allahabad is now lying very ill and she writes that she has no hope that she will ever be any better. She has dropsy and heart disease, and there seems to be a general breaking up of her system. She has spent a long life in India. She was married here in Allahabad to Mr. Owen 20 years ago, and there they have spent all but 2 years of their married life. They have one child, who is now 18 years old, a noble looking lad, if his picture is like him. He is at home at Princeton College. Mrs. Owen is an English lady, daughter of General Proctor, but is a very amiable and lovely woman. She went to America just before the Mutiny, to take her boy home, and returned just after the Mutiny. She did not know anything of it, until she reached Calcutta. On the river, she heard that many of the Missionaries had been killed. Imagine her joy when she found her husband safe. She seems very happy now though. She feels she has but a few days longer to stay, and rejoices in the glorious hope of going to be with Christ. She is willing to go, and is in a very happy frame of mind.

Mr. Brodhead and my husband have just returned from a trip to a Mela on the Ganges at Singarampur. They found about 10,000 people gathered there. The Mela lasted 3 days, and they, with their Readers and Catechists, kept up preaching pretty constantly all the time they stayed. Many thousands thus, heard the Word of Life. As the pilgrims arrived at the point where the Mela was held, or came in sight of the river, they would send up a great shout, "Long live Mother Ganges!" This would be taken up by others and prolonged until thousands joined in the shout of "Long live Mother Ganges!"

We will have Mr. and Mrs. Brodhead, Mr. and Mrs. Wyckoff, and all the little folks, with us on our tour. So that, with all the Catechists and Readers, we will have quite a large company.

I am glad to hear that Grandpa and Grandma keep so well. I dreamed that I saw them all last night, and Aunt Mary Ann, and Aunt Agnes, all, at home. But I waked, and found it all a dream. . . .

Now dear Father, and Mother, I must close. Here Stella is a kiss from your little niece Mary. With our united love to you all.

> Your affectionate daughter,
> Rachel L. Johnson

P.S. I hope that we shall soon have letters from the dear boys too. I wish we could have more details of their movements. The papers say Sheridan has gained a great victory in the Shenandoah, and Grant has gained some advantages in front of Richmond. Who is President? <u>Abraham Lincoln</u>, we think and hope.[8]

> In Camp Etah, India
> December 19th, 1864

Dear brother Frank,

I see by the paper that Sheridan has been moving about pretty briskly in the Shenandoah, so I hardly know where you may be now. Last accounts left you at Harpers Ferry. I trust that the same kind care keeps you still from harm and danger.

You will see by the date of this letter, that we are out on our tour through the District, and have wandered a long way from home. We are now at Etah, a native town about 80 miles from Futtehgurh. We, in company with the Brodheads and Wyckoffs, have been out about 3 weeks. We will perhaps return home about the last of the month. We march 6–8 or 10 miles a day, and stop two or three days in a place. You know, the people here all live in villages, and these plains are so densely populated, that the plains are dotted over thickly with these villages. Our object is to visit as many of these as possible, now during the cold weather, for at no other time can the Word of Life be made known to these so far removed from our Missionary Stations.

So while we with the little ones march direct from one camping place to the next, our husbands and native helpers, of whom there are 14, go

---

8. Sheridan won a series of battles in Virginia's Shenandoah Valley in the fall of 1864. Grant captured Fort Harrison but failed to take Fort Gilmer, outside of Richmond, in late September. Lincoln was reelected president over McClellan on Nov. 8, 1864.

Fig. 11. Will's sketch shows their missionary tents pitched in a mango grove.

off to the villages, scattered about at a distance of 2 or 3 miles from the road, and thus preach in a good many villages every day. The people are much better inclined to hear of this new religion than in the cities. They are more simple hearted, and kind, and our missionaries find it a great pleasure to sit down among them, and tell them the Good News. Doubtless much of the seed thus sown may bring forth fruit in the Masters own good time.

Every evening we all gather in our large tent, and each tells what villages he has visited during the day. It is very interesting to hear the different reports. In one village where they were preaching, they told them how the disciples were commanded to go to the people in their houses, and if they would not receive them, to shake off the dust of their feet against them. One old man speaking out, besought them not to do so against them.

If you could take a peep at us, you would see us with our tents pitched in a grove of nice large trees. We each have our sleeping tent, and then there is the large one for eating in and general use. We have just been taking a little lunch of bread and butter and corned beef, before our husbands went to the bazar to preach. We have dinner at 5 in the evening.

We had a sheep killed today, so if you will join us, you shall have some mutton for dinner.

Baby just got hold of my letter, and crumpling it all up, was about putting it into her mouth, but I have it safe again, so I will add a little more. Baby is 5 months old and can almost sit alone. She is as full of mischief as any little blue-eyed Mary could be. She is very good, and will sit for a picture the first opportunity, then you will know what a dear little niece you have got.

We will march tomorrow morning about 6 miles, so I must get my box in order. We send our tents, beds and boxes on ox carts, and go in our own carriages, as it is so much easier. We meet long strings of camels every day, sometimes 100 at one time. They come from Cabul, and are going to Calcutta. There are generally 2 or 3 men to about 20 camels. A man leads the first one, then a cord passes from its nose back through the nose of the 2nd, then to the 3rd, etc., on to the last. All are led by the nose. They follow along, one after the other. One morning there were 125 all passing in one long line. They have large sacks thrown across their humps filled with fruit and spices of different kinds. We got two small boxes of grapes from one grim looking Arab. The grapes are pulled off the stems, and laid in the box on a layer of cotton, so that they dont touch each other, then a layer of cotton, and another of grapes. They keep a long time, but must be used when they are opened.

> Your affectionate sister,
> Rachel

> Camp Etah, India
> November 19, 1864

My dear Sister,

. . . How I wish you could be with us now, while we are living out in the woods. It is so pleasant, and I know you would be happy to see the elephants and camels and deer. The children all raised a great shout awhile ago. They were laughing at a little baby camel passing by, running after its mother.

. . . Now dear sister, I leave you with a kiss from baby.

> Your affectionate sister,
> Rachel L. Johnson

> Futtehgurh, India
> January 21st, 1865

My dear Mother,

Mr. Johnson has just got his Yearly Reports ready to send to Dr. Lowrie. Altho I did not intend to write this mail, I find there is room for a little letter, so I will scratch off a few words to you in a great hurry.

. . . We were out in tents when I wrote last. We stayed out 4 weeks, then a week in Mynpurie. We are all very well now. I was not well, after we came into Mynpurie, but am quite well now. Baby has got two teeth, and is getting more, that gives her a little trouble. She is getting them much sooner than Willie did. . . . The Brodheads came up a few evening ago, and we had our babies vaccinated. There is always a good deal of small pox among the natives.

We have cold weather now, and have fire in our sitting room. I have a toothache ever since I came in, and it makes me feel very glum. Mr. Johnson had it nearly all the time he was out.

. . . We have had two weddings since we came home. Two of our native Christians (girls) have been married, and one more is to be next Tuesday. The last wedding was on Monday in Church, our Mission Church. Samuale, the young man, was very gay looking, with gold lace trimming on his fine white jaconet coat, and shoes that looked like gold, and his embroidered cap. The bride had a nice white dress and veil. After the wedding they brought us some sweetmeats, part of their wedding dinner. The bride always comes to the wedding crying, as tho her heart was broken. This is their custom. I told one of the women that, "They cry if they cant get married, and cry if they do."

Your affectionate daughter,
Rachel L. Johnson

Futtehgurh, India
March 6, 1865

My dear brother Sam,

I have been thinking this morning so much about you, that I have just put away all my little cares, until I write you a few lines. It is so long since we have had a letter from you, that I begin to feel uneasy about you. . . . Now dear brother, do not say you have nothing to write about, for you have always yourself. That is just the very person that I want to hear about. What are you doing? Where are you? Who are your chums, and all your little everyday doings and surroundings. Tell me all these, and then I can picture to myself how you look, and how you are living in camp.

We are rejoiced to hear rumors of peace again, and hope that they will end in something more than rumors this time. We heard by our last home letter, that you have been promoted to Captain Kerr. Well I am truly glad. No one dear Sam, more truly rejoices in your prosperity than your own sister. What are your present intentions, to remain in the army, or retire, when your 3 years are up?

We have just heard of the taking of Fort Fish. General Butler seems to have gone under a cloud.[9] The English will rejoice, they hate him so. Did I tell you that the Methodists have a Missionary here, a kind of bishop among them, named Butler? Well, about the time of General Butlers notoriety, somebody reported among the English here that the Missionary was a brother of General Butler's. So when he was making his collections, nobody would give him anything.

This last month my husband, with Mr. Wyckoff and Mr. Brodhead, and their catechists, were all out on a preaching tour for nearly two weeks. Mrs. Wyckoff came over here, and so Mrs. Brodhead and Mrs. Wyckoff and the little folks all stayed a week with me here at Rakha. We all stayed a week with Mrs. Brodhead at Barpur, so we were not so lonely as we would have been alone. The Wyckoffs will spend the coming hot season at Landour, on the Hills, as Mrs. Wyckoff's health is delicate.

We hear that two new Missionaries have sailed for India, but we expect the Board will send them to the Upper Mission, to take the place of Mr. Janvier and Louwenthal, who were killed a few months ago. We want another here at Futtehgurh very much. We will soon have a great change made in our station, as Futtehgurh will no longer be a Military Station. The Government has ordered the troops to some other place, where they seem to be more needed. There will not be so many Europeans here then. The station will be almost as small as Futtehpore is. It will not make much difference to us, as we have few acquaintances among the English people here, and dont care much for their society.

Well brother Sam, I must not allow you to forget our little Mary. Here she sits on the floor at my feet, playing with one of her papas slippers— looking up and scolding a little once in awhile, because I dont devote my attention to her instead of Uncle Sam. She is a very, good baby and a great pet of everyone.

Everything is quiet in India. There is a little war going on over on the frontier with some of the hill tribes that had been making some raids, infringing on the rights of her Majesty's subjects. There were a few troops sent to chastise the Bhooteahs [Bhutanese],[10] but there is always some little affair of this kind on hand with the frontier tribes. They are so far away, nobody thinks it worth much notice.

9. Benjamin F. Butler's joint army-navy expedition was turned back at Fort Fisher, N.C., on Dec. 25, 1864. A. H. Terry, however, took Fort Fisher on Jan. 15, 1865, and this closed Wilmington, the last major Confederate seaport.

10. The Bhutanese tribe lived in the Himalaya Mountains just east of Nepal in the region of Bhutan.

Our Mission is prospering, as usual. The Gospel is preached to many people. The good seed is sown, and though the harvest has yielded yet no plenteous return, we sow in faith, and wait with hope. . . .

Your affectionate sister,
R. Lillie Johnson

Futtehgurh, India
March 6th, 1865

My dear brother Frank,

We are all well and at home again. The Wyckoffs came over from Mynpurie, and our good husbands all went on a preaching tour for a couple of weeks. . . . Mr. Bradford, a young man in the Customs Department, went out with them, thinking he could do a little hunting in the jungle while they did the preaching. So we had some wild peafowls and ducks sent in from their camp occasionally, that was very nice. They had two camels to carry their tents, cooking utensils, etc., and they rode on horseback, themselves and catechists.

While they were out, they had quite an adventure with wild bees. The bees were on a tree near where they camped, and something disturbed them. They came down in swarms. They all fled to their tents, but the poor horses and Mr. Bradfords oxen had to suffer. The oxen were tied and could not get away. So the poor things, after fighting all they could, just lay down and gave up. Then one of the men thought of a plan of loosing them. By wrapping himself all up in an old carpet, this shielded him until he got up to them, and cut the ropes that tied them. The horses broke away from their fastenings and "skedaddled." Some of the natives were dreadfully stung. People in this country sometimes get almost stung to death by these wild bees.

. . . Now dear brother, about your leaving the Army. I would be glad if you should, and I think you are right about first getting a good education, and then deciding on your calling. You are older now and will feel the importance of improving your time at college, more than if you had gone younger. And whatever your position in life should be, a good education is most desirable, if it pleases God to spare your life. I hope you will spend it for Him in whatever calling you may be led to choose. But of the particular calling, we will talk again.

I am glad dear Frank that you have found friends in your wanderings, and I begin to suspect you have found some fair friends too. I am pleased too if you have some good friends among your female acquaintances, for I would not like to feel that, away from home, you were banished from all the kindly influences of female society and friendships. . . .

But what of India do you ask? I am sorry that I cannot tell you more of the progress of our work here. There is so much to be done, and so few to work, but we know that Indias day of rejoicing will come. The little leaven has begun to work and the work will go slowly, but surely.

Now Frank, I must say goodbye. Here is a kiss from our blue eyed Mary, and much love from us both. Write often and dont forget your affectionate sister.

R. Lillie Johnson

Futtehgurh, India
April 20th, 1865

My dear Father and Mother,

. . . I always like to write the same mail we get letters, for it stirs one up, and makes one feel that we must sit down and have a talk with all our dear ones. It is much easier to shake off the lazy feeling that the hot weather will bring with it, strive against it as we will. It is such a comfort to hear from you and know that all is well with you. It is always with a trembling heart I read, for we hear so often that there has been a "great battle and heavy loss on both sides," and then I think of the many homes that have been desolated, and I wonder and ask myself, "Is ours one of the bereaved ones?"

. . . Is it not wonderful, how seldom we lose a letter, though our letters have such a long way to travel. We still have to wait about 2 months generally for our letters from America, but you will be surprised to hear that you are getting so near to us by way of the telegraph. The new line of telegraph, from London to India via Constantinople, Persia, Kurrachee (in the west of India), Bombay, and Agra, has lately been completed. So now we have had news from London in 24 hours. Just think of that. The congratulatory message came through in 2 days, and the papers say they have had news in 24 hours. When the Atlantic cable is laid and in working order, we will only be a few hours distant from you. This is great progress from the days of the old "John Companys" first days in India, when they had to wait for all their news to come round the cape in sailing vessels. One of the old viceroys of India says in a Government Dispatch, "I have not heard any reliable news from London for 7 months." So the world moves on. Well—enough about the telegraph, you will perhaps like a little news from us as well.

Since I wrote, there has been no very interesting news—unless I should tell you baby had got 2 new teeth. She has 6 now, and this is good news for her, for they were a good deal of trouble to her for several days. She seems to feel the heat a good deal, and is just now stretched out on her little bed under the punka, asleep. She gets a bath every morning, and thinks it fine fun to get in the water, and dont like to come out of her bath tub. Water is a great comfort in the hot weather. Last hot season, I used to get up sometimes in the night, when it was too hot to sleep comfortably, and go and take a cold bath. That would cool me off and make me able to go asleep. We were sleeping on top of the house when I wrote last, but we had so many dust storms, that we had to come down several nights in the middle of the night. This is not pleasant with the wind blowing a hurricane, and so full of sand that you cant keep your eyes open; so we took down our tent, and now sleep down stairs. The way we get on top of our house is by a stairway outside. Now for a few months, while the sand storms come occasionally, we will stay down, though it is much cooler outside.

. . . A young man who attends our Boys school came in a day or two ago to talk to Mr. Johnson about the Christian religion. He says he has no faith in Hinduism, and he believes that ours is the only true one, and that Jesus Christ is the only Savior. But he says that his friends persecute him because he does not observe the Hindu rites as he used to do. He has a wife and children, and he does not feel that he can give them up. If he becomes a Christian, then they will not receive him, and he says they too will be left helpless. So this is his stumbling block. There seem to be a great many who are convinced of the folly of idolatry, but like the rich young man in the Gospels, are not prepared to give up all for Christ.

There has been a good deal of small pox among the natives, so they are very zealous in their worship of Seetla, the Goddess of Small pox, trying to propitiate her. I read a story in one of the papers about a man who had lost all his children by small pox, and when the last one was taken, he, in his anger, went and broke his idol incarnation of Seetla all to pieces, saying, "Why, when I have given you all my goods, could you not spare me this one?"

The Government tries to get the natives to be vaccinated, but they are very much opposed to it. Their Brahman priests tell them that it will bring on them the anger of the Goddess Seetla. So great numbers of them fall victims to this plague every year.

Little Mary has just got a new wagon, and she is very much pleased with it. The Brodheads children have gone with Mrs. Brodhead to the Hills to Landour. Mrs. Brodhead has been in very delicate health for some time, and she felt too weak to bear the hot weather. I miss her very much. Mr. Brodhead is alone down at Bharpur, but we see him almost every day. Mrs. Wyckoff has a little son, a few days old. They have quite a housefull of little ones now—four. They are all going to the Hills too, as soon as Mrs. Wyckoff is able to take the journey. The Walshes have sent up their two children too, so our house in Landour will be pretty full. We have not seen the Hills (or Himalaya Mountains) yet, and I hope it will not be necessary for us to go for a long time. I am sure I would not like to go and leave my husband down here, to bear the hot weather alone, but sometimes it has to be done.

Affectionately, your daughter,
R. L. Johnson

Futtehgurh, North India
May 17th, 1865

My dear Brother Sam,

We were delighted this morning to receive a good long letter from you, and another from Frank. What a nice time you must have had at home, both too at the same time. I can imagine how happy Father and Mother would be to have you all gathered home once more. What cozy chats by the fireside. How much you would all have to talk about. How changed too you would be, both now grown to manhood, and so many adventures to relate of the camp and battle field. What a precious meeting it must have been. How happy we would have been to have shared it with you—to have been all home again once more, if but for a little while. Well dear brother, I rejoice that this privilege was yours, and thank God he spared you both to enjoy it. He has been very good to you, and to us, in keeping us all safe under his wing through all these years that we have been separated.

When your letters came I was sitting out on the chibootra (a kind of raised platform made of brick and mortar and plastered or stuccoed all over) in the little garden plot, just in front of the house. Here we often sit in the mornings and evenings, while it is cool, to enjoy all the fresh air that is going. Well, it was not quite 6 o'clock in the morning, and I was just taking a cup of tea and a slice of toast when Bhawani, a one eyed Hindoo, came along with a very big letter. Mr. Johnson and I soon found out the contents, which were your letters, one from Pamelia Johnson, Professor Waugh of the Steubenville Seminary, who is an old classmate of Mr. Johnson's, and a letter for Mrs. Brodhead. You see, Dr. Lowrie puts all the letters for Futtehgurh in one big envelope, and then we each take our share. Well, we read the letters, and found all good news. . . .

Now brother Sam, that is what we were doing, but if you could have looked up the broad garden paths, you might have seen a wee brown head peeping out here and there. Little Mary is out taking the air in the little wagon, and looking as happy and roguish as any little girl you have seen. People say she is a very, pretty little Mary, and her papa and mama cant feel like disputing the fact, for she is very sweet in their eyes surely. We have a poor artist here, and we tried to get her picture, but she would not sit still. We will try again when she is a little older, and the first good opportunity we have. It is too hot now.

We have the thermometer at about 95 degrees in the house, outside it is something above what ours measure. Ours only goes up to 120. One day Mr. Johnson put the thermometer out, and it ran up to the top, so he had to bring it in for fear it would burst. With all the great heat, we had a very hard hail storm one night last week. I never heard harder hail. Those who saw it, say it was as large as a hens egg. I dont doubt it, for it sounded like a shower of brickbats. We had very hard thunder and lightening too. Not long ago I heard of a man being killed by the hail. He was caught out where there was no shelter. There are some very hard storms in India sometimes. I think I told you of the great storm that destroyed so many lives in Calcutta, and on the Island of Sangor below. The loss to the shipping was very great. The storm wave that was driven up the Hoogly was said to be 30 feet high, and swept every thing before it. Such storms do not come very often, but they do a great deal of damage when they do come.

We have just heard of the assassination of President Lincoln and Secretary Seward.[11] What a sad loss to the country the president will be; and how horrible that he should have fallen by the hand of an assassin. Seward is reported recovering. We will have to wait so long before we hear particulars—almost 6 months—then we will get accounts from the English papers, and 2 weeks after from our American papers. We get the New York Tribune, and see the Times too, which is sent to Mr. Walsh. So we get all the particulars, and keep well posted about the war.

What glorious victories have lately crowned our arms. Richmond taken. Lee surrendered. Early captured, Johnson beaten, and what next?[12] Surely the Confederacy has not a leg left to stand on. We look now for a speedy termination of the war. But we feel sad to think that the good honest President who so long and so wisely has guided the affairs of our country has fallen, and he will not be there to share the nations joy.

And what of Johnson, the Vice President? We have seen very disgraceful accounts of his conduct at the time when he was installed as Vice President, that he was so drunk he could not take his oath with decorum; that he made a very low and undignified speech before the Senate, that the senators and people hung their heads for very shame that they must have such a man to fill such a dignified office. And now, can it be

11. Abraham Lincoln was shot by John Wilkes Booth at Ford Theater in Washington, D.C., on Apr. 14, 1865; he died the following day. Also on Apr. 14, in a separate assassination attempt by Lewis Paine, Secretary of State Seward was severely injured, but he did recover.

12. Union forces entered Richmond on Apr. 3, 1865, and Lee surrendered to Grant at Appomattox Court House, Va., on Apr. 9. Maj. Gen. Jubal Anderson "Old Jube" Early was soundly beaten at Waynesboro in March 1865, but he managed to escape. Joseph E. Johnston surrendered to Sherman on Apr. 26 near Durham, N.C.

that a drunkard is to be the man who is to guide our battered ship safe through all the breakers ahead? God save our country![13]

The Indian papers say that Grant or Sherman will assume the reins, supported by the army, and we will have a Military Dictator to reign over us. But Mr. Johnson tells our English friends they dont know the soldiers they thus malign. They are not hirelings that have fought for their liberty, but brave men, sons of liberty, who will know how to preserve liberty, as well as fight for it. You are not the soldiers to follow a Dictator or support a usurper.

Well we must wait with patience to know the end of these troubles, and hope that God will soon give our bleeding country a blessed rest of Peace.

I am glad you think of going back to finish your college course, and I hope you will be spared to do so. Then whatever profession you may choose, I hope you will be a good and useful man.

Now dear Sam, I must say goodbye, with our united love to you.

Your own affectionate sister,
Rachel L. Johnson

Futtehgurh, India
July 15th, 1865

My dear Father and Mother,

Here it is mail day and no letters ready, and why you will ask. Well there are several reasons. Perhaps I ought to put the blame on little baby Kellogg, a little stranger that came to Rakha a few days ago. Our new missionaries, Mr. and Mrs. Kellogg, arrived here on the 20th of last month. On the 1st of July, the wee Miss Kellogg came, so we have not had our usual quiet household. They had a very long, tiresome voyage, and Mrs. Kellogg, in her delicate state of health, was not able to go on to Lodiana, where they were appointed. So Mr. and Mrs. Myers went to Lodiana, and the Kelloggs stay here. Mrs. Kellogg is getting on pretty well, and will be able to be up in a few days, I hope. The baby is a fine little girl and behaves herself remarkably well—sleeps day and night.

The Kelloggs are nice people and we will, I think, find them pleasant co-laborers in our Mission work. When Mrs. Kellogg is able, and they get

13. Andrew Johnson, a shrewd political choice as Lincoln's vice-president, represented the faithful, militant, Southern Unionist remnant. On inaugural day, Mar. 4, 1865, Johnson was suffering from a bad chest cold and exhaustion. Lincoln, however, insisted that Johnson be present to symbolically stand by his side at the inauguration. Unfortunately, Johnson drank a few too many slugs of the usual home remedy for colds and fatigue—whiskey and sugar—before the ceremony and was visibly "under the influence" for all to see, an embarrassment that plagued Johnson for years.

Fig. 12. Samuel Kerr photographed in his new captain bars in 1865 at age 24.

things ready, they will go to housekeeping down at Barhpur, in the Fullertons vacant house.

We were rejoiced to see you dear Mother, last mail, as you came peeping out of the folds of your letter, and brother Sam too. Your likenesses are both very good. Sam has changed a good deal. He looks more like the man than the boy.

. . . We rejoice that the war is now over, and that there is good hope that soon you will have quiet and peace over the land. What are you going to do with Jeff Davis and Company? Hang them? They certainly deserve it. The papers give a more favorable account of President Johnson than at first.

The boys are home now I suppose, if it has pleased God to spare them. When I think of the many bereaved hearts who will wait in vain for the coming of their dear ones home from the war, I thank God that our dear ones were spared so long, and still hope they are kept safe to the end.

The Doctor has just called to see Mrs. Kellogg, and he has lanced our little Marys gums, which has almost broken her heart. She is still sobbing over it in her sleep. She has nine teeth and four more nearly through. She has been very well through all the hot season and teething too. I expected she would grow thin, but she looks as fat almost as ever, and has begun to walk round after a chair. She stands alone and is busy in all sorts of mischief from morning till night. She was a year old last Monday, the 10th. . . .

> Affectionately,
> Rachel L. Johnson

[After the Union forces occupied Richmond, Lee retreated toward Appomattox through the small hamlet of Farmville, Virginia. In Farmville, Lee found Sherman's forces on his left and the remainder of the Union forces behind him. Lee led the Confederates in several final skirmishes, successfully holding off the Union forces at Farmville for several days. On April 7, Grant and Lee corresponded about a possible surrender; two days later Lee surrendered at Appomattox Court House.

Rachel and Will's joy over the news of peace at home turned to grief when word reached them that Sam had been wounded at Farmville on April 7 and had died on April 15 from a gangrenous leg wound. Sam had refused to let the doctors amputate his leg. The rank of major was conferred on Samuel Kerr posthumously "by a special commission from the President for meritorious and gallant conduct upon the field of battle."[14]

Frank learned of Sam's death as he headed home from the war to celebrate with his family. His daughter, Estella, wrote of that experience ninety-five years later:

> Papa was coming home on the train loaded with soldiers and boys with crutches, arms in slings and bandages. He hadn't heard from home for weeks nor had any word from Sam. Came to a junction station and pulled off on a siding. Looking idly out the window, back at the building, an old man with his back to him. He was startled at the resemblance, but knew it wasn't, his father would not be that far away from home. Still his eyes kept coming back to him. Another train pulled in. The old man rounded the corner and he could barely see him go into the far side. Pretty soon men came out carrying a box and Grandpa walked behind it and started to cross to their train . . . and he got a view of his father. He started to pound on the window and yell. There was a Sargent at each end would not let him out. The boys all started to make a rumpas. The Conductor came but he had to wait hours and hours until they reached Smith's Ferry but he knew what it meant. Grandpa was coming down the steps of the train when Papa went up to him.[15]]

14. Jordan, *Genealogical and Personal History*, 545.
15. Estella Kerr Moore, letter to David Kerr Fulton [1970], Presbyterian Historical Society, Philadelphia.

Futtehgurh, India
July 29th, 1865

My dear Father and Mother,

I wrote to you just two weeks ago, and the next day (Sabbath) came the sad news from you of dear brother Samuels death. It was then too late to write by that mail—if I could have done it. Even now I can scarcely write for the blinding tears that will come when I think that dear Samuel is gone. This is a hard stroke for us all. I cannot tell you dear Mother and Father how much I feel for you in this hour of bitter sorrow. It came so unexpectedly, just in the hour of victory, when the load of anxiety that had so long weighed upon our hearts was almost gone. We thought that now dear Samuel and Frank are safe through all the battles, and we will hear of them safe at home in a few days.

Dear Samuel, it was very sad for him to have none but strangers hands to soothe his last hours. While we cannot but feel that it would have been a great comfort to our hearts if he could have been at home, where loving hands could have tended him—where you could have watched over and been with him in his last hours—yet dear Father and Mother, let not this trouble your hearts nor ours. Let us thank God for the blessed hope that he was not friendless, though among strangers. Jesus, the best of friends, was with him and we know that His presence could make his dying hours peaceful and happy. Let us, while we sorrow, not sorrow as those who have no hope. It is a sweet consolation to think that dear Samuel has left us so much comforting evidence that he has gone to be with Christ. That we have nothing but pleasant memories of his life and sweet hope in his death.

I hope my dear Father and Mother, that you are both supported and comforted in your affliction. It was Gods will to take him from us. Though we cannot now see why he was cut off, just in the prime of his youth, when we hoped he was about to enter on a life of usefulness; yet, we shall one day know, and then, if not now, we will feel and recognize that it was done by a wise and loving Father, who knoweth what is best. Now he chastens us in his love. Let us pray for grace to kiss the rod and say in our hearts, "Even so Father, for so it hath seemed good in thy sight."

You my dear parents, have now nearly all your children safe home in Heaven. God has often afflicted you, but he has mingled mercy with it while he has smitten your hearts. You have the blessed memory of the joyful death of dear, sister Jane—how she was enabled to rejoice in the hour of death that she was going to her Saviour—then the lambs of our flock, are they not safe with the Good Shepherd—and now, while you have laid dear Samuels body by their side, you have the blessed hope that he is "Asleep in Jesus, blessed sleep." We weep for him, but he is happy—gone where all tears are wiped from off all faces. May we who are left have grace given us to live for Christ, and at last, be enabled to triumph over the last enemy, death, that all reunited may rejoice together in the better land.

I hope dear Mother, that this great cross that has been laid upon you will not be greater than you can bear. May God give you strength. It is a source of comfort to think that you had dear Samuel and Frank both at home for a little while with you, so short a time before his death. That meeting will be pleasant to look back upon. It seems a long time since we last saw your dear faces all. Samuel and Frank had changed no doubt a good deal—that I could see from their pictures—but they seem to me, as I think about them, the boys I left 4 years ago. It was 4 years yesterday, 28th, since we sailed from Boston. It seems a long time. So many changes since then.

Dear Stella too, I think of as the little Sister that then clung to me as we tore ourselves away in tears. I hope she will not forget us, and that she, while she mourns for dear Samuel, will think of that blessed land where we hope he is. I hope she will pray Jesus to help her give her heart to him, now while she is young. For he still loves the children, as He did while He was here on earth, and wills them to give their hearts to Him.

I cannot write of other things this time—my heart is too sad. I will only say that we are all well. Mr. Johnson and our little Mary and myself have all borne the great heat of this year remarkably well. The rains have set in and the weather is not quite so warm now. The Kelloggs are still with us. They will go to Barhpur in a few weeks, when their house will be ready.

With our united love and sympathy for you all, your affectionate daughter,

R. L. Johnson

Futtehgurh, India
July 29th, 1865

My dear brother Frank,

It is with a sad heart I write to you this time. I can hardly bring myself to realize that dear Samuel is indeed gone—that I have seen his face for the last time, and read the last message from him. The last letter he wrote to me was when he was at home in February. It was so full of hope. He was then looking forward to the time that seemed so near when he would be home again, ready to go back to his studies. But I trust that he is this day safe in the home of peace—his warfare ended—that now he enjoys the blessed rest of those who sleep in Jesus. I had felt when I received Mothers letter, written after the battles, before Lee's surrender, that you were both spared through them. . . . I feel that it would be a precious privilege if I too could have been with you all in the time of your sorrow. Oh, if I could have but gazed once more upon that dear face, before it was hid away! But this could not be.

I am glad that you were at home, and that dear Samuels body rests in the old graveyard, by the side of our other dear ones. It will be a comfort to Father and Mother, and you all, that he is not left like so many of his brother soldiers to sleep in an unknown grave. How very sad it was that none of you were permitted to be with dear Sam in his last hours.

I want you dear Frank, to write me all the particulars you were able to learn of his last sickness and death. You have doubtless heard more than you were able to write about in your letter at the time. The Chaplain, or officer you mentioned, Capt. Rickett, would doubtless be able to tell you much about those last days. How many days was he spared after his wounds seemed dangerous? Was he conscious until the time of his death? Who was with dear Samuel when he died? There are so many questions I would like to ask, but I hope you will tell me, dear Frank, all you were able to learn. Send me copies of his last messages to you and home. I love to read over the comforting words of the hymn that Samuel sung before he died. When I read it, the thought that now he sleeps that blessed sleep, comforts my heart in its sorrow. I have found the tune of "Rest" in the Christian Psalmodist. It is a sweet, sad air.

I have many things to write Frank, but I cannot now. Let us pray that this affliction will be sanctified to our heart, and that it will lead us to think more of that blessed sleep, that we all hope will end our labours here, when God calls us to rest.

Dear Brother, God has graciously spared your life, mid all the dangers that have surrounded your wanderings, and has ere this, I trust, brought you safe home. . . . What are you going to do now? You talked of getting a good education before you seek any particular employment. I hope you will, for then you will be fitted for being a useful man.

I hope you will write oftener to me now Frank. You and Samuel have always been very dear to me and all your interests. Now you and dear Stella are left. May God spare you long, make you a good and useful man, and a comfort to Father and Mother, and us all.

. . . With our united love.

Your affectionate sister,
R. L. Johnson

Futtehgarh
Aug. 10th, 1865

My Dear Friends,

Some of you have expressed some curiosity as to our fruits and flowers, and no doubt all of you would like to hear about:

Our Garden.

So I have spent all the morning in making out a plot of it and a list of its contents, which will give you a better idea of it than many pages of description. My wife, looking over my shoulder, says that "you will suppose we must have a slice of the Garden of Eden here." And indeed for the little space, the variety is something wonderful. Tropic and temperate fruits bow to each other on every side.

Tropic and temperate plants elbow each other along every walk. I have made a list of and marked the positions of the more prominent trees and plants and those whose names are known to me; but nearly as many more—mostly delicate little flowering shrubs, unfamiliar in look, and unpronounceable in name—hide themselves in all the nooks and corners, fringe the path borders and straggle over all unoccupied spaces.

Of fruits. Never have I seen so small a space produce such an interminable round. When we came here in January we luxuriated for weeks on delicious Seville oranges. Then for a few weeks we had plantains, from the row of broad leafie trees which extend along one end and (double) down one side of the garden. Next were the mulberries, but from some cause they did not quite come to perfection; and at all events, they have much less flavor than the same fruit at home.

About this time the gardner came to me for a great quantity of little muslin bags. I, much wondering, gave him some stuff to make them, and a few days after what should I see but the apple trees with innumerable white jackets in their leafy coats, and in every pocket a bunch of little growing apples. Some days afterwards the grape vine followed suit, and the vine trailing over the long arbor looked like a childs head in curl papers. These proved to be the shadows of coming events, and ere long nice mellow little apples began to appear on the table—the first we had seen in India that tasted like the genuine article. The figs now ripened but while apples were to be had no one would eat them.

A few days more brought the crowning delight of the season, the peaches. Of these there are two varieties, one flat with a flattened seed shaped much like a tomato is called the China peach. They are sweeter than the common peach but do not last as long. For weeks we had one dish of peaches and cream as regularly as the day came, and I think we have not enjoyed anything so much since we feasted on wild raspberries from Goat Island at Niagara.

The apricots were like small plums and were almost too sour to eat but made good preserves. The nectarines outwardly look like a greengage plum but within differ little from the peaches. The grapes were white and very sweet.

These are all foreign fruits—close on their heels came the prince of the natives—the Bombay Mango. This fruit looks like an enormous green plum, is 3 or 4 inches in length and something less in thickness—very sweet and very juicy. The old residents become excessively fond of it and say that it is only surpassed by one other fruit in the world, the mangoshen of Pava.

When the Bombay mangoes were gone we had the Desi ones for a month or so. These are the common fruit of this part of India, lining the roads shading the wells and cropping out in great orchards in every direction. I think it safe to say one half the trees we see are of this kind. Futtehgarh is a famous place for mangoes, many of which are almost equal to the Bombays though smaller and apt to taste a little of terpentine.

After this we contented ourselves with plantains or bananas, which are to be had the year round. This is a fruit shaped like a sweet potato, generally about 5 inches long and 2 inches thick, tasting something like a pear. Just now we have limes and guavas. This last is a nice looking fruit—sub acid—something between a quince and a pear, but with a strong fragrance that I do not like.

In the markets here I see also the Jack fruit which looks like an enormous thick-skinned gooseberry as big as ones head. I tasted it once, but never shall again—not but the taste is pleasant enough but the smell—oh pah! Did you ever when walking out come upon the remnants of a dead dog in some neglected valley—if so you can "eliminate a Jack fruit from the depths of your mental consciousness."

I must not forget the custard apple or Sharifa. It is a little smaller than one's fist, and with a thick furrowed covering like a pine-apple; but this easily breaks in the hand, and there appears a rich soft pulp, which in color, consistency, and taste always reminds me of ice cream, except that it is not so cold. To help the illusion, it is always dipped out or eaten with a spoon.

To wind up this dissertation on fruits, I have only to mention the melons, which, though not produced in the garden, are very abundant in the fields outside. The watermelons are good and cheap, large ones generally selling for 3 or 4 cents apiece. The muskmelons are smaller and rounder and I think a little inferior in taste to the Ohio ones as I remember them. Price, "two for a cent apiece" or less. But there is another kind with a smooth glossy rind like an apple, and tasting, too, much like a sweet and very juicy apple. These last are superb. Then there is a native melon—1 $\frac{1}{2}$ feet long—6 inches thick, which when ripe cracks open and reveals a snowdrift. It is however rather insipid unless eaten with sugar.

Loqats are a curious little tart fruit, much like an apple, only having one or two large seeds in the middle. The Bear bears a close resemblance to a half-ripe apple—poor eating—and quite small. Here and there. . . .

Yours sincerely,
W. F.   Johnson

[Flowers and shrubs identified in Will's garden diagram were: holly-hocks, flowing bean, Indian honeysuckle arbor, fragrant grass, flowering sage, silver bush, flaming bush, maiden's blush, stained mountain, crimson and yellow roses, an arbor of rose and yellow rose creepers, flowering flag, passion flower, white lilies, tuberoses, mignonette, portulaca, cypress vine, oleander, thorny cactus, juniper tree, fuschia, scarlet pointsettia, hedge of henna, a cedar tree, and unknown plants.]

SEVEN

August 1865–January 1868

FATEHGARH

⁂ IN AWE-FILLED NARRATIVES sent home to family in Pennsylvania, Rachel and Will described the natural beauty of India as seen on their preaching-camping tours. Rachel recounted their journeys and the magnificent and exotic sights, paying close attention to details—a shower of stars, a jeweled temple, a slender minaret of a mosque. In contrast to these wonders, Rachel expressed compassion for the miserable, filthy places in which the poor lived, where cholera took a heavy toll.

Will, who was now comfortably skilled in local languages, was welcomed as an old friend on repeat visits to villages during preaching tours. Described as "one of the most observant and sensitive of all the Fatahgarh missionaries," Will lamented that their work produced few converts to Christianity. He concluded, "It is every day apparent to me that there is in this district . . . a large class of persons, whose faith in Hinduism is entirely broken. . . . I believe that hundreds are intellectually convinced that Christ is true, the only saviour. . . . The social curse is to a Hindoo something dreadfully hard to bear. Probably, if any one were to preach a Christianity without the element of open confession, he would soon have in this region hundreds of adherents."[1]

In many of the letters sent home during these years, Rachel reverted to her middle name, Lillie, used by her family when she was a girl. Although her letters described a more settled home and work routine in India, a homesick Rachel wrote of the familiar, her youth, dreams of home, and thoughts of change in America since coming to India.]

Futtehgurh, July 31st, 1865

My Dear Uncle and Aunt,

I have just time before the departure of the mail this morning to apprise you of the arrival of Appleton's New Cyclopedia. It is indeed a noble gift. There are 16 large volumes of about 800 double columns

1. Alter, "Presbyterians in Farrukhabad," 24–26.

each, good type and very neatly bound in black cloth. Volumes of the like size and general appearance would usually sell from 8 to $10 apiece here, I think. The books came in beautiful order too. It will be very valuable to me, because students here have no large libraries to run to, to inquire into any subject that may puzzle them. . . .

Yours truly,
W. F. Johnson

Futtehgurh, India
August 30th, 1865

My dear Mother,

We have not had any letters from home since the one that brought the sad news of dear Samuels death. . . . I suppose that long ere this time, you have dear Frank home with you. What will he do now? Begin his studies again, I hope. How does Stella get on at school? I hope she has good teachers and loves her books.

One of the little orphan girls, blind Niddia, has just been in to say her lesson. We got a book for the blind not long ago, with the raised letters, and printed in the Hindustani language, so I am trying to teach little Niddia to read with her fingers. She has learned some of the letters, but has been sick so much, that she has not been able to come regularly. She is about as old as Stella and has a wonderful memory. She knows a great many hymns and sings like a lark. Her voice is very sweet and soft, and though she is blind, she always looks and seems to be very happy.

We are now alone again. The Kelloggs have gone down to Burhpur and commenced housekeeping. She is not very strong yet. We expected them up last night to tea, but her baby was not well, so Mr. Brodhead came without them. Mr. Ullmann has been over staying with Mr. Brodhead for a few days. He is not well, and he and Mrs. Ullmann will both go home to England in the cold weather.

The Fullertons have had a heavy cross laid on them. For some time, Mr. Fullerton had been troubled with his throat, in addition to other bodily ailments. Now the doctors all say he has cancer in the throat, and it may take him away any time, and there is no hope of a cure. He suffers a good deal, but has been wonderfully strengthened to bear cheerfully his affliction. They were preparing to go home in next December, but he will hardly be able to go. Poor Mrs. Fullerton, it is a sad trial to her and all the family. They have a family of 6 children, and will be left very desolate.

Here comes little Mary with her chatter. She can say several words, and is busy as a bee with her toys and play. She kisses her Grandma in her picture, and has a great many little accomplishments, that I know would interest her grandpa if they could see her.

Well dear Mother, I must leave you. Our love to you all. Your affectionate daughter,

Rachel L. Johnson

[In this brief note, Will announces to the Hookstown community that on December 6 another child was born to the Johnson family, Edwin Kerr Johnson.]

Futtehgurh, India
December 7th, 1865

My dear Friends,

Mrs. Johnson was intending to write to you by this mail, but is prevented by "good and sufficient reasons." Yesterday morning the even tenor of our household arrangements was disturbed by the advent of a new baby—a fine, hearty, little boy. And consequently, I am commissioned to present Mrs. Johnsons excuses, and to say that she will write when she finds herself able to do so. . . .

The doctor, who has just gone, reports mother and child as doing very well. Little Mary is very much pleased with her little brother, and is very fond of kissing and patting him.

I have just lately returned from a delightful trip to a meeting of the Synod of Northern India, away up at Amballa—within sight of the mountains. How inspiriting to us, who have seen hills but once since we came to India, was the sight of the spur of the great Himalayan chain only 38 miles away. I was greatly tempted to go on a little farther, and get a breath of mountain air. Both the Lodiana and the Furrukhabad Missions met at the Synod, and we made quite a respectable body.

On our way to the meeting, the Kelloggs and I stopped at the famous cities of Agra and Delhi, and saw some of the wonderful architecture of the old Mogul Kings. Some of the buildings erected by Shah Jehan, especially, are beautiful beyond all description. I suppose the Taj is, with perhaps one exception, the most beautiful building. It is built of white marble on a platform 400 feet square, also of white marble. The doorways and windows and interior of the building is most exquisitely inlaid with a mosaic of agate, carnelian, jasper, lapis-lazuli and such precious stones. Bayard Taylor's *India, China and Japan* gives the best description of the Taj which I have seen. But even that gives little idea of its marvelous perfection.

At Delhi, we went out 11 miles to see a wonderful tower 240 feet high, built away back in antiquity. No one can say when. It is called the Kutub Minar. From its top we calculated that about 1300 square miles of the earths surface lay within the compass of our vision, and almost the whole of this was covered with the debris of former cities—ruined while England was still the home of savage barbarians.

It was the most interesting trip. I wish I could speak of it more in detail, but it is time for me to close. . . .

Yours sincerely,
W. F. Johnson

Futtehgurh, India
January 20th, 1866

My dear Father and Mother,

I suppose you have heard by Mr. Johnsons letter of last month that we have another little assistant Missionary—and you, a little grandson. . . . Our little son was born on the 6th of December. He is a fine, little fellow. Cant say who he looks like yet. He is thriving nicely, though the poor child has not got a name yet. The difficulty is not so much in finding a name, as that there are so many pretty names. Mary is delighted with her little brother and calls him "Claude," the name of Mr. Brodheads little boy, who is her playmate.

Mr. Johnson, Mr. Brodhead, and Mr. Wyckoff are out preaching at a mela about 40 miles from here. I have been staying this week with Mrs. Brodhead at Burhpur. I feel pretty well now, though not quite so strong as I hope to be before the cold weather is over. We look for our husbands home on next Wednesday. Then in about a week after, they expect to go out preaching in the villages and will take us all with them. Mary has not been very well the last month, and is much thinner than she was. I hope the change will do her good.

Last week we had a meeting of Presbytery for the ordination of Baboo Jshuree Dass, who has been a licensed preacher for 2 years. He assisted Mr. Johnson in the Sabbath services and had been Head Teacher in the Boys School. He is now to be sent to take charge of the station of Futtehpore. . . . We are sorry to part with Jshuree Dass, but there was no one to go to Futtehpore, so it is placed in charge of a native pastor again.

. . . The mail is just in and I am delighted to find a letter from Frank, Stella, and Lizzie Harper. . . . It was quite a surprise to find you talking of Lizzie Stewart as Mrs. Harper, for I did not know she was married. . . . How strange it seems to think of all these changes going on among our old friends. I suppose it would seem just as strange for you all to see us come in with our little ones. . . . I was glad to hear that Frank is at College, and hope he will progress in his studies rapidly.

. . . We are looking for three new missionaries here this week on their way to the upper Mission. Mr. and Mrs. Alexander will be here soon. They are to be stationed at Allahabad.

Fig. 13. Rachel and her oldest daughter, Mary,
posed for this portrait in 1866 when a traveling
photographer took this picture at their home in
Fatehgarh.

. . . I am glad to hear that dear Grandfather and Grandmother are
with you. Tell them I love them just as well as when I was a little girl, and
thought there was no greater pleasure than a visit to Grandpaps. . . .
Well I must say Goodbye. Much love to all and kisses from the little ones.

Your loving daughter,
Rachel

Futtehgurh, India
March 7th, 1866

My dear Father and Mother,

We have the pleasure of sending you this time some very poor pictures of ourselves and little Mary. Mary's will not give you much idea of
the little blue-eyed, round-cheeked, roguish, little girl, that now plays
about the room—she is chattering with a native aya [nurse] in Hindustani—but it is the best we could get here now. . . . This one was taken
by a native artist, a Nawab from Lucknow. He brought his camera to our
house, and we tried several times; but Mary would not sit still, or would

not keep her face straight, out in the glare of the sun. Indeed, it was more than I could do to look out into the glaring sunlight, as you will see. These pictures will however help you to realize that we are still flesh and bones, and have not become myths, as we must seem to the little folks we left so long ago.

. . . But where is the baby? you will say. Well, here he is, asleep in his cradle. He was too sick to have his picture taken, but hopes sometime when he gets a little older to send you one. So this time, he will only send his name—which is "Edwin Kerr"—and ask you how you like it? He was baptized last Sabbath in the morning by Mr. Brodhead. In the evening his papa baptized 18 little ones! All are children of our native Christians. So you see our flock is growing. There will be a pretty large church after while, if the little ones only are trained up to be good men and women.

You ask me Mother if I am able to nurse my baby myself. I can now answer for Master Eddie that I am nursing him myself. As for Mary, she now eats rice and milk, dal (a native grain that we cook and eat mixed with rice), chupatties (a native cake that we all like very much. It is made of unbolted flour and baked like pancakes). She is fond of fruit too, and eats bears—not the four footed kind, but a little fruit that tastes something like a sweet apple and grows as large as a plum—plantains or bananas, and gooseberries, etc. We have a bush of mulberries in the garden now that are very good stewed. The Mango trees are in blossom, and they and the orange trees fill the air with their fragrance. . . .

. . . I hope Fathers oil interest still continues to give such good returns. Does he own a whole well, or part? I suppose Hookstown is illuminated entirely with oil—no more dark streets at night. How nice that will be. I suppose everybody will get rich now that lives in smelling distance of oil. I wish we had some of it here in its crude state, to feed our white ants on. It would not be so expensive as silk dresses. Did I tell you that they got into my box of warm clothes and ruined my silk dresses? They ate a path half round my brown silk, and a hole here and there in my black. So I think I cannot get a new one until that box of nicknacks comes out from home. Perhaps I will find a new one in it.

. . . With love to you and all.

> Your affectionate daughter,
> Rachel L. Johnson

> Futtehgurh, India
> March 7, 1866

My dear brother Frank,

We were very glad to hear that among all the Christmas rejoicings, you had time to send us a good long letter. We are also glad to hear that you are making progress in your studies and reaping some of the honors that fall to the good student. I am glad that you find favor with your fellow students and dear Frank, none will rejoice more in your advancement and success than we. We do pray that you may be led in the right way, and that God will, in his own good time, show you what work he has for you to do. It seems to me that it would be better for you to take the regular college course, especially as you feel undecided about your choice of a calling. You will certainly become a better scholar if you improve your time than if you hurry through. And you will be better fitted for whatever you then feel it your duty to do. We would be glad if you find the way plain, and decide to become a minister of the Gospel. It is true you may not reap so many earthly honors, but what reward better than that promised to those who turn many to righteousness. I hope dear brother, you will not give up the thought of preparing for the ministry because it will take so long. You are young, and have the prospect of being able to go on with your studies without hindrance, so that even it if takes "seven years," you will still be younger than many. Indeed, you will be younger than most of those who leave our Theological Seminaries. So dont make a hasty decision. I believe that you might become, with the help of Gods grace, a good minister. You have the talents and the means. I hope you will be enabled to come to a right decision when the time comes. Ask God in faith to guide you and he will direct your steps. . . .

It was with a sad pleasure that I read the tribute to the memory of dear brother Samuel from the Banner. I am glad to read of his worth and bravery, and that it was acknowledged by his Commanding Officers. Unspeakably precious is the testimony that dear Samuel did not forget to join with those who met for devotions, and was found with those who loved prayer and praise. The sweet hope that he died a Christian is worth more than the highest praise, tho we know he was worthy of it. Dear Samuel! I feel sometimes as tho it cannot be that he is gone. When I pray for you, his name too, involuntarily rises to my lips. But we have this blessed trust that now he needs not our poor prayers or tears. All is well with him.

Your affectionate sister,
R. Lillie Johnson

Etawah, India
May 17th, 1866

My dear Mother,

Since I last wrote to you about 6 weeks ago, our children have been very sick again. Mary is quite well now, but Eddie has never got well entirely since his first attack of bronchitis. He got a little cold and had another severe attack when he got a little better. We thought a change might do him good, so we came over here for 2 or 3 weeks. Mr. and Mrs. Sayre, our missionaries here, have taken their children to the Hills, as they were sick too. So their house is empty, and we are making ourselves at home—using all their housekeeping furniture as we need. This station has only been a Mission Station about three years, so there is only a little flock of native Christians here. Dr. and Mrs. Sherlock, our old Futtehpore friends, live here now. We see them every day, and they are very kind to us.

June 1st, 1866

I have so little time to write Mother, that I can only scratch off a few lines when I can get away from Eddie. He has been very ill since we came over. He has not got much better of the bronchitis, and now he suffers dreadfully with teething. He has two through, and four more very near, and he is not 6 months old until the 6th. I had hoped he would not get them until he grew stronger. He suffers so much, that sometimes he screams with pain nearly all night. I feel very much discouraged about him.

Mary is getting fat again and is as merry as a lark. The Brodheads are here now with their children from Futtehgurh. They will stay a week with us, then I hope Eddie will be well enough to go home. We have a better doctor here [Dr. Sherlock] than at home, so I dont like to go until baby is better.

I often wish—Oh! so much—that I could have you dear Mother with us. It would be such a comfort in our troubles, to ask Mother what to do.

June 2nd, 1866

Yesterday morning Mr. Johnson woke me with the pleasant news of letters from home. You may imagine how glad I was. I got up in a hurry and found letters from Mother, Frank, Stella, and Stellas picture. I was delighted to get it, and the letters too. How fast Stella is growing. I fancy she is as tall as I am now. She does not look much like she did when we left home. I dreamed the other night of paying you a visit and found everybody changed so much. I thought when I found the curl of hair in your letter that it was your hair, Mother. I was surprised to find Stellas so dark. I suppose you and father have a good many gray hairs now.

You have our pictures before this. So you think they are good? Mary's is so poor, I wish I had not sent it. She is such a winsome wee thing, it gives you no idea of her. She talks now and is very amusing to hear her chatter in Hindustani. She can say almost anything she likes. I have taught her some English words, but children here always learn Hindustani first. Mrs. Walsh said that when they took their children home, they did not know a word of English when they left Calcutta, and when they reached America, they talked English altogether. They soon pick up whatever they hear spoken around them.

Your affectionate daughter,
Rachel L. Johnson

Futtehgurh, India
Monday, July 1866

My dear Father and Mother,

It is now about two months since I wrote to you from Etawah. . . . Our little Eddie was then very ill. He soon got better, so we were able to come home again. Home is always the best place, and especially when there is sickness. . . .

. . . We found our village all quiet. Our home, with its pleasant garden and trees, looked very inviting after our long visit.

We had our communion 3 weeks ago, when Mr. Johnson baptized a convert from Hindooism of the writer caste. He is a very intelligent man and seems to be truly in earnest. He has had his share of persecution to bear too. He was employed as a writer by a bigoted old Hindoo merchant, and since he was baptized, he had lost his place. His wife says she wishes to become a Christian too, but her people are trying to keep her back. This old Hindoo offers her three dollars a month to support her, if she will hold on to her idolatry, and not disgrace them by giving up her old religion to become a Christian.

Your affectionate daughter,
Rachel L. Johnson

P.S. Dear Stella,

Mary says, send you a kiss. She is very well, and Eddie has four teeth and a little curl on the top of his head. That is all the hair he has. I can't keep it down, so I think he will be a curly head—like one who was very dear to us.

You must not think it was any want of love that we did not name him for dear Samuel, but I could not call him Samuel Kerr. I can think of but one with that name.

Love to Frank, and write to him often.

Your affectionate sister,
Rachel

Futtehgurh, India
September 20th, 1866

My dear brother Frank,

Mary found some little kittens in the orphanage adjoining the school room that interested her very much. Blind Susan has the care of the orphan girls, and she came in to ask me to go to see blind Phoebe, who is nearly always sick with asthma. The larger orphan girls are all married now, and living in homes of their own in the Christian village. They seem to be very quiet and well behaved women, and I hope will be examples for goodness and virtue to the heathen women around.

We have all had a good deal of trouble among our children from sore eyes this season. Eddie, poor child, seems to get his share of every sickness, and he has had it for several weeks. The kind of ophthalmia they have seems to be a disease of the eyelid, more than of the eye itself. The eye is affected painfully from the light, so that we have to keep them in a room partially darkened, which is a great trial to little folks. Mary is the only one of all the children that has escaped so far. Eddie is now almost well, I am thankful to say. Soon we will have the cold weather coming on, when I hope the children will get strong. Today it is raining and feels quite cool, or comfortable, I should say. This is perhaps the last of the rains.

I had a visit from a native lady the other day, who will, we hope, be baptized soon. She is the wife of Hindoo, Har Pershad, who was baptized a short time ago. She is a nice-looking woman, though she was decked out in ornaments rather profusely for our taste. Her arms were covered with bracelets of various kinds, from the hand to the elbow, nearly; fingers with rings (natives wear them on their thumbs too); and then toes and ankles must have a share of tinkling ornaments. Then she wore necklaces and a kind of ornamental headpiece of silver work worn above the forehead—a frontlet you might call it. The natives have a passion for jewelry, and will persist in putting silver ornaments, necklaces and anklets on their children, though they are so frequently stolen away, and murdered for the sake of their ornaments. Only a few weeks ago, one of the boys attending one of our bazar schools was missing. A few days later his body was found in the jungle—his ornaments gone.

It would seem very strange now, after our six years exile, to go home and find so many new faces filling the places of those who are gone— strange and sad. But I hope that we shall sometime again be permitted to meet our dear, loved ones who are left in the dear, old home. I often try to picture to myself how you all look there: Father seated in the corner with his newspaper, dear Mother in her rocking chair before the fire. I wonder, has 6 years made much change in their looks? Stella now almost grown to womanhood, yet I think her face is like it used to be. And Frank, you my careless brother, how can I tell what you look like, for you have not sent me your picture for nearly 4 years. . . .

We are not so far away now that you can send us a message on the Atlantic cable that will reach India in two days if not sooner. I see that a message of 20 words will cost $100 to America at present. We have had news from New York in the papers, only two days from America. But I think the terms will be lower by and by. It is a glorious success tho, is it not, to be able to bind the old and new world so closely together.

Your affectionate sister,
Lillie

Camp Ummedipoor, India
Tuesday, Dec. 18th, 1866

My dear Father and Mother,

We have been moving about so much during the last month or two that I have not been able to write as usual. We are now out on our yearly preaching tour and in camp today, about 100 miles from home and about 12 from the city of Agra. The Brodheads and Kelloggs, and 13 native preachers, are with us—or have been, I should say. The Kelloggs left us yesterday to go home; their child being sick and Mrs. Kellogg not well. We are all in good health. The children are getting quite rosy, being out in tents. Mary is getting her cheeks rounded out again and is very happy playing with Claude and Wilfred, Mrs. Brodhead's little boys. Eddie is the picture of health and good humor—the best of babies. I had his picture taken for you, but the little rogue would not be still and laughed; so you have not quite as good a picture. But it will show you what a fine big boy your little grandson is. I will send it as soon as we get to a safe post office. You know we are not out in the jungle now, and tho we may find an opportunity to mail our letters, they are not so sure to go from these little out of the way places.

We left home on the 12th of November to attend the Annual Meeting at Etawah. We had some difficulty in getting over to Etawah as the dawk gares had stopped running. So we divided our families. Mrs. Brodhead, Mrs. Kellogg, and I, and our children came to Bewar, 20 miles, in our own carriages. Mr. Brodhead and Mr. Johnson followed in a small wagon drawn by oxen. At Bewar we got doolies or palkis, which are only small beds with a frame covering over with a coarse cloth stretched over top and sides; you can lie down a good deal easier than you can sit up. A pole passes through the top and extends beyond at each end, so that the native bearers can carry it conveniently. 4 or 6 men are required for each doolie and they trot along quite briskly.

We had quite a large company when we all got started. We waited in the dawk bungalow, or travelers house, until our husbands came up. Then we had dinner and started on a little before dark. Mary and Eddie soon went to sleep, lulled by the seesaw motion of the doolie, as the bearers trotted along. Mr. Johnson and Mr. Kellogg went on in their ox cart, and Mr. Brodhead stayed back to take care of our company. You would have thought us a strange looking caravan as we threaded along the narrow streets of Bewar, with our troop of half naked grunting bearers, all humming or grunting in a sing-song chorus. Torch bearers were running along by the sides of our doolies, every little while pouring oil out of their little cans over their torches to keep them burning. On and on we went at a brisk trot until we had accomplished several miles. Then a relay of bearers changed, and so over 40 miles we plodded. Just before daylight we came to the railway track, and I knew we were at Etawah. A little farther on we entered the Mission Compound, where the tents dotted round told us we had reached our brethren.

The stars were falling in showers away off toward the Northwest, some leaving long trains of light. It was a beautiful sight. We were sorry we had not waked a little earlier, for those who were watching earlier said they were much more brilliant. The night of the 13th was the night the astronomers had predicted. There was a very unusual number and, tho not so many as fell 33 years ago—the night you used to tell us about—yet the sight was one I would not have missed for a great deal.

We found that our missionary friends were all there. The Scotts from the Hills, the Walshes, Alexanders and Dr. Owen from Allahabad, the Wyckoffs from Mynpoorie, the Sayres and our 3 families, made up all our Mission family—all there, not one left behind. This was the first meeting for many years in which some one had not been left at home. The meeting was a delightful one and lasted 8 days. The Missionaries met each day at 11; spent $\frac{1}{2}$ hour in devotional exercises; then the remainder of the day in business. The ladies generally stayed part of the day, as it was interesting to us to listen to their discussions. Then the evenings were seasons of pleasant, social intercourse. Most evenings an hour was set apart for a prayer meeting, when Dr. and Mrs. Sherlock always joined us. On Sabbath we had the morning service in Hindustani, and the evening sermon in English; the Lords Supper was administered. It was a delightful season to us to meet with our brethren and sisters in this heathen land around our Lords table; and sing together once more his praises in our own sweet native tongue; and listen to his word expounded in our own language. No words ever sound so sweet or go home to the heart like those we hear in our mother tongue.

So the time passed and all our friends prepared to leave. The Scotts went over to Futtehgurh, their old home, to see the native Christians. But we had made arrangements to go out on our preaching tour before going home. There was to be a large fair at Bateswar the next week, which our husbands decided to visit, to preach to the crowds. So, leaving us all in Etawah, Mr. Johnson with 3 of the brethren, went to the fair; where they, with their native helpers, preached several days. After their return we went by rail to Agra, where our tents had been sent to await us.

But I must take another sheet before I begin to tell of the wonderful old ruins and scenes we have visited.

Wednesday, 20th

We have been at this place longer than we usually stop. We marched here Monday morning, and we leave tomorrow. Today is the regular market day and our husbands have gone out into the market place to preach. The people have listened very well here, and they have had pretty large audiences. The village is not large. All the houses are on one narrow street, and there is nothing attractive about the place.

Our camp is just on the outskirts of the village in a little grove of trees. We have our flock of goats with us for milk for the children. Our bread and butter we brought with us from Agra, as we cannot get it by the way. Though the villagers have plenty of cows, yet they dont make butter, except near European stations where they can sell it to the Foreigners. They dont know how to make it, and think the milk boiled down into the ghee they use much more palatable.

We had a very amusing, but rather annoying experience, when we came up to Agra. The train got in about 11 at night, and we expected our own carriages to be waiting for us. But when we got to the railway station there was no sign of our carriages. So we were obliged to get three of the hacks, or carriages, to carry us all over the river to our camp, about 2 miles from the station. After a long drive we found our tents. As we had had no dinner, we felt rather hungry, and ordered the servants to get us a cup of tea. It came in soon, smoking hot. We were all stirring it, preparing to enjoy a nice cup, when Mr. Kellogg says, "Whats the matter with the tea?" Mrs. Kellogg tastes and says, "It is pepper tea." I took a pretty good sip—as I had a sore threat and thought it would be good for it—when much to my disgust, I found it was tobacco! Ugh! The stupid man had heated the water in a vessel in which he had stored his tobacco. We all had a laugh at our being so taken in, and sent the man off to try his skill in making another teapot full for us. It was one o'clock when we got ready to rest, and we all felt tired enough. Next morning we moved our tents into the old church yard that belongs to our mission, and pitched near the old church where Mr. Fullerton used to preach before the mutiny.

We have no missionaries in Agra now. The field is occupied by English missionaries, since we gave up our mission there. They invited us to tea one evening during our stay in Agra, but Mr. Johnson was not feeling very well, so we did not go. The rest all went and found them very pleasant people.

... Stella dear ... I wish you could see all the beautiful temples, mosques and palaces we have seen since we came out. But when we look at these poor, ignorant Hindoos, we cannot but long for the time when we may see them loving that Saviour whose love will one day open to our wondering eyes ... his far more wonderful temple in the New Jerusalem. . . .

Rachel L. Johnson

Futtehgurh, India
March 6th, 1867

My dear Father and Mother,

When I last wrote to you, we were away out in the jungle. From Ferozabad we marched to Shikohabad, a city on the railroad. Mr. and Mrs. Sayre, with their native preachers, met us at the last village. They spent Sabbath with us, then on Monday, we marched for Shikohabad and they went on their way. We camped in a beautiful grove of large mango trees. . . .

. . . Then we turned aside, and went up a little narrow lane, fringed on each side with tall grass crowned with its silvery heads.—This same grass, by the way, is full ten feet high. The oxen no doubt would prefer a more modest growth, but this is used for making chairs. It makes a very comfortable chair, woven together with twine. Our chairs we had with us were made of this sauta, as it is called. We went up this little road about a mile until we found a grove, not too far from the city. We turned in to wait for our camp. We spread our shawls under the trees for beds for the children, and sat down with our books to wait. By and by the carts came. Then there was hurry and bustle until the tents were up and in order. Then, towards evening, our husbands came in, tired and weary after their long walk.

Mr. Johnson had visited several villages and had preached, but in one or two he found, as he came up, the people all fled and hid themselves. He thought it very strange, until a few natives explained the cause of their flight. A murder had been committed, or at least the body of a native man had been discovered in a well near the village. Perhaps it was a traveller who had been murdered and thrown into this well to conceal the dead body. This is a common practice among the native people. I suppose you will think it strange for them to throw the body into the well; but here there are so many wells, all over the cultivated land, almost one for every field. They are not always very deep, but dug just deep enough to get water to water the fields nearby.

Well the native police were busy making arrests among the poor villages, fleecing them sadly, as they always do. For in such cases, those who are able to pay a bribe will get off, and those who cant, are sure to suffer. When they saw Mr. Johnson, with his catechists, coming, they supposed of course he was some Official Sahib coming to arrest them for the murder. So they fled at his approach. He passed on to other villages, as the people were too much frightened to hear preaching, and visited others on the way. You must remember that all the people here live in villages from the little nagra of a few houses, up to the large towns and cities.

We spent Christmas in camp in this grove. And we had the pleasant cheer of letters from you on Christmas morning. . . .

We made 3 marches from this place to Mynpurie, and spent a few days with the Wyckoffs. Mrs. Wyckoff came down from the hills in November. She looks well, and her two little girls and two little boys all look so rosy and healthy. The weather began to threaten rain, so we pushed on long marches, hoping to get home before the rain. But the last night in camp, the rain came down in torrents. Mrs. Brodhead and I took our children and slept in the large double roofed tent. Mr. Johnson and Mr. Brodhead took the small tent, which was soaked through in the morning, but we were quite dry. We reached home next day, through a steady drizzling rain—that would have been quite the thing for an election day, as it used to rain.

I was glad to receive a long letter from Frank last mail. I dont understand why he is not going on with his regular college course. Why does he turn aside to teach? Why not go through the college course first, and then he would be ready for whatever work he may choose?

I am glad to hear that you, dear Mother, keep so well. Mary was looking at your picture and she asked me if you wear a cap. She never sees any old ladies here that wear caps, so she noticed it as strange that you wore a "tope," as she called it—the native name for hat or cap or turban. Does Father wear glasses now? I suppose you both do when you read. I was glad to hear from Fathers letter so much news about the old neighbors—where they live and what they are doing.

With love to you all from us both. And kisses from Mary and Eddie.

Your affectionate daughter,
Rachel L. Johnson

Futtehgurh, India
March 19th, 1867

My dear Mother,

Mr. Brodhead goes today to Etawah to meet Rev. J. L. Scott and Mrs. Scott, who are on their way to Calcutta. They will leave for America via England in a few days. We are sending a little package for you which I hope will reach you safely.

When we were in Agra, an old, long-bearded, Cabul man brought a large bundle of goods to our tents for sale. He had some beautiful, Cashmere shawls, Lama shawls, soft as silk, and oh so many beautiful things. I bought two little scarfs, which I send you as a specimen of native embroidery. The dark-colored one is for Mother, and the Magenta colored

Fig. 14. Featured goodies in the baskets at this sweetie shop in the bazaar are *jolebies*, sweet and salty pretzel candies; *gulgullas*, doughnut holes made from wheat flour and molasses; *pakauras*, vegetables dipped in lentil flour batter and deep fried; sweetened puffed rice; *pera*, milk boiled down to a sweet solid; hot *gram*, chick peas; and *reowri*, sugar taffy wafers.

one is for Stella. They will keep your throat warm when you go out sleigh riding in the winter. These were made in Peshawar, away up in the north of India. Inside the little piece of bamboo you will find a little Delhi broach, I send as a present to Stella. The natives at Delhi are noted for their beautiful work in gold and silver. Some of it is exquisite, so delicate and beautiful. This little broach is set with emeralds, real stones. I bought it from a man from Delhi who brought jewelry for sale. The gold work I think you will admire as a specimen of native work, and I want dear Stella to wear it as a reminder of sister in India. Mr. Johnson puts in some photographs too of which he has written a description, and some of his pencil drawings about home. I must send off the parcel.

Your affectionate daughter,
Rachel L. Johnson

Futtehgurh, India
May 7th, 1867

My dear Father and Mother,

I will begin you a letter early this morning, for when the thermometer gets up above 90 degrees, as it will in a few hours, it is rather hot for such exertion of mind or body. Since I wrote to you last, we have received the long, looked-for box from home. Everything came safely, and we were very, much pleased with the nice things you sent. Mary was delighted with her hat. She is very fond of wearing something pretty. And Eddie looks very sweet in his. It just fits his head. Dolly was welcomed with a great many caresses and kisses. She had suffered a little in her complexion by her sea voyage (the glazing was discolored by the sea air), but a little rubbing up made her all right. I suppose Stella dressed her, so I told Mary she might call her Stella. She often goes to sleep with her in her arms.

The bonnet for me came very nicely, and I have worn it several times, calling on some of the lords of the land, the English. My dress will make up very pretty, and will be very serviceable. The gaiter boots fit my foot exactly. It is quite a comfort to wear a pair of American square toed shoes again. The English shoes are always very narrow at the toes. Mr. Walsh said that when he was in Europe, he always was able to find out his Yankee countrymen by looking at their boots. The childrens shoes will fit them in a few months. Their dresses I liked very much, especially the blue. My muslin and other things came all right. The socks for Mr. Johnson are of an excellent quality. Well, I need not say anything more, for you will gather from this that we were quite well pleased with our box, and send you many thanks for your kind remembrances.

I have just been out on the veranda the last two hours hearing the lessons of some ragged little Hindoo girls of one of our bazar schools. Some of them have learned to read very well, and have the whole of the shorter catechism at their tongues end—besides having committed a great many hymns. Some of the girls are very clever and learn very quickly. But they are married off at 11 or 12 years of age and taken out of school, so they are not able to make as much progress as our Christian girls. But they get a good knowledge of the Testament, and have a good deal of it stored away in their memories, so we hope the truths that they learn may often be blessed to their souls in after days. "Sow the seed in the morning, and in the evening with-hold not thy hand, for thou knowest not whether shall prosper either this or that."

We have just lost one of our best and most intelligent native Christians, Baboo Jshuree Dass. He was licensed to preach when we first came to Futtehgurh. He assisted Mr. Johnson in preaching at Futtehgurh, until he was sent to take charge of the station at Futtehpore, nearly 2 years ago. At our last Annual Meeting, he was sent back to Futtehgurh on account of his health having failed at Futtehpore, and it was hoped that he would recover if sent back to his old home. He was to be co-pastor with Mr. Johnson over our church here in Rakha. But his health has been failing ever since, so that he was not ordained. He gradually got weaker until last Thursday he obtained release from his sufferings. He died a most peaceful, happy death—witnessing to all around that his only hope was in Christ. He was a most exemplary Christian and lived a very blameless life. He was always a great student, very fond of his books. He had a very good knowledge of English, wrote an excellent book in English, giving an account of Hindoo Manners and Customs. He was a very good preacher and teacher. He leaves a wife, who is a very good Christian woman, and several children. The funeral service was held in the church. Mr. Johnson preached the sermon, and Mr. Kellogg closed with prayer. Then some 6 or 8 of the native Christians bore the body out and carried the coffin out to our little graveyard, followed by a large crowd of mourning natives. We all felt that he was one of the Blessed dead who had died in the Lord.

Since we wrote last we have all been well, the children are both very well. Mary looks better than she has ever done, and Eddie has grown to be a great strong boy, full of all sort of mischief—running all about the house and garden. He talks some and goes at such a headlong speed that he has many a broken head to weep over.

Mary says she is going to vileyat [distant country], that is, to America. We have a stairway outside of our house that goes up to the flat roof. Mary's delight is to go up and down the stairs. I told her that in her Grandpa's house there were stairs inside that she could go up and down herself. She thinks that will be one of her greatest pleasures, when she goes to see you. She wanted to start at once.

Your affectionate daughter,
Rachel L. Johnson

Futtehgurh, India
June 12th, 1867

Dear Frank,

 . . . The last letter I received from you left you at the Normal school. I hope this will find you back at college. We have not had any news from home for more than two months and it makes me feel that you are all Oh, so far away. When letters come often, it shortens the seeming distance wonderfully, and I feel as tho I could almost run over and see you all at home. . . .

This is the hottest part of the season and we have had some very, trying weather, altho this season has been cooler than usual, and now we will have the rains here very soon. I have just been out with the children (6 o'clock) to get a cool breath of the morning air. We went to the public garden—a very pretty place where the grass and flowers are always kept green by watering them. The garden is large, with nice carriage roads laid out, and pleasant little foot paths leading round among the flower plots. When we reached the garden, a sand storm came up and we were obliged to hurry home, with our eyes full of dust.

These sand storms are very unpleasant—sometimes the air is so filled with dust that you cant see anything outside, but they clear the air and leave it pleasanter after they blow over. We had a very hard storm a few weeks ago: a kind of whirlwind that uprooted trees, tore off their branches, and unroofed a great many of the native houses (which are mostly thatched with grass or tiled roofs). Hail too fell, about the largest I ever saw. A great many cattle and sheep were killed in some parts. Our mangoes were stripped from the trees, and the grapes injured very much. There are still some mangoes left—ripe and golden. Here Frank, is a plate of that beautiful fruit that would make your mouth water. . . .

Saturday Morning
June 15th, 1867

Good morning dear brother Frank,

Since I last had a chat with you, I had the pleasure of a letter from you. So you are teaching? Well, I hope you have had a pleasant school. Your term will be out before this time. Have you given up your college course? I hope not. . . .

Your box reached us after a very long voyage. You will doubtless have seen many changes in the fickle goddess of fashion while my bonnet was traveling down round the cape. But you are right when you say that we do not change our fashions very often; though we see very fashionable people here among the English civilians. Hats are so much cooler and convenient here, that ladies wear hats in place of bonnets, except on special occasions.

. . . Mary is sitting in the doorway playing with some toys she has just bought from a man at the door. She is much afraid of a visit from Master Eddie, who is a great piece maker. He is out in the garden with a native woman. Mary has learned all her letters and is very fond of her books. I cannot please her better than to "parhoo" her, as she says, which is Hindustani for teaching to read.

. . . Goodbye, dear Frank. May God bless you and make you useful.

Your affectionate sister,
R. Lillie Johnson

[Will added a note to Rachel's letter for Frank at what appears to be her urging.]

My dear Frank,

We were glad to hear from you two days ago, that you were well and flourishing. You have never told us, I think, why you left College. I was in great hopes you would have concluded to go on through your course of studies, enter the Seminary, and perhaps eventually join us here. We have plenty of hard work and some few drawbacks. But on the whole, ours is an unusually pleasant mode of life; and to one who loves the Master and his service, it has unusual attractions.

In the cold season, we travel a great deal here, preaching in every direction, and seeing many strange sights and people. This year we had a couple of magnificent trips, one to Agra and one to Gwalior. At Agra, we got several nice, little photos of views about there to send to our friends. I enclose a view of Agra city looking from the Fort, of which the prominent object is the Jumna Musjid[2] or principal mosque of the city. The Mohammedans have several other places of worship in the city, some of which are more pretty, but this is the largest. It forms a sort of outer bastion of the fort. The front, which faces you, is enclosed with a wall perhaps 15 feet high, the inside of which is lined with shops continued in a pillared corridor, which you see joining the Mosque. The Mosque stands on a platform some eight feet high, which extends far out in front for the worshippers to kneel on. The rest of the inclosure is filled up with piles of grain, forage fruits, etc., carts and laden oxen and asses, so that there is an ever-crowded bazar. Some of the booths and piles of grain and animals may be seen in the picture near the platform steps.

Back of the two mango trees you can see the thatches which project from the front of the shops to protect the wares and purchasers. There are two gates to this inclosure through which you get access to the Main entrance of the Fort. The top of the high arch of one of these gateways is visible in the left foreground. The view looks down from the lofty walls of the noble ancient fort of Akbar, the Great. This part is a mile and a half in circuit, and its embrasured battlements rise to the height of 70 feet about the level plain, so that you almost seem to look down upon the swelling, towering domes of the Musjid.

The two smaller arched entrances of the Mosque are, I should think, nearly forty feet high, from which you can get an idea of the size of the structure. The little pillared pavilions, along the top of the front, on the corners, and crowning the minarets are extremely graceful. The whole structure, as well as the Fort itself, is built of a dark red sandstone. The famous Jumna Musjid of Delhi is on the same general plan as this, but its proportions are infinitely more noble, and the vast quantities of black

2. "Jumna Musjid" translated means "a great mosque on the Jumna [Yamuna] River." Literally, the word "Jumna" means "collecting" or "uniting," because this is where worshipers gathered for prayers on Fridays at noon.

Fig. 15. A view of Agra from the ramparts of the old fort.

and white marble used in its construction greatly relieve the heaviness which this structure possesses.

Fancy yourself sitting in the pavilion on the top of one of those slender minarets. . . . Three of the most beautiful buildings in the known world are before you; perfect dreams of beauty in white marble, agate, jaspar, carnelian, and every stone you can conceive of. The Taj, the Pearl Mosque, and the Palace of Shah Jehan, are all before you. Oh what enchanting days we spent, rambling among these scenes.

In the immediate foreground you see a gun platform with two mantled port holes for the guns. Beyond and behind the Mosque, stretches for miles, the confused mass of irregular houses which make up an oriental city. The distant trees to the right embower the residences of the Europeans.

I hope you will be pleased with this addition to your Indian curiosities. But I have left myself no room to speak of other things. We are well and everything goes on after the old fashion. . . .

Yours,
W. F. Johnson

Futtehgurh, India
September 2nd, 1867

My dear Mother,

You ask why we never wrote about the famine? I did write about it, I am quite sure. But it was not in our part of the country. It was in the south of India. About a million people died. It was dreadful—the suffering of the poor natives. We all sent something towards their relief, but the help they received was not more than a mite among so many. Government gave a great deal, but it came too late to the rescue.

Mr. Johnson . . . is just counting out a bag of pice or cents, as you would call them, and now he is taking them out to the gate to distribute among a most, distressed-looking company of the poor blind, diseased, and lepers that have come for their monthly pittance. There are 40 or 50 I think, from the number I can see; and of course, we can't spare them each very much, but for a little, they can get a days food. As to clothing, they dont have much of that, only a very scant supply of rags. Fortunately for the poor creatures, these rainy days are warm, and they dont suffer on that account. There has been a good deal of cholera in the city for a month or so, and when we see the misery and filth in which the poor live, we cannot wonder that pestilence finds many victims among them. There has been no case of cholera among the European residents, and reports say that it has very much diminished in the city.

. . . Mary talks a great deal about Grandpa and Grandmama, and is trying to grow big as fast as she can, so that she can go to see them. We are glad to hear that you have such a good High School, and that dear Stella is one of the scholars. . . .

. . . We had one of the Methodist brother Missionaries with us a short time ago. Rev. Waugh—he was from Mercer [Pennsylvania], and knew Mr. and Mrs. Morton very well. He was on his way to the Hills where his family now is. We enjoyed his visit very much. It is refreshing to meet an American in this land. . . .

Your affectionate daughter,
Rachel L. Johnson

Chhibramau, India
November 21st, 1867

My dear Father and Mother,

. . . You will see by my date that we are not at home. A little more than a week ago we left home on our yearly preaching tour through the villages. We are now about 20 miles from home, at a large town called Chhibramau. Our tents are pitched outside of the town in a nice large grove of Mango trees. The children enjoy tent life, and feel like prisoners just out of bondage. They have been shut up all the long hot days in the house, and now they are free to run all about in the shade of these grand, old trees, from morning to night. Eddie is generally in full chase after a kid, or a chicken, or a crow, or something. Mary and Louise Kellogg are busy with their dolls, or running, climbing over the low mud walls of the neighboring fields. If by chance they find a little mound of earth, a hill they call it, they are delighted. They totter up and down until their little legs, unused to climbing, tire—or a misstep brings them crying back with a broken nose.

The people here receive them [Mr. Johnson and Mr. Kellogg] very kindly, and listen to the gospel more willingly than at any place we have visited. Two of our native Christians, with their families, have been living here for some time, and it seems to be a very encouraging place for an out station. There are a great many villages clustering around within a few miles, and we will remain here sometime—a month perhaps—so that these villages may be reached. We have with us 10 native helpers, catechists and readers, who all assist in preaching the gospel to these poor villages. Mr. Johnson and Mr. Kellogg go out on foot with these, morning and evening, to preach either in the bazar of Chhibramau or to some of these villages around.

Mrs. Kellogg and I hope to be able to see some of the women and talk with them. We had quite a congregation of women visit us in our tents at one village on our march. We camped near the village of Najipore, and while our husbands were out preaching, the women of the place all came to see us. I think there was about 80 there at one time. We told them as well as we could about the Good News of a Saviour who saves them from their sins, and of the folly of worshiping their idols of mud and stone; that all their bathing in the holy waters of the Ganges nearby could not wash away their sins. But oh they are so ignorant, their minds are in such utter darkness. It makes ones heart ache to see how little idea they have of their need of a Great Saviour. They seem very willing to hear all we had to say to them, and glad to have us come among them. When we left their village, the women came running to make their parting salams.

We do not expect to go home before the Annual Meeting in January at Allahabad. We will march from here to Kannauj, the old capital of India, which is now all in ruins. It is about 25 miles from here. From there we will march on to Cawnpore, preaching in the villages on the way, and from there go on the railway to Allahabad, about the 2nd week of January.

. . . Mary and Eddie are both getting on nicely. Eddie is almost as tall as Mary and talking and able to tell a great, long story about his and "shisters" doings. He is every inch a boy in all his works and plays. . . .

Always your affectionate daughter,
Rachel L. Johnson

Chhibramau, India
Nov. 22nd, 1867

My dear brother Frank and Sister Stella,

Just now I am sitting under some grand, old mango trees that shut out the sun and make a delightful shade. They are still covered with leaves, altho it is November. You know they never look bare and naked like the trees at home, for while the old leaves drop off, one by one, the new ones are quietly unfolding. By and by you find the old leaves covering the ground and the trees all clad in a new dress of quiet brown and green, that soon changes to a bright glossy green. It looks strange to us to see the new leaves of the mango taking a brownish tint, and thus reversing the order of nature as we saw it at home. The other trees are not like them in that particular.

Yesterday an old Hindoo came along with two little birds in a cage, that he said would perform some wonderful tricks. The children all gathered round and begged to see them; so we told him to show us what his little birds could do. He said to get some slips of paper and write the childrens names on them, and scatter them before him. Then whatever name we called, the bird would bring to him. So I did so, and Mary, Eddie, Louise and Allie sat down before the tent to see what was coming. He took the bird on his hand and first, giving it a few grains of rice, he told it to bring the names as we called them. It fluttered about picking up one paper, then another, until it had the right one. Then it flew back and put it in his hand, and so on, until it had given all the childrens names correctly. The secret of the little birds knowledge we thought was this: when it picked up the wrong one, the man kept on talking; and when it got the right one, he said nothing; and then it flew back to him.

He then took a rude little cannon, about 6 inches long, and put a little powder in it, and lighted the match. The bird fired off the cannon. He first lighted a little piece of cotton suspended over the touch hole; and the bird, by picking at a little string, caused the cotton to ignite the powder.

But after all his trouble training his little birds to perform such tricks, I thought it was not nearly so wonderful as the skill they show in constructing their nests in their native groves, untaught, save by the hand of Him who made them. These same little birds build those wonderful hanging nests that are sewed and woven together in such a way, that you think the little bird must have had some other needle than its little, sharp bill and claws to make such beautiful network. We found a tree not long ago with a great number of these nests hanging from the ends of the branches. They are nearly a foot long, 4 or 5 inches wide, something the shape of an egg with the small end elongated. In the lower end there is a narrow passage that forms the entrance to the nest. It is

Fig. 16. Rachel and Will's early missionary friends are featured in this photo-graph of the annual meeting of the Presbyterian missionaries in North India in Allahabad in January 1868. Back row, left to right: Emily Brodhead, Rachel Johnson, Benjamin and Nancy Wyckoff, James Alexander. Middle row, left to right: Samuel and Antoinette Kellogg, Augustus Brodhead, Will Johnson, Susan Alexander, Mrs. Owen, Mr. and Mrs. Edward Sayre. Seated, left to right: John J. Walsh, Mrs. Walsh, Julius Ullmann, Joseph Owen.

suspended by the larger end, and so the door hangs down from the tree and the bird is protected from intruders. We took some of the empty nests home with us, and perhaps sometime we may be able to send, or show you one.

We have plenty of companions in our grove. The squirrels chasing each other up and down almost every tree, and the hungry crows on the alert for every stray morsel of food. Yesterday Eddie came holding his hand on his head. He said a crow had scratched him. When he was chas-ing it, it had turned on him. I suppose he had something to eat in his hand. They are so impudent. At night we hear the barking of the little foxes, and sometimes the howling of the jackal. Wolves too sometimes come about the camp, looking with hungry eyes on our goats and their kids. We have watchmen all night to keep off thieves (men and beast). We get so used to these things here that it does not seem strange.

Always your affectionate sister,
Lillie

In Camp Poora, India
50 miles from Futtehgarh
January 4th, 1868

My dear Mother,

It is Saturday night and the rain is pattering down on the roof of our tents. The camp is all quiet, the children in bed, and their papa about joining them. It is so quiet that I feel that it is a good time to have a little talk with you, my dear Mother.

We have been marching almost every day this week—6 or 8 miles. Here we have pitched our tents to rest over the Sabbath. We were at Kannauj about two weeks after we left Chhibramau. . . . We are now about 30 miles from Cawnpore, which place we hope to reach by the 14th. Then we go on to the Annual Meeting at Allahabad for the 17th.

. . . We will have to remain here until the ground dries, and our tents too. But the hot sun soon dries everything, even in these winter days. How different everything here now from the cold, bare, ice-clad hills at home. The harvest of sugar cane has just been gathered. The children beg for the sweet juicy stalks of sugarcane. Altogether, it seems only winter in name.

Goodnight. A Happy New Year to you all in our dear old home!

Your affectionate daughter,
Rachel

EIGHT

March 1868–December 1871

FATEHGARH

⊄ BETWEEN 1868 AND 1872, four eventful years, Rachel's regular monthly letters became more irregular; they slipped to every three months, and then there were no letters from Rachel for two years, from December 1869 until they sailed for America in early spring 1872. Most likely Rachel's letters were lost; however, with both a growing family and mission, she may have been too busy to write regularly. Several letters from Will to his Uncle and Aunt and reports to the Board of Foreign Missions filled in critical details of those years.]

Futtehgurh, India
March 7, 1868

My dear brother Frank,

I am sorry Frank to hear you talk of giving up your college course, even tho you dont like Greek. It is but a small part of what is required of you to study, and no one finds all his studies equally interesting. Tastes differ. One likes languages, another mathematics, and another general literature; yet he who would be a scholar must study all, more or less. If you do not excel in Greek, I am sure, with a little application, you will be able to pass creditably in it, as well as your other studies.

Perhaps you think that if you do not become a preacher, all this unpleasant study and time is thrown away, but not so. All the labor and study, even if not of practical use, is improving to your mind, and will be of use in educating and enlarging your mind. It does one good to apply the mind to that which is not too easy and pleasant, even if our progress is not so fast as it would be if palatable as well. But why trouble your mind now about what you will be, even if, after a college course of two or three years, you should settle down to be a farmer? An intelligent, well educated man—be he farmer, or preacher, or lawyer, or physician, or mechanic—is all the better fitted to perform his work in life well, if you study well and improve your time as well as you can. Learn just as much as you can (even if Greek lesson is not the best learned). Spend some of your leisure time in general reading, books of travels, etc. There is plenty of good, interesting, reading matter in your college library. You may not always have access to so good a library.

Withal, take time for gymnastic exercises to keep your body in healthy condition, else your mind wont be able to do its work well. Why dear brother Frank, if you spend two or three years in such a good work as fitting yourself to be a good, useful, and intelligent, well-educated man, surely $6.00 a week, or much more, would be well—not "spent," but—invested.

. . . Your affectionate sister always,

R. Lillie Johnson

Futtehgurh, India
April 13th, 1868

My dear Father and Mother,

. . . Eddie is busy going round the windows looking out for wasps—with a stick to give them a tap. He is so full of mischief. Dr. Reed called this morning to see a sick girl and Eddie runs off to the garden and comes up with his hands full of roses for the Doctor. Mary is shy of strangers, but Eddy is afraid of nobody, black or white.

There are three boys of the 1st class in school here. They have come to Mr. Johnson to learn how to make a sun dial to measure the time. Mr. Johnson made one last week and put the stone on a little pillar in the yard. The school boys think it quite a curiosity. One of the boys is a son of Jshuree Dass, who died. His son is a very promising young man named Parmeshwari Dass. He was married lately to a native Christian girl in Allahabad.

We have had a very interesting young Bengali native with us for a few weeks past. He came here saying that he had long been convinced of the Christian religion; and that when his friends heard that he wished to become a Christian, they gave him poison. He managed to escape from them and came here, fearing that they would still pursue him and kill him. He seems to be very intelligent and sensible. He has good recommendations from his former employers—he was a teacher in Government schools—but he seems to be under a hallucination that everywhere he is pursued by his enemies trying to poison or kill him. We think that the poison he took may have affected his mind. Although he is perfectly sane on every other point, he cannot recover from this fear that has taken hold of his mind. He wants to be baptized. He says he has but one desire, to become a Christian. Poor man, he seems in great distress about both body and soul. Our Missionaries told him he must wait until they learn more of his state of mind. Altogether his is a most interesting case. He asked us to pray for his wife too, that she may be brought to believe the Christian religion. He seems to have a warm affection for her, and says she is kept back by her Mother, who is a bigoted Hindoo. They live in Benares.

. . . So you have new carpet for the Parlor? Well Mother, I would like to take a peep at it . . .

Your affectionate daughter,
Rachel

[In 1868 northern India had the hottest summer in any local resident's memory, and this heat was followed by a winter drought. In 1869 Will reported to the Board that "the Government meteorologist reports the daily average for June of this year is 30° Fahrenheit higher in the sun than ordinary years!!" These consecutive hot, dry seasons destroyed much of the grain harvest. Shrewd grain merchants bought the remaining short supplies and sold the grain at four times the previous year's price, leaving the poor to starve. Will reported that "orphans are being offered us, and we cannot always refuse them," even at a time when the mission had a "great deficit in orphan funds."[1]]

Futtehgurh, India
July 22, 1868

My dear Sister Stella,

. . . We have just passed through a very hot season, the hottest I think I have felt in India. The rains that usually set in about the middle of June, have this year been delayed until the 20th of July. So we have had a month longer of grilling than usual. We began to fear that the rains were not coming, like the famine year. A few weeks longer of drought would have caused the failure of the crops, and starvation among the poorer people. It seems strange that one year of drought should produce a famine in a land where the ground yields such bountiful crops. It would not be so if it was a Christian land. But here the mass of people are poor, and only manage to eke out a living at the best. When there is prospect of scarcity, the "bunnias," or grain merchants, buy up the grain and sell it at their own prices. So the poor starve, while their granaries are full. If there were plenty of railroads and means of communication, of course, they would not have it all their own way, as they now have. But we have now for two days been rejoicing in delightful, refreshing showers. Yesterday there was a nice, gentle rain almost all day. The farmers are busy plowing their fields, and everybody, and everything looks refreshed. In Lucknow the papers say that the very chickens were dying of sunstroke, and horses would drop down on the roadside in their harness.

1. "India Letters," vol. 11, no. 35, Nov. 15, and no. 36, Oct. 4, 1869.

Mary is busy writing you a letter, and she gets over her paper so fast I can hardly keep her supplied with paper. Eddie is out looking after the chickens, ducks and turkeys. He thinks the turkey gobbler a very, interesting bird. He feeds the fouls every day, and is very much offended if anyone else takes his work. He says the gobbler dances, which amuses him very much. Mary is able to spell "cat," and all such hard words. She is fond of her book, and has her lesson now everyday—tho I did not press her to learn while it was so hot. She has her slate too, and her little hands are busy making letters, or wonderful-looking dolls and animals. Mary has just taken her letter in to show Eddie. He says he will write one too, as soon as he gets his bath. Every morning they get into their big tub and have a good bath, which they enjoy very much.

Jai Ram, a little orphan boy, who is blind, comes to read at 11 o'clock. He is a nice, good-natured fellow, about 8 years old, and Mary is very fond of him. He learns very fast to read with his fingers, and is very quick in mental arithmetic. He can cypher out in his head some very mixed sums.

Here comes a dirty-looking native with a bag of jamuns, a fruit that looks like a blue plum, but it is not so good. It draws your mouth like alum. We first sprinkle salt over the fruit, then shake the jamuns, and the skin bursts. After standing a little while, they are ready for anyone who likes them. We had some pineapples the other day that were very nice. They do not grow here, and I have never been able to get them here before. They came from Bareilly, about 40 miles from here.

Well Stella, I want to write part of this letter to Frank, so I must not give you more than your share. . . .

Well Frank my dear brother, what are you doing with yourself these hot days? Where did you expend your patriotism on the 4th of July? Did Hookstown come out with a good show of loyalty and zeal in fire crackers, political meetings, picnics, etc.? I suppose President Johnson would enjoy his Fourth, now that he is safe for a few months longer. We are very much surprised that he was not found guilty. Is Grant to be the next President?[2] I suppose he has the hearts of the young men who served in the war with him.

Well Frank, we dont have any patriotic meetings here on the Fourth, but we are going to have a grand Eclipse of the sun next month. It will be total in central India, and parties of Scientific men are being sent out from England and the Continent to take observations. They expect some important discoveries and questions to be settled. The eclipse will

2. Andrew Johnson, who succeeded Lincoln as president in April 1865, had a stormy relationship with Congress. When Johnson removed Edwin M. Stanton, the secretary of war, and appointed Ulysses S. Grant, all without approval of the Senate, the House impeached him. He was tried in the Senate and acquitted by one vote on May 26, 1868. Congress never confirmed Grant in that position because Grant ran for president to succeed Johnson and was elected in November 1868.

be about $\frac{2}{3}$ of the suns diameter here, so we will have it pretty dark; and the natives will be awfully frightened. Then the old Brahman priest will have a good harvest out of the poor ignorant creatures.

We, that is the Kelloggs and ourselves, were at a grand wedding 2 weeks ago. Mr. Brown, a young man from Banda, was married to Miss Blunt of this station. The Episcopal chaplain performed the ceremony in the Church of England. He is one of the High Churchmen, and has almost as many forms and ceremonies as the Roman Catholics. The bride looked very nice in her white robes and veil and orange flowers, and the bridegroom looked exceedingly happy. After the ceremony, we went to Mr. Blunts, where they had a nice dinner prepared. The day was so hot that it was like driving through a furnace, but we did not like to decline going.

The Chaplain is a poor specimen of a Christian. He is fond of hunting and balls. Not long ago he was out in the jungle with his gun and while in pursuit of game, he walked into a well. Fortunately he was not alone, so he was rescued. A great many young men enter the Church of England and come out as chaplains in the Army, just because they have no other career open to them for making money. They get good pay, and a pension after a few years service; so they are oftener fishers for money, more than fishers of mens souls.

Mr. Walsh spent a week with us last month. The missionaries have just started a magazine for the native Christians in Roman Hindustani, and he is the editor. It is printed at the Mission press in Allahabad. The missionaries write the articles for it and it comes out monthly. There is so little Christian literature in the native language, that something of the kind will be very useful. Mr. Johnson is writing something for it now, I believe.

. . . Give our love to all our friends and take a share yourself.

Your affectionate sister,
Rachel

Futtehgurh, India
September 24th, 1868

My dear brother Frank,

. . . Eddie is making so much noise I can hardly get my ideas gathered into shape to write. He saw a boy show some tricks of a monkey and goat, a day or two ago, and he is going through the performance with great enjoyment—just as you boys used to do, standing on your heads, and cutting up all sorts of shines, the week after a circus came round.

. . . There is to be a meeting of the Presbytery here in October, and Mr. Ullmanns Theological class of native preachers are studying hard to pass their examination at that time. We are to have another meeting of Synod this year . . . at Saharanpore. . . . It is a long journey up there, but we hope the railway will be open that far by December. If so, we can go most of the way on the rail. The Reformed Presbyterian Missionaries of the Punjab want to unite with our Old School Mission at that time, if our Board at home will receive them under its wing. So you see the spirit of Union reaches over to India. What a grand church the Presbyterian will be when the different branches all unite, as they seem likely to do.

As soon as the weather gets cool enough, Mr. Johnson and Mr. Kellogg will be starting out to preach in the villages round about. Mrs. Kellogg and I and the little ones will go along in our tents as usual. We like to get out among the simple-minded, country villages. The people are so much readier to hear the Gospel.

. . . Here are the orphan boys who are learning to sew. I must see after them a little. Mary too has her needle and thread, and is wanting me to show her how to sew. And here comes Eddie. He wants to sew too, so I have my hands full. Mary is such a careful, little body, she will be able to help Grandma keep things straight when she goes to vilayat. . . .

Your affectionate sister,
R. Lillie Johnson

Futtehgurh, India
February 8th, 1869

My dear Father and Mother,

. . . I must introduce to Grandpa and Grandma a little stranger who lies sleeping in his cradle. He sends his "salam," and claims their notice as their new grandson—as yet without a name. He is three weeks old today: born January 18th. During these weeks, he has been a remarkably good boy, spending most of his time, day and night, sleeping—as good babies ought to do. Mary thinks there never was such a baby. She lavishes a great deal of affection upon him, almost smothers him with her kisses. Eddie too thinks his little brother very nice, and wants to know if he will grow big like he is, and be able to help shell peas—a work in which he is now engaged very busily (taking a little rest from other mischief).

I have been out of my bedroom for several days, and begin to feel pretty strong again. I have regained my strength quicker this time, not having had so much trouble with sore breasts as before, which always kept me weak for a long time. The children keep very well and Mr. Johnson has grown so much stouter than when we left home, you would be surprised I know.

The meeting of Synod was put off until the 20th of December, so I only went with Mr. Johnson as far as Mynpoorie, and stayed with Mrs.

Wyckoff while he was gone. Mr. Wyckoff has been laid up on his couch for about 3 months with a broken knee. His health is so poor that the Doctor has ordered him home.

. . . Mr. Brodhead has decided to stay another year. Dr. Owen goes home too, after about 28 years missionary labor in Allahabad. Mr. Wynkoop has arrived safely (the new missionary). He will remain in Allahabad this year. . . .

Is Frank preparing to teach at the normal school? It seems strange to me to think of you with only Stella at home with you. Stella goes to school almost all the time, I suppose; and I hope I will find her a good scholar when we go home.

We have pleasant cool weather now, and last week had a little rain. There is great distress in many parts of India from famine, but this part around us has been mercifully favored. Although grain is very dear, and the poor suffer some, yet they can get something to eat.

Your affectionate daughter,
Rachel L. Johnson

[The intense and prolonged heat caused more sickness among the missionaries than usual. Rachel reported many illnesses and deaths among other missionary families, and Will reported that there was almost constant sickness in the Johnson family.]

Mynpoorie, India
May 10th, 1869

My dear Sister,

. . . We have all been sick, but are all well again. We have come over to Mr. Alexanders for a change, hoping to recover fully, then go back able to do some work again. Mr. Alexander has taken Mr. Wyckoffs place here. . . . We had a sad time at Futtehgurh for the last few weeks. Mr. Kelloggs Allie was very ill, so that we scarce hoped for his recovery. Then Mr. Kellogg had an attack of pleurisy. Mr. Johnson had a bilious attack accompanied with boils that laid him up. Then Eddie had fever and severe cold. I was then laid up with fever and biliousness. To crown all, while I was sick, baby caught cold and had an attack of bronchitis. So you see we were a miserable set. We were too sick to help the Kelloggs in their night watching, and they too sick to help us in ours. The Kelloggs have gone to Landour at the Hills, as a last hope for Allie. He has chronic diarrhea. We are all feeling pretty well now, and will go home on Wednesday night. Baby is much better than when we left home, tho he has not a vigorous appetite yet. Mrs. Kellogg left me her pony to ride while she is gone, and I hope to have much benefit from riding it. Mary and Eddie are both pretty well, tho Mary is not so fat as she was.

. . . I wish I could get good likenesses of our children for you. I wont send any more until I can get good ones. Mary is quite a big girl—will be 5, July 10th. And Eddie is almost $3\frac{1}{2}$. Baby will be 4 months old on the 18th. He is a nice, sweet, little fellow. Other people say he is pretty, and of course we think so. We have named him Albert Orr, for Mr. Johnson's brother who died here in the mutiny.

. . . I dont know when we will come home, but most likely it will be within the next two or three years. There are so many of the missionaries recovering now, that it is very difficult to keep all the work at the different stations going on. Unless more men are sent out, it will be very difficult to get away. Perhaps some who are at home will return by that time. Then we can take our vacation too.

When I think of going home to leave our children there, it seems almost more than I can bear. But this is a trial that all our missionaries with families have to go through. . . .

Your affectionate sister,
Rachel L. Johnson

Futtehgurh, India
August 13th, 1869

My dear Mother,

I have not written to you for a good while. Although I dont feel much like letter writing this morning, I must send you a few lines. Baby is very sick with fever and diarrhea. We have to be up with him at night, so the loss of sleep and constant care of him does not give us much chance to do anything but snatch a little rest now and then in the day time, when we can get it. He is teething, which I suppose is the cause of his fever. But it seems very obstinate, and has reduced him until he is the mere shadow of what he was a few weeks ago. He feels so weak and miserable. Sometimes I feel very much discouraged about him, especially as his first teeth are not through yet. Dear little Bertie, he is such a sweet, merry fellow when he is well. Now he can scarcely give one wan, little smile.

We had a very, hot season, much hotter than usual, and it is not strange that we have all had more ailments than usual. It seems to me that we have not all been well at once since the hot weather came on. It is now the time for rain and we have had some very, refreshing rainy days. The trees and grass and fields are all beautifully green, and it does ones eyes good to look at them. We have had no rain for several days and we look anxiously for more, for if we have not a good supply this year, there will be a great scarcity. And grain, which is very high now, will go up to famine prices, and the suffering of the poor natives would be great. Last year there was little rain in many parts and famine in some. We here between the Ganges and Jumna rivers were more favored.

We received a letter yesterday from Rev. Campbell of Steubenville 2nd Church—Mr. Johnsons old pastor—telling us of the new interest that the Steubenville Presbytery has lately shown in the Missionary cause. They have formed all the Sabbath Schools into a Missionary circle, and resolved to raise funds to support Mr. Johnson in the Mission field. This is encouraging to see them waking up. They selected Mr. Johnson, as he is known to most of them, and they will feel more interest in one they know.

Dear Mother, I hope you all keep well. How I would like to see you all again. The journey home is but a short one now, only two months—Mrs. Wyckoff wrote after they reached America. Mr. Wyckoff was very much better. Lizzy Wyckoff did not like America as well as India. She said, "We were born there, and so we like India best."

Now dear Mother, I have written more than I expected, but I must go to Baby, so goodbye. With our united love to you all. . . .

> Your affectionate daughter,
> Rachel L. Johnson

> Futtehgurh, India
> September 22nd, 1869

My dear Father and Mother, Frank and Stella,

Since I wrote to you a few weeks ago, our hearts have been made very sad by the death of our darling little Bertie. For some weeks he had been suffering from diarrhea, brought on by teething. His head too was often very hot, and he sometimes had fever. Dr. Reed gave him medicine, but it did not help him. He seemed playful in the daytime, but at night he was very restless and evidently suffering pain. As time passed on and his diarrhea seemed about the same from day to day, he began to droop. He did not care for his toys. He wanted to lay his little head on my shoulder, and be carried from place to place. We at last determined to go over to our old friend, Dr. Sherlock at Etawah, 62 miles distant.

We left home on the morning of the 7th at 4 o'clock. We reached Bewar about 9 and stopped at the Government Rest House until 3 in the evening. We then started on in a comfortable spring wagon drawn by oxen. We travelled all night and reached our Missionary friends, the Sayres house, at 3 in the morning. It was a weary journey, for we slept none on the way; but the children slept—baby in his cradle. The road is perfectly level and very smooth, so there was no jolting.

Baby seemed to be rather benefited by the change. Good, kind Dr. Sherlock came twice a day to see him, and did all human skill could do.

But dear baby soon began to sink. His diarrhea continued, and altho we hoped to the last he would rally, on the morning of the 14th there was a change for the worse. At 2 o'clock in the afternoon, dear, little Bertie passed away. The little spirit entered on its joy and rest. The precious, little body rested from its suffering, and such an expression of rest and peace stole over the sweet face and the little folded hands, that our smitten hearts were comforted with the blessed assurance that our darling was safe—safe home in the strong arms of Jesus. He was so lovely and winsome in all his ways that everybody loved him.

We had seen Eddie so low and recover, that we hoped to the last that this blow would be spared us. . . . We brought our little Bertie home and laid him beside little Willie in our Mission graveyard. On Friday morning at daylight, we reached our desolate home. At noon we buried our darling. I cannot tell you how sadly we miss him every where. The native Christians are very kind and sympathizing in our troubles. They mingled their tears with ours, and spoke sweet words of comfort. . . . Sarah, one of the Christian women, told me she had laid 2 children in our little graveyard; another 6; and so on—they all have at some time tasted the bitter cup of sorrow. . . .

Our little Bertie is gone. I send you a curl of his hair. This and the one I keep is all thats left. We have no picture of his sweet face. You can never know what a dear, lovely child he was here below. But I trust we and our little ones all, will be gathered together in that blessed home where all our joy and love will be perfect and forever.

This has been a sad year in our Mission. God has come near to us all by affliction. Mr. and Mrs. Alexander of Mynpoorie are with us. 3 weeks ago they buried a lovely boy, 15 months old. His disease was like cholera. The Walshes have lost their daughter Emma, the oldest of the two daughters that came out almost a year ago. She died suddenly of brain fever. Mr. Henry at Lahore died of cholera last month—sick only 8 hours. He leaves a wife and 6 little children, all under 7 years. Mrs. Kellogg lay for weeks at the point of death, but God has raised her up again. Mr. Calderwood at Saharanpore buried his youngest. So you see, it has been a year of trial for all of us. God grant that we all may be made better by these chastenings.

Affectionately,
Rachel L. Johnson

Etawah, India
October 27th, 1869

My dear Brother and Sister,
You will see by my date that I am not at home. Mrs. Sayre is very ill with brain fever, and I have come over to help Mr. Sayre take care of her.

I brought Mary and Eddie along, and left their papa to keep house alone. I sit up almost every night. . . . I am now writing at 2:30 in the morning, while Mrs. Sayre sleeps. We keep ice in a bladder laid on her head all the time. The ice comes every night from Cawnpore by rail. It is made there in an ice machine—by evaporating ether, I believe.

The weather is getting cool now. We had such a deluge of rain this season, that the cold weather is coming on a month sooner than usual. We came all the way but 18 miles of our journey from Futtehgurh by ox wagon—slow traveling. . . .

. . . I expect to stay here two weeks longer, then go to the Annual Mission meeting to Mynpurie, where Mr. Johnson will meet us. The time of Meeting is Nov. 11.

Bewar—December 3rd, 1869

Dear Frank and Stella,

I left you abruptly more than a month ago and now I will take up the broken thread of my letter and try to finish this time.

We are now in camp, 23 miles from Futtehgurh at Bewar, a large native town. It is Saturday evening. The sun has just dropped behind yon grove of trees, and leaves a glow of gold behind. Soon he will be peeping in at your bedroom window, warning you that the early bird catches the worm. Then we will be shutting our tent doors and covering up under blankets and comforts to sleep soundly in the cool, fresh air. The noisy parrots are now coming home to their nests in the trees overhead and around. They are full of these pretty green chatterers with their bright red beaks. They look so pretty that one is disappointed that no sweet sounds come out when they begin to talk.

I must now come back and tell you why we are here. We left home on Friday to go out three weeks on a preaching tour. Mr. Johnson expects Mr. Alexander from Mynpoorie tonight with Mrs. Alexander and Herbert (a nice boy 3 years old). Mr. Heyl came out last night, and we expect Dr. Sherlocks sister-in-law, Miss Whittaker too. Then there are 10 native Christians. So we are quite a large party. I have charge of the provender and will have to get most of our eatables out from home— that is, what we cant get in the villages.

. . . We had a very pleasant Missionary meeting at Mynpoorie. We were 12 in all, Missionaries and their wives. We were there about a week. Mr. Johnson was not well during the meeting, and is not quite well yet. He was stooping to lock a box and took a crick in his back. He could not walk for several days. The Dr. said it was some derangement of the liver and kidneys. He is better, but not very vigorous. You will think truly that he is not very lean in flesh from the photograph we send you. Mary and Eddie are both very well.

. . . Frank, I received your last letter a week ago . . . are you going to be a M.D.? Well you ought to settle down to something, but if you dont intend to practice medicine, why spend time reading a little—a smattering of medical knowledge will not benefit you much. Settle down in earnest at one thing. Dont be changing your mind so often. . . . I hope you will do well in whatever you undertake.

You sent us glad news about dear Stella. Nothing could have rejoiced me more than to hear that she has chosen the good part [joined the church by confession of faith], like that other Mary, whom Jesus loved and commended. Dear sister, may the dear Saviour help you and Ella both to adorn the confession you have made, and ever keep you sitting at his feet learning of Him what he would have you do for Him.

Now my dear brother and sister, I must say goodbye. . . . With our united love to you all.

Your affectionate sister,
R. Lillie Johnson

[This is the last of Rachel's preserved letters for a little over five years. However, a few letters from Will and events documented in other sources maintain the chronology of the Johnsons' lives during this period.]

In Camp near the Mukkunpare Mela
40 miles from Futtehgurh
Feb. 2, 1870

My Dear Aunt and Uncle

A coolie is to come out from Futtehgarh today to bring us bread, butter and vegetables, and to take back letters to post. I embrace the opportunity to write to you and Maggie, and to send my photograph, lately taken at Futtehgarh. You will think that if India does not agree with me, it at least has not yet caused any great fading away. The likeness is considered a very good one.

We left home three weeks ago for a long tour among the villages; and if all is well, will not probably return for a month more. The Kelloggs, and the new missionary, Mr. Tracy, are with us, and we have six native preachers. Each of us preaches about twice a day.

We have had two adventures. One night thieves broke into our camp and carried off a catechists box of clothes from under his bed, and got off with their booty. The next night a wolf came into the midst of our tent, and carried off a goat from the midst of half dozen men who were loading a cart. Since then we have kept four or five night watchmen, and have great trouble keeping them awake.

In December we made a tour of two or three weeks in another direction with the Alexanders, and Mr. Heyl of Mynpoorie, and had very pleasant preaching. We hurried home to receive Dr. Prime (Eusebrius) and his party, who after all disappointed us.[3] They hurried around so much as not to see things to much purpose. He ought to have spent three months here instead of one.

I expect I shall have to go to America in a year or two, as the last, unprecedented, hot season used me up pretty badly. I fear I shall have to go to the Hills this summer, but do not intend to leave my station unless it cannot be helped. Ours is the only family in our mission which has held out so long, without either going to the Hills or to America.

We have been experiencing almost a famine in this part of the country for months past, and are yet. Grain is four times the price it was a year or two ago, and there is a great deal of suffering. But now the whole country waves with the finest crops which have been seen for years. In a month hence, if nothing happens, the trouble will be over. Though prices can hardly fall very low, as the country has been so throughly drained of grain, and such high prices were paid for the seed sown.

In spiritual matters there is nothing to remark but quiet growth—slow, it is true—but I think sure. The knowledge of Christianity becomes every day more wide-spread, though we are pained to see how unwilling men are to give up all for Christ. We have met some interesting persons since we came out. Time will tell whether or no they will come out on the Lord's side.

I sent you by Mr. Brodhead (of Princeton, N.J.), an Indian Choga, or cloth gown, such as gentlemen here draw on over their clothes when out driving in a cold day; or use as a dressing gown on winter evenings. They are cheap affairs, but I think them much more comfortable than an overcoat. I hope it will reach you safely and be of use to you in your cold drives to Steubenville.

Let us hear from you often.

Yours Truly
W. F. Johnson

[The summer of 1870 was exceptionally hot. With two little children and Rachel expecting a third, the Johnson family escaped the heat and "ran away to the Himalayas" with other missionary families. It was in "the hills" at Landour that Jane "Jennie" Rex Johnson was born on August

3. Samuel Irenaeus Prime was author and editor of *The Observer,* a private Presbyterian newspaper published in New York City from 1840 to 1848 and 1850 to 1884; secretary of the American Bible Society in 1848–49; and editor of *The Presbyterian* in 1849–50.

10, 1870. While in Landour, Will wrote and published teachers' tracts, a parable, a short treatise on idolotry, and a bazaar sermon with imaginary conversations between missionaries and villagers in which objections and questions were addressed and answered.

Will, Rachel, Mary, Eddie, and baby Jennie returned to Fatehgarh in the cooler season to resume their daily routines. A cooler-than-usual summer enabled Rachel and Will to remain in Fatehgarh in 1871.

The last letter from Will from the Johnson's first tour of service in India is full of anticipation of the family's upcoming furlough and their plans for their return journey to the United States in the summer of 1872.]

In Camp Khiurseypare
20 miles from Futtehgurh
December 18th, 1871

My Dear Uncle and Aunt,

We left our home a little over a week ago for an itineration among the villages of our district. Mr. and Mrs. Brodhead, Mr. Seeley (son of a Missionary who used to be here), and Mr. Wykoff are with us. Mr. Wykoff, who came out with us 11 years ago, has been at home in America for two years, and just returned a month ago, leaving his family at home. He thought he had made an arrangement for his children with an uncle; but just then the uncle fell ill, and is never likely to be better. So Mrs. Wykoff was left behind to arrange for leaving the children. She will follow after a year, if possible.

We have also 7 native helpers with us, beside servants. We have each (except Mr. Seeley, who has hardly got hold of the language yet) preached twice almost every day since we have come out.

The weather just now in these beautiful mango groves is delightful— very pleasant to sit about under the trees by day; but at night, I sleep under a heavy blanket and comforter. We feel a little nervous in the evenings about the children straying outside of the tent doors, as wolves have several times been seen quite close to the tents. But by day, no one thinks of any danger.

We expect to remain travelling until after new years day, when we return to observe the "week of prayer" in our churches at Futtehgurh and "the City."

My principle object in writing this note is to appraise you that we expect to visit America next Summer, to stay nearly 2 years. The principle reason for this is my health. I am not sick, but I find for two or three years back that my system is losing tone; and there are frequent symptoms that my liver is becoming affected, which is something never to be neglected with infirmity in this country. I got through this last hot season very comfortably because it was uncommonly cold; and the preceding one, by running away to the Himalayas. But the doctor tells me that I ought by all means to take a furlough. So we are selling off our furniture, and expect to spend the most of what remains of this cold season in making our preparations for the long journey. Fortunately it is not the long six months sea voyage that it required when we came out. The Suez Canal has made it nearly as cheap to go through Italy, and to traverse the Arabian and Mediteranean seas by fast steamers, as it used to be to sail about the cape.

Our plan is to go from Bombay by an Italian steamer (which are much cheaper than the English ones); from Bombay to Naples through the Suez Canal; thence by rail via Rome and Venice; across the Brenner pass of the Alps into Germany; and to reach England about June. I should like to spend a few days seeing the sights in London. After we reach America, I think we shall try and spend a week or two in Waterbury before we go West.

So if God wills, it will not be many months until we may see each other in the flesh. It is needless for us to say that the thought of such a meeting is a very pleasant one. We shall dream about it many a time before the fleeting days make it a reality. But on the other hand, it makes me sad to think of leaving all our work here—our plans uncarried out, our places to be filled by others—just when we begin to feel thoroughly at home in it. We use two languages here beside the English, and it takes years to learn to use them forcibly; so that men newly arrived from America can by no means fill the place of those who have long been here.

We are to be succeeded at Rakha by Mr. Tracy, a young man who has been two years in the country. He is soon to be married to a daughter of Mr Isaiah Dickey of Pittsburg, who came out a year ago as a female missionary.

We have not heard a word from you since our little Jennie was born, more than a year ago. I hope "no news means good news" in this case. But I must say Good Bye.

Lillie joins me in love.

Yours Truly,
W. F. Johnson

NINE

June 1872–November 1878

HOOKSTOWN, MAINPURI, AND ALLAHABAD

◈ IN THE SUMMER OF 1872 Rachel and Will Johnson set their feet down on American soil for the first time in twelve years. Rachel was thirty-five years old, Will was thirty-four, Mary was almost eight, Eddie was six and a half, and baby Jennie was not quite two years old.

Much had changed in Hookstown. Sam was gone from the family circle; Frank and his wife Susan were living in their own home in nearby Wellsville, Ohio; Stella was away at school and was consumed with her own plans and with her fiancé, John Langfitt from Pittsburgh. Rachel's parents, Mary and David, eagerly pushed things aside, and prepared the big brick house on the corner of Mill and Washington streets for Rachel, Will, and their three grandchildren. Sadly, days after Rachel and Will returned to Hookstown, Grandpaps died; by sheer will he held on tightly to his eighty-five years of living until he could once more see his grandaughter and wife's namesake, Rachel, whose thirst for books and adventure he had whetted and nourished in her youth.

Will traveled from the East Coast to the Dakotas, preaching and talking about missionary activities and needs in northern India; he was a charismatic promoter of foreign missions for the Board of Foreign Missions of the Presbyterian Church U.S.A. Rachel was a popular addition to his speaking engagements in western Pennsylvania communities; she spoke about the woman's role in the mission field.

The children reveled in life at their grandparents'. In the small town they had heard about all their lives they had an abundance of cousins and neighbors for playmates, new games to learn, and a new environment to explore. Motherhood and balancing the family's schedules absorbed most of Rachel's time. And midway through their furlough, Frank Orr Johnson was born on October 20, 1873. Another corner in the big house was cleared for the newcomer.

Indeed, private space must have been a rare commodity, for Stella moved back into the Kerr household to prepare for her wedding in early summer, 1874. The wedding date was chosen so that Rachel would be able to attend the marriage of her "dear little Stella," who was now a young woman of twenty-one.

After the wedding, the time Rachel and Will had been dreading rapidly approached. Although they were anxious to return to their work in India, they had decided for health and education reasons that Mary and Eddie must remain behind in Hookstown with their grandparents. In contemplating their leave in May 1869, Will wrote to his uncle and aunt: "One thing makes us afraid to think about going home—that is, we must leave our children behind when we come out again! Children so soon forget their absent parents that it is a very hard trial to think of." With many promises to write faithfully, the painful good-byes were said.

Will, Rachel, Jennie, and baby Frank arrived "home" in northern India in October 1874. When they were settled in their new mission station in Mainpuri, Rachel picked up her correspondence once again, much of which was with Mary and Eddie. Rachel described the everyday events of their lives in delight-filled tones, as a parent would to a child. She wrote about what would have pleased and interested her children. She and Will wrote touching letters about events both great and small: the pageantry of the Queen of England being proclaimed Empress of India, descriptions and drawings of toys a peddler had made and was selling for one cent each.]

                                        Mynpoorie Feb 5th, 1875
My dear daughter, Mary,

We had a nice visit at Futtehgurh, and I sent you a letter from there. We staid about 4 days at Rakha in our old home. Then we got all our things we left loaded on an ox cart, and sent them to Mynpoorie, where we live now. It is 40 miles from Futtehgurh.

. . . We got to our new home at 1 oclock at night. We opened up the house, put our mattresses on the beds, and slept till morning. Then we went over to the house where the young ladies live, and staid one day. Their house is in the same "compound" or yard—about as far from our house as Mr McFerrans is from your GrandPa's.

Our boxes with our clothes did not come in the same ship with us. We have just heard that they have arrived in Bombay and are now coming on the railway. They will be here in a few days. I wonder if the fruit is safe. We brought only our trunks with us.

Often I think about you, dear Mary and Eddie, and feel as if I would give a great deal to see you. Jennie talks every day about you, and does not forget you. She is very lonely with nobody to play with. She just now came in with a big bump on her forehead. She fell and hurt herself, so I had to put some arnica on the bump. She is now sitting by me with a looking glass in her hand, looking at herself. She is singing, or making up her song as she goes along. She says, "O Lord, dont let the lions eat me up." I dont know what made her think of them, for they are far away.

Frankie is very happy, toddling around. This morning an old German missionary came along and ate breakfast with us. He was telling us about the dawk carriage breaking down with him. Frankie was sitting on my lap watching him, and when we laughed, he laughed louder than any of us. He seemed to think something very funny had happened. The old man held out his arms, and Frankie went to him. He seemed much amused at his way of talking.

The next day after we got to our new home, your letter and Eddies and Stellas came. It quite cheered us up to have such nice letters and to hear all about you at home. Jennie says we have so many homes: one at grandpas, and here, and over where Miss Hardie and Mrs. Miller live in Futtehgurh.

. . . Jenny saved the ribbon on her hat the other day for you. She is learning to spell and make pictures every day. Jennie sends kisses to Grandma and Grandpa; and Frankie can make his salam very nicely now.

> Goodbye, with much love from
> Papa and Mamma

Mynpoorie Feb 5th, 1875

Dear Eddie,

I was so glad to get a letter from you too this last week. Jennie sat down and I read yours and Marys to her. When I read about Grandma cutting her fingers, her eyes filled with tears, and she said, "Oh it was dreadful! Poor grandma." I showed her a little cut on my finger and told her Grandmas was mended, I hoped, now like mine.

Jennie finds it hard work playing with nobody to help her. She has not forgotten Millie McCartney or Jimmy Bryan. Tell them Jennie and I saw a real monkey sitting on top of our house one evening when we were walking in the garden. If you had been here, you would have felt like helping it down stairs, wouldnt you? I see them often in the city when I go to see the schools.

A little girl at Rakha gave Jennie 3 little, red birds in a cage. She fed them for several days, but at last they got out and flew away. The wire was not close enough. A cat has killed two of our chickens. I think we will have to have him ducked, or put out of the way.

The clouds make today dark. I think it will rain. There is a great fair or mela not far from Mynpoorie tomorrow.

We took a drive with our new horse last evening, and met so many people. I saw two little boys, as big as you, riding on one donkey. It looked scared at our carriage. I think we must call our new horse "Fan"—a namesake for grandpas Fan. It is a reddish color and papa paid 42 dollars for it. It goes along very well so far.

I was glad to hear that you had written to Aunt Jane Johnson. How is Uncle Franks new house getting on?

I hope your teacher got well. How are you getting on at school? Have you had any sleigh rides? The native boys here have been putting out a little water in an earthen saucer, and gathering the thin bits of ice in the mornings to eat. You would hardly think it such a rare goodie.

Now my dear son Eddie. I must write a little to Grandpa and Grandma too. My heart longs to see you. When I write, I cannot keep back the tears when I think of you all so far away. I can only pray our Father up in Heaven to watch over you, and take care of you, and Mary, and all. Goodbye.

With love from papa and mamma

Mynpoorie June 29th, 1875

My darlings, Mary & Eddie,

I have just read over your letter again. I had so much written, when Jairoo and Nuttoo came in to say their lessons. . . . Jairoo says, send my salam to Mary and Eddie.

I am glad you are getting on so well in your Grammar and Geography. Can you find on the map the road you went home from India? Begin at Bombay, and go up the Red sea to Suez; thru the canal to Aden; then across to Naples in Italy. Then go to Rome, Florence, Venice, Munich, and Cologne. Then cross from Ostende to Dover—just across the straits of Dover—then up to London. Go to Liverpool, on the other side of England—where we took the Steamer for New York—and thence to Smiths Ferry, and Hookstown. Get Uncle Frank to help you trace out your path.

I was sorry to hear that Eddys first days labor fishing went to make the cats supper. Tell him he must remember, she has not learned, "Thou shalt not steal."

Frankie is awake now, sitting by me, amusing himself running a stick thru' a spool. . . . Jennie is not feeling well enough to write today. Papa is busy writing tracts and books in Hindi.

Our organ keeps in good tune, and we often play in the evenings. . . . How are you getting on with your music now? Do you play much?

Jenny says, "Let us go over when Mary and Eddie are asleep and surprise them." Tell Stella we had a hearty laugh at her picture of you all sewing carpet—Eddy helping too. When does she expect their new house to be built? I suppose Frank and Susan are very fine in their new house. I would like to see it.

Two little native Christian girls, named Rose and Mary, came to play with Jenny this morning. Jenny is always glad to find someone to play with.

We met an elephant, Eddie, when we took a drive. It turned off into a field until we passed, for fear the horse would not like to meet it. Frankie makes a funny face, stretching his mouth wide to show how the elephant looked.

Now dear children, I must say good bye. May God bless and keep you, and make you to love what is good.

> With love always, from
> Papa, Jennie, Frankie, and Mamma

[One of the teachers in the girls' school in Mainpuri became ill and left Rachel to take over her teaching responsibilities. In her annual report to the Board of Foreign Missions, Rachel said there were ninety children in the mission schools in 1875. She and two assistants, Mary Jane and Emeline, taught sixteen girls. "All attention is given to learning to read and understand their mother tongue," the Nagari script characters in Hindi and the Persian, Arabic, and Korna characters in Urdu. Rachel's mission work also extended to visits to local villages with a native Christian woman, Mulla. At first the women and children fled; then they became curious, especially with the singing, and gave them friendly receptions. Rachel and Mulla were commonly followed out of the village and asked to come again the next day.]

> Mynpoorie
> June 29th, 1875

Dear Father and Mother,

I have been writing to you all in turn, and this time it is yours. . . . We received Stellas letter, and Marys . . . and felt grateful to hear of your health and the welfare of all our dear ones.

We have had a few weeks of extreme heat. Almost every day the thermometer has stood in the house at from 98 to 100 degrees, from morning until night. We are now daily looking for the beginning of the rainy season, which will refresh us we hope. The clouds have been gathering up for a day or so, but as yet they have been clouds without rain.

Jenny has not been well for a few days. She seems feverish, and says today her head and back aches, and she feels miserable. She dont enjoy being sick. She came in to me and said, "I aint a bit happy here. I want to go back to Grandma, where Mary and Eddie are." Poor child! She forgets the long road that lies between us. I have just given her some pills, hid in a lump of jelly, which she took down very well. She is now taking a sleep, with Frank for company.

We are going over to Futtehgurh next friday. I hope the change over there will do the children good, and will brisk us all up a little. The Presbytery of Farrukhabad—which includes the Missionaries at Futtehgurh, Mynpoorie, and Gwalior, meets at Fattehgurh on the 7th. We will go a few days earlier to the Tracys.

Mr. Johnson is now reading over some of his translations to his moonshee, who criticizes, and makes changes he thinks needful.

. . . I have taken charge of the schools, that were under Miss Hardie's care, until she comes back. This, added to my other work, keeps me very busy. Yesterday Miss Blunt, a young lady who is employed as a teacher and bible reader by our mission at Futtehgurh, went with me to visit a school. We went into a village near by to talk to the women. Nearly all the women in the village were hurrying up their cooking to go off to worship an idol about 4 miles away, taking their offering of a brass bowl full of water and etc. with them. They said they hoped thus to propitiate the god, so that cholera and other sickness would not be sent on them. Poor foolish creatures. They had their long, hot walk in vain, and worse than in vain, for the exposure to the great heat was likely to bring just the calamity they feared.

On our way back we stopped in H. R. Wilsons house, one of our native Christians. We found his wife and family at home, and glad to see us. Their children were suffering very much from boils, which the heat brings on.

You would laugh, Mother, if you could see Frankie going about in his summer costume. He dont quite come down to the native fashion of a string of beads only, but he dont wear much—only a thin slip and his jangee [short drawers or breeches]. He has a crop of little boils on his face, that dont add to his beauty or comfort. I had one by my eye too, that gave me a very severe look for a few days. We hope that these little troubles will soon leave us when the welcome showers come.

> . . . With our united love,
> Your affectionate daughter,
> Rachel

Mynpoorie
October 12th, 1875

My dear Father and Mother,

One year ago today we were busy getting ready to sail. On the 13th we bid adieu to the shores of our dear, native land. When I think of our sad leave-taking of you all, our journey to Waterbury, then to New York, then across the ocean, down through England, across the continent of Europe, across the Mediterranean and Red Seas, and on to Bombay, then 2 days and nights by rail to Allahabad, where we found at last a resting place among friends, then on to our old home in Futtehgurh, and at last to Mynpoorie, where we found a new home, it seems scarcely possible that all has been crowded into one short year. I sometimes close my eyes and think of it all as a dream, and fancy my self waking up still at home with you in Hookstown. But, I dont dream long before some sound of the Hindoo tongue wakes me to realize I am in India.

Here on the veranda is Frankie, chatting in the language of the Hindoos to Eli Bup. Frankie, understanding all he says to him, and knowing enough to make his wants known. Pretty good for a youngster of 2 to learn the use of a language in one year, isn't it? But, poor boy, he has lost much of the strength and plumpness with which he started out from your arms on his travels. He has been sick for several weeks; his last 4 double teeth have given him a good deal of trouble. Diarrhea and fever have pulled him down, until he is quite weak and thin. We felt very much discouraged last week, but this last few days he is better, and his appetite is returning. We hope he will get over this trouble before long. The weather too is in his favor. We have now very pleasant, cool days. The nights are almost cold for our climate.

Jenny is still at Landour on the Mountains, but in two weeks more we hope to see her curly head appearing at the door, along with Mr. and Mrs. Lucas, in a dawk gari or carriage drawn by two old "crow-bait" horses. The driver will be making the walls ring with his bugle notes, which will sound sweet to us this time.

. . . This has been a very strange season. First it was hotter than the "oldest inhabitant" had seen for a score of years. Then we had more rain than that venerable had ever seen. Now it is colder than we ever saw it in October during our 13 years sojourn in India.

Mr. Johnson has been giving a great deal of time this year to translating "tracts" into Hindu. He hardly takes time to eat some days. And I, with the schools and classes of boys and girls at home, have tried to do something towards training up the girls and boys to be workers too, as they grow older, and go out to let their light shine amid the darkness around Mynpoorie. We have been very happy in our work, and have both had perfect health to carry it on. There was a great deal of cholera in the city, but it has passed away. We and all the native Christians have been kept, through Gods mercy, unharmed. The girl I mentioned before, dying of it, was not baptized—tho' her father is.

In December our yearly Mission meeting will be held in Etawah, 36 miles from here. We hope to go. Mr Ullmann, our German Missionary, will be our host on that occasion; but we always divide the table expenses, and each pays his share. Dr. and Mrs. Sherlock are still there, and we will be glad to see them.

. . . Well I must close. Good by, with much love from us all.

Your affectionate Daughter,
Rachel

Mynpoorie
January 23rd, 1876

My dear Son Eddie,

I suppose you have nice times these winter evenings, cracking the nuts you told me you had gathered. Dont eat too many. We had some chestnuts the other day that Mrs. Alexander brought Jenny. She roasted some and ate them, but she did not feel well after it, and had to take some medicine to take her pain away. Now she says, "I dont like to see chestnuts." She is now sitting with her paint box, coloring pictures in some old papers.

Did I tell you about the long-necked cranes we saw in a swampy field as we went to Etawah? More than a hundred were all together, and they were about as tall as Jenny. They were wild ones. In the wet weather they are busy looking for fish and frogs in the ponds. They had long red legs, gray backs, wings, and great, long bills.

You could see lots of elephants and camels if you was here. I was walking down to the gate, when I saw four big elephants coming. The biggest one had a scarlet cloth or blanket on, and bell tinkling on his neck, and a kind of silver chair or howda on his back, in which 4 people could sit. I asked the men with it whose elephants they were. He said, "The King of Rewah is sending them to Agra, where he is going to meet the Prince of Wales next week." There will be grand doings there, when the son of Englands Queen comes.

How are you getting on dear Eddie at school? When you hear the boys use wicked words, do not learn to say them; for God will not love those who swear and use bad words. When you kneel down and pray to your Father in Heaven, think how grieved he is if we dont do as he tells us in his holy Bible. He takes care of us, and loves us too.

Frankie has waked, and I had to go and call him in here. He and Jenny are now looking over her paint box, and Frankie is trying to arrange them to suit himself. He looks quite fat and rosy now. Jenny is not quite so fat as when she came home. She dont eat enough to make her grow, I tell her.

There is a little buffalo calf over at the Baboos, that you and Willie McCartney would think a wonder. It is so ugly. Our horse must soon start down on its long walk of 240 miles to Allahabad.

Now dear Eddie I must send off the letters. Let us often hear from you, my dear Son. May the Lord keep you and dear Mary safe, and help you to always do right, and love what is good. Papa and all of us send love.

Your loving, Mamma

[In 1876 Rachel and Will were reassigned to the larger mission station in Allahabad, where they had begun their missionary service almost sixteen years earlier. At the request of the Board of Foreign Missions, Will was spending more of his time training Indian helpers, teaching Hindustani to new American missionaries, and writing books and pamphlets in the Indian languages. He also was the editor of *The Makhzan* (The Christian Treasury), was secretary-treasurer of the North India Tract Society, translated a selection of hymns, and published several articles in Indian journals.]

Mynpoorie
January 21st, 1876

My dear Father and Mother,

I wrote to Frank and Stella a short time ago, telling you that we are soon to leave Mynpoorie and go to Allahabad. We will then be back where we spent our first few months in India. How do we like the change? you ask. Well, we will have the advantage of the society of our missionary friends, Rev. J. F. Holcomb, Mrs. Holcomb, Rev. S. H. Kellogg, Mrs. Kellogg, Rev. G. S. Wynkoop, and Rev. F. Heyl. There are a good many English people in the station, and it is a centre of heathenism, where there is plenty of work to be done, before Satan gives up his stronghold.

Mr. and Mrs. Alexander have arrived safely from America. They and Miss Scott and Miss Hardie have been with us for two weeks past. Miss Hardie left us yesterday, accompanied by Miss Scott, on her way as far as Allahabad, where she will join Dr. Brodhead and Lizzie Walsh. They will go with her to Syria, and leave her there. Then they will go back to America. Miss Hardie is very much broken down, but we hope the change of climate will build her up again. If she can work in Syria, she will be very glad to still remain in Mission work. If she is no better there, she must go home. We felt very sorry to part with her, and she too is sadly disappointed that she must leave India.

We will get off to Allahabad in about a week or so. Our furniture we will send (what we have not sold) in oxcarts. The distance is 240 miles. The carts will be about 16 days on the way. We will go by stage coach to Etawah, 36 miles, and thence by railway, a 10 hour journey to Allahabad.

John, Chester, Nuttoo, and Jairoo, the blind boy, all orphans who were with us at Futtehgurh, will go with us. John and Nuttoo have learned the printing business with Mr. Johnson; and John and Jairoo are studying, preparing for the ministry. They are all good boys and we hope they will make good men.

I hear a great noise outside, a wedding procession is passing. Drums are beating, horns are blowing, and guns being fired off. It sounds a good deal like an old fashioned serenade. The natives are very fond of a big noise when they do anything, be it worship or feasting. I often think it is well for their idols they cant hear, or the dreadful music screeching in their ears would torture them beyond endurance.

Mr. Johnson and Mr. Alexander have just returned from Etah, 36 miles distance. We have a few Christian families there, a kind of colony of native Xtians [Christians]. They went up to see how their work is getting on, and to hold a communion service. They had a very large heathen audience on Sabbath to hear them preach. They came back quite encouraged to hope for fruit from their labors there. They marched up and came back part of the way in a wagon drawn by a camel. Mr Alexander said the camel was so slow, he got out and pelted it with pieces of brickbats. We all laughed at their queer way of hurrying up the camel.

. . . Frankie talks Hindustani very well, and Jenny can talk their language as well as the little Hindoo girls do. Of course she always talks English to Papa and Mamma. It is surprising to see how quickly, and well, she has learned to speak Hindustani.

Mother, I am writing after all the rest are in bed. Jenny has a little bed at the foot of ours, and Frankie is tossing about in his, as if he had eaten too much beef and potatoes for his supper. We are all very well now, and the weather is pleasant as September at home. The cool weather is fast slipping away, and by the time this reaches you, it will be hot weather with us.

. . . Well dear Father and Mother, I am tired, and sleepy, and cold, so I will say goodnight! and go to bed. May the Lord keep you and all our dear ones safe and well!

Affectionately,
Rachel

Allahabad, Northern India
Saturday March 3rd, 1876

My dear Children,

I have just been telling Grandpa and Grandma about the wedding. . . . Nuttoo and his bride came in a little while ago, bringing us some of their dinner on a large tray. One plate had pullow, another curry, and the other two had native sweetmeats, some pomegranates and raisins. Papa ate very little, for he said he did not feel very well—his liver troubles him sometimes. I ate some pullow and curry, and then I set the plates out of sight in the cupboard, so that Jenny and Frank would not be tempted to want more than was good for them. The bride had changed her dress, and put on a nice chintz, black and white, and a white muslin chudder—or veil—with the edge embroidered with yellow braid.

Frankie and Jennie came in saying we had a very good dinner. I said, what did you have? Frankie said, "bahut achcha pullow"—that is, meat cooked with rice and some curry, also which had potatoes too mixed with the meat and spices. You asked me, Mary, for the receipt for curry. I will send you one, but I expect Aunt Susan will not like it very much at first, though everybody likes it after they eat it a few times.

Jenny is sitting reading for herself, and Frankie is gathering up his scraps of paper that he has been cutting. I told him to get a little box and put them in, and play boxwalla [peddler who sells door to door], selling them. So he is busy at work.

The river Jumna is going down again. It came up and washed away the cucumber patches the natives had planted, down to the very edge of the water. The great, long-legged birds stand out in the shallow water, looking for fish. The boats glide lazily down—some laden with grain, and some with cotton—their big sails spread to catch the wind. . . .

This last week I had to give vacation to my girls schools, as it was the Hindoo New Years festival, called the Holie. The Hindoos have a queer custom of sprinkling a red powder on each other during the festival. Every one you see has their turbans, coats, and veils all smeared over with this red powder. For several days, they continue to wear their clothes in this state. . . .

How is the school flourishing? I hope you will send us your reports again this year. We can see then how you are getting on in your studies.

. . . with love to you all, from us all.

Affectionately,
Your Mamma

Allahabad
New Years Day, 1877

My Dear Mary and Eddie,

I wish you many happy returns of the day. I often long to see you once more, but I try to be patient, till the time when our Father will bring us together again. I hope you will, neither of you, ever forget that you are as near to the hearts of papa and mama as ever, though great seas roll between us. We are very much interested in all we hear of your welfare and progress, and are glad to get so many nice letters from you.

We are very busy here in these days. The annual meeting of the missionaries of our mission has just been held at our place. Some of them have not gone back home yet, so mama cant find time to write to you by this mail. There were 8 gentlemen and 6 ladies at the meeting. Most of these were with us for 10 days. Then besides, we had a number of visitors: Dr. and Mrs. Newton and two children were here several days; and just now, there is a Rev. Douglas, from Canada, here. He intends to start a new Mission in Central India. We had a big tent pitched out in the yard to dine in, and it was much more convenient with such a large crowd than it would have been to eat in the house. . . .

They are having very gay doings now here in India, especially at Delhi. The queen of England is being proclaimed Empress of India. All the great Rajas and nobles of India, and the rulers of the land, are gathered at Delhi to celebrate the affair with great pomp. They have a city of tents pitched on the great plain outside of Delhi. Some 20 or 30,000 troops are gathered there to do honor to the occasion.

They say there are 1000 elephants gathered there. It is a custom of the native Kings to paint their favorite elephants with all the colors of the rainbow, and deck them out with silver saddles, rich embroidered blankets, and garlands of gems and coins. You can imagine there will be a very gay scene. I heard that one great raja, who went through Allahabad by railway, employed 10 special trains to carry him, his wives, nobles, retainers, and their stuff. I should think he would not want to travel often by railway.

Since the cold weather began Jennie and Frankie are getting quite hearty and strong again. . . . Just before the Annual Meetings, we were out in tents on a preaching tour for some 10 days, and the children enjoyed the playing about in the grove very much. It was like a continual picnic to them. Mama has bought a little mite of a pony to carry her to her girl's schools in the city, and the children enjoy a ride on his back very much. When we were out in camp, and wanted to come home, we could only get our carriage within a mile and a half of our camp. We did not know how to get the children across to it. At last, we concluded to put Jennie in the saddle and Frankie on behind her, and a man led the pony. Mama and I walked. We made a merry party, winding through the fields, and scrambling over the ditches.

Mama sends you some beautiful New Year's cards, to remind you that she has not forgotten you. . . .

Your loving papa, W. F. J.

[Back in America, in 1875, Frank and Susan had a baby daughter, Helen Rachel, who weighed just two and three-quarters pounds at birth. By this time the Kerrs had lost a son and a daughter in childbirth, and they lost another child in 1876, prompting Frank to give up carpentry and set off to study medicine at Western Reserve University in Cleveland with the hope of saving lives.

Stella and John had a baby daughter, Rexa, in 1876. There was much excitement among the nieces and nephews with the birth of each new cousin.]

Allahabad
January 25th, 1877

My dear Sister,

I was very glad to have a letter from you last mail. We were favored with letters from you all, coz Mary Johnson, and Maggie Blakesley, within a few days. We often say, you don't know how much good it does us to hear from you all. How much I wish I could sit down, and have a talk, instead of this cold pen. There is so much I want to ask you.

What a comfort your sweet babe must be to you. Jennie says, "Wouldn't you like to see Aunt Stellas and Uncle Franks babies?" I say, "Yes, indeed."

. . . I am glad Frank likes his new work, and I hope he will succeed. But he and Susan will need a good deal of patience in beginning their new life. Doctors and doctresses out here get plenty to do. Miss Seward has been our doctor for the children, since we came here. She seems to understand her work. She took a regular course in Philadelphia. But the natives dont like to take medicine long. Unless they get well right away, they go back to their native doctors. The old man, who owns one of the houses where I have a girls school, has dysentery. He told me his native doctor told him to eat nothing, and drink only buttermilk for 40 days! He is trying it, and if it dont kill, he will likely be cured by that time.

Tell father of the good luck of a native carpenter who was doing some work for us. One morning he didnt come. In a few days his old Mother came, and said he was in jail, for debt. She wanted some money to get him out, but couldnt raise enough, fortunately. A few weeks after January 2d, he appeared one morning, looking very happy. He said, on the day the Queen became "Our Empress,"[1] he and some other prisoners were called up, and asked by the jailor how much they owed? He said, 20 dollars. The reply was, "Go free. The command of Her Majesty is that your debts be all paid." So, he got his debt paid, and was fed for a month. He seemed in fine spirits. I told him he ought to be very thankful for being put in. He said he was, and to prove it, he wanted immediately to borrow some money, to go and make an offering to his idol god. He

---

1. In an extraordinary ceremony called "a Festival of Peace," Queen Victoria was proclaimed Empress of India in 1877.

didnt get much. All prisoners owing less than 100 rupees (or 50 dollars), were released on that day.

I have been making some green tomato pickles today. Mrs. Holcomb gave me the recipe, and I think they are very nice—especially in the hot weather. I find Marian Harlands Common Sense Cookbook very good—though I dont cook apples her way. I wish I could try it. I am going to make guava jelly tomorrow. I got 6 for a cent. They are as big as pears, and make nice jelly. We have more vegetables in our winter time than any other time. We have just been having some oyster soup, which Mr Heyls mother sent him from America. It was nice, but I dont care very much for it. I would prefer some of Mothers chicken soup.

. . . Do you think there is any danger of war at home? The papers talk very bumptious about the President-elect—or not elect.[2] The danger of war on our side of the world seems a little less.

. . . Kisses to the babies, you and yours.

Your affectionate sister,
Rachel

Allahabad
North West Provinces, India
August 14, 1877

My dear Children,

. . . As I now write, the punkah wala has stopped pulling the punkah, and my sleeves look as if they had been dipped in water. The drops of sweat fall off my chin, and every pore seems to be a channel for a small stream.

Frankie has gone out into the yard. Your papa has gone to prayer meeting. I have a headache, but the home mail goes tonight. The steamer that takes the English mail sails on Saturday, and we have to send on Wednesday from here to catch it.

Today Jennie wrote [from her boarding school in the Hills at Landour]: "I had a birthday party. 12 little girls came. Mrs Holcomb made me a nice birthday cake with frosting on it, and 'Jennie' in pink letters on the top of it. We had tea together, and had such a nice time." August 10th, Jennie was 7 years old. Quite a big girl now. Frankie looked vexed, when I told him about Jennies big cake. He said, "She for-

2. Although Samuel J. Tilden won 4,284,757 popular votes and Rutherford B. Hayes won 4,033,950 votes in the presidential election of 1876, Hayes had one more electoral vote than Tilden. When the election returns from four states were questioned—Republican election boards in three Southern states had thrown out enough Democratic votes to certify the Republican candidate, Hayes, and a western Democratic governor had replaced a Republican elector with a Democratic one—a joint session of Congress declared Hayes the president on Mar. 2, 1877. McPherson, *Ordeal by Fire*, 587–90.

got to give me any." I comforted him by explaining, it was not that she forgot him, but that the 500 miles between prevented her doing what I am sure was in her heart to do, if it had been possible.

A few minutes ago a man brought a small alligator to the door to show us. He caught it in the river in his fishing net. It was still living, and he had its long, savage-looking mouth tied, so that it couldn't bite him. From tip of nose to tip of tail, it was about 4 feet long. It had a black and white back, striped all down to its toes. Its eyes were grey, and as I shook my handkerchief at him, he blinked. I suppose he thought—if alligators do think—I would like a bite of you. The rope was tight around his nose and one leg, so I felt safe in taking liberties with him. We have seen the remains of much larger ones, found in the Jumna river.

. . . Tell Mother I have been making my "Singer" sing, making a new dress. Did I tell you I have got a Singer Machine? It came from London, and cost us 45 dollars when we got it here. It runs beautifully. There is a box to cover the top.

This morning I was out to see a school, about a mile and $\frac{1}{2}$ away, and came home half roasted. The pony didnt mind the whip a bit more than a fly. I suppose he felt the heat too.

Now dear Mary and dear Eddie, I must say good bye. With kisses from Frankie,

Love from Papa and Mama

[Many of Rachel and Will's letters between August 1878 and October 1880 are missing. Although Rachel was busy with her family and her teaching, there is no indication that she did not write regularly. Since David and Mary Kerr had always generously shared Rachel's letters with family and friends, it is likely that the letters were not reclaimed, returned, or filed away as carefully as in earlier years. Afterall, with Mary and Eddie now living in their home, life certainly was not as methodical as it had once been. Fortunately, several of Will's letters to the children provide some information of the Johnson family's activities in India.]

Allahabad
November 22d, 1878

My Dear Daughter Mary,

We have been very much pleased during the past years to hear so often from you, and of you, and to get such good accounts of your progress. You seem to be getting on well with your studies, and trying to improve your mind, which is a great pleasure to us. It is a still greater comfort to us, in our long separation from you, that you are among those who have "named Christ's name." We trust you are trying to live as a Christian should. If I dont write to you very often, you know it is not because I do not love you and Eddie very much indeed, but because I am able to write very few letters. I still keep hoping for the day when I might write letters as I used to, but it seems as far off as ever. Meanwhile, we very often think of you both. Your names are often on our lips. When we see something very nice, we often say we wish Mary and Eddie could be here to see this; or, we think it would be pleasant if we could send this to Mary and Eddie.

I think your Mama will tell you of a very pleasant trip we made to Benares, as we came down from the hills. But, I believe she has not told you of one of the things which was about the most interesting to me, of all that we saw in that interesting old city. That was a place called Sarnath, about 6 miles from the city. We hired a carriage for a $, and Mr. Lambert, your mama, and I drove out one lovely afternoon. When we came within 2 miles, we could see two great ruins, looming up out of the black plain. The first one was a great mound of broken brick, crowned with a large brick tower. This tower had been all dug away about the base, till it looked just ready to topple over. A great hole yawned in the side of the mound, for it had been cut open in search of treasure. We all groped down into this excavation, and then climbed up into the tower. The sun was just setting. We looked out through the arched openings in the top of the tower. On every side, we looked out on wide plains, green with every sort of growing crops. These, glowing in the evening sunlight, made a most exquisite picture. Many of the little fields were filled with growing rice, which shows, I think, the prettiest green in nature.

This place, though very curious, was not, after all, so very old. At least, the mound is old, but the tower has been built for an observatory by the Mohammedans, say, within 300 years. But, across the fields we could see the Sarnath tower, which has an antiquity of another earth. It is not on a mound, but rises . . . for perhaps 150 feet out of the flat plain. It seems to have all been cased with cut stone, but for part of the height, these have all fallen away, and left the solid core of brick. There is no room in it. There used to be idols of buddha on it, but these have been carried away. This place is immensely ancient. This is a Buddist monument, and that religion vanished from this part of the country some 1400 years ago. I have a book of travels by a chinese traveller named Fa Hian, who came to India in A.D. 399. He speaks of this Sarnath. He calls it the "Temple situated in the Deer park of the Immortal." He says men built a temple there, because Buddha there became immortal; and there began "to turn the wheel of the law"—that is, began to preach the Buddhists faith. So that this dome, which marks the birth of a religion held by $\frac{1}{3}$ the people of the world today, is well worth a visit.

Within a few miles of this spot (and some are close by) are many old Buddhist cloisters, where the priests lodged. They are marked all over by images of a wheel. Some are in excellent preservation. One, on the Ganges bank, is 120 ft long by 22 ft wide. The roof is supported by 4 rows of beautifully carved stone pillars. The Mohammadans now use it as a mosque.

Near to Sarnath is a beautiful little lake (about as large as Hookstown), and we wandered about its banks till nearly nightfall. We found many porcupine quills scattered about, which we gathered, and brought away as momentos of our visits. It was long after dark when we rattled back over a fine road, to and through Benares. So ends our visit to a place built, I suppose, about the time of the Apostles.

We were glad to hear you had such a pleasant visit to Steubenville. Now that school has begun again, we hope you will work hard. Among other things, dont neglect to cultivate your music.

Your loving Father,
W. F. Johnson

Allahabad
November 22, 1878

My dear son Eddy,

We have again got back to our old home on the Ganges, and are beginning to get our house into shape again, so that we can be comfortable. What with the rains, the white ants, moths, and thievish servants, a house from which the owners have been absent for some time has a very forlorn look. If you take down all pictures and ornaments from the walls and put them away in boxes, take up the carpets and pile them on the beds, let the servants tumble things about for 6 months, and get all ones books and papers mixed up, you may be sure it is a troublesome job to get things to rights again. While we were away, somebody opened the lock on our cupboard, and stole our cooking utensils. As we only use copper pots to cook with in this country, this is quite a loss to us. We think we know who stole the things. When the parties were taxed with it, they said little, but ran away early next morning. This looks as if their consciences were not very clear.

We were much amused by a man who came to the door with toys for sale—such as are used by native children. As nearly all natives are very poor, they cannot afford to pay very much for their childrens toys, so all the sorts this man had were at a cent apiece. Now what sort of toy could you make to sell for a cent? It would not be very nice, would it? But some of this man's were quite ingenious. I have made a picture of one above, thinking you might like to try your skill in copying it. I think your Uncle Frank, at your age, would have much enjoyed such an experiment. This toy is a light wheel with a sharp edge. Bulging out in the centre, it is suspended, so as to turn very easily on a fixed axle. Then, when you blow in the tube b, the wind coming out at the hole c, strikes the edge of the wheel, and makes it turn with immense speed. Now is not that a fine cent's worth? Mica is best for the wheel, as it is very light and strong; but a thin card would do. The pieces of which the wheel is made are shaped like this $\sqrt{}$; and the small sides are pasted onto a round piece $\odot$, with a hole for the axle to go through. The edges are joined by pasting paper over them.

There is another sort of toy, for a cent, which shows 4 snakes fast to a stick by their tails. Their heads are suspended from a X on the top of the stick by 4 horse hairs. When the stick is twirled, the snakes coil about, and strike out at you, in the most lifelike and vicious way. The snakes are made of a peculiar grass. You could not make them in America because you have no grass strong enough.

But I must not take up all my letter about toys. . . . This morning I wakened before Daylight. I heard, from a village half a mile away above us on the river bank, a high, clear voice crying again and again: All——— a——— h hu Akb——— a——— r——— God is great! He prolonged the last syllable of each word very much, and gave the words a wild, strange sound. This was the Muezzin, or Mohammadan call to prayer. As 1 of their prayer times is in the early morning, he was calling to awaken good Musalmans [believers in Muhammad] for this purpose. It was a very pleasant sound with which to begin the day. God is great! With them, no doubt, it is a form. With us, such a thought should be always present. But I have come to the end of my paper, and must say Good Bye.

Ever, Your Father, W. F. J.

TEN

October 1880–April 1884

ALLAHABAD AND LANDOUR

⌘ FIVE YEARS AFTER RETURNING to India, Rachel gave birth to Walter Frederick. Will reported that Rachel was gravely ill the following summer, yet another exceptionally hot season in India. Since Freddie could not stand the heat either, Rachel took the children to the hills, leaving Will in Allahabad.

Jennie continued her studies at the Woodstock School for missionary children in the hills at Landour; Woodstock was a boarding school for girls, but boys could be accepted as day pupils. Thus, during the school year Rachel kept a home for the children in Landour, so that Frank could enroll as a day pupil at Woodstock and Jennie could live more cheaply at home.

Rachel's daily letters to Will during those long separations were personal, loving, direct, and full of gossipy observations and conversations, bits of business, outspoken thoughts and feelings, and deep expressions of love for her absent husband. Rachel spoke of being "glad and proud" to receive some "good, old-fashioned" love letters from her husband after more than twenty years of marriage. These letters were dotted with casual Hindi words which Rachel and Will must have used in a familiar way in their every-day conversations at home. Rachel signed these letters to Will with the familiar name from her youth, Lillie.

In Allahabad Will continued to preach, write, translate, and edit. In one letter Rachel described Will's effective use of a "magic lantern," or light projector of gelatin images, in conducting a service for crowds of sixty to one hundred, attentive listeners, seated on carpets outside under large trees.

In America, Mary, at age sixteen, followed her mother's footsteps to the Female Seminary in Steubenville, Ohio. A year later, in 1881, Eddie went to the preparatory school his father had attended in Canonsburg, Pennsylvania. Rachel wrote personal, private letters to Mary and Eddie at their schools, which was a change from the earlier family letters that were intended to be passed around among the relatives.]

Landour, Himalaya Mountains
October 5th, 1880

My dear children.

There! I see I have begun on the last page by mistake. Well, I did not sleep any until 3 A.M. last night; and it dont make one feel very bright, especially when I am myself almost an invalid yet. Baby had a severe cold, with sore throat and fever, the last 2 days. He was so restless, we got little sleep. I am thankful to say that he is better today. . . .

The weather is clear and cold now, and sunshiny. The Mountains look lovely. We will go down home about the last week of October, I hope. Your papa would have gone 10 days ago, if I had not been taken ill. Now he will wait until we hear that the weather is cool enough in Allahabad to take the children down without risk of fever.

We received one letter from you since I wrote, and a picture of a very, nice-looking, wee girl—but no name. . . . I think she must belong to Stella from her looks.

. . . I was surprised to hear that Frank has sold his house. What next? Tell him I want to know all about his plans. I hope he is not going to move west. I want him to be near home when we get home again.

Well Mary dear, are you at school at Steubenville, or where are you? I feel that I hardly know where to look for you these days. I think of Eddie these bright October days, as busy looking after the thieves among Grandpas grain. Dear Eddie, be very careful of that gun, that you dont let it wound you in some of your hunting expeditions. Some boys are careless about carrying about loaded guns, but I hope you will be very careful not to run any risk. . . .

The carpenters are busy preparing the roof of this house with a covering of corrugated iron, in place of the grass one now on it.

Allahabad
November 11th, 1880

My dear children,

Here we are at home again. We left the mountains on the 26th, and came down to Rajpore at the foot of them (if mountains have a foot) in the evening of that day. If you could have looked around on our side of the world with a spy glass, you might have seen a procession filing down the mountain side about 3 o clock. Jennie and Frankie in one "dandy," carried by 4 men (two alternately). Your papa in a "jhanpan," which is suited for heavier people, and takes 4 men, with 2 or 4 more to change with. Baby and I were in another of the same. The men went along at a trot, and we found the air losing its coolness and becoming more like the balmy spring air, rather than the cool autumn air of the top, as we wound down the mountain side.

Fig. 17. Landour, the summer mountain retreat where missionary families went to escape the intense heat of the Indian plains.

Baby was in high spirits, crowing and trying to dance a hornpipe in my lap. At last, as the stars came out, he was filled with wonder, for he had not been out stargazing up in the cold. He got much excited over the sparking lights. As one very bright one came in sight, he stretched out his little hand, and motioned to it to come to him, saying ao! ao! (in Hindustani)—which means "Come! Come!" He enjoyed the journey, and so did we all.

We got to the hotel at Rajpore a little after dark, had our tea and went to bed, expecting to start by daylight for Saharanpore. The dawk gari didn't come until 8 A.M., and we were ready waiting, so off we started. They gave us pretty good horses, and they had fresh ones every 8 miles.

We looked back and up at the big mountains, with their grand peaks towering up among the clouds. The houses looked like white spots sprinkled over their sides, growing smaller as we rattled on. 7 miles passed and we reached Dehra—that beautiful place where hedges of roses scent the morning air, and the gardens are full of beautiful flowers. Everything grows with tropical luxuriance. The "morning glories" we saw here and there clambering over the roses were about 4 times as large as they grow in Hookstown. Such beauties! The fuchsias too are mammoths. Though they grow in full beauty on the mountains, I never saw such large, perfect ones as I saw at Landour. The tall bamboos in large clumps, nodded their graceful, drooping heads over the entrance to the mission compound as we passed by.

. . . As we began to ascend the Sewalik Mountains, they hitched on an additional pair of horses, and we were taken up at a good pace. If horses go at all in the dawk, they always go at a trot, or a gallop; varying the journey by sometimes stopping "stock still." The coaches gariwan—or driver—then lashes the poor brutes. Another man or two turns at the wheels and shouts. At last, away we dash again. We hold our breath, wondering if the rickety harness—plentifully patched up with ropes and strings—will hold together. Having reached the summit, two of the horses are taken out. The drag is put on the wheels, and now we begin to descend. At first slowly, then faster and faster. On we go, plunging around sharp curves, when the driver frantically blows his bugle to warn any unwary traveler or lumbering cart coming up hill out of sight around a corner. On we go. The poor bony horses, propelled by the heavy carriage, seem scarcely to touch hoofs to the hard, smooth, metalled road. If one should stumble, what then? But all safe at last. After many windings, we reach the bottom.

As we change horses for the 2nd time in the descent, we find, spread out on the plain, the tents of the Goorkha regiment. The men are busy cooking their noon meal. They are coming home from the war in Cabul. They look happy to get back. The men are from Nepal, and look more like Chinese than natives of India.

We arrived safely at 4 P.M. o'clock in Saharanpore. We expected to stay all night at Rev. Calderwoods, but found that the 3 o-clock train for Allahabad had been delayed. We had just time to buy our tickets, and get our luggage into the train, when we were off to Allahabad. A ride of 26 hours brought us home on Thursday evening, just about dark. Tired, hungry, and dusty, we were glad to see the old house on the Jumna again. We felt that after all, "there is no place like home." The mosquitos organized a band at once to celebrate our arrival. I was obliged to hunt out our mosquito curtains at once. They seem to find baby very sweet. Even in the daytime, the poor child is teased and bitten by them, until his face is quite full of marks.

Several of the native Christians met us at the depot on our arrival. The next day, men, women, and children came flocking in to welcome us back.

We find the weather here quite warm. There was so little rain here in Allahabad this year, that it makes the hot weather linger longer than usual. Baby felt the heat more than the rest of us, and he has not been well since we came. Frankie has a very bad cough this last week, and we think it may be whooping cough. Baby too coughs a little, and I fear that they will both have it. I am sorry that baby should get it while he is teething, for that seems enough trouble at one time.

We received letters from you both, just before we left the mountains. I suppose Father and Frank are very much elated over the Republican victory: "Garfield elected!" We don't get our political enthusiasm up much out here, but we generally take it for granted that the Republican man must be the best one. I hope he will prove so. . . .

Affectionately,
Mamma

[A preserved fragment of a letter from Will reveals more clearly the mission work in which he was engaged, the centrality of Allahabad, and the nature of Rachel's illnesses at the time.]

Allahabad
February 14, 1881

My Dear Aunt Jane,

. . . with the best intentions in the world, I make a very bad correspondent. My correspondence as editor of the Makhzan i Masihi, as manager of the Northern India Tract Society, and latterly also of the Northern India Vernacular Education Society, is very large, and often gets dreadfully in arrears. In fact, my life here at Allahabad is like that play of the jugglers, where he devotes all his energies to keeping a lot of balls in the air, and where the slightest pause brings a lot of them about his ears. No doubt a life of this sort is useful, but it is often wearying. I wish, on occasion, I could escape to the comparative quiet of some other mission station. We scarcely ever go anywhere, see anything, or visit anybody. Perhaps two or three times a year we make a formal call on somebody. But we have no associates here.

Once in a while though, the steady stream of work is interrupted: in the hot weather, by illness and a flight to the Hills; and in the cold weather, by persons passing through Allahabad. At the railway bridge close by our house, the three great lines of Railway—Lahore, Calcutta, and Bombay—meet. So most travelers in India pass through Allahabad. As it is a run of 24 hours or more to the end of these lines, travelers like to stop and rest here. Americans and Missionaries often stop with us. From November to February, we often entertain such parties. Mr. Lucas, and Mr. and Mrs. Newton, the elder, have thus stopped with us this season on their way home. Miss Hutchinsen, Miss Walsh, and Miss Perley of Mainpuri made us long visits. Miss Butler called to see us on her way to Gwalior.

Just now Wynkoop, who used to live here, is back on a visit. His mother is with him. He has taken a vacation of 6 months from his church at Washington, D.C. They are having a grand tour. They left America in October; came via California, China, Japan, Siam, Ceylon, Madras, and Calcutta. They came here day before yesterday in good health and spirits, and are staying with Mr. Heyl, on the other side of this house. They report a very encouraging state of things in China and Japan. There are many conversions, and the work is spreading rapidly.

Last season as we found Frankie could not bear the heat, I sent off Mrs. Johnson and the children to the Hills in April and undertook to keep house here alone for the summer. About August 1st, I got a telegram to hurry off to Landour, as Mrs. Johnson was very ill. She had three such attacks during the summer, and was more ill than she had been before in India. We came down again in October, and she has been pretty well since. Frankie and the baby caught the whooping-cough about the time we came down, and are not over it yet. Strange to say, I caught it from them, and have been "barking" for two months. At first it was very severe. For a long time it interfered much with my preaching—though the daily grind of the desk went on the same as ever.

We are making great efforts to utilize the new generation of readers, who are growing up in the native schools. We are preparing and circulating vast numbers of small Christian books in the vernaculars. I have had a larger share in this work than perhaps any body else in North India. The two Societies, that I have spoken of above, put in circulation something like 150,000 of such books and tracts per year—a large share of these being written or translated by me.

Besides this, I have had this last year another similar work on hand. A childrens Society in England is trying, through me, to put in circulation 40,000 Hindi and 40,000 Urdu tracts of 4 quarto pages each. Each tract has one full-page picture. As Urdu has to be printed by lithography, the paper for these was sent out from England with the pictures ready printed. I am having the letter-press pages set up in type, and then stereotyped in Calcutta. These will be sent to England, the picture plates added, and the whole printed there. They will then be sent to me to distribute. There are 8 different tracts in Hindi, 8 in Urdu, and 5000 of each. . . .

Yours Truly,
W. F. Johnson

Upper Woodstock
Tuesday, April 19th, 1881

My dear Husband,

This is a bright, lovely day . . . baby is asleep, and Jennie and Frank are at school. Frankie felt very bashful about making his first entree, but I suppose he has kept his courage up, as he has not returned in such haste as last year. After breakfast he remarked that the thought of going the first time made him feel a little sick at his stomach. Poor boy! It is a trial to face so many girls, and no boys. He thought he would not mind if Edwin was here to go with him.

Mrs. Seeley had a fainting spell this morning. I was called in from my chhoti haziri [little breakfast], but by the time I had hurried on my dress, she had revived. She is very imprudent about getting up from bed, and thinks she cant manage without it; but others do, and I think she could if she would be more persevering. I fear she will get thrown back by it. Her baby is very thin, but healthy. She is much worried about his hand. Two of his fingers are grown together. The doctor pooh! poohs! it, and says he can soon put them right. On the 10th day he will separate them. He says it will be quite safe and easy to do so.

. . . Miss Perley has been quite ill with very severe headaches, that leave her head very sore to the touch, and quite prevents her studying or writing. They come on every morning and last till evening. What is to become of poor Miss Perley, I cant tell. I suppose this will be a new grievance against the married missionaries . . . "she must have perfect quiet and constant care"—neither of which any of us can give her.

Mr. Calderwood called on Mr. Seeley and wasnt in 5 minutes "until he began about Woodside." He said "our Mission action has caused consternation in New York!" "They have had one meeting of the Board and called another. We, as a Mission, have insisted on the recall of Mr. Woodside or we appeal the case to the General Assembly." Mr. Seeley talked very plainly to Mr. Calderwood, and told him that their condemnation of a man, without a hearing, by prejudiced judges, was unheard of in church courts. He asked him if Woodside had been given copies of charges sent home against him! If there was ever a case of persecution, I think the Lodiana Missionaries are guilty of it.[1]

Mr. Seeley says Mr. Herron invited him and Ewing to dine at Synod with them. At the table, in reference to Woodstock School, he said that, "when he was at home, he had offered the Board to manage it without any expense to them. He would pay all the teachers salaries from the school receipts, if they would only make it over to him." Do you see the iron hand under the velvet glove? He will never rest satisfied until he gets himself worked in again. The wretched hypocritical man! I dreamed saturday night that Mr Woodside was dead, but that Mr. Herron wouldn't let his grave be closed. He kept turning him over, and calling everybody to come and see him in his corruption. I cant get the horrible dream out of my mind.

. . . Here is Frankie home from school, and I hear him and the khan in a takrar [dispute]. The khan is not a nice man with children. He distinguished himself this morning, by going into Mr. Seeleys drawing room for coals to kindle his fire, and dropped some on the durrie, and left several holes behind him. The wretched fellow. I fear he is no prize.

Baby seems well today, but fretful. I hope the boxes will soon come, as I have no table cloth until they do.

Well, here is the last corner, so I must stop. There were many inquiries about you and Mr. Heyl. Give him my salam, along with that of the Woodstock ladies, and faith—

Love from yours, all,
Affectionately, Lillie

April 20th, 1881
Landour, Upper Woodstock

My dear Husband,

This is another bright day. We are all well and enjoying it. Jennie and Frankie are at school. I felt relieved after Frankies first introduction, but he complained of "one biggish girl who wanted to kiss him." He is be-

1. Missionaries from the Lodiana Mission and those from the North India Mission came together socially in Landour during the hot seasons and when their children attended Woodstock School. Apparently, in 1880, the Lodiana missionaries sent a poor report back to the Board of Foreign Missions in New York about Rev. John Woodside, principal of the Woodstock School, and requested that he be removed. Based upon that report, the Board removed Mr. Woodside, prompting the North India missionaries to write a contradictory report requesting that Rev. Woodside be returned to his position as principal or they would appeal the Board's action to the church's General Assembly for resolution.

ginning the arduous labors of studying "Grammar, Geography, Arithmetic, History, Reading, Writing and Spelling." So you see, he is likely to have enough to do to keep him out of mischief.

I felt quite fatigued after my mornings work coaching and cramming him with the distinguishing marks of the "Noun, Article and Adjective." This was a review lesson, and he, being new at the work, felt quite a load on his mind. He was not satisfied unless he had it all, as he wished to be head. He came home at noon, stowed away a bun and 2 biscuits, and went back for History and etc.

I went down to see the Woodstock ladies last evening, and saw Mrs Seeley. I had a long chat with her, and found her full of enthusiasm as usual. . . . She has engaged a French teacher in Calcutta. She heard of her thru' Mrs. Elmslie, who was trying to get her one. She will likely be here next week if Mrs Miltre is favorably impressed by her. She is full of accomplishments and likes a challenge!

. . . Life seems very humdrum up here. No word of my horses yet. I moved Miss Walshs sewing machine in out of the hall today, and will try to hem some jharrans [dust cloths]. That is all the material I have to work on. By the way, did you find in your drawer the new piece of flannel I left to make you new shirts, and some old baby skirts, to reback the old ones?

Here is Fred, scolding me because I dont take him. He is very gabardast [demanding] since he came up. There seems to be no special news here.

> Will love from us all,
> Affectionately, Lillie

> Landour, Himalaya Mountains
> April 23d, 1881

My dear Son Eddie and Daughter Mary,

Here we are, up on the mountains again—we, that is Jennie, Frankie, Baby, and I. Your papa we left in Allahabad. The weather had become very hot there, and I came to bring Jennie and Frank out of the heat, and send them to the Woodstock School. If they had had any accommodation for boys, we would have sent them as boarders, and I would have staid in Allahabad too. But this is a girls boarding school, and so they could not take Frankie, except as a day scholar, boarding at home.

On last thursday, one week ago, at 7 P.M., we got on the train at Allahabad, and came directly to Saharanpur without stopping, except to change cars at noon on friday. We got to that place about 5 in the evening of friday; stopped a couple of hours at our missionary's house, Rev Calderwoods; then we got into a "dawk gari"—or carriage—that brought us to the foot of the Mountains.

We traveled all night, and dozed along as best we could crowded in one carriage. The bottom has no seats, so we stretched ourselves out on our mattresses and pillows. About every 6 or 8 miles, a fresh pair of horses are posted. As we approach the place, the coachman blows his horn, as a signal for the horses to be got ready. Arrived, he dismounts, takes out the tired horses, and disappears, leading them off in the darkness to their stable. This is generally a picket place under a tree near by.

The coachman must take time for a smoke at his hookah, and we wait as patiently as we can. Sometimes the stopping wakes up the children, and sometimes they doze on. I often get out and stretch my cramped limbs, by walking about a little. I feel very impatient as time passes, and no horses come, tho I hear voices in the distance. I dont like to call out, to hurry up the coachman, for fear of waking up the baby. At last they come. I scramble in and settle myself. . . .

At last we drive into Rajpur, the town at the foot of the Mountains, where we leave the carriage. We drive to a hotel. It is not quite daylight, but the servants are astir, and we unload sleepy children, baggage, and all. I pay the coachman a fee for his arduous labors (not landing us in a ditch on the way). I order tea, toast and milk, then open my trunk, and get out warm clothes for us all to put on before ascending the mountain. I order 2 Jhanpans to carry us up the mountain, and 1 pony for the native who accompanies me. It is about 8 miles up the zigzag road to our house at Landour.

By the time we have got on our warm dresses and trunks repacked, it is daylight, and the tea, toast, and butter are ready. We eat our little breakfast, and make over our baggage to the hotel keeper. He weighs all the trunks, bundles, and etc., and makes them over to some hill men to carry up, giving each man 40 pounds as his load. Each gets about 20 cents for carrying up his load, and delivering it safely at "Upper Woodstock" house in Landour. They carry the weight on their backs. The jhanpans are ready, and wraps and shawls put on.

The sun is shining brightly, and the blue haze is lifting from the mountain sides. The air is just cool enough to be pleasant. As we ascend, the view of the Dehra Valley is very lovely. The Sewalik Mountains rise like a wall beyond, shutting in the lovely valley with its great tea plantations dotted here and there over its miles of level plains. Above us, and on either side, the Great Himalayas tower up in all their grandeur. Their sides slope down in frightful precipices.

We jog on about half way up, then stop to rest. We get out our lunch basket, and supplement our breakfast with a little more. We get a drink from the cold mountain spring, and then move on. About noon we reach "Upper Woodstock." Mr. and Mrs. Seeley of Futtehgurh have been there for about a month. She was ill when she came up, but Mr Seeley comes out to greet us. We hear that he has a little son, 2 days old; so Mrs Seeley is, of course, not able to be up to welcome us.

Our side of the house is ready—fires burning and all. So we settle down at home at once. . . .

The change from the heat of the plains to the cool air up on the mountain top is very great. We have to keep pretty close to the house for a few days until we get used to the cold. Baby had fever for a couple of days from the sudden change, but is now well again.

I left your papa well, but of course he will be lonely with us all away. What will he do for somebody to make a noise in the big rooms, with Frank and Fred away? Jennie too, can make her share. Baby runs everywhere and is a very happy little tot. I would much rather be at home than up here, but there seemed to be no other arrangement possible, than for me to come.

. . . I have taken up so much of this letter telling you about our journey, that I have no room left for much else. More again soon. Now my dear children, good bye. With much love always, from your affectionate Mother,

RL

[In the following letter Jennie wrote to her father of some of the more basic observations in her life.]

Upper Woodstock
May 9th, 1881

My dear Papa,

I have not gone to school today because I have got a sore throat and a swollen eye. Mama said I had better not go. I am first in all my classes, except in History and Grammar I am second.

One of the cows died day before yesterday. We make our own butter. Yesterday evening the Khansama went off to see a brother of his at Mrs. Hathaway's, so the gualla took the opportunity to water the milk, and put milk in his own bartan [vessel]. This morning, of three jars of milk, we got only one "chatak" of butter—just when we need it most, for Misses Ward and Lathrop are coming to dinner.

The wild rose and sweet briar bushes are all in bloom and smell very sweet. . . .

In starting, I forgot my big doll behind.

There is a little bird that comes and sits on our big oak tree every night, and sets up a "too toot" all night long. Yesterday a raven carried off one of Mr. Seeleys chickens. It left go when it got to the slide of stones at the back of the house, so their mater ran down the hill and caught it. It was not much hurt.

I suppose mama has told you that the Seeleys baby's second and third finger grew together. The doctor made a little cut and put a ring on.

Well, he came today and cut the rest of it. Mrs Seeley is very nervous, and she staid in here till the operation was finished—poor thing. I am sorry for her, she was crying so. But it is finished and she has gone back.

Frankie is back from school. As I have nothing more to say, so goodbye, with love. Do write to me.

Your loving daughter,
Jennie

Landour
Tuesday—May 10th, 1881

My dear Husband,

This is another bright, sunshiny day; but notwithstanding the brightness, there seems to be some clouds in the house—and rain too, I judge, from the sounds in the back room. Frankie came home at noon. It seems all who had been guilty of saying "ohhhh!", when a girl dropped some ink spots, were requested to "stay in." But the attractions of bread and honey at the top of the hill were too great for Frankie, and he "skedadelled" when school was "let out." When he went back at 2 o clock, some of the sufferers assured him that his turn would come in the evening, and he would have to stay in until prayertime. Discretion getting the better of his valor, he retired up the hillside. I persuaded him to face the danger, but he came back again. As it was then late for his afternoon class, I thought it hardly worthwhile to send him back through the hot sun the 3rd time. Now he is repenting that he didn't stay, fearing the dreadful tomorrow. Poor boy! I fear he will often have much trouble, unless he learns to discount a little more the idle talk of his schoolmates. Fancy the sufferings of such a sensitive child among a lot of teasing boys, ready to play on any such weakness.

Wednesday morning

Your mondays letter was delivered to me just as I was dressing. . . . I am sorry to hear that you are not feeling well. I hope it is nothing serious. Put a mustard plaster on that sore spot, and see if it wont relieve it. If it gives you more trouble, ask the Doctor about it.

. . . See Mrs. Scotts note enclosed.[2] My answer to her was in one word, PREPOSTEROUS!!! I am astonished at Mrs. Scott for supposing that we would listen for a moment to such a proposition. Fancy the delights of

2. Mrs. Scott managed the living quarters for the students at Woodstock, as well as the home rental properties for missionary families. To increase fiscal profits for the school, Mrs. Scott seems to have proposed accepting fifteen additional students and housing them in the other half of the house in which Rachel and her children were living. Rachel felt strongly that this would not be satisfactory and that the children could go to other denominational boarding schools that still had vacancies.

living in Upper Woodstock with 15 children in the other side! The truth of the matter is, she has been too greedy about taking in many scholars. She has 75 boarders. Now that paragon Bringle comes along, and begins to croak, she gets scared. She lies awake, and goes wandering about, inspecting and writing letters at "4 A.M." Mr. Seeley's reply was that "the plan was utterly impractical. He felt quite sure she would not get one vote in the Mission in favor." Her note was sent to both of us, as a private note. I told Mr. Seeley, if he didn't want it, I would send it to you—to amuse you with Mrs. Scotts nightmare. I felt quite indignant with Mrs. Scott for suggesting such a thing.

My advise to her, when I see her, will be to make her school a more select one. Be more particular who she takes, and limit her number to her accommodations. She can afford, now that she has got a big name, to dispense with some of the "riff raff." I dont exactly see how she can suppose "Providence is making this a solution of the missionary children question," by taking away their only refuge. There is Caineville—not full, the Kassouli School and the Methodist Grand Select School—without pupils almost (Miss Latterop tells one). Let the suffering public send theirs to them. Mrs. Frazer told me she met 3 girls on the road by "Jerypani," running away from Cainville. They told her, "they beat us, and we are running away to Rajpur." A little farther on, she met a governess and a Sahib in hot pursuit. So they have their troubles there too it seems—though of a different kind.

. . . The "Great light of Gregson" preached on Sunday to an interested congregation. "Itching ears" were left tingling with such great and grand(?) illustrations as the following: "He understands God best, who best comprehends the Great Circle that God described in eternity!!" I should not have said "illustration," for as far as I could gather, it had no possible connection with either what came before or followed. . . . Mr. Gregson, you know, failed to be here at the appointed time, so Mr. Seeley was asked to take the Services for Sundays. Mrs. Smith first asked him if he would be willing, and he assented. Then Mr Anderson, who is now on the Committee, wrote to Mr. Webb, who was willing to have Mr Seeley, but said, "of course, we cant pay him anything." Mr. Anderson wrote asking him to preach, and enclosed Mr. Webbs note—so that he wouldnt indulge visions of rupees to follow, I suppose. Mr. Seeley preached 3 sundays, and he said he hasn't even had a thank you! He met Mr. Gregson yesterday in the bazar and had a long chat. Mr. Gregson never alluded to his services. I suppose he thought it was sufficient honor for a broken down Missionary to be allowed to do his work, even if he drew the Rupees.

. . . Well I have no more news now—and Fred is up, hanging on to me wanting consolation for bumping his head—so dearest, good bye. With love from all of yours,

Lillie

Landour
Saturday, May 14, 1881

My dear Husband,

I was very glad this morning to receive the anxiously, looked-for epis-
tle. It came all safely wrapped in its big envelope. Jennie was much concerned about its contents. She thought "Papa might write her a big letter
too." Well, my darling, I must not attempt to answer it today. I must have
a chance to do its loving pages justice, at least more so than I can in this
fragment of a broken, worn-out day, full of interruptions: the sweetie
man is howling at one door, the kaprawala [clothing or fabric man] at
another; the honey wala has just been relieved of his burden; the dhobie
[washerman] just attended to; the bazar durzi man [tailor] attended to—
I am getting him to finish off my dress, and he brought me cloth to
match it at last; the roti walla [baker] is screaming kai roti [how much
bread]?; Mrs. Scotts khid [shortened form of Khidmati or servant] just
brought some salad for us; the berry men with the yellow raspberries
relieved of $\frac{1}{2}$ a basket; the khan given his masala [seasoning] for a curry
for dinner; Freddie just out of his nap wanting "dudh" [milk]; the bihisti
[water carrier], remembering I arrived just a month ago friday, must
needs have his talab [salary] just now; Frankie reading me striking pas-
sages from his book; and Jennie just back from Miss Lathrops, where
she had gone to greet the newcomers. So is it any wonder I found it
rather uphill work writing the last sheet of Marys letter, and that I can
give you only a very common-place, scrap of a letter today?

Well Daulatu is lying in wait for the mail, and you know I would not
be late for anything, when you are the expectant of a letter. So my darling, excuse this scrawl. . . . With much love from yours, and your own
loving

Wife Lillie

I enclose Marys letter for you to forward. Cant you add some? Correct
any omissions, I havent time to read over.

May 15th, 1881 Friday night
Landour, Himalaya Mts, India

My dear Daughter,

I was very glad to get the letter you wrote me on that sunday evening,
telling me something of your heart life. I have often wished you would
do so, and felt that drawback about family letters. There is always so
much that a child feels like telling to a mother's ear alone, that you
ought and should write, feeling that she alone is receiving your confidence. Yet you do not feel free to write if others must see your letters. I
quite understand my daughter the difficulties you speak of, and why you
could not. But, as you say, it may have been, and no doubt was, blessed.

This was the means of sending you to the Great Comforter, in whose ear we can pour out all our sorrows. I feel sure that He is ever ready to sympathize with us, and able to help us—however small and petty our vexation might seem to human ears. Yet our dear Saviour knows how hard it is to bear the little thorns that rankle, and how much grace we need to bear lifes little worries. When some great trouble comes, we brace up our courage to meet it, feeling that now we must have special strength to bear the burden. We go to the Great burden bearer and get the needed strength. He does not tell us to Cast only thy great burdens on the Lord, and He will sustain thee; but, "thy burden," whatever it be, bring it all to Jesus. "Come unto Me." "Let not your heart be troubled." His ear is never weary. His eye follows us. His hand is always outstretched to help and guide us, if we will but grasp it.

I cannot tell you dear Mary what an unspeakable comfort it is to me, to know that you have found this Great Comforter to be your comforter—this precious Saviour to be yours. Live near to him. Love and read his precious promises, and go to Him daily for that strength you need to help you serve him faithfully. You can do much to commend the religion you profess by living a consistent Christian life among your schoolmates. Always try to show the loving, forgiving, spirit of Jesus. Be patient under provocation, returning good for evil. In short, try to be like Him in all things. You can do much to win others to love your dear Saviour too.

Do the young ladies still have their Sabbath evening prayer meetings in the Class rooms? We used to have such pleasant little meetings for prayer—10 or 12 meeting in one room. Are your roommates good, earnest, Christian girls? I hope so. You will then be helps to each other.

. . . I cannot tell you how my heart longs for you, to see you, to clasp you again in my arms, my darling children. I know your hearts have often felt desolate, and ached with a longing for your parents love and sympathy. When I think of this, often I cannot keep back the bitter tears. But my darling, I know this cross is done for our Master, and there is a need be in it. All I can do is to carry my grief to Him. . . .

Affectionately,
Mama

Landour
May 30th, 1881, Monday night
My dear Husband,

I was very glad this morning to find that my letter from you was one of the good, old fashioned kinds—a true love letter. It makes my heart glad, and proud too, to think that my husband—after 20 + years of wedded love—can find it in his heart to write of his love. A very pleasant kind of "dotage," that will, I trust, affect us both, and cling to us through the years to come. It will gild our years with a brightness that shall grow clearer to the end.

. . . When I think of the wealth of love that cheers our hearts in our absence, and hopes that brighten our future, how blessed our lot. How great the love that has portioned us our part in this worlds drama! My darling, it is good for us to own up sometimes a few of the loving kindnesses that gladdens our lives. We feel a "praise God!" for all his goodness to us, and to ours, welling up in our hearts. Of all our blessings, what gives our hearts so much joy is our love to each other. How its absence would shadow every other blessing. It would leave a feeling of unsatisfied longing for that sweet communion of feeling, and sympathy in each others trials, that now doubles our joys and halves our sorrows.

Yes, my dear Willie, I feel that the deep, full current of our love, tried and true, brings us greater happiness than even the sparking flow of stream that danced so merrily, hopping over all obstacles in its earlier course. Perhaps it was more to our minds fancy—or hearts rather—in those days when youths prism, tinted with rainbows, even the rocks that loomed up to cause the foam and whirlpool commotions that often stirred the stream. Now that we look at things more in the clear, white light, it seems good to go hand in hand—heart in heart—trustingly, lovingly on. Not forgetting that the heart still longs for the tokens of love. The sweet assurances that all is well. This seems to me too to be all that is needed to add much to our enjoyment of our love. This thread of gold that runs through all the web, should not be hidden, but kept free from the tangled threads that often hide its brightness. Why should the love that so brightens life in every relation, be so often hid down in the heart—half ashamed to show itself, though of such heavenly origin it always adds so much sweetness to the cup of life. Yes dearest, let us cherish its expression. Rejoice in its security and live in its blessed atmosphere. It will keep our hearts pure and healthy, and we will be able then to Rejoice always in love.

Now my darling, I must bid you a loving good night.

This pen is too slow and poor to tell you the thoughts of my heart. But present or absent, I am your loving wife

Lillie

[In this letter to Will, Rachel is "riled up" over the accusations of Miss Seward, who had accused Rachel of failing to show proper courtesies toward a young female missionary who passed through their station. Rachel took great insult and told Will that she had not received any notice of the young woman's arrival in Allahabad. Tensions did exist between the single and married women in the mission. The role of the single woman was not clear; their presence was a threat to the wives of missionaries, as it was not uncommon for one of the mission's single women to become widowed missionaries' second wives.]

Landour
Wednesday June 8th, 1881

My dear Husband,

I have just been giving the Khan a few hints on butter making—not very encouraging work, when I find my practical illustrations yesterday didn't stay in his head 24 hours. His theory is, as soon as a few globules appear, to collect them on his hand and arm—like the coolie who brought the bees to Mr. Hunter the other day. He brought a swarm, hanging on his hand and arm, for sale, and got his rupee. Mr. Heyl was out when he came, and he said it was getting pretty "heavy" by the time he came.

Today we have a downpour of rain. It has been coming down steadily for the last 8 or 10 hours. I heard it very heavy about 2 A.M. At 4, baby waked for a cup of "du du" [milk], and I didnt go to sleep again, thinking about some news Mrs. Ewing told me a day or two ago.

I dont know why it only took hold of my thoughts so forcibly at that untimely hour. It was this. You perhaps remember that Mrs. Perkins wrote one time last year to Mrs Ewing, urging her to be a peace-maker between the mission and single ladies—and especially Miss Seward. Well, she being looked on as an unprejudiced party, thought it would be well to write a plain letter, stating the facts about the relations of the Mission to Miss Seward, and to show how impossible it is to get on amicably with her. She told Mrs. Perkins all the circumstances of her arrival, her writing to outside people, and etc.

Mrs. Perkins now writes, saying that a letter received from Miss Seward throws new light on matters. It has made them look at things somewhat differently, since Miss Seward has sent her a copy of a letter written to Mrs. Johnson from London, "asking her to receive Miss Butler on her arrival." Seems Ewing left the letter of Mrs. Perkins in Fatehgarh, but has sent for it, that I may see exactly what she says.

You remember that Miss Seward said nothing to me on arrival, about having written to me. But some days after, when Misses Hutchinson and Perley went up to lunch, she said to Miss Hutchinson, "she wondered if I had received a letter from her from London." Miss Hutchinson said "she thought not, as I had not spoken of it." The next time I saw Miss Seward, I said to her that I was surprised to hear that she said she had written, as I had not received any letter; and that when she was writing again to Miss Butler, I hoped she would not fail to say that I had not received any letter from her, or any notice of her coming—lest she might think I had not been courteous in not replying. You know we are always ready to entertain our missionaries passing through.

Miss Seward said, "Oh, I dont just remember when or where I posted your letter . . . and I dont think I ever mentioned it to Miss Butler." . . . So the matter dropped. I didnt think from her hesitating, doubtful tone, that she quite felt sure that she ever had more than intended writing. But she has produced "a copy!" of a letter—so hurriedly written, by the way, that she couldnt remember when or where she had posted it, and hadn't even thought it worth while to mention to Miss Butler, the party concerned. But now she sends this to Miss Perkins, with the intention I suppose, of showing how badly Miss Butler was treated by me, and herself so discourteously as to not get even a reply. The Old Shaitan [satan] seems to be still abroad, walking to and fro in the earth. . . .

When Mr. Robinson wrote to Mr. Heyl asking him to ask me to take in Mrs. Lochs friends, I asked Mr. Heyl to keep a copy of his reply and Mr. Robinsons note. . . . I may want them to help straighten out the tangled web. If Miss Seward is going to act so abominably, she will only lose in the end by driving away every feeling of sympathy and forbearance towards herself. I feel that she may "paddle her own canoe" as far as I am concerned, hereafter. I have helped push her off "the snags" she has washed on heedlessly, and daringly, often enough. I am tired of the worry. If she treats those who have sincerely tried to be friendly in this way, she will have to reap as she sows. There might as well be an end of the hypocritical kind of friendship now as later. You will see that I am "riled." Well, patience dont seem to be any longer a virtue. I dont like this kind of warfare, being shot at in ambush like the Boers carried on their war; and not giving me once a chance to reply, except by accident, when one has a good supply of ammunition. When I see Mrs. Perkins' letter I will be able to judge better of the amount of damage done, so till then, I wait patiently as I can.

. . . Well my dear, I was sorry to see you are "depressedly" this morning. Cheery! and dont use up your eyes altogether. I hope to hear that you are in better spirits tomorrow. I am glad to hear that you are getting the permit ready to come up, and I think you must come before the 11th hour. Well my darling, only much love from yours.

Lillie

Landour
Saturday June 11th, 1881

My dear Husband,

In spite of the assurances of the oldest inhabitants of these hills, that this is only the "chhota barsat" [small rainy season], the rain continues.

. . . Frankie went down to Miss Lathrops to spend an hour or so. They all make a good deal of him, and he is very fond of going over for a chat. Mr. Hunter is very fond of children too. I told him I thought it would be too rainy for calls, but he said, "it wasn't good to break your promise, just for a little rain." So, he took advantage of a break to go. Now he will find it pretty wet to come back, unless the rain holds up again.

Col. Buckley is overseeing the job of putting up railing on Woodstock road, which will be a needed improvement.

The boy who died at Mr. Stokes' school had Scarlet Fever, and it has caused quite a scare. The parents have taken away their boys, as there have been 3 cases since, but no more fatal ones as yet. This is a new scourge for India, and the Doctors say they have never seen it here before. I heard that it was brought up from the plains.

Now my dear, this is such a cold, dark, dreary day, I fear I have not been able to cultivate much sunshine, to sprinkle over my letter—if you can sprinkle sunshine, but kya karen [what can be done]? I have some in my heart. Still, how could it be otherwise, when I soon hope to welcome my darling Willie home to his loving wife.

Lillie

[In 1881 Will escaped the heat of Allahabad and joined his family in the hills. The highlight of this pleasant, wet summer was the birth of daughter Dora Elizabeth, "Bessie," their eighth child.]

Upper Woodstock, Landour Hills
August 14th, 1881

My Dear Mary and Eddie,

I have not time to write you much of a letter today, but I have a nice little bit of news to give you. You have another little sister, born last Monday, the 8th. Every body says she is a very, pretty, little baby, and certainly she is a nice, plump, little youngster, and is a model of good behavior. Mamma thinks she looks like Mary, and I see more resemblance to Frank. The rest say, "Oh, she is a Johnson anyway." Mamma and baby are doing very nicely. Jennie pretty nearly had a birthday gift, as her birthday is August 10.

The Ewings, who live in the other half of this house, had a little daughter born on the 10th. Pretty good for one house in one week! We had the two babies weighed: Miss Johnson weighed $7\frac{1}{2}$ light; and Miss Ewing, 8 lbs heavy. You know the proverb that "Precious things are put up in the smallest parcels." Well, they are both very promising young damsels.

We are having dreadful weather up here. Almost incessant rain for a month past. One can hardly get out to take any exercise. It is very handy for Jeannie and Frank that their school is so close. Even as it is, we sometimes have to have them carried in a kind of long chair by two coolies, when the rain is too persistent.

The children enjoy their studies very much. Jennie is, I think, the youngest of a class of 15; but she manages to stand [a]head a good part of the time. Frank is not so lucky. His English is very much mixed with Hindustani, and he does not easily expresss himself in English. He generally vibrates about the middle of his class. Little Fred is fat and hearty, but not very happy, as the fleas are a great plague here. He scratches until he is covered with marks. Poor fellow, he will think it very hard to have the new baby usurp his place with mamma. . . .

Your loving papa,
W. F. Johnson

"Upper Woodstock," Landour, India
August 14, 1881

My Dear Aunt Jane,

. . . What dreadful news this is about the attempted assassination of Garfield![3] In spite of the predictions of the end of the world in this year, we seem to be some distance off from the millennium yet.

I hope the prosperity of the country, about which the American papers boast so much, will show itself in increased pushing on the work of Foreign Missions, but there seems little hope of this. We learned last week that our work, which has been "running close-reefed" every since the panic, is to be still farther cut down next year. Why, we cannot conceive. But people will be wondering why Missions dont flourish more in India? I wish we could have a new Board! But this is "telling tales out of school" and I must stop.

Mrs. Johnson writes in kindest regards to all your circle.

Yours ever,
W. F. Johnson

"Upper Woodstock," Landour, India
August 20th, 1881

My dear children,

It was very pleasant to me as I lay upon my bed to receive such nice, long letters from each of you, and to find your picture enclosed. It seemed almost like seeing you after a long absence. Both of you have

---

3. President James A. Garfield was shot on July 2, 1881, by a mentally disturbed office seeker. He died on Sept. 19, 1881.

grown so much, and look so much older than in your last pictures. Eddie has grown to be almost a man. I was glad to see that he looked so strong and healthy, with his fine, broad shoulders. He has not changed in the face so very much.

Mary too, if not very tall, you look as though you had not been starved at school, and seem to have kept in good health and conditions. You are just as tall as Mrs. Alexander, if you are past 5 feet. She is up here now, in a house above us. When I look at her, I think of how big you are.

Jennie is now 4 feet 11¼ inch, and growing fast. If she dont stop soon, she will be the taller of you two. I cant tell yet whether the wee Miss Johnson will be of the tall or short kind, but she is now rather of the "petite" style. Freddy is fat, and saucy, and has hair like gold in color.

Well, my dears, I will stop now and finish tomorrow. Jennie and her papa are down at Woodstock School. This is the close of the Quarterly examination. Today the girls play musical exercises to show their progress. Their marks for the last quarter will be read out to the visitors and scholars.

Friday

Now I must write you a little about the Examination yesterday. Miss Fullerton and Miss Griffith, two of the teachers who taught in the Public schools in Philadelphia before coming to India, have introduced the method of Examination they followed there into the Woodstock school. At the end of every 3 months, the girls have to pass an examination. The questions must be all answered in writing. Each girls papers are then examined, and they are marked accordingly in each study. The one with highest marks is read out as 1st of her Class (100 is perfect). Jennie is in a class of 15—all older than herself—and she had the honor to be 1st in her Class this last quarter. . . .

The smaller scholars had only a verbal examination, and were not marked. They had a "spelling bee," in which Frankie distinguished himself by spelling all the girls down. Then he said he went down on "conceit," spelling it "conceat."

We were much pleased, dear children, to see such good Reports for both of you. There is nothing that you will find greater pleasure in, in after years, than in the reflection that you have improved diligently the opportunities you now enjoy to get a good education. It is the best legacy you can have. There is nothing we desire more than to fit you to be useful and happy. Above all, we pray that your talents and your gifts' may all be consecrated to the service of the Master, whose service brings peace of mind, happiness here, and joys beyond all we can know. . . . May this grace be given to us, and to you my darling children, one and all!

God has been very good to us, and I feel that I owe him a special thanksgiving for the returning health and strength he is giving me. I am sure you too will rejoice in his goodness to us.

My dear Mary and Eddie, I must say goodbye! With much love always from us all, and the assurance that you are daily remembered affectionately by your loving,

                                                        Mama

                                                    Allahabad
                                                    November 29th, 1881

My dear daughter,

... Mr. and Mrs. Wynkoop have left for America. She was a very nice old lady, and has always been a great traveler. Now, though she is past her 3 score and 10 (I should guess), she is very brisk and as fond of going as ever. ... While she was here one morning, a carriage drove up, and a very brisk, elderly man came in, saying, "I am Cyrus Field of America. Are the Wynkoops here?" He said his wife was ill at the hotel, so Mrs. Wynkoop and I went over to see her. She had been suffering from dysentery, and was able to do little sight-seeing in India. He, you know, is the great telegraph man—who laid the Atlantic Ocean Cable and all. Mrs. Field is a very, pleasant lady. Mrs. Wynkoop had known her at home, and they traveled to China together.

... I hear a little voice calling Mamma! As I look round, here comes Freddie's silver head. He walks now, and sometimes tries to go down the steps, ending in a tumble with a swollen lip and various bruises.

... Now my dear daughter, I must say goodbye. Papa joins me in love to you, and all our friends ...

                                                Your Affectionate, Mama

Kisses from Jennie, Frankie, and Freddie.

                                                    Allahabad, India
                                                    February 6th, 1882

My dear Son Eddie,

Will you excuse this blot? I have just been telling Mary that I am coddling myself in bed today, trying to get rid of a bad cold. Jennie, Frank, Fred, and baby are all out under the shade of a big tree, that stretches out arms about 40 feet long. It makes a nice shade. Just now the weather is not very cold and not very warm, so the children like to be out of doors. Baby is just over the fever and worry of vaccination. Fred is full of mischief, pulling about his little wagon. Jennie and Frank are obliged to fall back on their books for most of their amusement.

Frankie might tell of his elephant ride and elephant scare, if he was more used to the use of the pen. But perhaps I had better do it for him.

A few weeks ago, Miss Walsh and I, with Frank and baby, went to a photographers, who lives about 3 miles from here. We went in a palki carriage—that is one with closed top, and door in the side.

As we entered the city we passed 5 or 6 elephants, and a procession of people. There was a procession of young men, carrying maces—long pointed staves, with the ends covered with silver (or something that shone like it). As we arrived near the market, the street is rather narrow and there is always a great throng of native carriages. In this crowded thoroughfare, we met a large procession of fakeers coming to the mela. They also had elephants, mace bearers, and camels, with big drums suspended over their sides. On each was a man thundering away, making all the noise he could on those drums.

We soon found that we could not make our way through the crowd, so the driver got down, and held the heads of his old crowbaits. They seemed really a little frightened, and the crowd got denser every minute. The procession we had passed was a delegation from another band of fakeers, coming down to meet the one coming in. As they came up, the jam became worse. A number of the elephant drivers stopped the elephants very close to our carriage. The mahawat, or driver, sits on the neck of the elephant, and guides him by touching him up with a sharp piece of iron. We shouted at them to move away, for the elephants seemed restless, and not well-trained—and doubtless, not used to white faces. But we couldnt make the driver hear. He was so taken up with watching the procession of nearly-naked fakeers passing by.

We were in a great fright, for we couldnt get the sliding door of the carriage to move, to close it; and close, peering in—not a foot away—was the angry-looking, little eyes of the elephant, tossing his trunk about. Every moment we feared that he would give us a blow with it. Frank huddled up into the corner. I got my arms around baby, to ward off the blow from her, if it came. Miss Walsh screamed at the driver, and at the bystander natives, to make them move on, but nobody listened.

We were kept in this state of painful suspense for about 15 minutes, though it seemed an age. At last the fire-eyed monsters moved off. The filthy, nearly-naked, fakeers passed on, shouting, "long live Gunga" (the goddess of the Ganges); and we were freed from our uncomfortable situation.

Frankie was very much frightened. When we got home, he asked me to "look and see if his hair hadnt turned white." He said there was a girl at Woodstock school whose hair had turned white, partly, when she was scared with a bull; and he felt sure that "he couldnt have been worse scared." His locks, however, are still brown, in spite of the scare....

Your Affectionate,
Mama

Allahabad
March 22nd, 1882

My dear Mary and Eddie

This morning I went to three zenanas [section of a Muslim house where women of high-caste families were secluded], and to visit two girls that were formerly in school, but have grown too large to go to school. Now they are betrothed, and have passed through the first marriage ceremonies, but have not gone to live at their husbands homes yet. They are young women of 12 years, and 10, respectively. One named Paoty, and one Kokan. They read Hindi pretty well, and write the same character.

Fred has been in the hands of the barber, and looks funny with his hair cut short. He is full of fun and mischief. He has just come to me to soothe his wounded feelings after a fall. Baby, "Dora Elizabeth," is asleep. (How do you like the name? Every one calls her "Bessie." Still, we have named her "Dora Elizabeth.")

Jennie was trying herself against the wall, and reports herself "$\frac{1}{9}$ inch taller than Mary"; so you see she is improving the time growing. Frank is a big boy too. He is very fond of his books, and kite flying too these days, though it is so hot, he dont get out more than an hour or so for that purpose in the evening.

We were very glad to receive letters from you both. . . . I hope that the smallpox epidemic has disappeared. It is a frightful disease. I went to one of my schools the other day, which is kept in a gardeners house. They took me into a little yard, and showed me a stunted tree, that she said is much worshipped by the women in the city during a smallpox epidemic. They bring offerings to propitiate the goddess of smallpox, or so the woman told me. She found it a very good business, keeping this tree.

With our united love to you dear children, and all our friends.

Your affectionate
Mother

Landour, Himilaya Mountains
June 14th, 1882

My dear Children,

Here I am, up among the clouds. As I write, they are apparently having a race from the valley below to the mountain top above. A big bank of cloud comes rolling up the ravine on one side and another up on the other, then there is a break, and the sun shines out. Then in a few minutes again, all is mist and cloud, shutting out the beautiful valley below. Bye and bye will come a patter on the roof for a little while, then perhaps a beautiful sunset. The far-off mountains to the west are all flooded with gold and purple. Here and there is a beautiful peak of cloud, with a deep margin of silver or gold, suggesting the silver lining and flood of light visions: the entrance to that city whose streets are paved with gold. The cloud scenery here is certainly grand. But when they begin to pour down torrents day and night, then we begin to long for cloudless skies again.

Well, to come back down to earth—You may fancy us scattered about in the various rooms of Upper Woodstock. Baby is asleep, and I am writing near her. Frank is reading in the sitting room. I found him a few minutes ago in a row with a man outside who is cleaning out the spouts. Frank was anxious to occupy a seat on the upper rung of the ladder, and as he was in the way—and also in danger of getting a tumble (for the cross pieces are only tied on the ladder)—I had him come in. He is solacing himself with a book. Jennie is just home from school, and she has taken a book to amuse herself with while she rests after her climb up the hill. She says it gave her a pain in her side. She is growing too rapidly for her strength. We measured a few days ago, and she is $\frac{1}{2}$ inch taller than I am. So she bids fair to be the tall one of the family.

I suppose this is your resting time from lessons, Mary. I sent you a book for your birthday. The girls here are very interested in getting their friends to write their names opposite the day of their birth, and add the year, if they please. I didnt write in yours, for fear it might be an excuse for some zealous Post office official to confiscate the book.

How are you getting on in your studies Eddie? Do you like Greek?

I am surprised to find that I cant finish my letter, as the postman is here.

> Love to all, from us all,
> Your affectionate Mother

> November 30th, 1882
> In Camp Kuranah,
> 10 miles from Allahabad

My dear Daughter,

. . . The catechists and native helpers often ask, Are Mary and Eddie coming back to India? We reply that we cannot answer that question yet. The Lord will make that matter plain when the time comes to decide. If we are good soldiers, ready to do service wherever sent, the place matters little. You can serve Him now while at school, and honor and glorify Him, by being diligent and faithful in all your duties, by being kind and gentle, imitating his loving Spirit in all your intercourse with your companions. Live daily near to Jesus, remembering that all your strength to do right, to resist temptation, comes from Him. Strength to succeed in your studies, both physical and mental, are His gifts. He is best pleased when we look up to Him for all, and bring back all we are and do, and lay it at His feet, thus. He would have us to be His, and He our all.

I forget where I was in my account of our travels when I wrote last. . . . October 9th we left Landour, leaving Jennie with Mrs. Scott at school as a boarder. We reached home safely. Found your papa well, and the Ewings, our neighbors in the other half of the Jumna Mission house, all well—except Elinor, their oldest little girl had sore eyes. It was not easy to keep Fred from playing with her, and the result was he got sore eyes too. For the next 3 weeks he had to be kept mostly in a darkened room. This was a great trial to him, and to me too, for having been away so long I found so much to do.

Our Mission meeting on November 9th came on, and all our missionaries came, with the exception of 2 of the ladies, Mrs. Tracy and Mrs. Woodside. We were 19 at our table, and there were 12 children—though some were too small for a seat at the childrens table (3 at least). We had a big tent in front of the house for a dining room, and the gentlemen held their business meetings in the church near by.

The meeting lasted 9 days, and was a pleasant one—barring the anxiety over sick babies and all. The result of the appointments for the year was, Mr. Alexander is to come to Allahabad; and Mr. Lucas, just back from America, goes in his place to Mynpoorie. We will now have 4 missionaries instead of 3 in Allahabad.

The Church Mission (all missionaries in Allahabad) had a Conference a week earlier, and we were all invited to dine with them. After the meeting was over, we decided to come out for a preaching tour in tents; so last Wednesday all our tents and luggage was packed on carts, and we came here.

Now dear, daughter Mary, all the family join in love to you, and all our friends.

Your Affectionate
Mamma

December 4th, 1882
10 miles from Allahabad,
In Camp Kuranah

My dear Son Eddie,

. . . We came out here nearly 2 weeks ago, and your papa, Mr. Ewing, and the 3 native preachers, are busy preaching in the villages around about. They go out in the early morning, each missionary taking one or two of the native preachers along. They walk 1, 2, 3 or 4 miles, until they find a village; preach, and return to a 10 o clock breakfast. During the day, your papa is busy writing tracts, or books, in Hindustani, or proofreading for the native Christian press—one of the best in all India. It is managed entirely by the native Christians. Caleb, a licensed preacher—one of the boys brought up in the Allahabad orphanage 30 years ago—is the Head Manager. He is also pastor of the native Christian church at Kuttra, 8 miles from where we live.

In the afternoon, at 2 or 3 0 clock, they generally go out again to the town near by, and preach in the streets. . . . If it is the market day, they take their stand near where the buying and selling is going on, thus they get large audiences of hearers. Many hearers have no other opportunities of hearing about this new way to be saved, save as the missionaries during the cold season make these itinerant visits. Some of our best Christians are those who have thus heard the Word preached by the wayside, and after perhaps many days they have found their way to some missionary station, where they have received further instruction and been baptized.

Your papa has made good use of a magic lantern—given by a sabbath school in Washington D.C., for use in our Chapel in Allahabad—in bazar preaching (i.e. to weekly outside audiences of people passing by).[4] He has a good supply of Bible pictures; and every night at dark, the screen is stretched out under a big tree, and the magic lantern put on a table behind it. A big durree (a coarse carpet) is spread in front for the people to sit on (no chairs). The audiences have been very good—varying from 60 to 100 many nights. Your papa has printed off a number of Hindi hymns on gelatine sheets, and he uses these in the magic lantern very effectively.

The evening service begins by throwing one of these hymns on the screen. Your papa, Mr. Ewing, and the catechists all sing (Frankie too helps), then a Bible picture is shown and explained. This furnishes the text for a short sermon. Then another picture, and hymn, then another short sermon; and so an hour, or perhaps a couple of hours is spent. The people are quiet and orderly. Occasionally some small boy may begin to talk, and the audience, untrained to church services, reserves the right to speak out in meeting. They make comments freely on the pictures as they appear, but keep pretty quiet during the discourses. One small boy the other night made a rather loud "wah"! When taken to task by his elders sitting near him, he said that a boy at his elbow had "kan men phunk diya" [blown in his ear]; so you see, "boys will be boys the world over." I dare say the boy got his ear smartly twisted (In India, a favorite punishment) by some of the sage old men sitting near, as a reminder to restrain his levity. But a Hindoo miscellaneous crowd is, as a rule, much better behaved than an English or American one.

Write often as you can Eddie. . . .

With affectionate love always,
from your Mamma

4. The magic lantern was an arc lamp amplified with oxygen to project pictures on a cloth screen; it was used in preaching to large gatherings.

[A sample of sisterly correspondence is included here, with a letter from Jennie to her sister Mary in the Steubenville Seminary.]

Allahabad
January 17, 1883

My dear sister Mary,

I am ashamed that I haven't written to you before, so I will write now. Papa went to the Conference last month, and Mamma took charge of Auntie Ewings babies so that auntie could go too. They say Calcutta is a very, dirty place, and full of bad smells. Papa came home from the Conference nearly two weeks ago, and ever since, we have had people stopping here on their way up country.

. . . I went to a party at Mr. Gordon's. He is principal of the Government high school for native boys. The Gordons are East Indians, but they are very, nice people, and I enjoyed myself very much.

It seems so funny to think that I have a sister almost "grown up." I think we may go home next spring (1884). Wont it be nice to see you all again. You will be out of school when we come home, wont you?

I didn't get the prize in my class last year, because I wasn't there the first term. But I was first in both the last examinations. I am going up when school begins this year.

Now goodby, with lots of love to all,

Your loving sister,
Jennie

[Will wrote the following letter of consolation to his Aunt Jane when he heard of his Uncle David's death. Will's words of comfort to Aunt Jane revealed his great love for his uncle and aunt.]

Allahabad
March 22, 1883

My Dear Aunt Jane,

A letter from our Mary this morning, as also one from Dr. Reid, tell us of the great sorrow which has befallen you. Although the Foreign mail left only yesterday, and what I write cannot go for nearly a week, I feel that I must write to you at once—just as I would have, had it been possible, gone to you at once.

You will not need any assurance from me, how Deeply I sympathize with you in this affliction. Other people used to speak of his many, noble qualities, but I think most of this: he was the only Father I ever knew. And whatever I have, or have become, I owe largely to him. Although I must sometimes have tried his patience sorely, he never seemed to lose faith in me.

How vividly those old, home days come back, now that we are irrevocably separated from them. The days when Pamela, John and I were children together, and the later days when Walter and Alice were joined to us. What a strong and manly man he seemed to me in those days; a man for other men to lean on. Very reticent too, for the most part, he seemed, with the reticence which belongs so strongly to his Scotch-Irish race; but I used to wonder how he opened his heart sometimes, when, at rare intervals, some genial visitor afforded him an opportunity. Happy days they seemed for him and for you, as for the rest of us. But, when we think of it, how far off they are!

God has been very good to us all; so many years of quiet happiness, and I trust of usefulness as well. In place of the one, "Two Ridge" home, we now have several homes scattered far and wide. In the case of such a life, extending I think beyond the three score and ten, full of beneficent activities; one must, even in their sorrow, mingle much thanksgiving. In thinking of his life and death today, one text keeps ringing in my head: "Like as a shock of corn cometh in, in his season." Except the pangs of separation, in respect to which our poor human nature is not to be reasoned with, what is there to regret in such a fully ripened, well-rounded life? "In his season," the eye of the Master marks when the time for the Reaper has come. He knoweth best! He doeth all things well!

It was a great comfort to hear from Mary the particulars of all that happened, but I hope when you feel able, you will write to me yourself. At such a time, one feels that those of us who are left should draw more closely together. We were so sorry to hear of poor Alice's illness at the time of trial; she has been so long and closely associated with her father, that the blow would fall very hardly upon her. Of your own affliction, what shall I say! I suppose no one can have any conception of what the rending of these lifelong ties can mean, until they have been in a position to have felt the same. But one thing I know, you learned long ago where to look for a consolation that never fails; and how to lean upon an arm that never disappoints. As one by one your treasures are gathered thither, your heart will more and more be drawn to the Better Shore.

Still we must never forget our duties to the living. Those who have gone before, no longer need our loving ministry, for "The Lamb will feed them, and lead them unto living fountains of waters; and they shall serve him day and night." He, who is all love and compassion has wiped every tear-drop from their eyes, and lifted every burden from their hearts. But here, how much there is that needs our sympathy and our help. I think that for the Child of God, there is no alleviation of heart-sorrow like that smile of the Master, which is obtained by service rendered to Him, here, where he has appointed it.

And now, my Dear Aunt, I must close. What is there that I can say except to give my tribute of affection, and of an esteem that was very high, to him who has left us, and my deep sympathy with you in your mourning. Words are but poor, cold things, where feelings of the heart are concerned; but, remembering what he was to my youth, you will understand what I want to say.

Almost my first thought when I heard the news, was of regret that I had not gone home, when I first thought of doing so; so that I might have seen him once more in the flesh. But I am not sure that such regrets are right. When we have weighed our duty in the light of present facts, and have decided according to them; duty is not changed by new facts, which may be disclosed afterwards. Yesterday was ours, today is ours, tomorrow is Gods. Still I cant help feeling that it will be a different home-coming now, to that to which I had been looking forward.

I was sorry to hear from Mary's letter that Uncle John is looking very frail. Time is passing. The night cometh! I find quite a touch of silver in my own hair; and these fast-growing children remind me that I am no longer young.

. . . We are all in usual health. Jennie went away to School at Woodstock March 1st. We expect to send Frankie with some friends to Upper Woodstock. We will remain ourselves here all the hot season, if all be well. Already the winds begin to blow, and we shut the house doors to keep out the hot blasts; still there is comparative comfort indoors for a month longer, and this not an unhealthy season. Our mission is prospering and we are very busy as usual. Mrs. Johnson is much grieved at the sad news, and wishes me to express her loving sympathy, and say to Alice and the others how much we both feel with you in this stroke.

Do write to us when you can.

Yours Affectionately,
W. F. Johnson

[In earlier letters Frank Kerr gently teased his sister about not being up on the latest fashions. Rachel still wore the same hooped skirts, fitted bodices with tiny waists, and proper hats with embroidery, ribbons, lace, and flowers that she took with her to India nearly twenty years earlier. A major style change in America in the 1870s, the demise of the hoop skirt, caught up with Rachel in June 1883 when she encountered the Salvation Army's "Hallelujah Lasses." In addition to questioning these young missionary women's effectiveness, Rachel commented on their style and propriety in her letters to Mary and Eddie.]

June 16th, 1883
Allahabad

My dear Daughter,
We have been thinking much about you this week, and of the scenes through which you are passing—or rather the part you are acting in

the closing exercises of your seminary course. The goal for which you have been striving has been reached. We rejoice in the success that has attended your efforts to make the most of your opportunities. We send our hearty and loving congratulations, that the reward of your diligence and perseverance has been the 1st honor of your class. We feel grateful to Dr. and Mrs. Reid for their happy home they have given you, and the many kindnesses that have made your school life such a happy one.

How well I remember the excitement that the last week brings—the mingling of gladness and sadness: the joy of the going home, and the sorrow of the parting with dear friends, as we each hurriedly bid each other a long adieu. Few of us never again meeting, as our paths in life diverged from the old Seminary.

. . . We were glad to hear from Eddie that he is getting on so well in his preparation for College. I suppose he has, ere this, received the answer to his inquiry about going to College this Fall. At first his papa did not think it the best course, but afterwards wrote to go ahead and try to enter this year. . . .

. . . We have just had a visit from some of the "Salvation Army." The delegation came from Bombay, and call themselves the "Hallelujah Lasses." There were 2 English girls dressed in plain muslin dresses (such as you use as under clothing), made without ruffles or trimming. On their heads they wore the native chudders—one a red one and the other a green one—in place of hats. They held meetings on the street corners, getting someone to interpret into Hindustani for them. Then they had an evening service in the Methodist church. There was a crowd of the poorer class of European people—that frequent the theatre oftener than churches—and a few natives. I do not think the street of a heathen city is the best sphere of work for the lasses, for they do not get women to listen to them, but a sneering rabble of Mohamedans, whose insulting talk would bring blushes to their cheeks, if they understood how they looked upon them. They are misunderstood, and do harm here to the cause they would help. These seemed to be uneducated girls, and have so special gifts for such work. . . .

Now my dear child, with much love from us all—Kisses from Freddie and Bessie.

Your affectionate, Mama

June 16, 1883
Allahabad

My dear Son,

I imagine you are now enjoying the lovely June weather, while we are in the midst of our roasting. We are now much in the condition that our cooks here call "half done," when they bring a piece of meat under-done. They always count the hot season about $\frac{1}{2}$ over now. If we have a good, rainy season, the worst $\frac{1}{2}$ is gone; and if we dont, much the hardest to bear is to come. This last week we have had some refreshing showers and the burnt-up grass is already showing signs of life in the roots, by the delicate green blades that are shooting up so fast we can almost see them grow.

. . . I have told Mary about the visit from the "Salvation army." I went to one of their services in the Methodist Church. They sang indiffer-ently, and talked a good deal, saying very little in substance. Altogether their meeting was not a success in any respect. They know nothing al-most of the Hindustani language, and make themselves the laughing stock of the Mohammadans—who are so vile themselves, that they dont understand the possibility of pure, good women going about in the city, talking to the rabble. Some of the Mohammadans talk was like this: "These women have failed to get husbands in their own country, and now they come here putting on native dress, hoping to get some of us to marry them. We are not going to be taken in by them, etc."

I think that these "Hallelujah Lasses," as they sensationally parade their names, make a great mistake in their way of trying to do good. Captain Thomson said, "I am a poor, uneducated girl." She seemed to be without any peculiar gifts to instruct others. I think some are drawn into the army here, for the sake of the sensation they make. There has been a good deal of petty persecution by the police, and some have had the honor of martyrdom in jails, for marching with music and holding meetings on street corners. The authorities pretend that there was dan-ger of stirring up the natives, but if they had only let them alone, there would have been no danger.

I hope you are able Eddie, to master all that list of studies. It must take hard work too. Well, my dear boy, it rejoices our hearts to see you able and willing to work hard and faithfully. We know with such a spirit, you will succeed. Dont neglect to take exercise enough to keep your body in health too. Students often forget the importance of keeping up their physical vigor.

. . . Your papa joins me in love, and Fred and Bessie send kisses to their big brother.

Affectionately,
Mama

July 10th, 1883
Allahabad

My dear Daughter,

Our little Mary, 19 years old today! We rejoice with you my darling child, that another year has been added to your life. Especially do we rejoice in the mercies that have crowned it. May the song still be of "Goodness and Mercy" all the days of your life to come, and when the journey is ended, then a welcome home.

We have been thinking and talking much about you these days. Your school days are now over. What next? You too have doubtless been considering this question. In your last, you say that you have been thinking of teaching and would like to do so. Have you any prospects of a situation as teacher? There is no object in being in too much haste about going into the school bonds. You doubtless will be all the better in health, if you rest a little from brain work. We have just received Eddies letter in which he said that he was going over to Steubenville to your Commencement.

. . . The 4th has come and gone with us, without a ripple to mark it as "The Glorious Fourth." Not a bit of powder burned, nor a bit of bunting afloat in its honor in this hot, barren land. Jennie said that some of the American girls in school asked for a holiday on the 4th, but as the English girls are such a large majority, I suppose it was not thought expedient to remind them of the auspicious fourth July—which they might not consider a day for special rejoicing. There are enough of our countrymen and women in Allahabad to have made a large dinner party, but with the thermometer away up—no rain and everybody gasping with the heat—we thought it best to suppress our patriotic celebration until cooler weather.

. . . We will feel interested in all the particulars about your last days at Steubenville. I begin to feel old when I think of having a daughter just finished her course at Seminary. I remember at the Reunion, some of the pupils of the first generation said they didnt realize how old they had grown, until they saw their classmates.

I have been writing with difficulty, Bessie is so fretful today. Now my dear, with our affectionate greetings and love.

Always your loving,
Mamma

[In December 1883 Rachel and Will began selling their furnishings in preparation for their return to America, which was to be in time for Will to be the North India Mission's delegate to the General Assembly meeting of the Presbyterian Church U.S.A. in May 1884.]

Allahabad
December 12, 1883

My dear daughter,

How are you getting on as "village school ma'am"? I hope that you find much that is pleasant in your new work. I know that you will need much patience and perseverance, but I trust that you will have strength and courage for each days burdens as they come.

We were very much pleased to receive your letter, and the Souvenir of your last days at Steubenville. We read it with great interest, and think it a very good piece of "patchwork." One of which you have no reason to be ashamed. The seams were all well done and the corners neatly joined. The effect, on the whole, very good indeed. We understand what you say about the difference time and place always make on such pieces of work.

We are now beginning to take some active measures about getting rid of our furniture and the stuff we have gathered. The easiest way here is to make out a list of things, with prices marked, and people buy the "pig in the poke" without seeing what it is. If things dont sell, then they are sent to the auction rooms. They dont bring much more than $\frac{1}{2}$ their value generally there.

We have not decided what date we will leave India, but it may be that your papa will have to go as a delegate to the General Assembly in May. The Farruckabad Presbytery have some business before that body, and they wish one of our missionaries to be present to present their case in its true light.

The time will soon pass when I hope we will gather a happy family in the dear, old home. Until then my dear child, may God bless and keep us all, and bring us together in peace.

Now goodbye. Love from us all,

Affectionately, Mama

[The last letter before the Johnsons returned to America was from Jennie. It was written to her brother Eddie from Paris.]

April 19th, 1884
Hotel Du Palais
Champs-Elysees, Paris

My darling brother,

We received your letters day before yesterday, and very pleased we were to get them. Papa had Mr. Wallis send the letters here, as we were going to stay longer than we at first expected. The home-mail arrived at Allahabad the day before we sailed from Bombay, so we didnt get it till now.

. . . We got here on last Thursday, and have been sight-seeing almost ever since. Mamma caught a bad cold on the train coming here, so she was in bed for two or three days when we first got here. She and Papa have gone out shopping and the children are asleep. Frank has been

Fig. 18. Before leaving India for their second furlough in 1883, the four young-est Johnson children posed for this portrait. Left to right: Frank, Jennie, Bessie, and Fred.

playing with the draughts-men, trying to turn on the gas (though it is only about 4:30); now he has climbed out of the window into a sort of garden outside. I am sitting in the Hotel writing room, and every few minutes you can hear the omnibus horns blowing.

We have three rooms on the second story of this hotel, and are very comfortable. We have Breakfast at 8 A.M., Lunch at 1 P.M., and the Table de Hotel is at 6:30.

We met a very nice American family here when we came. . . . It was a real relief to meet some "free and easy" Americans again after seeing so many stiff English.

Papa, Frank and myself went to the Jardin des Plantes this morning. It is a Botanical garden, but it also has a collection of animals, birds, etc. There were two rather young elephants, a gnu, antelopes, deer, hyenas, tigers, panthers, bears, lions, pythons, boas, other snakes, lizards, cock-atoos, swans, pelicans, and all sorts of birds. The biggest python must have been nearly 10 inches round at the thickest part and about 12 ft long. We also went to see the aquarium at the Trocadero. There are some immense salmon trout there, and some of the prettiest, colored, little fishes I ever saw.

Bessie is up, so I must stop writing, and go upstairs to her. The chambermaid broke Papa's ink-bottle, so we cant write unless we come all the way down here to do it.

Apr. 20th

This is Sunday. As Papa and Mamma have gone to the Madallyne, I am trying to coax a gold pen—that hasnt been used for about 20 years, I think, judging from its stiffness—to write. . . . We think of leaving for London on Tuesday or Wednesday of this week. We dont want to sail from Liverpool later than the third of next month. I dont quite realize yet that we are going home. . . .

It is awfully cold here now. It snowed a little, day before yesterday. The only place one can keep warm is in bed . . . my hands are so cold that I can hardly write. This isnt much of a letter, but I hope you will excuse it, as we will see each other soon. It is about time to get ready for dinner, so I will say goodbye. Please give my love to all our home-folks, and accept a big bit of the same for thyself.

Your loving sister,
J. J.

ELEVEN

October 1884–July 1888

PENNSYLVANIA AND NORTH CAROLINA

⦃ WILL AND RACHEL SEARCHED their souls before they left India in 1884. Though Will was recognized as a valued language scholar, preacher, teacher, and editor in India, he and Rachel decided to follow their hearts and remain in America with their children. It had been ten years since they had seen their two eldest children. Mary was now twenty years old and teaching school, Eddie was nineteen and attending college, Jennie was fourteen, Frankie was thirteen, Freddie was five, and Bessie was three years old. Rachel and Will resolved that there would be no more lengthy separations from their children; the pain of separation from Mary and Eddie had been too great.

When Will returned to America in 1884 he resigned from foreign mission service and enrolled as a doctoral student at Western Theological Seminary in Pittsburgh. Rachel established the family home among their many Johnson aunts, uncles, and cousins in Washington, Pennsylvania. Will returned to his family from seminary studies on weekends, when he wasn't preaching in Nebraska, Iowa, Kansas, Illinois, Kentucky, the Ozarks, or Minneapolis. He also filled a summer pastorate in Baltimore in 1885 and 1886. Mary accepted a teaching position in Washington; Eddie attended Washington and Jefferson College (merged in 1865) and lived nearby; and when Jennie was sixteen, she attended Washington Seminary for Women. So, although all the Johnson children were together with their mother in and around Washington, Pennsylvania, Will frequently was the absent family member.

Rachel became a frequent speaker at women's missionary society meetings in western Pennsylvania, eastern Ohio, and northern West Virginia. After a series of speaking engagements, Rachel wearily spoke of longing for more time to herself. Jennie echoed those sentiments, and lamented that the housekeeping responsibilities fell to her when mother was on "the circuit."]

October 16th, 1884
Washington, Pennsylvania

My dear Brother,

I suppose you received a letter from me about the same time today that I received yours. I had the pleasure of reading it at the dinner table.

. . . Tell Susan I put up my quinces, but didn't get any jelly made. I wish Aunt Liz would make up a bushel for me with butter and jelly. I would pay her whatever she said was right. I could get it when some of us goes over to Fathers. But perhaps she has too much work on hands to do, and she would not like the bother. Eddie is very fond of the tomato butter, and the little folks too. I did not think they would like it so well, or I should have made more.

. . . Mr. Johnson writes, on Monday last, that he had 2 hearings before Synod of Nebraska, and preached in the evening in the Congregational Church to a very large audience. He went via Burlington, Iowa— where his cousin, Rev. Calvin McClintock, lives—to Bloomington, Illinois. I think he may be home next week, but he didnt say. Dr. Mitchell wrote for him to try and visit Synod of Louisville, the 18th, 19th (Saturday and Sunday next).

The ladies of Pittsburgh want me to come over to their Presbyterial meeting on Wednesday, the 24th. If I go, it will be for a day only.

. . . Love to all.

Affectionately, your sister,
Rachel

October 16th, 1884
Washington

My dear Father,

. . . I hope that you and Mother are both well and enjoying the quiet. We are all well.

Mr. Johnson is enjoying his western trip and has spoken before the Synods of Nebraska, Kansas, the Ozark Presbytery, and held several other meetings. The Western people are very much interested in Home Missions work, but have given him a very kind reception. They seemed glad to hear what is being done for the heathen in India too. He says the climate of Nebraska is very pleasant at this season. I dont know when he will be home, but expect him early next week unless the Secretaries have sent him further orders. . . .

We like the Washington folks very much so far, but have been out very little. Fred and Bessie are getting used to their new home. They missed the children, the horses, cows, and chickens, and talked a great deal about you all. I think they were a little homesick, but didn't know what was the matter.

We want you and Mother to come over and visit us before the cold weather comes. I wish that our house was a little nearer the centre of the wheel. We are on the rim. The situation has its advantages in summer, but its disadvantages in winter.

. . . The political excitement is very great over here, and the rejoicing over Ohio news, very loud. Some of the clubs were out with tin horns, blowing Blaines trumpet, and relieving their feelings.[1]

Remember us to our friends. With love to Mother and yourself from us all.

Your Affectionate Daughter,
Rachel

Pittsburgh Union Station
Thursday, 11:30 A.M.

My dear Husband,

I have been so busy that I have had no chance to write the last day or so. Mary and Fred went over to Fathers. Having received an urgent letter. . . . I left Jennie in charge this morning and came here on the 9:30 train to speak to a Missionary Meeting. The Program left me out, and had you and Dr. Kellogg listed. . . . The Mercer trip almost used up my voice. Spoke 8 times in Mercer, Grove City, Slippery Rock, Fredonia, Greensburg, Jamestown and then home. It began to get monotonous. I got tired of myself. I told Mary, I felt that for my own sake I must write up something new. . . . I have 3 other invitations ahead: Freeport, Mt. Pleasant, Ohio, and McKeesport, next week. I begin to feel like saying with Bessy, "I wants myself a little while."

. . . Well good bye! With love affectionately,

Yours, Lillie

[Rachel's letters from 1885 are missing. Will continued his itinerating on behalf of foreign missions for the church and pressed on in his studies toward his doctorate. Mary wrote to her cousin Helen, one of her Uncle Frank's children, and filled in a few more details on how the family spent their days in 1885–86.][2]

---

1. Despite the tin horns and trumpets in Washington, Pa., Democratic candidate Grover Cleveland defeated Republican candidate James G. Blaine in the November 1884 presidential election.

2. One sad family event should be noted. Will's sister, Maggie Blakesley of Waterbury, Conn., died in July 1885 following an illness of several weeks that left her paralyzed. Fifteen years later, at age sixty-two, Will concluded a lifetime effort to locate his last surviving sibling, a brother, Richard, who had run away from the western Pennsylvania family enclave as a youth. Will succeeded in his search and found Richard living on a farm in Para, Ill. Will traveled to Para for a brief visit, and they had a joyous final reunion in 1900.

Washington
April 1st, 1886

My dear Helen.

It is very hard nowadays for one to get up resolution to write a letter. I never have time except sometimes at night, and that is the only time I can enjoy a good read. So of course, I let the letter-writing slide. Therefore, give me lots of credit for this.

We are all well. Mamma went early Tuesday morning to the Womans Annual Missionary Meeting held at Wheeling. She came back last night. The meeting passed off very pleasantly.

The college has a short vacation now, so Ed is at home. He is engaged in sawing brackets with Frank's scroll-saw. He has just finished an elaborate one. Neither Frank nor Jenny have any vacation before June. In fact, Frank's school doesn't close till the 2nd week in July. He groans over that. Fred and Bessie are both very busy playing these days. They are both learning to read.

Tell Grandpa his apples are greatly appreciated. I suppose Grandma is home now. . . . It won't be long until the meeting of Presbytery. Will Uncle Frank or Grandpa be over then? It meets here you know.

Mamma is going to two or three more Missionary meetings this month, so I will get plenty of house-keeping. . . . Papa is over at the Seminary as usual. He comes home every Friday night to Monday morning, when he doesn't have another engagement to preach. . . .

With lots of love to everybody. Your affectionate Cousin,
Mary

Washington
Saturday, May 22, 1886

My dear Brother,

. . . This week is Assembly week and Mr. Johnson is, I suppose, in Minneapolis. He left on Monday evening, and I have not yet heard from him. I suppose some other Johnson will pass on the letter, when they have digested its contents. The Post Office officials here do not have time apparently to distribute letters into their proper boxes—it takes so much of their time collecting foreign stamps off our letters and papers, which come minus frequently.

. . . When I wrote to Father, I did not known where Mr. Johnson would be engaged during the summer. He since received, and accepted, an invitation to preach July and August in that same 1st Church in Baltimore—Dr. Leftwich, pastor—where he preached last summer. Mr. Davis, Elder of 1st Church of Pittsburgh, asked him to preach for them, but he had accepted the other. It is better in some respects, tho' being so far away is a drawback.

. . . I have been staying at home the last few weeks, and find plenty of work in the home department. This week, Susan, we have been busy over a blue, polka-dotted sateen for Mary, and a brown calico for Jennie. Bessie has a gingham waiting its turn, and I dont know when my blue calico will be ready—soon I hope, if we can keep on busy next week. Frank and Fred can be suited easier in ready-made. Now I want to touch up my wee garden, which isnt much of a credit to the family.

The oil derricks are plenty as flies. They are going up on all sides. Folks are bent on pumping Mother earth dry. When all the oil and gas comes out, what next? Has the excitement taken well in Hookstown vicinity? I dont like to think of Mill Creek valley defiled by oil. It brings a bad class of hangers on.[3]

Do write and tell us all the news, especially about the home news. . . . How is the new baby? Has she got a name yet. The family join me in love to you all. . . . Well, good night. If I dont soon stop, I will be gaining on Dr. Brownsons sermon tomorrow.

Your Affectionate Sister,
Rachel L Johnson

Washington
May 28th, 1886

My dear Father and Mother,

. . . I was glad to hear that you and Mother think of making us a visit this summer. We will be very glad to see you.

You will be astonished at the number of derricks that armament the hills around here. There are 4-5-6 in almost every direction. Everybody bent on getting a share of the riches hid down in the interior of old mother earth. New houses are springing up all over town, like mushrooms growing up in a night, almost. A new one is going up in the vacant lot to the west of Mr. Thomas's house. A derrick is up, and boxing begun on Judge Harts lot, facing back on the new road opened up parallel with Beau Street last year. The oil boom has made business brisk in Washington, but I think the once quiet, old town will lose much in many ways, and have a very oily smell after awhile.

I heard from Mr. Johnson that they are enjoying the meeting at Minneapolis. They visited St. Paul and had other excursions planned. He was stopping with a Mrs. McNair—an old lady with her 2 million. . . . He preached in St Paul on Sabbath last, in 1st Baptist church.

---

3. The first oil well was drilled further north in Titusville, Pa., in 1859. The oil industry in the 1880s was the scene of dramatic economic expansion, competition, and innovation. The oil-rich fields of western Pennsylvania were the central focus of this frenzied activity. John D. Rockefeller was setting the pace and buying up the competition through his Standard Oil Trust.

Fig. 19. In 1886, just after Will received his doctorate from the Western Theological Seminary in Pittsburgh and before the family left for Biddle University, Rachel and Will posed for these formal portraits.

He reports Dr. Margue makes a good Moderator. He was here at Commencement last year. It was his son who forgot his speech on Commencement day.

The weather is very cool and we keep the gas turned on pretty nearly all the time. The company said they would give us 4 months in the year, but the bills still come—75 cents for each fire; except kitchen and dining room, 1 dollar each.

The children all keep well. They often plan to go to Grandpas. I want to go over and see you all after schools are all over sometime.

With love from us all to you all.

> Your affectionate daughter,
> Rachel L. J.

[Will completed his Doctor of Divinity degree at Western Theological Seminary in the spring of 1886. Rachel remained in Washington with the children for the summer while Will filled his two-month pastorate in Baltimore. That fall Will accepted an elected appointment to the presidency of Biddle University in Charlotte, N.C. (now Johnson C. Smith University). Rachel's responsibility was to begin packing up the household belongings again for the move to their new home and next adventure together in Charlotte. Mary, Eddie, and Jennie remained in Washington, where Mary was teaching and the other two were attending school.]

October 17th, 1886
Hookstown

My dear Children,

As this is the last night in the old home before leaving, I will write you a few lines, which you can pass on from one to the other. The night is cool, and as we have no gas to temper the cold, I cannot write much.

. . . Father is well and has been busy picking apples. He sold about 88 barrels, and has plenty left. Frank has helped a good deal. As a reward, his Grandpa gave him a bright silver dollar saturday evening—a pleasant surprise to him.

This morning we missed the big family bible, and I looked all about for it in vain. It then struck me, that in lifting the valise (which I had sent over for repairs), it felt heavy. I knew Bessie and Company had been traveling on Saturday evening, so I looked in it. There, sure enough, was the big bible, a cyclopedia, etc., all strapped and buckled up.

. . . I received a telegram from your Pa saying the goods had arrived, so I go tomorrow at 12:50 to Pittsburgh. We will leave on tuesday morning at 8 A.M. for Charlotte, on the Penna line—according to your Pas instructions.

. . . I hope the unsettled business will soon be all settled, and you will have a satisfactory arrangement for your necessary expenses. I am sorry Jennie, that you had to ask Miss Sherrard to give you some rupees. I think I can spare you a few—which I send in this. Out of, give her what you borrowed; when I get down we'll straighten up the arrangements for the future. I dont know how much I will need on the way. I dont like to shave too close. Eddie, what is the custom about paying for room and board quarterly??

I look forward to two, tiresome days for the children. I shall be thankful when the journey is over. Mother is in her usual health, but not strong. Well I must stop, and prepare my past for what is before us.

May the Lord bless and keep you all. With a loving good bye.

Your affectionate,
Mother

[Biddle University was founded in 1867 under the guidance of the Committee on Missions for the Freedmen of the Presbyterian Church U.S.A. The primary purpose of the university was set forth on its letterhead: "The special object for which this Institution was founded is the training, right in the midst of the work to be done, of colored men, to be the teachers, and preachers, and educated leaders of their race. It is organized with Theological, Collegiate, Preparatory, and Manual Training Departments."

Although the Presbyterian Church had been involved in religious instruction of blacks from their earliest days in America, the slave masters
had openly opposed it during the 1840s and 1850s, "fearing that it
might inspire a desire for literacy training which was out of harmony
with their status in a slaveholding commonwealth." The slave masters
felt that religious instruction excited the black students and white in-
structors alike, and there was no way to separate religious from civil instruction. Thus, prior to the Civil War, the education of blacks in open
meetings or schools did not occur, but quiet instruction and study by in-
dividuals did.[4] Following the Civil War, the social and political climate
surrounding education for blacks was still tense. It was divided into two
schools of thought: there were those who felt the training should be lim-
ited to agriculture and the manual arts, and those who felt the training
should be the same as that offered any white student.

Biddle University began by providing black men with a liberal, clas-
sical education and, for practical reasons, added an industrial arts
department while Will was president. Will took a strong advocacy
stance and urged those who "doubt the ability of the colored man to ac-
quire, and the tact to make good use of the higher education should . . .
look into these class-rooms and see for themselves the work that is
done."[5] During Will's tenure at Biddle University, his primary goal
was to increase scholarship funds to enable more young men to attend the university. The success of that effort was measured in a 22
percent increase in the student population during his administration.
In addition, an Endowment Fund was established to provide salaries
for professors, the first black professor was hired, and plans were developed to build a dormitory for students. Will's "administration was
especially noted for the higher elevation of the standard of scholarship
in the school." Perhaps the most sensitive and significant event during those turbulent days was effecting a smooth transition from Will's
presidency to that of Dr. Daniel J. Sanders, the first black president of
Biddle University.[6]

Rachel's letters from North Carolina focused on student, faculty, and
visitor personalities, on events, and on the environment of Charlotte in
the 1880s, as well as on the development of their children. Her letters
were written to her brother, Frank, and to Mary, Eddie, and Jennie, who
remained in Pennsylvania.]

4. Ernest Trice Thompson, *Presbyterians in the South*, 210–11.

5. *Minutes of the General Assembly of the Presbyterian Church, U.S.A.*, May 1891, 262.

6. *Johnson C. Smith University Bulletin*, 14; Inez Moore Parker, *The Biddle–Johnson C.
Smith University Story*, 14.

October 30th, 1886
Biddle University, Charlotte

My dear Son,

Another Saturday evening has come. The ringing of the bell reminds us that it is prayer meeting evening. The College Chapel is heated by big heaters that are not yet in blast this season. A sudden cold wave has come, and wood fires are blazing on the hearths. Old fashioned andirons are doing service. Stoves are being brought out of the lumber room, and we are trying to find out what kind will best suit our big room. The study, and a room adjoining, are the only low ceilinged and small rooms in the house. A big stove in necessary for the sitting room, and it heats the bedroom above—having a drum on the pipe above. This will cost about 25 dollars (!) they tell us, and burns hard coal.

I think living will be even more expensive here, than in Washington. Have to pay more for almost all that is not grown here. Today we bought sweet potatoes for 75 cents a bushel, apples 25 cents a peck, and walnuts 25 for ½ a bushel. I am put to great inconvenience on account of the loss of the damper of the stove.

Fred has been groaning for bed. He has gathered quite a lot of hickory nuts. He says to tell you that rabbits are plenty, for he saw them in wagons going to market.

Monday morning

That ink was horrid I see, so I'll try your papas bottle.

Yesterday your Pa, Frank, and I went with Mr. Duncan to church at 11 A.M. We all attended Sunday School at 9 A.M. Mrs. Beatty always plays the organ, and a young colored student the cornet; then over 80 boys sing, as only darkies can. They have very musical voices, and many of them are well trained. Mr. Hutchinson is a good singer too. He is a young Professor—looks some like the Mr. Fulton of '85 class. Has his brisk manner. I had to stir briskly to get all ready for Sunday School at 9, and ready also for church, as we left immediately after. . . . The carriage and horse were somewhat aged. I almost wished for Barney, as we fell behind the public conveyances in general.

There is a 1st and 2nd church here, as in Washington, and they are alike in many respects. Dr. Mattoon goes to 1st and the others to 2nd. The Pastor of 2nd, Mr. Fair, is more sympathetic with our work. The 1st church Pastor, Mr. Miller, is opposed to any elevation of the colored folks—but his people, Dr. Mattoon says, do not agree with him on that subject.

In the evening at 7, we have our own service in the College Chapel, which is a beautiful room. Large, airy, and nicely finished, with great windows 10 feet high—the upper part is colored glass. The two rows of

tall, slender, graceful, columns that support the centre, are quite ornamental. A gallery runs across the back part. A large platform, with reading desk at the opposite end, is for the Rev., or officiating Rev.

Professor McMeen preached a very good sermon on Christ in the
Storm. He is a good speaker, and graphic in his description, and earnest
in his appeals. Professor Beatty preached the Sunday previous a very
good sermon, but read so closely, that it was not so effective. My opinion
is that for the average audience, a sermon not so good, well-delivered,
touches the hearts of the people more effectively than a very, good one
read closely and monotonously. You young men in College ought to remember this, and strike out in society, cultivating the power of expressing your thoughts extempore. Nothing but practice will enable most
people to achieve a comfortable freedom of the use of the tongue in
public. Mr. Fair preached a very good sermon on, "We know that we
know Him."

It is very convenient for me to go to night service here, tho Fred and
Bessie dont keep awake very well. But it is so near, it dont matter so much.

. . . Your pa and I are talking of a trip to town to get stoves. Fred and
Bessie are out after nuts.

. . . With our united love, affectionately,

                                                              Mamma

                                                November 2nd, 1886
                                                Biddle University

My dear Children,

We went today to town and saw all the glory of Charlotte. If you had
taken a birds eye view at 2 P.M., you would have seen a 3 seated carriage,
with a pair of coal, black horses, and a coal, black driver, draw up to the
door. Your Papa and I, Frank, Fred, and Bessie, all soon seated ourselves
in beside the driver. Your Pa and I on the back seat, and Fred and Bessie
opposite. The roads are again getting dusty. As there is a "Fair" in Charlotte, it keeps the dust flying with so many wagons coming in.

We pass a number of small frame houses. Just below our Compound
is our one grocery, where we can get eggs, butter, etc., of poor whites.
Farther on is a cotton gin at work. The boss is an ex-slaveholder. Then,
as we have "eaten the air" (hawa khageko gayh) for another ¼ of a mile,
we pass the Charlotte gold mine. We hear them thumping and pound-
ing, day and night. They get enough to make it pay, they say.

A creek meanders at the bottom of the valley (in spots at least). We
cross a bridge, and as we gently rise, that big, square, bare, stone house
is the place where Stonewall Jacksons sister-in-law lives. Some fine residences begin to show, and here is the depot, just on the edge of town. We
drove on past the Mint—ornamented by a big, United States eagle,

which must have hung it head in shame a few years ago. There are fine houses with nice, big lawns here and there; then big, business houses of all kinds; as many as ½ dozen big churches—or more—; other fine residences, big, grassy yards, old trees and flowers; ladies out sprinkling their choice plants; and colored nurses with the little ones out for an airing.

In a corner of a quiet street, a large, gray, stone building set back among old trees and large, grassy lawns all around, and 2 young ladies sitting on the ground in the shade, doing fancy work, suggests a young Ladies Seminary. So it is, our Jehu informs us. The young ladies filed into the 2nd church on Sunday, just as we drove up. There were about 100 or so.

We stopped and got stoves for our 3 rooms. One big one, which heats sitting room and bedroom above it, and a "Franklin" for parlor. These all burn the hard coal. We came home at 4 P.M., having driven all about the town.

Fred saw a pair of little ponies driven down to a circus tent, that suited his taste exactly. We missed them as we were in buying stoves. . . .

Wednesday
Today is cloudy and looks like a shower is coming. I see the darkies pouring in at the college, as if winter was nigh. The mud gets pretty deep here, and mules are used for hauling a good deal.

. . . There was a slight tremor of earthquake here on Sunday, not so much as the first one. The windows rattled enough to call Freds attention. He said, "Mama, that was another of them things."

Well how are you all? What news? I dont know if you like these joint letters, but I will change after while. The mail closes soon, so I must stop.

With our united love,

Your loving Mamma

[Mary accepted a teaching position in Claysville, just west of Washington, Pennsylvania. She was a short eight miles from Jennie's school and nine or ten miles from brother Ed at Washington and Jefferson College. Mary wrote the following chatty letter to her family in Charlotte.]

Claysville, Pennsylvania
November 28th, 1886

My dear Home-folks:

I must not omit my letter today, for Institute begins tomorrow. What with instruction all day, and lectures every night, it will be a busy time.

I am going up on the 9 A.M. train tomorrow. There will be quite a crowd of teachers get on here, for those who have been away are home (Mag Gamble among the number). I am to stay with Ella Wade, you know; and I am looking forward to the week with almost as much pleasure as any children anticipate their weeks's holidays. I did not go up to town for Thanksgiving, because we had only the one day, and I was going so soon anyway. . . . Just think in one more week, half the term will be gone. I cannot realize it.

O. yes! I had a visitor Monday morning (of all times), a Mr. Fish.[7] He visited all the rooms. Miss Kelly's first—for which I was devoutly thankful.

While I think of it, I must tell you something little Willie Fish got off the other day. Miss Kelly was at a dinner Thanksgiving at Mrs. Botkin's father's (Mr. McKee's). Mr. Fish, his mother, a younger brother (Grant Fish), and Willie were there too. Miss Kelly sat next to young Mr. Fish at dinner and they talked, of course. Well, old madam glared at them with her one eye, until everyone noticed it. After dinner Miss Kelly sat on the sofa beside Mr. Grant Fish, and the madam looked at them until they seemed paralyzed into silence. Then she would talk to some one, and they would fall into talk again, and she would glare at them again. She is a regular dragon. I am coming to Will's remark. There was something said—I don't know what—about the school, and Willie chimed in, "Uncle Grant likes the school-teachers pretty well." Miss Kelly said the poor, young man's face was scarlet.

On Wednesday evening Mr. Spindler called, but Ella Noble was up in my room, so he wouldn't come in. But he made me promise to come up to Mary's when she left. Mary came in shortly afterwards herself, and after Ella left we went up and spent the evening together very pleasantly. The fun of it is, no one knows the nice times we three have together, nor how often they occur. Mary and I keep our own counsel. No one is the wiser, and the gossips of Claysville have one thing the less to talk about.

There was a union service Thanksgiving morning. Mr. Spindler happened to sit near me, and he leaned over and asked where he could see me that after-noon. He had some sentences—the analysis, diagrams, etc.—he wished to talk over with me. I told him I was to be at Mary's for dinner, so he said he would be up in the after-noon. He can't bear to come here.

Well, Mary had a splendid dinner: roast turkey, delicious pumpkin pies, and all the other things belonging to a Thanksgiving dinner. I am there so much, it seemed quite a family party. Mr. Spindler came about

7. Mr. Fish was a school administrator who was making rounds inspecting teaching in his classrooms.

four, and stayed till after six. We "carried on" a while, then we discussed the sentences (pretty, tough ones they were), while Mary pretended to snore on the sofa. A little after six we came away. Afterwards Mary came down, and Ella Noble, Mag Gamble, she, and I went to prayer-meeting together.

Friday afternoon I was up at Mary's after school, and behold Mr. Spindler came up. He had intended going up to Washington that evening, but his wash-woman hadn't his things ready; so he said he believed he would get some oysters and have a stew. Mary said, "If you'll bring them up here, I'll cook them." O course he took to the proposal very rapidly, so the result was we had a little impromptu oyster-supper that night. Mr. Anderson got home from the store just as it was ready. He presided over the feast, so there wasn't a vestige of impropriety. We didn't start home till half-past ten. Mrs. Gamble remarked drily that it was rather late when I came in, but she didn't know Mr. Spindler had been there. I 'spect she thought John Anderson brought me home.

However, she can't say much to me now, for a certain young man has been to see her daughter twice since she came home. I don't know how late he stayed, but I went to bed after eleven last night and he was still here. There has been fire and light in the parlor ever since Mag came home. I never set foot within the parlor till last night, and wouldn't then, if I could have escaped it without being rude.

There is no fire place in the room where Mag has to sleep, so I asked her to sleep with me. This has pleased the old lady evidently, and she has one of her kind spells on at present. May it last!

Yesterday I paid my board up to tomorrow. For six weeks she charged me $18.00, throwing off $1.30 for the time spent in Washington. That makes $32.73 I have paid altogether. Whew! but it takes a slice out of $33 a month.

. . . Jen sent word for me to come up Saturday and spend today with her, but I couldn't possibly go. Had a big (for me) ironing to do, which took me the whole morning. I get my washing done every other week and pay fifty cents. I iron myself—sometimes here, sometimes up at Mary's.

Sue McLane said Jennie got to spend the day at Baird's Thanksgiving, and Ed was at the Seminary for dinner. I think Ed must be getting to be one of Miss Sherrards pets.

. . . I think, Mamma, you must find it hard to get acclimatized, or what is wrong that you are "a little sick" so often? Do you have a great deal to do or not?

. . . Just think, not four weeks till Xmas. I wish we could spend it together, but if we waited till then, we must put it off till the Fourth of July.

Love to Papa, Mamma, Frank, Fred and Bessie.

Your affectionate, Mary

Biddle University, Charlotte
Saturday, December 4th, 1886

My dear Son,

This is a real winter day—thermometer down to the snowing point, and the ground covered with a white robe of snow an inch deep. A few flakes still falling. The cold morning, and the shivering boys in Chapel at 9 A.M., brought your Papa home in search of some extra clothes, so I have been culling out old overcoats-etc. Your heavy one made happy a young theologue, who thought it a beautiful fit. He has been sick a good deal this year, so his case seemed more urgent. When the barrel Dr. Brownson wrote about arrives, we will be able to make some more of them happy. The cold here seems to chill a person about as much as the greater cold. I suppose it is the sudden change.

December 4th reminds me that the 8th is on Monday next. You will then have reached that milestone, where the boy stands up a man and claims all the rights and privileges of an American Citizen. Well, my dear Son, accept our congratulations. May the same loving care that has kept and guided you these 21 years, still guard and guide you through the rest of your pilgrimage. We have many mercies in the past to call out our songs of thanksgiving, and the future is safe if we "Commit our way unto the Lord."

We wished to send you some token of our affectionate remembrance of your birthday, but in our isolation, we could not get any thing appropriate. We decided to send you the enclosed engraving [money enclosed], hoping you will be able to exchange it for something that will pleasantly commemorate the day. Wishing you many, happy years to come, full of happiness and usefulness.

Fred celebrated his birthday on the 2nd by a party. The tea party was given for him and Frank, as he was "in transitu" on his birthday. They had Edward Laurence, Rob Duncan, Lucian Beatty, Edgar Beatty, Tony Beatty, and Bessie Duncan to take tea with them. After tea they had a lively romp for a couple of hours.

This has been a quiet week—seasonal calls from some of our neighbors of the Faculty and their families, and calls from prospective teachers among the students. They are leaving for a 2 months session of teaching, by means of which many of them have to eke out their partial scholarships.

. . . The wind is howling a regular dirge, and "the day is dark and dreary." Write soon. With loving remembrances from us all.

Your Affectionate Mother,
R. L. Johnson

Biddle, Charlotte, North Carolina
January 5th, 1887

My dear daughter [Jennie],

We received your letter and were glad to hear that you were having such a merry time. I hope you escaped any serious effects from the cold you said you were trying to ward off the day you wrote.

. . . We are in the midst of a real, wintry, snow storm, that looks more like it belonged to the Arctic regions, than the sunny south. It has been very cold for several days. This morning it began snowing, and now the flakes are falling thickly. . . . Your papa says the study is so cold, he had come in by the big heater. Frank got chilled yesterday, sitting in the cold class-room, and is now in bed trying to get his skin and liver in working order again. I gave him a hot foot bath—always the best remedy for most of the ills the flesh is heir to—and some warm tea, and he retired.

Fred and Bessie are out in the dining room playing with Noah, Japheth, Ham, Shem, and their ark full of animals—most of whom find difficulty in even standing. Already, in one short week, many have lost from one to two legs, and some even a head. I fear they will soon be without a menagerie, excepting stumps.

The tree stood in the parlor until today. Fred said he, "felt like chopping all the time," when he got his hatchet. And he was very anxious for Sunday to come, so that he could use his purse. He put his "dime offering" in, and enjoyed giving it out of his new purse.

We have had Prayer Meeting every evening this week, and will continue the meetings at 6:30 instead of 7, so that the boys can get their lessons afterward. The colored Sabbath School had their tree New Years Eve. I used the contents of Miss Pennie Bairds last barrel to good purpose. I made a lot of pink tarlaton bags for the candy, and a card accompanied each. The warm jackets, hats, etc., were put up in parcels. Mrs. Laurence supplemented with some things her sewing class had made from her barrel, so they thought they fared very well this year.

. . . I see in the Makhzan that a gentleman in the West gave Chicago Ladies Board 600 dolls toward the girls school at Allahabad. He and his wife went as missionaries 30 years ago, but health failed and they returned. He went into business and has always felt a debtor to the Foreign Board for the cost of sending them to their field of labor. He now gives this sum to refund that expense.

Well Jennie, I must sent this out into the snowstorm or it wont leave for Washington tonight. . . . All join in love, with Your Affectionate Mother,

R. L. Johnson

Biddle University, Charlotte, N.C.
January 22, 1887

My dear Son,

. . . We are all well now. Frank and Fred both have exchanged bone-set for the ordinary tea diet, and are again able for a game of shinny.[8] Your Papa has just gone walking over to town. Bessie is playing the "90 + 9" on the organ.

Last night we had another social meeting, this time at our house. I think I told you that we met at Laurences last week to talk over the plan of a sociable once a week. Mrs. Beatty and Mr. Semple were appointed a Committee to arrange some entertainment for the evening. What it should be, we did not know. They had first a song quartette ("Take Her Up Tenderly," etc.) by Mrs. Beatty, Mrs. Laurence, and Professors Semple and Hutchinson. Then a piece read by Mrs Lawrence, another by Professor Hutchinson. They brought out their games of Authors, and their parlor quoits. Part of the company pitched quoits, and some engaged in their various amusements. Another song, "Home Again," and at 10 P.M. they adjourned.

. . . The colored boys are all out this evening, playing ball I think, from the sound. They are not allowed to leave the grounds without permission, so they have to take their exercise in the grove. . . .

With our united love.

Your Affectionate Mother,
R. L. Johnson

January 29th, 1887
Biddle University, Charlotte

My dear Son,

This is Saturday, and Frank and I have just got home from a walk over to Charlotte. The rain came on just as we were starting back, and as the red clay mixed up with the water, we had a slippery, nasty walk back. The occasion of our trip, was to see the Post Master about Franks Boys Paper. It came at last, in the form of a bound volume, October 1885–86; but at the custom house, it was opened, and arrived with the back torn off. From May to October is missing. The Post Master said he would write, and see if the missing part could be found. I fear the prospect is not cheering of ever hearing how those thrilling stories end.

8. "Boneset" is the common name for a plant used for a wide variety of medicinal purposes. Rachel used it in tea to settle her children's upset stomachs. The name came from the belief that this herb flower could help set broken bones. Shinny was a simple form of field hockey played with a curved stick.

... We have not had another visit from the drunk man. He was a Mr. Henderson, a white man. He lives in the country, and prides himself on his politeness—when sober. When told by a colored man how he had behaved, he said to, "Ask Mrs. Johnson to please excuse and forgive him, as he knew nothing at all about it."

... Your Papa has received his appointment as Delegate to General Assembly from India. It meets at Omaha. I dont know whether he will go or not. Our plans are unsettled for the Summer. School closes early in June–1st Wed, I think it is. The Professors here generally scatter off North. . . . The summer here is pretty hot. Mr. Beatty and his family are the only ones that generally remain. He says the northern climate does not agree with him. He has suffered so much from rheumatism.

The street cars have lately been started in Charlotte, but I fear they are not very profitable. I saw no less than 4 empty cars driving along this morning in Charlotte. They only come down to the depot, and the worst part of our walk is this side, so we didn't trouble them. I dont think Southern people will crowd in them much, for they never seem to be in a hurry.

This is a dull day, and I feel like it. With our united love, and kind regards to all our old friends.

Your Affectionate,
Mother

Biddle University, Charlotte
Monday, March 7th, 1887

Dear Eddie,

I sent you your Pas money order for 10 dollars, which I hope reached you safely. A letter from Uncle Frank says that Father will send you some more, as soon as he can get it collected. So I hope the financial straits will soon be over.

The colored folks in Biddle village have got into their new church. Mr. Graham, colored graduate of Biddle University, is their pastor. Professor McMeen preached for them yesterday, and I staid after Sabbath School. They have quite a good congregation, and they showed a row of the shiniest shoe leather on the mens side I have seen. Good shoes and swell neckties seem to be the fashion among them, as far as they can raise them. Some of the men and women are very good, respectable, intelligent-looking specimens. 20 years out of slavery has done wonders for them. I could not help thinking this as I looked around and thought of their former state—"driven like cattle," as my old cook said they once were, as a drove of oxen passed by, and suggested old sights to her.

Things are going smoothly in College. Your Papa gave them a lecture on India, illustrated by Magic lantern pictures on friday night. They seemed to enjoy it, and wonder at the beautiful palaces, temples, and tombs the heathen had built.

. . . Bessie is complaining of her eyes hurting today, so she has to rest from reading, much to her grief. Fred has just reported a new nest full of eggs under the porch. Brownie had stolen their nest, and there has been clucking for a week. He has two setting hens trying our patience for a week past.

The roads are getting dry, but full of holes. The soil dries up very quickly. The last day I was in town they had been watering the street!

. . . I dont think of any news. Life here hasnt much variety. . . . Frank is looking for a letter from you. The white boys have got a ball in partnership, and play base ball on a small scale. Fred is full of zeal, and talks "bobs and balls," and plays very well for a 7 year old.

With love from Papa, myself, and the rest,

Your Affectionate Mother,
R. L. Johnson

Biddle University, Charlotte
April 28th, 1887

My dear Brother,

Your letter came yesterday and I was glad to hear from you all. It was very good of you to write, when you were tired and weary from your labors and watchings, as you must have been. I feel very anxious about dear Mother, for if she cannot digest her food, I fear she will get still weaker. She must be quite feeble from what you say. Does she try milk diet, or raw egg in milk or beef juice? Mrs. Woodside, an old lady in our India Mission, got in a state when her stomach couldnt bear any thing solid. She used to pound and mince up raw beef, pour a very little water on it; put it in a jar; close it with dough; set it in a pot of boiling water, and boil it several hours. The juice would all come out, and leave the hard, dry fibre in a lump. This, with a little salt in it, made a nourishing beef tea. How I wish I was where I could help dear Mother, for she needs some one to save her trouble and care, to save her strength.

Did I ever thank you and Susan for your kind and cordial plans for the summer? The College here closes June 1st. . . . I hope we shall be able to come part of the vacation, if you will allow us to arrange in some way, that we will not be too many. I want to be a help, and not lay burdens on those that, however willing, I know have burdens heavy enough.

. . . The children send love, in which we both join.

Your affectionate sister,
Rachel L Johnson

[Just as the Johnson family was beginning to settle back into life in America, Will received strong urgings from the Board of Foreign Missions to return to India as a professor and director of the Theological School in Saharanpur. Although his service at Biddle University was highly valued by the Board, members argued that other able men were available to replace Will in Charlotte, but the demands of the position in India made it a much more difficult position to fill.]

New York
June 15, 1887

Rev. W. F. Johnson, DD
My Dear Brother,

We have sad news from India again: Mr. Ewing's complete break down in health. He is coming home, with perhaps little hope of his going back. His a serious case of nervous prostration, loss of sleep, no rallying power, apprehension of still more serious condition, and the Doctors' imperative orders. Dr. Wherry is to come home next spring, for somewhat similar causes. Mr. Seeley, so they write, will also have to come home next year. Mr. Pollock, as you know, has lately arrived, and cannot now go back—if ever. Mr. Woodside is in England. His wife is seriously out of health.

Dr. Wherry looks urgently to you, Dear Brother, to come and take his place in the Theological School. I had hoped that Dr. Brodhead might be able to go to Saharanpur, or some station. This was before we heard of these discouragements; but he decided adversely. His State of health will not warrant his going back, much as he would be glad to go.

Well. Can you go? At an early day, for I am sure it would not be easy for you to change your engagements immediately. But if you could arrive early in the next sessions, your arrival would hold the school together, and the prospect of it would make up for some delay. I fear it will be very difficult to fill two such vacant chairs, or rather vacant places filled, thus far, by two such men.

I send you a copy of the last Catalogue. Perhaps you have already seen it. A good foundation has been relaid. I think you had much to do with this School, down to the time of your coming home. You know well its importance, and what it needs for enduring influence and growth. And your dear wife would exert the finest influence over both the students and their wives—Hindi, like most of them, being married. But of course I need not plead the case with either you or her. I am sure your going back all depends chiefly on whether you can go.

I highly value your present post of service as of more moment for years to come than the Presidency of any out of fifty of our Colleges. So I believe, or I think, of the future of the colored people in this country, and of our American land and people. But I hope your place at Charlotte could be soon supplied. At Saharanpur, the case seems to me very different; and the School there is one of the greatest importance to many millions.

How much I wish I could see you to talk over this subject, and others subjects! Amongst others, the action of the late General Assembly on union missions. It seems to me, in the face of Presbyterian Church principles, not to be the place to begin foreign union, by severing Presbyterian foreign Missionaries from the Home Church. Only through its own presbyteries, can the ministers of our Church be members of our body at all. Ah well! Can this last?

With kindest regards to Mrs. Johnson and yourself,

Yours sincerely,
John C. Lowrie
[Secretary of Foreign Missions]

Excuse my writing in haste.

[In 1887, other complicating family events kept intruding upon Will and Rachel's long-range plans. Rachel's solicitous recipe for beef broth to strengthen her mother was not adequate. The Johnsons' festive summer plans for a Hookstown vacation took a sad turn when, on July 7, Rachel's mother died. Rachel and the younger children stayed in Hookstown through the summer providing what support she could for her grieving father.

David Kerr insisted on remaining in his own home alone. Frank and Susan temporarily set aside their plans to move out of the county so that they could remain near their father and coax him into their family circle. Rachel and the younger children returned to be with Will and to start school in Charlotte in September; Mary, Eddie, and Jennie remained in Washington.]

"Memorial Hall"
October 15th, 1887

Dear Papa and Mama,

Was glad to hear from Mama's letter that you had all arrived safely at your destination. Your Washington, D.C., sight-seeing must indeed have been under unauspicious circumstances. Still, you would get a good, general idea of the situations and general appearances of the different buildings. I think I would prefer seeing it in sunshine, to in shadow; nevertheless, you may sometime in the future get to see it again. You will enjoy it all the more, having seen the two views.

I suppose, in spite of forlorn aspects of the house, you would feel like you were once more getting home; and err this, you have gotten everything in its place once more. Did your canned fruit succeed in staying in the cans, and all your luggage arrive safely?

Suppose the University is in full blast, and you all have your hands full of work. Does your new cook succeed in upholding the high standard of Mrs. Pheifer?

I have not had any direct word from Hookstown since you left. . . . I expect to hear soon, and will drop you a card as soon as I do. School is progressing and we have enough to do to keep us out of mischief. . . . We get well 'wakened up these cold, misty mornings crossing the Park going to breakfast. This morning was almost "bitterly cold." There was a very, heavy frost. I never saw the leaves falling off the trees so suddenly as they have, or are doing, this fall. The long dry spell appears to have left them in such a condition, that the first frost sends them "helter-skelter." I suppose the Hickory-nuts, Chestnuts, Butternuts, etc., are making many country youths and maidens rejoice. I wouldn't object to a ramble through the woods myself.

I suppose you have seen what trouble Rev. Leiper, of Reading (formerly of Claysville), has gotten into on the charge of preaching some of Dr. Talmage's sermons. In todays Gazette, Talmage says it doesn't hurt him any, if the preacher can stand it. This he said in Reading, so there must be some truth in them.

Must close as 'tis 11 o'clock. Time for bed on Sabbath night. With love to all. Write soon and often.

Affectionate Son, E. K. J. [Eddie]

Friday, November 18, 1887
Biddle University, Charlotte, N.C.

My dear Friends,

. . . We are all well, and enjoying this nice Indian summer weather. The Synod met here 2 weeks ago. We had some of the Ecclesiastical notables, who came to feel the pulses of the Colored brethren, to see if they were beating regularly. They wished also to find out if they were anxious to be seceded from the northern General Assembly and formed into one of themselves, where they could grow on ad infinitum. Dr. George R. Hays spoke in the interest of the Centennial Fund, to stir up the brethren. Dr. Montfort and Dr. Patterson were taking notes on the Union question.

Mrs. Patterson came along. They were going on for a tour thru' South Carolina and etc. The roads were muddy, and it was a rough ride in to town from here; so they did not stay with us all the time, as we had expected.

The event of last week was a Ladies Foreign Missionary Meeting in the 1st Church. Societies sent delegates from some other churches in Presbytery—I mean white southern Presbyterian Churchs. The 2nd

Church has 125 ladies enrolled in its Society, and the 1st about 70. . . . The Reports showed a great interest in the work and liberality in the churches. The 2 churchs here head the list in the Southern Presbyterian Church, giving more in proportion than any others. They asked me to give them a talk about India, which I did at the Ladies meeting at 11, in the 1st church. In the evening there was a General Missionary Meeting, addressed by Mr. Johnson and Mr. Cochran, pastor at Steel Creek, 10 miles from here. There was a large audience, and all seemed interested.

Mrs. General Barringer had invited us all to stay and dine there, and also invited several ladies to tea to meet us. Mrs. Laurence and I staid and had a very pleasant evening. General Barringers family includes Mrs Barringer, a boy, her 2 sisters, Mother (an invalid), and cousin (the Miss Long). I have mentioned this as being the first entertainment of the kind that we have been favored with.

This week we had a visit from a man named Jackson. He said he lived in West Virginia, 5 miles or so from Steubenville. He looked a good deal like he belonged to the genus, tramps. He decorated his neck with a pocket kerchief, pinned with a safety pin—no collar apparently. His hair was long and flowing style. His shoes needed new strings, for he had been supplied with stray ravelings. But shabby clothes may conceal much excellence, so we gave him the best treatment we could. He said he "thought missionaries were very sociable, hospitable people," which was quite flattering. He was here 2 nights and a day. Said he was going South for his health, but wouldnt say just where. Gave no account of himself, although I, at various times, worked the pump handle vigorously. I dont know yet who or what he is. He was an inveterate asker of questions about everybody, so I asked him his fathers name. He told me, "Jackson"—which was news(?), as he called himself by that name. He seemed to know about the Johnson and Orr families, and nearly everybody in Steubenville, tho' I didnt find that he had a personal acquaintance with any of them. He said he had been the guest of Jeff Davis! I can imagine him sticking himself into the White House itself, if Mr. Cleveland wouldnt invite him out. He has no delicacy about claims, but marches right in and takes possession.

. . . Well Good night.

P.S. Dear brother, I wrote last night to you and this morning your letter came. I am glad you are all better. Why is it there is so much sore throat in Hookstown? Is it the low water this year? I feel so worried about Father living on alone—and sick—with no one to take care of him. But if he wishes to stay on alone, of course you cant help it. I hoped Stella would stay awhile, and make him comfortable, but you say she only staid $\frac{1}{2}$ a day. I understand the difficulty of Father boarding at your house. He will not resist temptation when appetizing things are before him, and his stomach will not bear the strain now. He has no use to go here and there, and I would not encourage him to go away. He would be miserable. There is no remedy for age and its infirmities, but care.

. . . This is a dark day. Looks like our nice weather was over. The rain must be coming, tho' we have had a good supply. We have a rose bush in full bloom, Sue. I would like to send you a bouquet. With love to all.

Your affectionate Sister,
Rachel L Johnson

[David Kerr died on November 25, 1887, four months after his wife, Mary, died. Over 100 years later, the landscape of Beaver County, Pennsylvania, remains dotted with the distinctive, bold brick houses and other structures that David Kerr built. They remain as sturdy memorials to this skilled craftsman.

The death of his parents changed Frank's plans once again. He and Susan decided to buy the family home on Mill Street and settle in Hookstown.]

Charlotte, N.C., Biddle University
December 13th, 1887

My dear Brother,

We were glad to hear from you again. . . . I infer that you are remaining in the old home. We are so glad you feel inclined to buy the old home and farm. I hope there will be no difficulties in the way of your doing so. No arrangement could be so satisfactory to us, indeed I cannot bear to think of any other. You may feel sure that we will be willing to settle on a fair price, and I trust that Stella will too. I heard from her just after she got back home from Hookstown, but she made no allusion to any business matters. The plan you suggest of sending a copy of the Will to each one, will be satisfactory to me.

. . . The verse you suggest for an inscription on Fathers tablet is very appropriate.[9] The last hope, especially comforting, in this unsatisfying world. I was thinking that Psalms 116:15, "Precious in the sight of the Lord is the death of his Saints," would be a suitable inscription over one who so eminently lived the life of a saint, as dear Mother did. Perhaps Stella would like to suggest something too. Did Father give any directions as to the kind of stone and etc. he would desire? We were talking it over, and agreed that the same money expended on one good heavy substantial stone, with inscriptions on both sides, would be a more lasting

---

9. Unfortunately, the ravages of time have taken their toll on the tombstone and inscription Frank carefully selected for his father. In 1992, David Kerr's name, life dates, and the image of an open book—the Bible—are all that can be discerned from the face of the stone.

memorial, and less likely to yield to the ravages of time. It is an object to avoid anything that will soon not be firm thru' frosty winters.

Mrs. Davidson, our help, is sick with rheumatism. Her husband died the day Mother left us, and she has lost all her children within a few years. She is a very nice, quiet, well-mannered woman, attends to her own business, and does it well too. I miss her sadly.

Write soon again. With much love from us all, to you all.

Your Affectionate Sister,
Rachel L Johnson

Biddle University, Charlotte, N.C.
January 30th, 1888

My dear Brother,

. . . I received you letter last week, and dont feel sanguine about Stella accepting your offer on those terms, tho' I have heard nothing from her since negotiations began. She has never written anything about the settlement of things. Perhaps my heart has been too much set on having you settled in the old home. I know that this is what Father wished, and Mother too no doubt, if she had expressed her feelings.

Eddie says he does not think Stella has a desire to buy the property, and I dont know what John would find to do in his line in Hookstown. In our talks while together, she never proposed such a plan, so I do not think she will want it much. But I fear if there is a Sale, some outside person will bid it up on you.

I feel like saying this, that as far as my share is concerned, I will be better satisfied to take the $\frac{1}{3}$ of the sum you offered—$3500 for the old home lots and farm—if you will buy it, than more from an outside party. I make you this standing offer: I will accept the third of thirty five hundred, as my share, if it should be bid above that sum, if you buy the old home. If it is bid off for a lower sum than $3500, I will be satisfied with $\frac{1}{3}$ of the amount.

Now I fear you think I am like the unfortunate widow, but I have done, and will say no more. I have honestly desired the property to fall to you, more I think if I know my heart, because I felt it was to your future interest, and comfort, than as a matter of selfish consolation to my own feelings—though that has had a large place too in my heart. If Stella has accepted your last offer, of course, I abide by my former offer, to make up the difference on her share. Yes, we understood your generous offer to not charge the 5 per cent on the $3500.

Of course I shall be very glad to share expense of stones for Grandfather and Grandmothers graves. I cannot bear the thought of their precious dust sleeping there unmarked. It was a painful thought to me, ever since Susan and I visited their graves. I am glad you suggested doing this for them. They always have a loving remembrance in my affections.

If you have a Sale of the household goods, could you make a copy of the list of house furniture with appraised value, I would select some things. I dont need a Sewing Machine, as mine is good. I would like a feather bed. The little brooch is one I gave Mother before I went to India in 1860. I think you may give it to Mary. I hope we shall be able to make you a visit this summer, but our plans are all unmade. Thanks to you and Susan for your kind invitation. We will be able soon to settle on some decision, I hope. It is not long now till winter is over.

> Your affectionate Sister,
> R. L. Johnson

> Biddle University, Charlotte, N.C.
> March 8th, 1888

My dear Niece "Rachel,"

Your very welcome letter was received on Monday, and I thank you for your nice letter, telling so much that I wanted to know about how things were disposed of at the Sale. I was very glad to hear that your Papa had bought the dear old home and the farm. I hope you, Jennie, Edith and Nellie will enjoy playing out in the nice shade in the hot summer days, and eating mellow apples as they drop—almost hitting you on the head. Fred and Bessie will be glad to join you in a romp sometime.

We are not certain yet what arrangement we can make for the summer, but I want to come and make you a visit if it is possible. We are very much obliged to your Papa and Mama for their very kind invitation.

It seems sad to think of going back and finding no Grandpa and Grandma there; but we must think of them in a happier home, with dear, little, sunny-faced Olive, where no sickness comes. Though we dont know how near that beautiful place is to us, which Jesus has got ready for his children, we know their happiness is greater than we can imagine. If we could ask them, they would say they did not want to come back into this world of trouble, after living with Jesus in the place he has prepared for them. Let us all try to please Jesus every day, so that we may go to be with them when He calls us.

Have you and Jennie been going to school this winter? Fred and Bessie say their lessons to me every morning after breakfast. This morning Fred had a headache, so I let him off.

Two little colored boys came in a few minutes ago for a pair of Bessies old shoes. One boys name was Duke. His mother used to cook for me last year, but was sick this winter. I have a Mrs. Ship now to help me. Her husband died before Christmas. He was a bad fellow, and had been stabbed several times, so that he almost died; but at last he died of consumption, after all his fights.

The colored public school is to have an exhibition up at Biddle friday night. They have it in the Presbyterian Church, and have speeches and singing. Mrs. Pheifer, my old cook, wants her girl to look very gay, I suppose, as she is making her a blue dress, trimmed with wide lace.

. . . The sun shines today and the wind is cold, but the hyacinths are out in bloom—the violets too—though I am shivering by a big fire. Bessie is reading to Fred, to amuse him, while he is resting his head. Frank is in class at the College. He has very good teachers, and is getting on well in his studies. He is a good speaker for a boy of 14. I heard him not long ago speak at one of Professor Hutchinsons entertainments.

Tell Jennie she may look for a letter soon. . . . Mary has less than 2 weeks of school left, then you will probably see her before she comes to her new home South. Love to you all.

Your Affectionate Aunt,
Rachel L. Johnson

Dear Brother and Sister,

I received the good news that you are to stay in the old home with sincere thankfulness. I trust that you will never regret the investment, and be happy and contented, and prosper many years under the old roof tree.

I think of many questions I would like to ask, but will have to wait until I see you. I was surprised that Stella bought the frame house, for I did not suppose she would want it—either as an investment, or to live in. What does she intend doing with it? I hope you will find the farm a good investment, and get your money with interest in bountiful crops. It is a great advantage to have pasturage, etc., of ones own, and I am glad you got it.

My offer stands. We will settle on that basis in our final adjustment of matters. . . . I suppose from your letter that Stella was satisfied. I thought she would have bid off the Sewing Machine. What did she get of the furniture? Thanks Susan for bidding off the articles I mentioned. How was it that there was counter bidding by Stella when there was more than one in the list to be sold?

. . . We are looking for a visit from Mr. Blakesley [Will's brother-in-law] from Waterbury, Connecticut, next week. He was to have come this week, but was detained by business.

. . . Has the Western fever got epidemic again? Helen speaks of several going West? I should think the blizzards and cyclones would make old folks glad to stay among the Pennsylvania hills. . . .

Well it is now about dinner time, and here comes a hungry lot of youngsters, and "Dr" looking tired and hungry. So Good bye. With much love from all, and Your Affectionate Sister,

Rachel L Johnson

[On a hot July morning in 1888, as the Johnsons were on their way home from church, the horse drawing the buggy bolted, and Rachel and Bess were thrown out of the backseat. Bess was badly bruised; but Rachel, who landed on a rock, suffered grave injury to her spine and was paralyzed from the chest down. She died from her injuries three days later, on July 18, 1888.[10]

A month before her mother's death, Mary had accepted a teaching position in Charlotte to be near the family once again. After Rachel's death, Mary quickly took on the role of mother to Frank, Fred, and Bessie and supported a heartbroken Will.]

July 19th, 1888
Biddle University, Charlotte, N.C.

My dearest Uncle Frank and Aunt Susan,

Papa has written you the particulars of Mamma's sad accident. Yesterday he telegraphed to you the news of her death. It was so sudden at the last. We are all stunned by the shock. That very morning she seemed better, and we felt encouraged to hope she might still get well. But the paralysis extended to the lungs. She complained of phlegm in her throat, which we could in no way relieve. Very suddenly, she strangled. In a few seconds it was over.

The doctor said it was not the phlegm, but the paralysis of the lungs that really ended it. It must be for the best, but it seems so hard.

It happened yesterday, a little after one o'clock. If you could only have been here! But none of us foresaw that the time would be so short. God help us all in our trouble.

She is to be buried this evening at five oclock. The weather is very warm, you know.

Will write again when I can. With much love from us all.

Lovingly, your niece,
Mary

10. *Charlotte Chronicle*, July 17, 19, 1888.

Epilogue

THE CHILDREN RALLIED AROUND their father and redesigned their future plans. Eddie graduated from Washington and Jefferson College, and from Western Theological Seminary. He had planned to marry Ida Gantz, following graduation in 1890, and together they were to go to India with Will as missionaries. Tragically, however, Ed died from typhoid fever three days before their wedding. Again the family mourned.

When Jennie graduated from Washington Seminary in the spring of 1891, they all moved to Wooster, Ohio. With promised assistance from a host of missionary friends who had retired and now lived in Wooster, Will rented a house to make a home for Frank, Jennie, Fred, and Bessie. Jennie was placed in charge of that project. Frank entered Wooster College as a full-time student; Jennie entered as a part-time student, but her primary responsibility was to keep the home and take care of Fred and Bessie.

When things were running smoothly in Wooster, Will and Mary returned to India. Mary served as her father's secretary, assistant, and companion for the next thirty-five years. Many of those years were spent at the Saharanpur Theological School where Will was a professor, translator, and author.

After sixty-six years as a missionary in India, five years as president and professor at Biddle University, and as an author of 400 books or "tracts," many of which were translations of classics and other teaching materials into Hindi and Urdu,—Will died in 1926. He never remarried. His ashes were buried in a mountain graveyard in Landour, India.

After her father died, Mary returned to America and lived with her sister Bess, until her death ten years later in 1936. Mary never married.

Frank graduated from Wooster College and McCormick Seminary. He married Annette Thackwell and they spent seven years as missionaries in the Punjab, India. For health reasons they returned to America, where Frank served as a pastor in several churches in and around Pittsburgh. He and Annette had a son and a daughter. Frank died in 1939.

Fig. 20. In 1890, just months before Ed's death, the Johnson children posed for this family portrait. Left to right: Jennie, Ed, Mary, and Frank are in back, with Fred and Bessie in the foreground.

Jennie graduated from Wooster College, where she met and married William Thomas Mitchell. Together they had two sons and a daughter and served as missionaries in Mainpuri, India, from 1896 until 1930. They retired in Wooster, Ohio, where Jennie died in 1951.

In 1898, at age nineteen, young Fred, like his brother Eddie, died of typhoid fever. He had gone home to Hookstown, where his Uncle

Frank—who has become a beloved, and well-respected country doctor—gave Fred the finest, most loving medical care possible. Fred died in the house on Mill Street where he and his mother were born.

Bess became a nurse. For many years she worked with Dr. C. E. Gibson in his private hospital in Beaver, Pennsylvania. Bess, too, never married. Following her retirement, she moved to Fredericksburg, Ohio, where she was known to all around as "Aunt Bess" and as a great storyteller. Aunt Bess died in 1970.

It seems fitting for Rachel to end her own story, with selected musings from that wise Valentine essay she wrote in 1852:

> How silent and noiseless is the tread of time as he pursues his ever onward march, bearing all things before him and sparing none. . . . Yet what is it but the shadow of a man—a moment as it were of eternity—a fleeting Span which hasteth to be done, which soon will be lost forever. Lost on eternity's shore.

Bibliography

Alter, James P. "Presbyterians in Farrukhabad, 1838–1915." *Indian Church History Review* 10.1 (1975–76): 83–126.

"American Presbyterians in India/Pakistan: 150 Years." *Journal of Presbyterian History* 62 (Fall 1984): 189–282.

Bausman, Joseph H. *History of Beaver County, Pennsylvania, at Its Centennial Celebration.* New York: Knickerbocker Press, 1904.

Beaver, R. Pierce, *American Protestant Women in World Mission: A History of the First Feminist Movement in North America.* Grand Rapids, Mich.: William B. Eerdmans, 1980.

Bishop, Chris, Ian Drury, and Tony Gibbons. *1400 Days: The Civil War Day by Day.* New York: Gallery Books, 1990.

Boatner, Mark Mayo III. *The Civil War Dictionary.* New York: David McKay, 1987.

Brice, Nathaniel, comp. *A Romanized Hindustani and English Dictionary, Designed for the Use of Schools and for Vernacular Students of the Language.* 3d ed. Benares: E. J. Lazarus, 1880.

Brown, Arthur Judson. *The Foreign Missionary: An Incarnation of a World Movement.* 2d ed. New York: Fleming H. Revell, 1907.

——— . *One Hundred Years.* New York: Fleming H. Revell, 1936.

Brown, Joe David. LIFE *World Library: India.* New York: Time Inc., 1961.

Caldwell, J. A. *Caldwell's Illustrated Combination Centennial Atlas of Beaver County, Pa.* Pittsburgh: Otto Kreps, 1876.

Catton, Bruce. *The American Heritage Short History of the Civil War.* New York: Dell, 1960.

Cockshut, A. O. J. *Truth to Life: The Art of Biography in the Nineteenth Century.* New York: Harcourt, Brace, Jovanovich, 1974.

Collier, Richard. *The Great Indian Mutiny: A Dramatic Account of the Sepoy Rebellion.* New York: E. P. Dutton, 1964.

Cosens, R. R., and C. L. Wallace. *Fatehgarh and the Mutiny.* Lucknow: Newul Kishore Press, 1933.

Craven, Thomas, comp. *The New Royal Dictionary: English into Hindustani and Hindustani into English.* Revised and enlarged by J. R. Chitambar. Lucknow: Methodist Publishing House, 1932.

Crumrine, Boyd. *History of Washington County, Pennsylvania, with Biographical Sketches.* Philadelphia: L. H. Everts, 1882.

Dickson, Mary. "The Orr Family." Presbyterian Historical Society, Philadelphia.

Divine, Robert A., T. H. Breen, George M. Fredrickson, and R. Hall Williams. *America, Past and Present*. Vol. 1. Glenview, Ill.: Scott, Foresman, 1984.

Eddy, Sherwood. *India Awakening*. Forward Mission Study Courses. New York: Missionary Education Movement, 1912.

Embree, Ainslie Thomas. *1857 in India: Mutiny or War of Independence?* Boston: D. C. Heath, 1963.

Epstein, Barbara Leslie. *The Politics of Domesticity: Women, Evangelism and Temperance in Nineteenth-Century America*. Middletown, Conn.: Wesleyan Univ. Press, 1981.

Fullerton, R. S. "Mr. Fullerton's Narrative of Events at Futtehgurh." *The Foreign Missionary* 17 (May 1858): 51–61.

Gupta, Pratul Chandra. *Nana Sahib and the Rising at Cawnpore*. Oxford: Clarendon, 1963.

Hays, George P. *Presbyterians: A Popular Narrative of Their Origin, Progress, Doctrines, and Achievements*. New York: J. A. Hill, 1892.

Heuser, Frederick J., Jr. *A Guide to Foreign Missionary Manuscripts in the Presbyterian Historical Society*. New York: Greenwood, 1988.

Hibbert, Christopher. *The Great Mutiny: India 1857*. New York: Viking, 1978.

History of Beaver County, Pa. Philadelphia: A. Warner, 1888.

Holcomb, Helen Harriet. "Sketch of the Furrukhabad Mission." In *Historical Sketches of the Indian Missions of the Presbyterian Church in the United States of America* . . . Allahabad: Allahabad Mission Press, 1886.

Home and Foreign Record of the Presbyterian Church in the United States of America. Philadelphia: Presbyterian Publication House, 1854.

Hunter, Jane. *The Gospel of Gentility: American Women Missionaries in Turn-of-the-Century China*. New Haven: Yale Univ. Press, 1984.

"India Letters, Furrukhabad or Lower Mission." *Foreign Missionary Correspondence of the Board of Foreign Missions, Presbyterian Church in the United States of America, in the Office of History Presbyterian Church (U.S.A.)*. 1857–84. Microfilm series, vols. 8–13. Presbyterian Historical Society, Philadelphia.

Johnson C. Smith University Bulletin. Vol. 1, no. 4. Charlotte, N.C.: Johnson C. Smith Univ., 1935.

Jordan, John W., ed. *Genealogical and Personal History of Beaver County, Pennsylvania*. Vol. 1. New York: Lewis Historical Publishing Co., 1914.

Kaul, H. K., ed. *Travellers' India, an Anthology*. Delhi: Oxford Univ. Press, 1979.

McMahon, Arnold B. *Beaver County Album II: A Collection of Historical Photographs of Beaver County, Pa.* Rochester, N.Y.: Graule Studio, 1984.

McPherson, James M. *Ordeal by Fire: The Civil War and Reconstruction*. 2d ed. New York: McGraw-Hill, 1992.

Malone, Dumas, ed. *Dictionary of American Biography*. Vol. 5. New York: Charles Scribner's and Son, 1958.

Metcalf, Thomas R. *The Aftermath of Revolt: India, 1857–1870*. Princeton: Princeton Univ. Press, 1964.

Minutes of the General Assembly of the Presbyterian Church, U.S.A. New York: Presbyterian Board of Publications, 1891.

Mitchell, Rachel C. Conversations with author. Wooster, Ohio. 1985–86.

Parker, Inez Moore. *The Biddle–Johnson C. Smith University Story*. Edited by Helen Vassy Callison. Charlotte, N.C.: Charlotte Publishing, 1973.

Price, William H. *The Civil War Handbook*. Fairfax, Va.: L. B. Prince, 1961.

Report of the Furrukhabad Mission of the Presbyterian Church in the U.S.A. for 1862–1863. Allahabad: Furrukhabad Mission Press, 1864.

Sherrard, R. A. "The Johnston Family and Its Connections." Presbyterian Historical Society, Philadelphia.

Simmons, Henry E. *A Concise Encyclopedia of the Civil War*. New York: Fairfax Press, 1986.

Spear, Percival. *India, a Modern History*. Ann Arbor: Univ. of Michigan Press, 1972.

Sweet, Leonard I. *The Minister's Wife: Her Role in Nineteenth Century American Evangelism*. Philadelphia: Temple Univ. Press, 1983.

Swyrydenko, Nicholas, ed. *Information Please Presents the Book of Facts*. New York: Del, 1979.

Thomas, Claudia Newel. "John Arbuthnot." In *British Prose Writers, 1660–1800, First Series*, edited by Donald T. Siebert. Detroit: Bruccoli Clark Layman Book, 1991.

Thompson, Ernest Trice. *Presbyterians in the South*. Richmond: John Knox Press, 1963.

Tracy, Jane. "The Development of Women's Work." In *After One Hundred Years: North India Mission*, edited by H. R. Ferger. Bangalore: Scripture Literature Press, 1936.

Walsh, J. Johnston. *A Memorial of the Futtehgurh Mission and Her Martyred Missionaries: With Some Remarks on the Mutiny in India*. Philadelphia: Joseph M. Wilson, 1859.

Walton, Denver L., ed. *The Beaver County Bicentennial Atlas*. Beaver, Pa.: Beaver County Bicentennial Commission, 1976.

Webster, John C. B. *The Christian Community and Change in Nineteenth Century North India*. Delhi: Macmillan, 1976.

Welsh, E. B., chmn. *Buckeye Presbyterianism*. Wooster: Committee of the United Presbyterian Synod of Ohio, 1968.

Welter, Barbara. "She Hath Done What She Could: Protestant Women's Missionary Careers in Nineteenth-Century America." In *Women in American Religion*, edited by Janet Wilson James. Philadelphia: Univ. of Pennsylvania Press, 1980.

The Western Theological Seminary, General Biographical Catalogue. 1827–1927. Presbyterian Historical Society, Philadelphia.

Yule, Henry, and A. C. Burnell. *Hobson Jobson: A Glossary of Colloquial Anglo-Indian Words and Phrases, and of Kindred Terms, Etymological, Historical, Geographical and Discursive*. 1903. Rev. ed. edited by William Crooke. Delhi: Munshiram Manaharlal, 1968.

Index

—letters written while tenting (1864–82): 199, 201, 228, 239, 240, 243, 254, 301–2

Johnson, William "Willie" (Rachel and Will's son), xv, 157, 183, 185, 187

Johnson, William F., v, 28, 200, 233, 242, 313, 318, 341; as author, 248, 257, 262, 264–67, 281–83, 302; at Biddle University, 318, 320; conducting services, 191–92, 197, 202, 223, 226–27, 235, 303; conversions, 206, 218, 226, 245; courtship and marriage, 10, 14, 26–45, 64, 277, 291–92; education, 9, 14, 313, 315, 318; health, 131–32, 147–48, 151, 157, 160, 170, 181, 250, 254, 257; mission appointments, 56, 85, 176–77, 260, 267, 331, 341; parenting, 260, 313; as pastor, 132, 194, 239, 256, 268; preaching, 81, 98, 106, 108, 113, 116, 128, 221, 259, 313–16; as teacher, 8–9, 17, 219, 267, 268, 341; tenting (1863–82), 174, 198–203, 228–32, 239–43, 249, 254–55, 257, 270, 302

—letters received: from the children, 287, 323, 331, 332; from Rachel, 283–84, 288, 290–91, 293–94, 315

—letters written: to Margaret Blakesley, 183; to the children, 188, 269, 272–73, 275, 295; to David and Jane Johnson, 218, 255, 257, 281, 296, 304; to David and Mary Kerr, 94, 113, 131, 142; to family in Hookstown, 157, 176, 214, 220; to Frank and Sam Kerr, 61, 92, 237

Johnson, William and Elizabeth (Will's parents), xv, 9

Johnson C. Smith University. See Biddle University

Kanpur, 14, 16–17, 86, 140–44, 227, 254. See also Sepoy revolt

Kellogg, Samuel and Antoinette, 209–10, 213, 219, 235, 240, 242, 248, 267, 315; health, 250, 253; tenting, 228–30, 239–43, 249, 255

Kerr, David, III (Rachel's father), xv, 2–4, 6–7, 223, 332, 335

Kerr, David, II, and Rachel (Rachel's grandparents), xv, 7–8, 189, 259, 336

Kerr, Frank (Rachel's brother), xv, 2n. 3, 4, 167, 342–43; education, 140, 224,

244; family, 259, 270; future plans, 91, 94, 104, 204, 214, 224, 237; homes, 278, 335, 338; as physician, 255, 270–71; as teacher, 232, 276; wartime service, 140, 150–51, 160, 165–69, 172, 180–81, 192, 196–99, 204, 207, 211

Kerr, Jane (Rachel's sister), xv, 2, 4, 7, 104, 212

Kerr, Mary Swaney (Rachel's mother), xv, 2–4, 6–7, 121, 184, 332

Kerr, Stella. See Langfitt, Stella Kerr

Landour, 133, 256, 265, 277, 279, 286–97, 300–301

Langfitt, John, xv, 259, 271

Langfitt, Stella Kerr (Rachel's sister), xv, 7, 23, 39, 55, 59, 95, 255, 335–36; family, 259, 271, 278

Laurence family, 326–28

Lincoln, Abraham, 39, 68, 91, 149n. 2, 159, 168, 178n. 14, 180, 183, 195, 209n. 13; assassination, 208; election, 77, 199

Lowrie, John C., 29n. 2, 31, 201, 207, 331

Lucas, James J. and Mary, 265, 282, 302

Mainpuri, 110, 142, 148, 153–55, 187, 232, 260, 342

Malaria, 101, 106, 147, 183

Maps, 66, 67

Mattoon, Dr. Stephen, 321

Measles, 13, 91, 184

Melas, 80–81, 171, 198, 221, 261. See also Ganges River

Mission business: appointments, 56, 267; finances, 107, 110, 151, 159, 161, 168, 179, 194, 296; General Assembly, 309–10, 316, 329, 333; ordination, 221; presbytery, 248, 264; reports, 68, 148, 179, 201, 244; synod, 220, 248, 250, 333. See also Missionary meetings

Mission compounds, 77, 88, 90, 127

Mission societies, 10, 252, 333

Missionaries (American): and the British, 53n. 6, 86, 161–62, 170–71, 178, 203, 248, 311; and House, 107–8, 124–25, 134; and Indians, 15, 17, 112, 123, 253, 281, 307–8. See also Politics; Press; Sherlock, Dr. and Mrs.

Missionary meetings (annual), ix, 107,
110, 115, 117, 194; in Allahabad, 56,
242, 243, 270, 302; in Etawah, 188,
228, 265; in Fatehgarh, 175–76; in
Mainpuri, 148, 151, 154, 254
Muhammedans: beliefs and practices,
151–52, 276; and Christians, 85, 112,
128, 163, 174, 307–8; mosques, 76,
96, 237–38, 275
Munshi (language teacher), 79, 98, 110,
113, 122, 129, 133, 139
Muslims. *See* Muhammedans

Norton, Captain, 33, 34–36, 40, 41, 49,
50–63, 69, 118
Nundy, Gopi Nath, 1–2, 65, 85, 107,
127, 149
Nundy, Mrs. Gopi Nath, 68, 88, 99

Oil, 93, 223, 317
Orphans, 1, 135, 190, 197, 219, 226–27,
246–47, 249, 268, 302
Owen, Joseph and Mrs., 155, 170, 173,
198, 229, 242, 250

Paris, 310
Politics: American, 8, 45, 67–68, 87,
272, 315; British, 14–16, 85, 105, 142,
195; British-American war rumors,
124, 127, 160, 162, 178; Indian, 14,
142, 185, 188, 203, 231, 280
Porter, Sepora, 12, 19
Prayer services, 79, 257
Presbyterian Banner, 28, 29, 79, 118, 129,
132, 134, 224, 311
Press: American, 92, 129, 166, 208;
British, 68, 91, 124–27, 134, 164,
174, 195; Indian, 92, 134–35, 174,
195, 209
Prime, Samuel Irenaeus, 256
Punka fan, 89, 93, 101, 137, 274

Queen Victoria, 260, 270, 271
Quinine, 100–107, 148, 171

Rakha, 176, 177, 182, 188, 190, 258,
260. *See also* Fatehgarh
Reid, Dr. and Mrs., 304, 307

Revivals, 4, 15, 23. *See also* Christian faith
Royal visits. *See* Edward VII, Prince of Wales; Queen Victoria

Saharanpur, 249, 280–81, 331–32, 341
Sahib, Nana, 16, 142
Salvation Army, 306–8
Sarnath, 274
Sayre, Edward Halsey and Mrs., 162,
178, 180, 225, 229, 231, 242, 253
Schools in India, 62, 196; mission, 67,
75, 107, 122–23, 168, 190–91, 196–
97, 245
Scott, James L. and Eliza, 125, 151, 154,
162, 169, 176, 180, 194, 229, 232; at
Landour, 182, 288–89, 302
Seeley, George A. and Jennie, 257, 283–
87, 289, 331
Seminaries for women: in Charlotte,
N.C., 323; in Steubenville, Ohio, 8–
14, 157n. 5, 277, 304, 309; in Washington, Pa., 313, 323, 341
Sepoy revolt ("the Mutiny," "the Great
Revolt"), 14–17, 68, 85, 86, 127,
140, 188, 190, 198; memorials, 141–
44, 227
Servants, 76, 82–84, 102–3, 105, 109,
119, 145–46, 152, 159, 290
Seward, Sara, 271, 292–94
Sherlock, Dr. and Mrs.: in 1861, 88, 90,
101, 104, 108, 115, 123–24; in 1862–
63, 126, 130, 136, 141, 150, 158, 161;
at Etawah, 168, 225, 252, 254, 266
Smallpox, 22, 128, 164, 182, 186,
206, 300
Steubenville, Ohio, 9–14, 17–25, 256,
310. *See also* Beatty, Charles and Hattie; Seminaries for women
Suez Canal, 258

Teachers, Indian, 221, 234–35, 245,
262–63, 268, 302. *See also* Munshi;
Nundy, Gopi Nath
Tenting, 110, 173, 179, 181, 199–201,
228–32, 239–43, 249, 255, 257
Tents, 80, 149–50, 200. *See also* Tenting
Theft, 84, 255, 275
Transportation in India: boat, 58, 62,
75; camel, 175, 268; dak gari, 65, 69,
71–72, 115–16, 148, 153, 267, 285;

Affectionately, Rachel
was composed in 10' ITC New Baskerville leaded 2 points
on a Xyvision system with Linotronic output
by BookMasters, Inc.;
printed by sheet-fed offset
on 60-pound Glatfelter Natural Smooth acid-free text stock,
Smyth sewn and bound over 88' binder's boards
in Holliston Roxite cloth
with 80-pound Rainbow Antique endpapers,
and wrapped with dustjackets printed in two colors
on 80-pound enamel stock with film lamination
by Braun-Brumfield, Inc.;
designed by Will Underwood;
and published by
The Kent State University Press
KENT, OHIO 44242